The easy Guide to Your Walt Disney World Visit

2020 Edition

Dave Shute & Josh Humphrey

Theme Park Press
The Happiest Books on Earth
www.ThemeParkPress.com

Editor: Bob McLain
Layout: Artisanal Text

ISBN 978-1-68390-241-6
Printed in the United States of America

Theme Park Press | www.ThemeParkPress.com
Address queries to bob@themeparkpress.com

To my mom and dad, for introducing me to Disneyland, Disney World...and everything else —Dave

To my mom, dad, brother, and friend(s)—without your help and guidance this would probably be a prison memoir rather than a Walt Disney World guidebook —Josh

Contents

Introduction

Congratulations. You are about to embark on a trip filled with magic and memories to one of the world's most popular vacation destinations. But with a Walt Disney World trip comes hundreds of decisions, from when to go to where to stay to what to eat to which attractions to experience. Walt Disney World spans more than 39 square miles and includes four major theme parks, two water parks, an expansive shopping and dining district, a 24-screen movie theater, more than 20 Disney-operated resorts, dozens of restaurants, hundreds of attractions, and a whole lot more.

That's where we come in. Whether this is your first or your fiftieth visit, this book will prepare you and your family to make the best choices, eat at the restaurants that provide the most value, make sure you experience the best Disney has to offer, eliminate as much time waiting in line as possible, and guarantee that your experience at Walt Disney World is stress-free.

This guide is written to help all visitors plan better vacations, whether you're a first-timer still unsure of how Space Mountain and Dumbo the Flying Elephant are different, or if you're an experienced returning visitor trying to decide whether you want to pick Na'vi River Journey or Flight of Passage as your Pandora FastPass+ choice at Animal Kingdom. We'll introduce each topic and then expand on it with tips and tricks so first-time visitors are quickly brought up to speed and returning visitors will learn new strategies to maximize their time and money.

Why this book in particular, you ask? Dave and Josh share thousands of theme park visits, hundreds of hotel room stays, and far more theme park meals than either of them would probably like to remember. Their experience culminates in this carefully crafted guidebook designed to be the framework for every step of your vacation planning. Both are firm believers that a little planning goes a long way. By spending time mulling the many options now, you'll set yourself up for the best vacation possible.

Getting free updates. We will update this 2020 edition several times between its initial late 2019 publication date and the late summer of 2020, when our 2021 edition will come out. In the meantime, we are offering free updates!

To get your free update forward your confirming Amazon email (that is, the email titled "Amazon.com order of The easy Guide to Your Walt Disney World Visit") to easyguidewdw@gmail.com, and then, whenever an update to the 2020 edition comes out, we will email you instructions on how to get yours (as a PDF).

Sit back, relax, and enjoy the planning!

CHAPTER ONE

How to Use This Book

This chapter serves two primary purposes: introducing the topics of the rest of the book, and boiling down our recommendations into an easy-to-digest list. First-time visitors will benefit from clear, actionable advice, while those returning to the Most Magical Place on Earth can compare and contrast our thoughts with their own experiences.

Subsequent chapters offer detailed information on the whys and hows behind the recommendations summarized in this chapter, and add hundreds of detailed and up-to-date thoughts, reviews, and tips. For example, you may be interested only in eating at one or two sit-down restaurants. Instead of forcing you to read through a hundred reviews, we've listed the best values and the most immersive experiences here in an effort to speed up and simplify the planning process. And you never know, as you read the later reviews of our favorite restaurants, something else might catch your eye.

While you can skip around the book, we suggest that returning visitors pay special attention to the material on the new FastPass+ system (much different than the old FASTPASS) in Chapters 6 and 9, and to the new date-based ticket pricing approach in Chapter 8, and that first-timers should consume the full text from beginning to end—perhaps a chapter per night with the help of a glass of wine and a roasty, toasty fire. The chapters build on each other, with decisions made during Chapters 2 and 3 affecting the choices you make in Chapters 4 and following. Chapters 8 and 9 come full circle and serve as the road map for your entire trip.

Changes, corrections, updates, links to larger color versions of key charts, and such, can be found at yourfirstvisit.net/easy-guide-2020-changes.

Why Age and Height Matter [Chapter 2]

Children of all ages enjoy wonderful visits to Walt Disney World every single day of the year. However, if this may be your kids' only childhood visit, consider going when your youngest child is at least 8 or 9, and your shortest child at least 48 inches tall.

Many of Walt Disney World's best and most popular attractions require riders to be 44" to 48" tall, and kids around the third-grade-age are mature enough to appreciate the layers and nuances of each Disney experience. Those already planning to return may want to start earlier, when the kids are younger and all aspects of the Disney magic are open to them. While toddlers and younger kids are charmed by and enamored with the Disney princesses, older kids may be less enthusiastic about a sit-down meal with Belle and Cinderella. Starting young offers an opportunity to enjoy many varied trips as the kids get older. But starting too young and too short on a once-in-a-lifetime trip means passing on several of Disney World's best rides. Chapter 2 describes how easy it is to design an itinerary with kids (or adults) of any age.

How Long to Stay [Chapter 3]

Wonderful Walt Disney World vacations come in all shapes and sizes, with guests enjoying trips that last anywhere from just one day to as long as several weeks. However, for a once in a lifetime trip, we recommend spending nine days in Orlando.

Guests planning to return enjoy the ability to ease into visiting the theme parks with shorter trips of four or so days, knowing they can catch missed attractions and experiences in the future. Those planning once-in-a-lifetime style vacations are best served pushing their stay to eight or nine days. This affords the opportunity to enjoy most of the best of Walt Disney World, and also allows a mixture of longer days in the theme parks tempered by more relaxing downtime back at the resort. While a longer trip will be more expensive than a shorter one, fixed travel costs and the way Disney prices tickets make the per-day costs of a longer trip typically much lower.

By booking FastPass+ experiences in advance and touring the theme parks intelligently, those returning to Walt Disney World may experience a wide selection of their favorite attractions during shorter visits. First-time visitors spending just a few days at Disney World will be able to maximize their time and money by putting our advice into action and making carefully thought out decisions in advance of their arrival.

RETURNING VISITORS NEED TO KNOW:

- At Hollywood Studios, Star Wars: Galaxy's Edge is the main event, opening with two all-new rides, new dining, and what will be one of the most immersive theme park environments ever created. Mickey & Minnie's Runaway Railway, being built in place of the Great Movie Ride inside of the Chinese Theater, should open in spring 2020.

- Also at the Studios, Toy Story Land opened in June 2018, including two new rides, Slinky Dog Dash and Alien Swirling Saucers, meet-and-greets, new dining, and a new entrance to Toy Story Mania.

- Animal Kingdom has expanded its after-dark hours and offerings, especially with Tree of Life Awakenings and Rivers of Light. Two new rides, the world-class Avatar Flight of Passage and the less interesting Na'vi River Journey, opened in an entirely new land, Pandora: World of Avatar, in May 2017.

- At Epcot, IllumiNations was replaced in October 2019 by the temporary show Epcot Forever. The temporary show will then be replaced by a new permanent show, HarmonioUS, in 2020. Also expected to debut in Epcot in 2020 are new offerings in France, including the new Ratatouille ride, and possibly late in the year the new Guardians of the Galaxy ride—although 2021 may be more likely for that. Frozen Ever After, a ride based on the popular movie, has replaced Maelstrom in the Norway Pavilion. Anna & Elsa meet in a new building next door. Wait times for Frozen Ever After routinely eclipse 75 minutes, making it a top FastPass+ priority. Waits for meeting Anna & Elsa have proven to be much shorter, often peaking under 30 minutes. Disney added a third theater to Soarin', in turn raising capacity by 50% and reducing standby waits. It has also received a new film and is now called Soarin' Around the World.

- At Magic Kingdom, Disney expanded Fantasyland by adding Storybook Circus, where you'll find the Dumbo ride and Barnstormer roller-coaster. Seven Dwarfs Mine Train, a headlining addition and a top FastPass+ priority, is located across from the Winnie the Pooh ride. Mickey's Royal Friendship Faire is the name of the new Cinderella Castle stage show that includes appearances from *Tangled*, *Frozen*, and *The Princess and the Frog* characters, in addition to Mickey and friends. The evening parade is gone, and Wishes was replaced by a new show, Happily Ever After.

- Disney Springs (formerly Downtown Disney) has added more than two dozen new places to eat and over 50 new stores. Parking and traffic are improved with three new multi-level garages, the widening of streets, and the addition of pedestrian bridges.

When to Go [Chapter 4]

If you can, visit Disney World at some point between the day after Martin Luther King Day in January until the Sunday a week before President's Day in February, or the three weeks beginning the Sunday after Thanksgiving.

In picking dates, it's important to consider crowd levels, pricing, weather, possible refurbishments, and special events. Our specialty is honing in on the less crowded times to visit, when wait times are lower at attractions, lines are shorter at stores and dining venues, and there's less congestion inside the parks. Lower crowds means being able to do more in a less stressful environment. From there, we typically prioritize lower resort pricing, followed by weather, refurbishments, and special events.

Based on these factors—but especially low crowds and lower prices—we recommend the following weeks:

- From the day after Martin Luther King Day in January until the Sunday a week before President's Day in February
- The Sunday after President's Day through the first week of March
- The week that begins the Sunday after Easter until mid-May
- From the day after Labor Day through the rest of September
- The last third of October

- November after Veterans Day until the Saturday before Thanksgiving
- The three weeks beginning the Sunday after Thanksgiving

Josh recommends the late January and early February dates, with the lowest prices (prices go up February 13), comfortable daytime temperatures, and some of the lowest crowds of the year. Dave recommends, most years, the three weeks after Thanksgiving, which marry below average-crowds and prices with Disney World's Christmas displays and offerings like Holidays Around the World and Mickey's Very Merry Christmas Party.

Those embarking on a possible once-in-a-lifetime trip should note that the peak of the hurricane season ends in early October, and that a few rides are almost invariably closed for refurbishments in January and early February.

If these dates won't work, Chapter 4 offers a blow-by-blow overview of everything to expect all year long.

RETURNING VISITORS NEED TO KNOW:

- Disney World crowds are about as high as they've ever been, and many of the new crowds are coming during periods that used to be much slower. There are still much better and much worse times to go, but starkly low crowds are a thing of the past.
- Price seasons at the values and moderates have changed over the past few years, the net effect being that late summer and fall dates are no longer in the lowest price seasons.
- Disney started charging different prices for different dates for multi-day tickets in October 2018. The highest-priced dates (around Christmas 2020) are 30–45% more expensive than the lowest dates of 2020, and higher priced periods largely mimic high-crowd periods. We expect a ticket price increase in 2020 that likely will increase these differences even more.

Where to Stay [Chapter 5]

Stay at Disney's Art of Animation, Pop Century, Port Orleans French Quarter, Port Orleans Riverside, Caribbean Beach, Coronado Springs, Wilderness Lodge, Grand Floridian, Contemporary, or Polynesian Village.

We suggest that you stay in a Disney-owned resort hotel. While more expensive than hotels operated by third parties, they are also typically:

- Much more fun
- Much more convenient
- Much more "Disney"

The Disney-owned hotels also offer unique perks, including:

- The right to book FastPass+ reservations for key attractions beginning 60 days in advance of arrival, and to attend Extra Magic Hours ("EMH"). At press-time, non-Disney guests (except those at the Swan, Dolphin, Four Seasons, Shades of Green, Hilton Bonnet Creek,

Waldorf Astoria, and the Disney Springs Resort Area hotels) are not eligible for EMH and can only book FastPass+ 30 days in advance.

- The right to book dining ten days further out than non-Disney guests, which can be critical for high-demand meals like dinner at Be Our Guest Restaurant.
- Free airport transport to and from your hotel via Disney's Magical Express.
- Free and frequent transport from your hotel to the parks, water-parks, and Disney Springs.
- Free parking at the parks.
- Access to the various Disney Dining Plans, a convenient budgeting tool even if they often don't present much actual savings.

Perhaps even more important than any of these quantifiable perks is the comfort and safety of staying inside the "Disney bubble", far removed from the hustle, bustle, and worry of the outside world. Staying on property is the easiest way to forget about life's problems and truly enjoy an immersive experience together. While a vacation staying off-site is generally less expensive at first blush, consider additional expenses like resort fees, car rental, and the price of your time. There is no more convenient way to experience Walt Disney World than staying at one of their resorts. There is a reason Disney commands premium prices and why so many return visitors stay on property over and over again. Strongly consider the additional cost of an on-property stay and find out for yourself.

Disney groups most of its hotels into three price types, which are from least to most expensive Value resorts, Moderate resorts, and Deluxe resorts. Among them we recommend, depending on budget:

Value Resorts
Art of Animation, Pop Century, All-Star Movies

These resorts are among the least expensive on property, offer dedicated bus service, have great food courts, and offer newer rooms. Art of Animation is the newest Disney resort on property, and Pop Century is a short walk away. Refurbed rooms at Pop Century, All-Star Movies, and All-Star Music (which began its refurb in September 2019) offer coffee-makers and queen beds—both firsts among standard value resort rooms. Art of Animation and Pop Century are also the only values on the new Disney Skyliner gondola line to Epcot and Disney's Hollywood Studios.

Moderate Resorts
Port Orleans French Quarter, Port Orleans Riverside, Caribbean Beach, Coronado Springs

French Quarter enjoys the smallest footprint of the moderate-level resorts and all rooms are just a few minutes away from the resort's amenities, including the bus stop, food court, boat dock, and resort concierge. Riverside is much larger, but offers better amenities, including a table service restaurant and several quiet pools.

Caribbean Beach is also rocketing up this list. In addition to being the only moderate resort on the Skyliner system, it's also the hub, which means it will offer direct service to Epcot and Hollywood Studios. Coronado Springs is moving up as well, after adding in July 2019 three bars and two restaurants to what was already the best set of amenities at a moderate.

Deluxe Resorts

Wilderness Lodge, Grand Floridian, Contemporary, Polynesian Village

The Grand Floridian is Disney's flagship resort and its most opulent, providing several of its nicest restaurants, beautiful pool and garden areas, and a convenient location to Magic Kingdom. The Contemporary is a magical space and just a short walk away from Magic Kingdom. Theme park view rooms in the tower look over Cinderella Castle and the monorail zooms through the center of the resort all day. The Polynesian Village combines South Seas theming that kids find fun and adults find charming with great convenience and strong dining. The Wilderness Lodge with its glorious lobby and lower prices—but smaller rooms—rejoined this list after it completed a multi-year refurb in July 2017.

Chapter 5 includes in-depth reviews of every Disney-owned hotel.

RETURNING VISITORS NEED TO KNOW:

- In March 2018, for the first time, Disney began charging for overnight parking at its hotels—apparently because it could.

- Over the last 18 months, Disney has added about 15% more rooms to the list of those eligible for Extra Magic Hours and able to book FastPass+ at 60 days. On the list of non-Disney resorts with these perks are the Swan, Dolphin, Four Seasons, Shades of Green, Hilton Bonnet Creek, Waldorf Astoria, and the seven Disney Springs Resort Area hotels.

- Five person rooms are easier to find, as Caribbean Beach completed a refurb that added many in 2015, and DVC studios that sleep five are now available in the Polynesian, Grand Floridian, Wilderness Lodge Boulder Ridge, BoardWalk Inn, and Beach Club DVC offerings.

- Major work is complete at Disney's Wilderness Lodge and Caribbean Beach. Each resort saw a decrease in the number of rooms available, but an increase in the amenities offered with Wilderness Lodge adding a new pool and Caribbean Beach seeing additional dining. Work at Coronado Springs ended in July 2019 with the resort adding far more rooms, in addition to new amenities such as a waterside bar and rooftop restaurant. After a recent refurbishment, Pop Century became the first value to offer queen beds and coffeemakers. Similar refurbishments are complete at All-Star Movies and underway at All-Star Music, with Sports likely next. French Quarter recently completed a minor refurbishment project, while a similar project is underway at Port Orleans Riverside. Old Key West and Animal Kingdom Lodge are also undergoing refurbishments with more on the way.

How to Spend Your Time [Chapter 6]

Set daily plans from the example itineraries and "cheat sheets" we provide.

Planning your time at Disney World can be broken down into three parts:

- Dividing your days among the parks
- Picking the best parks for each day
- Setting your plan for each park day

There are two easy ways to use this book to plan your time at Walt Disney World, each designed around Disney's new FastPass+ program:

- For those who can use them as a starting point, we provide sample 9-day, Saturday-arrival itineraries.
- For everybody else, we provide "cheat sheets" for designing your visits that work for both younger and older kids, and for longer and shorter trips.

Here's an excerpt from one of the example itineraries:

Meals:	Thursday	Friday
Breakfast	*Hotel Room*	*Hotel Room*
Lunch	**TBD** Cinderella's Royal Table**	Sunshine Seasons
Dinner	Magic Kingdom or Hotel Counter	Epcot or Hotel Counter
Parks, Etc.:		
Very Early Morning		
Early Morning	At Magic Kingdom by 8.15a	At Epcot by 8.15a
Late Morning	Magic Kingdom	Epcot
Early Afternoon	Magic Kingdom	Epcot
Late Afternoon	Magic Kingdom	Epcot
Evening		
Late Evening		
Notes:		
Parade	Afternoon Parade	
Evening Show		
Park-Open Target	Peter Pan	Soarin' Around the World
FastPass+ to pre-schedule	Seven Dwarfs Mine Train, Haunted Mansion, Enchanted Tales with Belle	Test Track, Turtle Talk with Crush, Mission: SPACE

And here's an example from one of the Cheat Sheets:

TWO-DAY EPCOT EARLY ARRIVAL PLAN, MORNING, DAY 1

Use FastPass+ at The Seas with Nemo (9:30am – 10:30am), Turtle Talk with Crush (10:30am – 11:30am), Frozen Ever After: 1pm – 2pm or whenever is available

1. Ride Soarin': 9am – 9:25am
2. Ride Living with the Land: 9:30am – 9:45am
3. Visit characters if desired: 9:55am – 10:10am
4. Ride Journey into Imagination with Figment: 10:15am – 10:30am
5. Ride The Seas with Nemo and Friends with FastPass+: 10:40am – 10:55am

6. See Turtle Talk with Crush with FP+ and Look Around the Seas: 11am – 11:45am

7. Have lunch – something in World Showcase makes the most sense: 12pm – 1:15pm

8. Ride Frozen Ever After with FastPass+: 1:30pm – 1:45pm

9. Book a 4th FastPass+

Chapter 6 includes in-depth reviews of all the theme park attractions and explains theme park touring strategy in detail.

RETURNING VISITORS NEED TO KNOW:

- Disney's new FastPass+ program, explained in this chapter and in Chapter 9, has profoundly changed the best ways to plan for and tour the parks. Never have advance planning and thoughtful itineraries paid off more, and never has lack of planning (or planning too late...) hurt more. This guidebook is part of the first guidebook series written from scratch for the era of FastPass+.

- FastPass+ allows you—and pretty much requires you—to book well in advance times for specific rides on specific days, beginning 60 days ahead if you are staying at a Disney-owned resort (or the Swan, Dolphin, Four Seasons, Shades of Green, Hilton Orlando Bonnet Creek, the Waldorf Astoria, or a Disney Springs Resort Area hotel) and 30 days ahead for everyone else.

- So many attractions offer FastPass+, and so much capacity is allocated to it, that standby waits for the majority of the rides are longer than they were prior to the implementation of the FastPass+ initiative.

Where to Eat [Chapter 7]

Target your dining venues based on our recommendations, our reviews, or simply where you are when you're hungry!

First-time family visitors to Walt Disney World need to know three things about dining:

- Several dining venues are among the most memorable and delightful experiences Walt Disney Word has to offer.

- Table service reservations open 180 days in advance. Availability at the most sought-after restaurants is taken almost immediately.

- Disney World dining is expensive. Expect to pay 25 to 40% more on-property than you would for comparable meals off-property. For most (but not all) visitors, the Disney Dining Plan won't save any money.

For families, we recommend:

- The Princess meals: *Cinderella's Royal Table* at the Magic Kingdom and *Akershus Royal Banquet Hall* at Epcot. The first has the better setting, the second is much less expensive.

- Dining with Tigger, Pooh, and friends at *Crystal Palace* in the Magic Kingdom.
- Dining with Mickey and Friends at *Chef Mickey's* at Disney's Contemporary Resort, *Tusker House* at Disney's Animal Kingdom, and *'Ohana* breakfast at Disney's Polynesian Village Resort.
- Dining in the Beast's Castle at *Be Our Guest* in Magic Kingdom.
- Various degrees of wait-staff induced silliness at *50's Prime Time Café* at Disney's Hollywood Studios and *Whispering Canyon Café* at Disney's Wilderness Lodge.
- The *Hoop-Dee-Doo Musical Revue*, a fun, energetic dinner show with interactive elements and plenty of audience participation at Disney's Fort Wilderness Resort.
- Exotic settings in the local versions of national chain restaurants like the *Rainforest Café*, in both Disney's Animal Kingdom and Disney Springs, and *T-REX* in Disney Springs.

For couples seeking a romantic atmosphere and the best food, we suggest:

- *California Grill*. Located on the 15th floor of the Contemporary Resort, it offers breathtaking views of Magic Kingdom during the evening fireworks, in addition to a great menu focused on fresh ingredients, sushi, and contemporary cocktails.
- *Flying Fish*. Located amidst the hustle and bustle of Disney's BoardWalk, this delightfully intimate restaurant welcomes guests with luxurious details and a menu featuring some of the freshest—and best—seafood on property.
- *Victoria & Albert's*. Offering impeccable service and astonishing attention to detail, dinner at this Grand Floridian restaurant is a truly memorable experience.

Chapter 7 includes advice on the Disney Dining Plan and in-depth reviews of all the major Disney World dining options, plus suggestions on the best quick service options.

RETURNING VISITORS NEED TO KNOW:

- Remarkable new dining has opened in the last few years, particularly in Disney Springs (Morimoto Asia, The BOATHOUSE, and Homecoming), but also in Magic Kingdom (Be Our Guest, Skipper Canteen) and Disney's Animal Kingdom (Tiffins).
- While prices are up everywhere, Disney World has seen strong increases in counter service prices, the more expensive of which now approach the price of the least expensive table service options.
- While we still don't particularly recommend the various Disney Dining Plans, they have gotten much more flexible and diner-friendly over the last few years.
- For the first time, in 2018 Dining Plans began to include one alcoholic (or "specialty" for those under 21) drink per meal credit.

Which Tickets to Buy and
How Much to Budget [Chapter 8]

Big budgets allow for more extravagances, but a vacation can be tailored to just about any budget. Realistically, for a first visit, a family of four is looking at spending more than $4,000.

"What should we budget?" is the hardest simple question for this book to answer. This is because smaller families, families whose kids are younger, families staying at a less expensive hotel, families going during a less expensive period, and families on shorter trips will pay less. Larger families, families where everyone is older than nine, families staying at a more expensive hotel, families going during a more expensive period, and families on longer trips will pay more.

- A parent and one younger child with three days of tickets and three nights in a value resort during one of the less expensive periods could spend as little as $1,500 in Orlando.
- Add another parent and another younger child and this trip jumps to $2,600.
- Stretch the visit out to the 8 nights and 9 days we recommend for "only visits" and the in-Orlando price exceeds $5,500.
- Stay this long in one of the more expensive deluxe resorts instead, and the price is more than $9,000.
- Shift to the most expensive times of the year to visit at this deluxe resort and add $3,000 more.

(All the figures are before transportation costs and souvenirs.)

The good news is that budgeting for a specific trip is relatively straightforward, once you've made the key decisions outlined in this book.

RETURNING VISITORS NEED TO KNOW:

- Hotel, ticket, and dining prices have seen major increases the past few years, at the same time as the range and availability of discounts that Disney offers has been severely scaled back.
- In October 2018, Disney shifted multi-day ticket pricing to prices that vary by dates of use. The effect was to raise prices for most ticket types and lengths, and add complexity to the ticket buying process.

How to Set Everything Up and
Get Everything Done [Chapter 9]

Your plans should be firm at least 181 days before your arrival date. Then see the To-Do List for exactly what to do, and when, to prepare for your trip.

There are three key dates to consider:

- Restaurant reservations open for booking 180 days before a potential dining date.

- For those staying at a Disney-owned resort or another eligible hotel, FastPass+ reservations can be booked beginning 60 days before their arrival date.

- For everyone else, FastPass+ reservations can be booked beginning 30 days before planned use.

Building a To-Do List is keyed to these three dates because booking as early as possibly will result in the widest selection of available experiences. Chapter 9 covers exactly how and when to make these decisions.

RETURNING VISITORS NEED TO KNOW:

- FastPass+ reservations are, along with good daily plans, the critical part of designing a lower-wait, lower-stress trip. The most options and best rides will be available at the beginning of your booking window. Which FastPass+ to book is explained in Chapter 6, and how to create FastPass+ reservations is explained in this chapter.

- You make and manage your FastPass+ and other reservations through the My Disney Experience website and app—creating and using a account is also explained in this chapter.

- Finally, for Disney-owned hotel guests, there are no more room keys. Customizable MagicBands, also explained in this chapter, serve as room keys and link to all your other reservations and tickets, and will be shipped before departure to U.S.-based addresses.

Disney World planning may feel like a daunting task. Don't worry. You're in good hands. The following chapters offer a step-by-step walkthrough of the entire planning process, offering just the right amount of detail so you can make informed decisions. When everything goes according to plan and the group asks, "How did you make this trip so wonderful?" you can respond with a smile, "It was pretty easy, actually."

CHAPTER TWO

Why Age and Height Matter

Children of all ages enjoy Walt Disney World in their own ways, whether by meeting the characters, riding the thrill rides, or blending both roller coasters and princess breakfasts into an overall itinerary. When deciding whether it's time to book a first trip, consider the ages and heights of the kid(s) and what they can and will be able to experience once they arrive. If one or more of the kids are under 48 inches tall, they will run into attractions they aren't able to experience due to height restrictions. If they don't have the intellectual and emotional maturity of the typical eight year old, other rides for which they are tall enough may be too frightening, or just a little too sophisticated for them to fully enjoy.

If your kids aren't eight or older and over 48" tall, and this is a once-in-a-lifetime trip, you need to decide whether you should wait until they are tall enough and mature enough to enjoy everything Walt Disney World offers. Even with height restrictions and the possibility that the content of an attraction like Living with the Land will fly over their heads, younger and shorter kids typically have as much fun as their older counterparts. But while pictures of the kids when they're young enough to sit on Mickey's lap might initially seem like a more precious proposition, trips with the kids when they're older may be more enjoyable and more memorable for all involved. Those already planning on a return visit benefit from enjoying a wider range of experiences over many years, in addition to more flexible planning. The good news is that no matter whether or not you're already planning a return visit, it's easy to design an itinerary around the unique needs of kids of any age.

This chapter first discusses trips with kids of various ages. It then covers handling a single visit with kids of wildly different ages.

Visits by Age and Height

PRESCHOOLERS

Preschool age children especially delight in the magic of meeting the Disney characters. They are young enough that they still believe they are meeting *the* Cinderella and *the* Winnie the Pooh. Pictures of the kids entranced with characters like Snow White and the Seven Dwarfs will turn into memories that last a lifetime. Some kids remain shy or apprehensive about meeting the characters. Mickey is, after all, an alarming five feet tall. Goofy, with his oversize top hat, stretches over six feet. With apprehensive

Comprehensive Guide to Rides

Key: **E=Epcot, AK=Animal Kingdom, HS=Hollywood Studios, MK=Magic Kingdom**
<u>Underline</u>: Favorite of older kids; *Italic*: Skippable for older kids

PRE-SCHOOL KIDS

Avoid	**E**: *Gran Fiesta Tour (Mexico)*, Innoventions, *Journey into Imagination with Figment*. **MK**: Carousel of Progress, Hall of Presidents.	**E**: Impressions de France, O Canada!, Reflections of China, Agent P's World Showcase Adventure.	**E**: The American Adventure, <u>Mission: Space</u>, <u>Soarin'</u>, <u>Test Track</u>. **AK**: <u>Avatar Flight of Passage</u>, DINOSAUR, <u>Expedition Everest</u>. **HS**: <u>Fantasmic!</u>, <u>Rock 'n' Roller Coaster</u>, <u>Millennium Falcon: Smugglers Run</u>, <u>Rise of the Resistance*</u>, <u>Tower of Terror</u>. **MK**: Haunted Mansion, <u>Space Mountain</u>, <u>Splash Mountain</u>.
Other	**E**: Living with the Land. **AK**: *Conservation Station*, Primeval Whirl, *Wildlife Express Train*. **MK**: Country Bear Jamboree, *Enchanted Tiki Room*.	**E**: Remy's Ratatouille Adventure* The Seas with Nemo and Friends, Disney & Pixar Short Films. **AK**: Gorilla Falls, Na'vi River Journey, Exploration Trail. **HS**: Mickey and Minnie's Runaway Railway*. **MK**: The Barnstormer, Swiss Family Treehouse.	**E**: Spaceship Earth. **AK**: It's Tough to Be a Bug, Maharaja Jungle Trek. **HS**: Indiana Jones Epic Stunt Spectacular, Slinky Dog Dash, Walt Disney Presents. **MK**: Big Thunder Railroad, Pirates of the Caribbean, Seven Dwarfs Mine Train.
Best-Loved	**AK**: *The Boneyard*, Dinorama, Triceratops Spin. **HS**: Disney Junior: Live on Stage, Alien Swirling Saucers. **MK**: Astro Orbiter, Prince Charming Regal Carrousel, Dumbo the Flying Elephant, Magic Carpets of Aladdin, Mad Tea Party, Tomorrowland Speedway, Tomorrowland Transit Authority PeopleMover, Tom Sawyer Island, WDW Railroad.	**AK**: Finding Nemo the Musical, UP: A Great Bird Adventure. **E**: Frozen Ever After. **HS**: Frozen Sing-Along Celebration, Lightning McQueen Racing Academy, Voyage of the Little Mermaid. **MK**: It's a Small World, Liberty Belle Riverboat, The Many Adventures of Winnie the Pooh, Monsters Inc. Laugh Floor, Under the Sea: Journey of the Little Mermaid	**E**: Epcot Forever/HarmonioUS, Turtle Talk with Crush. **AK**: Festival of the Lion King, Kali River Rapids, <u>Kilimanjaro Safari</u>, Rivers of Light. **HS**: Beauty and the Beast, Muppet Vision 3-D, Star Tours, <u>Toy Story Midway Mania</u>. **MK**: Afternoon Parade, Buzz Lightyear, Enchanted Tales with Belle, <u>Happily Ever After</u>, Jungle Cruise, <u>Mickey's PhilharMagic</u>, Peter Pan.
	Skippable	**Other**	**Favorite**

* Preliminary ranking of attraction not yet open

THIRD GRADERS AND UP

and shy kids, run a search on YouTube for "Disney World characters" and watch some interactions leading up to the trip. This will familiarize the kids with what to expect and reduce many of the first-time jitters and the tears that accompany them. While preschoolers will be too short or young for many of the premier attractions, there's still plenty for them to experience, especially at Magic Kingdom.

But they shouldn't try everything. Some attractions are simply too scary or intense for preschoolers. To help you figure out what is what, in the chart on the facing page we have sorted every attraction based on how well kids of varying ages are likely to enjoy them.

For example, in the bottom left box we have The Boneyard, a richly themed playground at Disney's Animal Kingdom. Younger kids love to play there, but most older kids will find it juvenile. The upper right box contains several of Disney's best attractions, many of which aren't suitable for younger children due to height restrictions or scary content. Most older kids (and their parents) love these attractions, which is why they fall into "favorites" for third graders and up, and into "avoid" for preschoolers.

With preschoolers, try to match their interests, stamina, and routines with what the family plans to accomplish...or you'll have the joy of experiencing the same tantrums every other parent is enjoying come 3pm.

When the meltdowns begin, it's not uncommon for Josh to turn to Dave and say, "It must be 3 o'clock." Indeed, even more common than Mickey bars and WDW t-shirts are the afternoon hissy fits. Be realistic about how long the kids are going to be able to go. While Disney World might be a magical place, pixie dust does not seem to increase kids' stamina or reduce their inclination to break down when they're overstimulated and ready for a nap. Plan a daily afternoon break for when crowds, wait times, and heat peak. This will rejuvenate the kids and their parents and prepare them for a fun and relaxing evening back in the parks.

YOUNGER SCHOOL-AGE KIDS

Kids between five and eight are young enough that they still enjoy most character meets and some of the other sillier entertainment that older kids may have lost interest in. They are also beginning to approach the height required to enjoy Disney's more thrilling major attractions.

The chart below illustrates which attractions shorter kids are disqualified from riding. Unfortunately, this chart could double as a list of Disney World's best and most popular attractions (with the exceptions of Alien Swirling Saucers and Barnstormer), including almost all of the headliners at each park. With a single trip on the horizon, if you can't wait until the kids are 48" tall, consider waiting until they are at least 44" tall. They'll then be eligible for every ride on property but two. And the two they aren't eligible for aren't necessarily deal breakers. Primeval Whirl is an off-the-shelf carnival ride, which has recently gone to seasonal operation. Rock 'n' Roller Coaster is located inside a relatively nondescript building at the end of a long road on Sunset Boulevard at Hollywood Studios. Simply avoid it and the kids won't feel like they're missing anything.

Keep in mind that "Tall enough for" doesn't necessarily translate into "ready for". Moreover, many of

Height Limit	Attraction	Those Less Than the Indicated Height Can't Ride					
		32"	35"	38"	40"	44"	48"
48"	Primeval Whirl	X	X	X	X	X	X
48"	Rock 'n' Roller Coaster	X	X	X	X	X	X
44"	Avatar Flight of Passage	X	X	X	X	X	
44"	Expedition Everest	X	X	X	X	X	
44"	Mission: SPACE Mars	X	X	X	X	X	
44"	Space Mountain	X	X	X	X	X	
40"	Big Thunder Mountain	X	X	X	X		
40"	DINOSAUR	X	X	X	X		
40"	Mission: SPACE Earth	X	X	X	X		
40"	Rise of the Resistance	X	X	X	X		
40"	Soarin'	X	X	X	X		
40"	Splash Mountain	X	X	X	X		
40"	Star Tours	X	X	X	X		
40"	Test Track	X	X	X	X		
38"	Seven Dwarfs Mine Train	X	X	X			
38"	Slinky Dog Dash	X	X	X			
38	Smugglers Run	X	X	X			
35"	The Barnstormer	X	X				
32"	Alien Swirling Saucers	X					

Caption: Disney World Rides Excluded by Height

Disney World's best attractions are like a Pixar movie in that there are layers of substance and humor that guests of all ages enjoy for different reasons. Kids between 5 and 8 understand and enjoy the attractions on a basic level, but nuances and deeper meanings are often lost.

KIDS BETWEEN 8 AND 88

Kids who are eight or older are tall enough, old enough, and mature enough to enjoy all of Disney World's rides and entertainment. Unfortunately, they may be getting too old to be swept up in the magic of breakfast with Cinderella inside the Castle. Most remain happy to participate, if for no other reason than it makes mom happy.

With just one planned trip, consider waiting until the kids are around this age. Returning guests that begin visiting when their kids are younger enjoy the widest range of experiences over many years. Cherish the memories of their first visit with Mickey Mouse and look forward to pretending you're not afraid when junior first starts begging to ride Expedition Everest.

Trips with Children of Different Ages

There are several ways to plan trips around kids of wildly different ages and maturity levels. The underlying problem, as discussed, is that kids of varying ages enjoy different things. This is not unique to Disney World. At home, young kids may like playing with Legos, while older kids have moved on to the Xbox One X. At Disney World, kids may occasionally want to or need to split up in order to experience certain attractions. Disney has made this relatively easy by building playgrounds and diversions aimed at younger kids in close proximity to the thrillers. Here are a few other ideas:

TAKE ADVANTAGE OF RIDER SWITCH. Commonly referred to as "Child Swap", Rider Switch allows those eligible and willing to experience an attraction with a height requirement to ride, while others either wait alongside them in line or do something else. Most attractions require the group to approach the attraction's entrance and present the child too short or too leery to board the ride. The Cast Member will hand the group a Rider Switch pass. The members of the group experiencing the attraction wait in line. Members not experiencing the attraction may wait at the same time or head elsewhere. Once the group has experienced the attraction, up to three people can use the Rider Switch pass to enter the FastPass+ line, eliminating much of the wait. This can include a member or two of the original group. For example, let's say a family of four wants to experience Test Track, but one child is too short. Parent 1 and the older child wait in line and ride, while Parent 2 and the younger child head off to Innoventions to play. Once Parent 1 and the older child are off Test Track, up to three members of the family may use the Rider Switch at the FastPass+ line. That means the older child that previously rode Test Track can ride again alongside Parent 2. Parent 1 can then take the younger child elsewhere—perhaps to the interactive play area at Mission: SPACE's exit.

HAVE PART OF THE FAMILY FOCUS ON RIDES FOR OLDER KIDS, AND THE REST ON ATTRACTIONS DESIGNED FOR THE YOUNGEST. Split the family up, with older kids and a parent on one set of rides, and the littler ones on another age-appropriate set. This works particularly well if one parent has little interest in the thrill rides and coasters anyway. You can build completely different itineraries and FastPass+ selections for the two groups, or have some experiences in common and some different.

CONSIDER CHILDCARE SERVICES. Disney vets use an independent in-room babysitting service called "Kid's Nite Out" for kids between six months and twelve years old. At press time, rates start at $18 per hour for one child and go up to $26 an hour for four children (four hour minimum). There's a $2/hour surcharge after 9pm and a one-time transportation fee of $10. Babysitters arrive armed with age-appropriate games, crafts, and books.

Families visiting with kids of any and all ages thoroughly enjoy their Walt Disney World vacations, but keep in mind that the experience will be quite different depending on who it is you're taking. Groups consisting of families with kids of varying ages will need to make some compromises, but the good news is that the vast majority of your time can and will be spent together as a family.

CHAPTER THREE

How Long to Stay

This chapter addresses the decision-making process for how long to stay at Walt Disney World. Guests planning to return enjoy the ability to ease into visiting the theme parks with shorter trips of four or so days, knowing they can catch missed attractions and experiences in the future. Those planning once-in-a-lifetime style vacations are best served pushing their length of stay to eight or nine days. This affords the opportunity to enjoy much of the best of Walt Disney World, and also allows a mixture of longer days in the theme parks tempered by more relaxing downtime back at the resort. Shorter stays are often rewarding and enjoyable for everyone involved, but the limited time necessitates skipping key experiences and requires a more ambitious schedule with fewer opportunities to relax.

We'll first cover the basics: budgets, time, and the ages of the kids. Then, in the next section, we'll address the importance of taking time away from the parks to relax, followed by a section about allocating time for an "only" trip.

Budgets, Time Available, and Ages of the Kids

Most prospective guests will choose a length of stay based on three primary factors: budget, time constraints, and kids' ages. Mom might only be able to get a Monday through Wednesday off work, necessitating a shorter five-day trip that begins with travel early Saturday and ends with travel late Wednesday. A budget might be stretched too thin for a seven-night stay at a moderate resort, but work with fewer nights at a value (Chapter 5 explains the difference between "moderates" and "values"). A family with very young kids may find that a delightful trip lasts only three or four days.

The good news is that guests with a wide range of budgets and trip lengths can thoroughly enjoy their visits. The bad news is that, like most things, (within reason) more is better.

A longer trip means more relaxing, more theme park visits, more Mickey ice cream bars, and, ultimately, more flexibility. Longer trips also have lower per-day costs. Most travel costs are fixed regardless of how many days you spend in Orlando. If airfare and related costs are $1500, the per-day travel cost on a five-day vacation is $300. On a ten-day trip, the per-day travel cost drops in half, to only $150 per day. Second, while Disney World's new date based pricing adds much variation to the cost to add a day, typically in 2020 it costs just $9 to $17 per ticket per day to add a fifth through a tenth ticket day. Of course, extra days come with other costs like dining, souvenirs, and lodging, but even so, one long stay is often much less expensive than two shorter stays.

If this is a once-in-a-lifetime visit, we recommend trying to stretch your vacation dollars to eight nights and nine days. This allows for the equivalent of a day and a half or so at each of Animal Kingdom and Hollywood Studios, in addition to one-and-a-half to two days at Epcot and two or three full days at Magic Kingdom. The longer trip length also offers flexibility in late arrivals and early departures. You may elect to leave Epcot one afternoon at 3pm to head off to the Grand Floridian Resort & Spa for afternoon tea with Alice from *Alice in Wonderland*. With an eight-night stay, there's plenty of time to return to Epcot without fear of missing anything. On a four-night trip, there's more pressure to stay in the park and tour until the last member of the family drops. It's either that or potentially miss out on key attractions that could be made up with a longer stay.

If time and budget don't allow, a shorter trip can be perfectly enjoyable, particularly if you're already planning a trip farther down the road. Two trips spread out over the years offer an opportunity to enjoy two potentially different experiences, while also providing more time to save for the hefty costs. (It also affords a great opportunity to purchase two of our guidebooks, which is pretty fantastic in itself.)

Deciding on a trip length that maximizes value and enjoyment varies a bit based on age:

KIDS FIVE AND YOUNGER tend to enjoy Magic Kingdom the most, where Fantasyland and most entertainment offerings cater specifically to their heights and maturity levels. Kids at that age may have no interest in visiting Disney Springs or Epcot. In this situation, a three- or four-day trip focused on visiting Magic Kingdom offers plenty of time to visit over multiple half days, in addition to affording opportunities to head back to the resort for naps.

MOST KIDS BETWEEN FIVE AND EIGHT will still prefer Magic Kingdom over the other major theme parks, but will get more out of trips to Animal Kingdom, Epcot, and Hollywood Studios. Plan to spend at least a half day at each of these three, pushing the number of theme park days up to five or six.

MOST KIDS EIGHT AND OLDER will be tall enough to ride every major attraction, including the thrill rides at each theme park, and mature enough to enjoy them all. Still plan at least two days at Magic Kingdom, but also include full days at each of the other major theme parks (and, if you can, even more) to take care of attractions like Test Track and Rock 'n' Roller Coaster.

The Value of Time Away from the Parks

Many first-time visitors equate time away from the theme parks as time wasted or value lost. This seems logical. After all, if theme park tickets are going to cost $350 a pop, we better be in the theme parks waiting in line for *something*. But don't make this common rookie mistake.

Touring the theme parks in Florida, by their very nature, is exhausting—particularly during the unrelenting summer when it's 85 degrees by 10:30am. It's a lot of standing. It's a lot of walking. If the kids are in strollers, it's a lot of pushing. In fact, it's not uncommon at all for guests to rack up five or more miles a day walking through the theme park. Just a quick lap around Epcot's World Showcase Lagoon is 1.2 miles. And that's without doing anything!

Time spent together back at the resort hotel will likely be some of the most fun, most rewarding experiences of the trip. One of Josh's favorite memories from his first visit to Disney World is sitting on the beach at the Polynesian with his brother, mom, and dad holding a Mickey ice cream bar in one hand and a hot cocoa in the other. Dave has fond memories of playing on the beach at the Contemporary with his mom and sister while his dad napped back in the room. Spending time with loved ones is a big part of a vacation and spending relaxing time together with Walt Disney World as the backdrop is an integral part of the experience.

Afternoon breaks are particularly necessary with young kids (or dads) who will be bombarded with sensory overload virtually every moment they spend in the parks. A child that's spent a few hours back at the pool will be a much happier camper when it comes time to stake out a spot for Happily Ever After that night. And, as an added bonus, those afternoons are also the busiest and hottest parts of the day at the theme parks. Where would you rather be? In a 25-minute-long line for a $5.50 Smartwater in the scorching afternoon sun, or back at the resort sipping a Mai Tai on the beach?

If It's Your Only Visit, Aim for Nine Days in Orlando

Returning visitors have the flexibility of choosing to spend less time at the theme parks and more time enjoying their resort and the other amenities Walt Disney World offers. But the four major theme parks—the Magic Kingdom, Epcot, Disney's Hollywood Studios, and Disney's Animal Kingdom—are the heart of a Walt Disney World experience. To fully appreciate the best they have to offer, you need about nine days:

- About a day and a half each at Animal Kingdom and Hollywood Studios
- At least a full day and an additional evening at Epcot
- Two to three days at the Magic Kingdom
- The equivalent of a day or two taking it easy

Add it up and you're looking at about seven full days in Orlando with a combined park and travel day on both ends, bringing the total number of vacation days up to nine. But if you can't make nine days work—don't despair, just move on to the next section!

SHORTER "ONLY" VISITS

Shorter "only" visits are doable with some compromises:

FIVE FULL DAYS To see most of the best of Disney World, five full days in the parks are about the minimum—two in the Magic Kingdom, and one more in each of the other three parks. Working some of this park time into your arrival or departure days will give you some needed time off in the middle of your visit.

SIX FULL DAYS Adding another day lets you have more time off and more time in the parks.

LONGER "ONLY" VISITS

If you are fortunate enough to enjoy more than nine days in Orlando, first prioritize time spent away from the parks. Time is a luxury at Walt Disney World, and more time means more sleeping in, more late park arrivals, and more time relaxing at the pool. Late arrivals are particularly advantageous with the invention of FastPass+, which offers the ability to schedule three high priority attractions for later in the day, far in advance of setting foot inside the theme park.

CONSIDERING ARRIVAL DAYS

If you are planning a nine-day visit, we suggest a trip that spans the nine days from Saturday to the following Sunday because it best fits the typical week off of work. The sample itineraries presented in Chapter Six will guide you through planning such a visit.

Of course, flexible visitors may prefer to arrive another day of the week, for the sake of saving time and money. Disney World tends to be busiest on weekends as local passholders push up attendance. If possible, design your vacation to maximize the number of weekday theme park visits. Disney's new date-based ticket pricing model (see Chapter 8) means that for short visits with three ticket days or fewer, having your first eligible park day be a Monday will commonly minimize your ticket costs. As a bonus, Disney resort rates are often higher on Friday and Saturday nights by $20 to $150, and typically lowest Mondays, Tuesdays, and Wednesdays. Avoiding the more expensive resort nights and park days will save money and reduce waits.

Airfare may be cheapest on Tuesdays and Saturdays, and there may be other travel expenses that can be reduced by traveling on certain days. Guests with flexible schedules should use services like kayak.com or google.com/flights to search out the cheapest or most convenient itinerary possible.

When deciding how long to stay, keep in mind that most travel costs are fixed, and the per-day cost of theme park tickets typically goes down as more days are added. Longer vacations allow more flexibility, in addition to providing more opportunities to experience everything Walt Disney World has to offer. Shorter Walt Disney World vacations tend to be more of a whirlwind experience. That isn't necessarily bad, but the go, go, go mentality often leaves first-time visitors thinking they need a vacation from their vacation upon returning home.

CHAPTER FOUR

When to Go

In picking dates, it's important to consider crowd levels, pricing, weather, possible refurbishments, and special events. Our specialty is honing in on the less crowded times to visit, when wait times are lower at attractions, lines are shorter at stores and quick service venues, and there's less congestion inside the parks. Lower crowds means being able to do more in a less stressful environment. From there, we typically prioritize resort pricing, then ticket pricing, followed by weather, refurbishments, and special events.

CROWDS Historically, Walt Disney World has been the most crowded when hordes of U.S. school kids are out of school: from early June through the third week in August, Thanksgiving week, Christmas and New Year's weeks, President's Day week, the spring break month of March; and the weeks before and after Easter. Recently, however, summer crowds have been more moderate. Other dates see an ebb and flow of mostly low and moderate crowds, all noted in the month-by-month calendar that follows.

Galaxy's Edge is scheduled to be fully open by 2020, and may drive daily attendance significantly higher at the Studios in the months after the opening of Rise of the Resistance in December 2019. We expect that the months following the full Galaxy's Edge opening will largely be business as usual at the other parks, while the Studios sees higher waits, particularly at the thrill rides.

RESORT PRICING Disney resort pricing is constantly fluctuating, so much so that the same exact room can increase in price 50% or more from one night to the next. For example, at All-Star Sports, the rate rises from $112 on February 12 to $193 on February 13, an increase of 53%. Picking less expensive dates may save $150–450 per night at the deluxe resorts. Disney used to name periods of different prices "Price Seasons": value, regular, summer, fall, etc., but abandoned this practice in 2018. We are sticking to the traditional price season names for simplicity and comparability. Fortunately, the less crowded times are also often the least expensive.

TICKET PRICING On October 16, 2018, Walt Disney World shifted to date-based ticket pricing, which means the per-day cost of theme park tickets changes based on how much demand Disney expects there to be for a given date. This pricing is based on the first day that the guest is able to use the ticket. Much more detail about this new style of ticket pricing can be found at the beginning of Chapter 8. Generally, ticket prices are higher during times when family travel is easier and crowds are naturally heavier. Disney has stated that the new pricing model is intended to distribute the crowds more evenly throughout the year. At press time, the most expensive tickets in December 2020 are as much as 45% higher in late December than they are in the least expensive times of the year—later January, later August, and most of September. We expect a ticket price increase in 2020 that will expand this range even more.

WEATHER The main weather points that concern us are summer heat and humidity, erratic winter highs and lows, and the peak of the hurricane season from mid-August to early October. Many of the least crowded and least expensive stretches suffer from weather issues, but none of these issues is routinely as challenging as the heat and humidity of the summer months.

REFURBISHMENTS Disney announces refurbishments about eight weeks in advance, making it difficult to plan a vacation around an unexpected major refurbishment. Fortunately, refurbishments follow a pattern, and we've identified when they're less likely to occur. In addition, it's rare that more than one or two major attractions are closed at the same time.

SPECIAL EVENTS Certain guests may want to plan a vacation around a special event like the Epcot Food and Wine Festival. Our month-by-month calendar identifies these special events and offers some advice on taking advantage of them, or how best to avoid them, depending on your needs.

Based on these factors—but especially low crowds and lower resort and ticket prices—we recommend the following weeks throughout the year:

- From Martin Luther King Day in January until the Sunday a week before President's Day in February
- The Sunday after President's Day through the first week of March
- The week that begins the Sunday after Easter until mid-May
- September after Labor Day through the end of the month
- The last third of October
- November after Veterans Day until the Saturday before Thanksgiving
- The three weeks beginning the Sunday after Thanksgiving

Josh recommends the first three weeks in May, the month of September, or the two weeks after Thanksgiving. Dave recommends the two weeks after Thanksgiving, which marry average to below-average crowds and prices with Disney World's astonishing Christmas displays and offerings like Holidays Around the World and Mickey's Very Merry Christmas Party.

Those embarking on a possible once-in-a-lifetime trip should note that the peak of the hurricane season ends in early October, and a few rides are usually closed for refurbishments in January and early February.

This chapter begins with summaries of what you can expect from weekly crowds, resort prices, ticket prices, and weather.

Next, it presents detailed over-views of each of the months of the year, discussing prices, weather, crowds, refurbishments, special events, and recommended times to visit that month.

Finally, for first timers who may never return, it presents Dave's chart that ranks all the weeks of the year based on crowds, pricing, weather, and other essential variables.

Crowds and When to Go

When considering "low crowds", remember that Disney World comprises four of the top ten busiest theme parks in the world, by overall attendance. Magic Kingdom averages around 57,000 guests per day. The days with the lowest attendance tend to see slightly north of 34,000 guests, while anything over 55,000 will result in much longer lines. Epcot averages about 34,000 guests per day. It's rare that the park sees fewer than 20,000 people, while anything above 35,000 will result in longer lines.

Each park suffers from bottle-necks and narrow walkways, in addition to succumbing to peri-odic mass exoduses from shows throughout the day. From there, certain attractions are extremely popular, with demand far out-stripping supply. For example, let's take a look at Frozen Ever After, the re-imagining of the old Maelstrom ride in Norway. The attraction moves around a thousand people an hour. On an average day with Epcot open from 9am to 9pm, there are 12,000 rides to share with 34,000 people. And it takes just 1,000 of them (or just 3%) in front of you to hit a 60 minute standby wait.

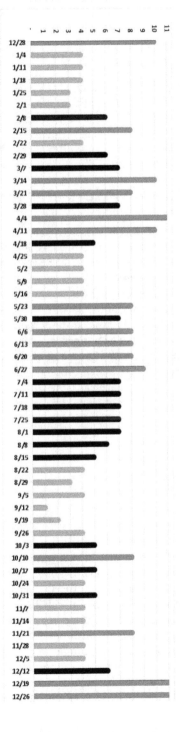

Walt Disney World 2020 Crowd Calendar

Don't be too discouraged, however. Just because everyone else waits 75 minutes in line doesn't mean you have to. Our touring tips and the cheat sheets that follow in Chapter Seven will reduce waits to virtually nothing, except perhaps in the new Galaxy's Edge land in Hollywood Studios.

Over the past several years, Disney World has tried various strategies to shift guests away from what would otherwise be naturally crowded times like major holidays and summer vacations. At the same time, the parks have reduced capacity during less popular times of day and cut operating hours during less crowded periods of the year in an attempt to lower costs. Economic and political strife, particularly in some major South American countries, have also contributed to lower international attendance.

The results, so far, have been lower attendance in the summer, higher attendance in the fall, especially the two weeks around Columbus Day, and higher standby waits during many periods of the year.

Resort Prices and When to Go

For its resort hotels, Disney traditionally assigned dates to a specific "price season." These price seasons did not mean anything so simple as fall or winter. Rather, Disney changes prices more frequently than that. In 2018, it made two changes. First, pricing now changes more often over the course of a given week, so the price for the room on a Monday or Wednesday night is often different than the price paid on a Thursday or Sunday night. Second, Disney World seems to no longer be using its traditional names (or any names) for these price seasons. We believe that each of these changes is a step on a path to much more varied day by day prices over the course of the year. For example, in 2020 a standard view room at the Beach Club is offered with 38 different prices.

In the material that follows, for consistency and clarity we will be using the traditional Disney price season names:

- Value
- Fall
- Regular
- Summer
- Peak
- Easter
- Holiday

The first two seasons are always the lowest-priced, and the last three always the highest. Disney groups hotels into value, moderate, and deluxe resorts (more on this in the next chapter). At Disney's value resorts, Summer rates are much higher than Regular rates; at its moderates, Summer and Regular are about the same over a multi-day visit; and at deluxe resorts, Summer rates are lower than Regular rates. Moreover, deluxe seasons change according to a different calendar in the summer and fall than value and moderate seasons do.

The chart (next page, top) shows different resort prices at Disney World during 2020. It does not refer to the seasons themselves, as it's more

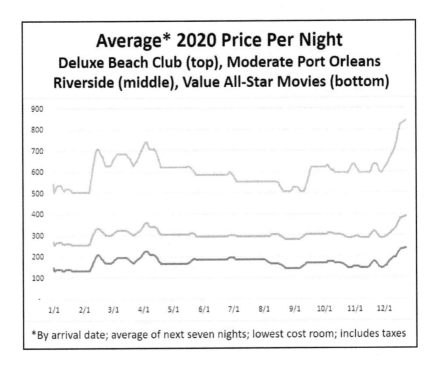

Average* 2020 Price Per Night
Deluxe Beach Club (top), Moderate Port Orleans Riverside (middle), Value All-Star Movies (bottom)

*By arrival date; average of next seven nights; lowest cost room; includes taxes

useful to show actual prices. The chart picks an example from each group, and to smooth out fluctuations that come from various upcharges, especially on weekends, averages prices over a seven-night stay.

Ticket Prices and When to Go

As of October, 2018, all theme park ticket prices now vary depending on the dates that a guest intends to use them and the length of the ticket. This means that there are now hundreds of different price points that a guest may pay to visit Walt Disney World for anywhere between one and ten days. For example, in 2020, a five-day ticket sees a price of $442 at the least expensive times, and a price of $605—37% more— in the most expensive dates of 2020. In the chart (next page, top), we use the cost of several lengths to illustrate the price fluctuations in 2020.

The chart (next page) shows how much more expensive a ticket of each of these lengths is compared to the lowest price for that ticket in 2020, by the first day the ticket is eligible to be used for. What you'll see in the chart is something like a crowd calendar, as ticket prices are higher during the holiday, spring break, and common vacation periods that are most convenient for families with children to go to Disney World, and lower during the beginning-of-semester periods like January and September that are least convenient.

We have much more on Disney World tickets in Chapter 8.

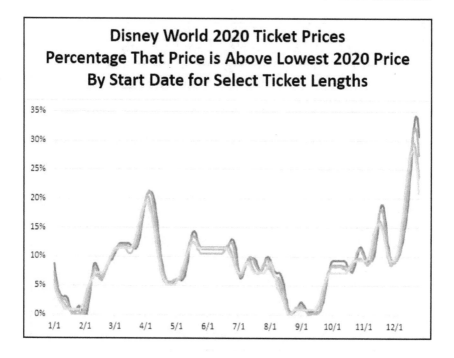

Weather and When to Go

The chart (below) shows the range of high temperatures at Disney World. The middle line is the average high. There's a 20% chance highs will be lower than the lower line, and a 20% chance that highs will be higher than the higher line. Note the big range of temperatures in the winter months.

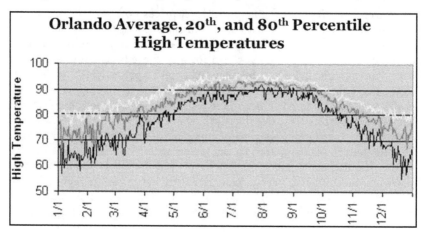

When to Go (Month by Month)

JANUARY

TICKET PRICES Medium-length tickets (4–7 day tickets) begin the month high priced—which we define as in the upper third of the year's prices. By January 5, they fall to low levels—which we define as in the lower third of the year's prices. After the 20th, ticket prices are at the lowest levels of the year for many lengths. For more specifics, and other ticket lengths, see Disney's ticket price calendar, explained in Chapter 8, at https://disneyworld.disney.go.com/admission/tickets.

RESORT PRICES Most of late January enjoys the least expensive resort pricing of the year, but January 1, 2020, with Holiday season pricing, is among the most expensive nights of the year, and the marathon (January 9–11) and Martin Luther King Jr. (January 17–19) weekends also see higher pricing.

WEATHER It's the coldest month in Orlando, with erratic temperatures and an average high of 69 and an average low of 50 degrees. Historically, it rains on 22% of days.

CROWDS Many U.S. school districts continue winter break through the first week, causing some of the highest crowds of the year to persist through the first Saturday of the new year. Crowds are lower the rest of the month, with two major exceptions over the marathon weekend (1/8–1/12) and Martin Luther King weekend (1/18–1/20). Historically, the period between the Tuesday after Martin Luther King Day through the Thursday before President's Day Weekend in February has been one of the least crowded times of year to go. Over the past couple of years, lower crowds have been offset by higher wait times, in large part due to reduced staffing. It's still an above average time to visit, particularly for those that follow our touring advice in Chapter 6, but it's far from the "dead" time of year that it would have been before 2017.

REFURBISHMENTS January usually sees the most refurbishments, including brief closures at most resort pools and typically lengthier closures at a few other attractions. The vast majority of attractions remain operating. Typhoon Lagoon likely will be closed into March.

SPECIAL EVENTS THAT MAY AFFECT CROWDS OR YOUR STAY:

- The WDW Marathon impacts transportation on the morning of the half- and full-marathons. Take Disney transportation.
- Several holiday events continue through the first week in January.
- Beginning in mid-January, avoid the large tour groups that become common.
- The Epcot Festival of the Arts will return in 2020, beginning January 17 and adding to weekend crowds at Epcot. The festival brings presentations, seminars, activities, shows, and kiosks in World Showcase offering food and beverage samples.

- Pro Bowl events will occur at the Magic Kingdom, Disney Springs, and especially ESPN Wide World of Sports the days before the game on January 26.

BEST TIME TO VISIT January 20 and later has cool weather, some of the lowest crowds of the year, the lowest ticket prices of the year for many ticket lengths, and the lowest Disney hotel prices of the year.

FEBRUARY

TICKET PRICES Medium-length tickets begin the month low, shifting to average levels around February 11. On February 17, they return to low prices, then become average later in the month. (For definitions, see "January)."

RESORT PRICES The lowest resort pricing of the year continues up until the Thursday before Presidents Day (2/13), when prices rise to the expensive Peak season. Peak pricing continues through the week following President's Day. Prices fall back to average February 23, 2020, and stay at that level into early March.

WEATHER The average high is 72 degrees and the average low 53, but temperatures are erratic and highs can get into the low 80s or dip well below 60. Precipitation is relatively low, but it does rain on about 23% of days.

CROWDS Crowds are below average to average through the Wednesday before President's Day weekend, when crowds are well above average (as well as in the week following it). Crowds return to average from the last week in February through the first week in March.

REFURBISHMENTS Most refurbishments will be completed by mid-February. Typhoon Lagoon likely remains closed.

SPECIAL EVENTS THAT MAY AFFECT CROWDS OR YOUR STAY:
- The Epcot Festival of the Arts will continue until February 24. See "January" for details.
- The Princess Half Marathon (Feb. 20–23) is scheduled the weekend after President's Day. It affects transportation in the early morning on Sunday and keeps crowds above average until the Saturday following President's Day.
- Superbowl Sunday (Feb. 2) sees few locals visiting, reducing crowds.
- Valentine's Day (Feb. 14) makes it harder to secure dinner reservations, but does not affect attendance.

BEST TIME TO VISIT A trip before peak resort season pricing goes into effect on February 13 is best, with these weeks seeing the lowest resort prices, low to average ticket prices, and some of the lowest crowds of the year.

MARCH

TICKET PRICES Medium-length tickets begin the month at average levels, and largely stay average until March 6, by when they are all high. Prices briefly drop to average levels for most on March 22, but then are high again by March 29. (For definitions, see "January)."

RESORT PRICES March 1–5 is Regular season with average pricing across the resorts. Peak season pricing begins March 6. Because of the later Easter in 2020, Regular season pricing returns on March 22, then Peak pricing return March 29.

WEATHER Temperatures warm, but remain erratic. Expect highs anywhere from the mid-60s to the mid-80s with an average high of 77 and an average low of 57 degrees, with minimal precipitation.

CROWDS Expect average crowds the first week of the month, followed by some of the heaviest crowds of the year the rest of the month due to spring breaks.

REFURBISHMENTS Pool closures remain common, and Typhoon Lagoon likely will be closed until mid-March. Attraction closures are less common.

SPECIAL EVENTS THAT MAY AFFECT CROWDS OR YOUR STAY:

- The Epcot International Flower and Garden Festival will begin March 4 and continue until early June. The festival brings millions of flowers, Disney-themed topiaries, and special activities around the park, in addition to kiosks in World Showcase offering food and beverage samples that generally cost $2–$7 each. The festival does not adversely affect daily crowds.

BEST TIME TO VISIT The first week of March will have the lowest crowds, ticket prices, and resort prices of the month.

APRIL

TICKET PRICES Medium-length tickets begin the month at high levels, and largely stay high until April 17. Prices then drop to a mix of average and low levels for the rest of the month. (For definitions, see "January)."

RESORT PRICES Peak prices continue through April 4, then the even higher Easter prices begin April 5. On April 19, prices return to Regular levels.

WEATHER April warms up to some of the most comfortable weather of the year, with an average high of 82 degrees and an average low of 62. Precipitation remains low with chances at 18%.

CROWDS Easter crowds mean that April will be rough by the fourth, and heavy crowds will continue through April 18. The next week will see moderate crowds, and crowds will be low by April 26.

REFURBISHMENTS Pool closures are rare; few attractions are closed.

SPECIAL EVENTS THAT MAY AFFECT CROWDS OR YOUR STAY:

- The Epcot International Flower and Garden Festival continues through the month. See "March" for details.

- The Star Wars Rival Run weekend is April 16–19. It affects transportation in the early mornings, but will have little additional impact on crowds.

BEST TIME TO VISIT Begin a trip at least one week after Easter Sunday when crowds and resort prices fall from some of their highest levels of the year to average and ticket prices drop to a mix of average and low levels.

MAY

COST Medium-length tickets begin the month at a mix of average and low levels. By May 18, all become high, and largely stay at that level until May 27. Prices at the end of the month are average. (For definitions, see "January")."

RESORT PRICES May 1–21 is Regular season, with average resort pricing, before prices rise from May 22–24 for Memorial Day. Then it's Summer season, when Value resort prices are higher than Regular, but lower than Peak. Moderate resort Summer prices are about the same as Regular, and Deluxe Summer prices can be lower than Regular season by 5–10%.

WEATHER Temperatures rise significantly in May, with an average high of 87 and an average low of 69 degrees. The weather gets wetter and more humid as you move closer to June.

CROWDS Crowds typically are average to lower than average through the Thursday before Memorial Day weekend. The Memorial Day weekend will be busy, but not as busy as other major holidays like Easter.

REFURBISHMENTS Rare.

SPECIAL EVENTS THAT MAY AFFECT CROWDS OR YOUR STAY:

- The Epcot International Flower and Garden Festival continues through May. See "March" for details.

BEST TIME TO VISIT Any time between May 1–16, with mostly low ticket prices, average crowds and resort pricing, cooler and drier days than later in the month, and the Flower and Garden Festival in full swing.

JUNE

TICKET PRICES Medium-length tickets begin June at average levels and become high by June 11. They remain high the rest of the month, peaking for date/length combinations that include the Fourth of July. (For definitions, see "January")."

RESORT PRICES All of June is Summer season. At the Value resorts prices are higher than Regular, but lower than Peak. Moderate resort Summer prices are about the same as Regular, and Deluxe Summer prices can be lower than Regular season by five to ten percent.

WEATHER June is hot, with an average high of 90 and an average low of 72 degrees. Precipitation inches up with a 38% chance and the highest accumulation of precipitation of the year.

CROWDS June is among the busiest months as schools let out for summer, but summer crowds the last few years have been lower than they were before. South American tour groups can drive crowds significantly upwards, though this is less of a factor while economies there remain weak. If the summer returns to historical norms, daily crowds will be lower than Easter or Christmas weeks, but busier than just about any other time.

REFURBISHMENTS Rare.

SPECIAL EVENTS THAT MAY AFFECT CROWDS OR YOUR STAY:

- The Epcot International Flower and Garden Festival continues through June 1. See "March" for details.
- Tour groups are common in June and July. If you see (or hear) a group of young kids walking around behind a 20-year-old carrying a flag, head in the opposite direction.

BEST TIME TO VISIT The first week of June will have slightly lower crowds than later in the month, in addition to reduced precipitation and slightly lower temperatures.

JULY

TICKET PRICES July tickets see some higher prices for shorter tickets keyed to the Fourth of July, and a mix of mostly average and a few lower prices the rest of the month. (For definitions, see "January.")

RESORT PRICES All of July is Summer season at the Value and Moderate resorts, but with an uptick over the Fourth of July weekend. At the Values, prices are higher than Regular, but lower than Peak. At the Moderates, prices are about the same as Regular. At the Deluxes, the first few days are Summer season, with prices that can be lower than Regular season by five to ten percent. After July 4, pricing at the Deluxes is reduced even further to Value Season 2 and some of the lowest prices of the year.

WEATHER July is among the hottest months in Orlando, with an average high of 91 and an average low of 74 degrees. Even worse than the heat is the humidity, which averages about 75%. Rain showers also increase in July, with a 49% chance of precipitation on any given day.

CROWDS Fourth of July crowds are the largest of the summer. Traditionally, the rest of July is the first or second busiest month overall because almost all U.S. kids are out of school, but see the note for "June" about recent lower crowd levels. International visitation is also at its highest point of the year.

REFURBISHMENTS Rare.

SPECIAL EVENTS THAT MAY AFFECT CROWDS OR YOUR STAY:

- Magic Kingdom offers a special fireworks show on July 3 and 4. The July 3 show is slightly less crowded. Epcot hosts special events and meet and greets in the United States Pavilion throughout the Fourth, and will likely offer a special Epcot Forever show with several extra minutes of intense fireworks. The Magic Kingdom show is the best, but Epcot crowds are more manageable.

- Tour groups remain common.

BEST TIME TO VISIT As late in July as possible is best. International visitation wanes and pricing at the Deluxes is lower.

AUGUST

TICKET PRICES Medium-length tickets begin the month at average levels and then drop to largely low levels on August 16. Some lengths see their lowest prices of the year later in the month. (For definitions, see "January.")

RESORT PRICES Deluxe resort prices continue low throughout August, dropping even a bit more on August 21. Summer season at the Values and Moderates continues through August 8. On August 9, the Values drop a bit and the Moderates increase a bit to the Regular season, and then on August 23 both drop to the Fall season, one of the lower-priced seasons.

WEATHER August is one of the hottest months in Orlando, with an average high of 91 and an average low of 75 degrees. Peak hurricane season begins in the third week. Hurricanes rarely directly impact Disney World or lead to the park closures we saw in 2016, 2017, and 2019, but they and lesser storms may affect flights and bring nasty weather. Showers and thunderstorms are common in the afternoons, with a 43% chance of precipitation.

CROWDS The first two weeks in August are as crowded as the rest of the summer before crowds diminish beginning the third week in August as kids start the new school year.

REFURBISHMENTS Rare.

SPECIAL EVENTS THAT MAY AFFECT CROWDS OR YOUR STAY:

- The Epcot Food and Wine Festival will likely begin in late August. It runs every day through mid-November. It's a fun event with interesting food, educational classes, and several expensive dinners. There are also bands performing throughout the Festival outside at the American Gardens Theater for free. During the festival, Epcot is extremely busy on weekends, and weekdays in World Showcase are also busier.

- Mickey's Not So Scary Halloween Party will likely begin in mid- to late August on select dates. It requires a separate ticket to attend. The party runs from 7pm until midnight, with ticket holders typically allowed to enter as early as 4pm. The party's main features are a unique parade, fireworks show, and trick-or-treating throughout the park. Most rides are operating. This event closes the Magic Kingdom at 6pm for visitors without a ticket to the Halloween Party. The Magic Kingdom is actually less busy on days when there is a Halloween Party because it closes early. If you have park hopper tickets, you may want to start at Magic Kingdom and then hop to another park to end the day. Without a park hopper, consider visiting Magic Kingdom on a party day then a dinner reservation at one of the resorts connected by the monorail. Tuesday parties are the least crowded.

BEST TIME TO VISIT The last week of August is the least crowded since early May, and sees lower resort prices and low ticket prices.

SEPTEMBER

TICKET PRICES Medium-length tickets are low—sometimes lowest of the year—in September until the 30th, when they shift to average. (For definitions, see "January.")

RESORT PRICES September sees a mixture of Value, Fall, and Regular resort price seasons. All prices are average or (most commonly) below average.

WEATHER September is just barely cooler than the summer months with an average high of 89 and an average low of 74 degrees. Humidity remains extremely high, and there is a good chance thunderstorms or rain will disrupt most afternoons and some evenings. Historically, it rains 40% of days in September. Peak hurricane season continues.

CROWDS We expect September, after Labor Day, to be a good month for crowds.

REFURBISHMENTS The frequency of attraction refurbishments increases with the lower crowds. Expect a few rides to be down.

SPECIAL EVENTS THAT MAY AFFECT CROWDS OR YOUR STAY:

- Mickey's Not So Scary Halloween Party includes many September dates. See "August" for details.
- The Epcot Food and Wine Festival continues every day through mid-November. See "August" for details.

BEST TIME TO VISIT After Labor Day, and before fall breaks start hitting at the end of the month, will have low crowds, and some of the lowest resort and ticket prices of the year.

OCTOBER

TICKET PRICES Medium-length tickets are almost all at average levels in October until October 29, when they become high. (For definitions, see "January.")

RESORT PRICES Most of October is a mix of Fall season and Regular season, with resort pricing slightly below average. Columbus Day weekend (Oct. 9–11) is the exception, with average to higher pricing.

WEATHER Weather cools slightly with an average high of 84 and an average low of 68 degrees. Precipitation is much lower than the summer months, with a 26% chance of showers on any given day. Peak hurricane season ends early in the month.

CROWDS Crowds are heavier in October than in past years with domestic school schedules moving toward fall breaks largely before or after Columbus Day. South American attendance is also higher in the first two weeks, culminating in the largest crowds of the month over Columbus Day weekend. If you are flexible with your dates, hold off until after October 24.

REFURBISHMENTS Expect a couple minor attractions to be closed briefly throughout the month.

SPECIAL EVENTS THAT MAY AFFECT CROWDS OR YOUR STAY:

- The Gartner Symposium likely will return to the Swan, Dolphin, Beach Club, and Yacht Club in mid-October. Epcot-area resorts will be sold out, and most nearby restaurants will be booked solid for those dates. The convention does not affect theme park attendance, except for Epcot, which is busier in the evenings.
- Mickey's Not So Scary Halloween Party includes many dates through October. See "August" for details.
- Epcot's International Food and Wine Festival continues daily through mid-November. See "August" for details.

BEST TIME TO VISIT October 24 through the end of the month is the best time to visit in October, with average crowds, cooler weather, and plenty of opportunities to enjoy Mickey's Not So Scary Halloween Party and the Food and Wine Festival.

NOVEMBER

TICKET PRICES Medium-length tickets begin the month largely average but shift to high levels by November 16. Prices remain high through November 27, and then are all average. (For definitions, see "January.")

RESORT PRICES At the values and moderates, resort prices begin November at lower Fall season rates, then kick up for the "Jersey Week" weekend 11/5 through 11/7. Prices return to Fall season 11/8, then increase 11/21 for Thanksgiving, returning to Fall rates on 11/28. Prices at the deluxes begin the month in the Regular season, then go up for the "Jersey Week" weekend 11/5 through 11/7. Prices at the deluxes return to Fall season 11/8, then increase 11/24 for Thanksgiving, returning to Fall rates on 11/28.

WEATHER It's noticeably cooler than September and October, with an average high of 76 and an average low of 59 degrees. November introduces more variability in high and low temperatures than the summer. Humidity is also substantially lower, with a 23% chance of precipitation. For those who like warm, but not uncomfortably hot temperatures, November is the perfect month to visit.

CROWDS Crowds are surprisingly light for the majority of November, with two major exceptions. The first is November 5–8, due to a phenomenon known as "Jersey Week" combining with the Wine and Dine Half Marathon. All New Jersey schools are off the Thursday and Friday of the first full week of November, and many families from the state travel to Disney World during that week and/or weekend. This raises crowd levels noticeably, particularly at Epcot and Magic Kingdom. Second, Thanksgiving week is very crowded.

REFURBISHMENTS Typically a few minor attractions.

SPECIAL EVENTS THAT MAY AFFECT CROWDS OR YOUR STAY:

- Mickey's Not So Scary Halloween Party may end October 31, or may have its final 2020 date on November 1. See "August" for details.

- Mickey's Very Merry Christmas Party will likely begin November 7 and happens several other evenings throughout the month. It requires a separate ticket to attend. Like Mickey's Not So Scary Halloween Party, it includes a unique parade, fireworks show, and special stage shows. Cocoa and cookies take the place of trick-or-treating candy. It runs from 7pm–12am, with ticket holders able to enter as early as 4pm. Because of the 6pm closures for regular guests, other nights that have late closures and fireworks are wildly crowded at the Magic Kingdom. Unlike the Halloween Party, where the first few parties typically are the least crowded, the first few Christmas Parties typically sell out due to elevated crowds for Jersey Week and the Wine and Dine Half Marathon.

- Epcot's International Food and Wine Festival continues daily through mid-November. See "August" for details.

- The Epcot International Festival of the Holidays (formerly Holidays Around the World) will likely begin November 27. Storytellers tell holiday stories and explain unique traditions in many of the World Showcase countries. Santa Claus meets in the U.S. Pavilion. The Candlelight Processional is an amazing stage show featuring the voices of famous celebrities, a large choir, and a 50-piece orchestra. The show, which tells the story of Christmas, is put on three times throughout the night (5pm, 6:45pm, and 8pm) and lasts about 40 minutes. Epcot Forever, the nightly fireworks and laser show, may also include holiday-exclusive highlights. The festival will increase crowds to the World Showcase in the evening, especially on the weekends.

- While the Osborne Spectacle of Dancing Lights is no longer offered, Disney's Hollywood Studios has improved its holiday decoration game considerably over the last few years. The Sunset Seasons Greetings projection show on Sunset Boulevard, the Jingle Bell, Jingle BAM! projection show, the Echo Lake and Toy Story Land decorations, and a whole lot more will all likely return on November 7 and run through the end of the year.

- Animal Kingdom began offering a broader suite of holiday programming in 2019, and we expect this to return in 2020.

BEST TIME TO VISIT November 8–20 is the best time to visit with the lowest crowds of the month and low resort pricing, although visits that begin later in this window will see higher ticket prices. You'll have plenty of opportunities to see the Magic Kingdom Castle Lighting and to attend Mickey's Very Merry Christmas Party.

DECEMBER

TICKET PRICES Medium-length tickets begin the month at average levels, and largely stay average until December 10, by when they are all high and stay high for the rest of the month, with the highest ticket prices of the year between December 16 and December 31. (For definitions, see "January.")

RESORT PRICES Fall season continues with resort prices slightly below average through December 6, 2020. Regular season pricing begins December 7; Peak season, with well-above-average pricing, begins December 11; another price increase begins December 18; and the highest prices of the year, the Holiday season, begin December 25.

WEATHER Expect erratic temperatures throughout December. It is not uncommon for one day to be in the low 60s and the next day to be in the high 70s. Nonetheless, the average high is 72 and the average low is 53 degrees, making most afternoons comfortable and most evenings a little chilly. Precipitation remains low with a 22% chance.

CROWDS Crowds are typically just below average to average through the second week in December. Crowds will then begin to build everywhere late during during the week of the 12th. Starting December 19, some of the heaviest crowds of the year arrive, with the highest crowds of the year from December 25–31.

REFURBISHMENTS Expect minor attraction closures for brief stints.

SPECIAL EVENTS THAT MAY AFFECT CROWDS OR YOUR STAY:

- Pop Warner brings its youth football Super Bowl to Disney World over the second full week of December. Pop Warner does not have a substantial impact on theme park attendance, but it does have a serious impact at the resorts where kids and their families stay. Pop Warner families typically receive hefty discounts at the All-Stars, Coronado Springs, and Caribbean Beach. If planning a trip over the second full week of December, consider booking another resort to avoid thousands of largely unchaperoned kids.

- Mickey's Christmas Party continues through several dates in December, with the last party scheduled for December 20. See "November" for details.

- The Festival of the Holidays in Epcot runs through December 30. See "November" for details.

- Evening holiday shows will continue at the Studios. See "November" for details.

NEW YEAR'S EVE CELEBRATIONS Magic Kingdom hosts identical fireworks on December 30 and 31. The 30th is slightly less crowded, but both days should fill to capacity in the afternoon. Epcot will host a special Epcot Forever show on the 31st with several minutes of outstanding fireworks at the end. Dance parties throughout World Showcase continue into the late night. Animal Kingdom is the least crowded park to visit during the day.

BEST TIME TO VISIT Try to end the trip by December 12 to take advantage of below-average crowds, average to below-average resort pricing, and everything the Christmas season has to offer.

When to Go If It's Your Only Visit

A family looking at a once-in-a-lifetime trip should visit at a less-crowded time when refurbishments and weather are less likely to negatively impact the trip. Based on both this and the delights of the Disney Christmas program, Dave has ranked all the weeks of the year for first-timers who may never return, in the chart on the following page.

Choosing dates is easiest for those with flexible schedules. For vacationers with school-age children unwilling to take them out of school, or other date constraints, picking a date among the less desirable times of year may be a bit daunting. The good news is that you're in the best possible position to make an informed decision. From there, we'll help you save money and time in the following chapters, regardless of when you ultimately choose to visit.

Walt Disney World Week Rankings 2020

Arrival Date	Week Rank	Comments	Crowds	Values Prices	Moderates Prices	Deluxe Prices	Other
		Bold=Recommended week for first time visitors who may never return					
12/28/19	44		Higher	Higher	Higher	Higher	Some Xmas Program
1/4/20	51	Marathon 1/8-1/12	Low+	Lower	Lower	Lower	Ride Closures Common
1/11/20	50	Marathon 1/8-1/12	Low+	Lower	Lower	Lower	Ride Closures Common
1/18/20	52	MLK 1/20	Low+	Lower	Lower	Lower	Ride Closures Common
1/25/20	49		Low	Lowest	Lowest	Lowest	Ride Closures Common
2/1/20	48		Low	Lowest	Lowest	Lowest	Some Ride Closures
2/8/20	53		Moderate	Low+	Low	Moderate-	Some Ride Closures
2/15/20	40	President's Day 2/17	High-	Higher	High	High	
2/22/20	**10**	**Mardi Gras 2/25**	Low+	Moderate	Moderate-	Moderate	
2/29/20	14		Moderate	Moderate	Moderate	Moderate+	
3/7/20	16		Moderate+	High	High-	High	
3/14/20	42		Higher	High	High	High-	
3/21/20	34		High-	Moderate	Moderate-	Moderate	
3/28/20	17		Moderate+	High	High	High	
4/4/20	45	Easter 4/12	Highest	Highest	Higher	Higher	
4/11/20	43	Easter 4/12	Higher	Higher	High	High	
4/18/20	13		Moderate-	Moderate	Moderate	Moderate	
4/25/20	**6**		Low+	Low+	Low+	Moderate	
5/2/20	**7**		Low+	Low+	Low+	Moderate	
5/9/20	**8**		Low+	Low+	Low+	Moderate	
5/16/20	**9**		Low+	Moderate	Moderate	Moderate	
5/23/20	39	Memorial Day 5/25	High-	High-	Low+	Low+	
5/30/20	18		Moderate+	High-	Low	Low	
6/6/20	37		High-	High-	Low	Low	
6/13/20	38		High-	High-	Low	Low	
6/20/20	36		High-	High-	Low	Low	
6/27/20	41	Fourth of July 7/4	High	High	Low+	Low	
7/4/20	19	Fourth of July 7/4	Moderate+	High-	Low	Lower	
7/11/20	20		Moderate+	High-	Low	Lower	
7/18/20	21		Moderate+	High-	Low	Lower	
7/25/20	22		Moderate+	High-	Low	Lower	
8/1/20	23		Moderate+	High-	Low	Lower	
8/8/20	32		Moderate	Low+	Moderate-	Lower	Peak Hurricane Season
8/15/20	30		Moderate-	Low+	Moderate-	Lower	Peak Hurricane Season
8/22/20	27		Low+	Low	Low	Lowest	Peak Hurricane Season
8/29/20	26		Low	Low	Low	Lower	Peak Hurricane Season
9/5/20	28	Labor Day 9/7	Low+	Low	Low	Lower	Peak Hurricane Season
9/12/20	24		Lowest	Low+	Moderate	Lower	Peak Hurricane Season
9/19/20	25		Lower	Low+	Moderate	Moderate-	Peak Hurricane Season
9/26/20	29		Low+	Low+	Moderate	Moderate-	Peak Hurricane Season
10/3/20	31		Moderate -	Moderate	Moderate+	Moderate	Peak Hurricane Season
10/10/20	33	Columbus Day 10/12	High-	Moderate	Moderate+	Low+	
10/17/20	12		Moderate -	Low+	Moderate	Low	
10/24/20	**5**		Low+	Low	Low	Low+	
10/31/20	11	Jersey Week	Moderate -	Low	Low+	Moderate	
11/7/20	**4**		Low+	Low	Low	Low	Some Xmas Program
11/14/20	**3**		Low+	Low	Low	Low	Some Xmas Program
11/21/20	35	Thanksgiving 11/26	High-	Moderate	Moderate+	Moderate	Some Xmas Program
11/28/20	**1**		Low+	Low	Low	Low+	**Xmas Program**
12/5/20	**2**	Pop Warner Week	Low+	Moderate	Moderate	Moderate+	**Xmas Program**
12/12/20	15		Moderate	Higher	High	Higher	Xmas Program
12/19/20	46		Highest	Highest	Highest	Highest	Xmas Program
12/26/20	47		Highest	Highest	Highest	Highest	Some Xmas Program

CHAPTER FIVE

Where to Stay

In this chapter we suggest that first-time visitors stay in a Disney-owned resort hotel, either a value, moderate, or deluxe resort, based on budget. Returning visitors should also consider a Disney-owned resort, in particular because of their FastPass+ advantages compared to most alternatives. Specifically, we recommend:

- **VALUE** Art of Animation, Pop Century, All-Star Movies
- **MODERATE** Port Orleans French Quarter, Port Orleans Riverside, Caribbean Beach, Coronado Springs
- **DELUXE** Wilderness Lodge, Polynesian Village, Contemporary, Grand Floridian

The chapter begins by addressing the advantages and disadvantages of staying on-site in a Disney-owned hotel. We then discuss the key differences between Disney's value, moderate, and deluxe classes, and take a look at what specifically differentiates resorts within each class. Next we provide detailed reviews of all the Disney-owned resorts by resort class. The chapter finishes with alternatives to staying in a Disney-owned resort.

Stay at a Disney World Owned Resort

More than 20 Disney-owned resorts dot the 40+ square miles that comprise Walt Disney World.

Another dozen hotels owned by third parties are also on Disney World property. Most of these are located in the far southeast corner of Disney World near Disney Springs (formerly known as Downtown Disney). Third-party hotels much closer to the parks include the Swan and Dolphin, both about a 10-minute walk to Epcot and about 15 minutes away from Hollywood Studios. Another is Shades of Green, an armed forces recreation center with lodging for military personnel and their families, located right across the street from the Polynesian. Finally, the Four Seasons Resort Orlando, between Fort Wilderness and Port Orleans Riverside, is the only five-star resort on property, and offers luxurious amenities, including the best pool complex in all of Disney World. There's more on these non-Disney owned hotels on Disney World property, and also off-site options, near the end of this chapter.

The Disney-owned resorts are usually more expensive than hotels operated by third parties, but they are also typically:

- Much more fun
- Much more convenient
- Much more "Disney"

The Disney-owned hotels offer unique perks that third-party operators could never dream of providing. The most advantageous perks include:

- The right to book dining ten days further out than non-Disney guests, which can be critical for high-demand meals like dinner at Be Our Guest Restaurant.

- The right to book FastPass+ reservations for key attractions beginning 60 days in advance of arrival. All non-Disney guests (except those staying at the Swan, Dolphin, Four Seasons, Shades of Green, Hilton Orlando Bonnet Creek, Waldorf Astoria, or a Disney Springs Resort Area hotel) can book only up to 30 days before use—which may mean some attractions aren't available for pre-booking, and others may be available only at less convenient times. The newest and most popular rides are hardest to pre-book, so the 60 day access can be quite helpful.

- Free airport transport to and from your hotel via Disney's Magical Express.

- Free and frequent transport from your hotel to the parks, water-parks, and Disney Springs.

- Free parking at the parks. Somewhat scandalously, Disney ended free overnight parking at its hotels in March 2018, aligning its practices with every other hotel on property.

- Access to the various Disney Dining Plans, which are a convenient budgeting tool if your family eats the way they are designed to feed you, and may save you a bit if your kids are younger than ten and you plan on several character meals.

- Eligibility for Extra Magic Hours (EMH)—extra time in the parks before or after regular open. We used to recommend avoiding parks on days they offered EMH, but fin d that crowd patterns have recently changed enough that this perk has become more valuable. We get into the pros and cons of EMH in more detail next.

While it's easy to read a list of definable resort perks, it's more difficult to describe to a first-time visitor how it feels to be caught up in the immersive atmosphere of the Walt Disney World bubble in a Disney-owned hotel. There are very few vacation destinations in the world that truly allow visitors to escape the harsh realities of life and instead be immersed in the fun and fantasy of a make-believe world. An inclusive on-property stay offers just that—from the time Magical Express picks you up at the airport to the moment they drop you off again, there's nothing to worry about at Disney World.

Extra Magic Hours: The Complicated Perk

Extra Magic Hours (EMH) are one of the best-known perks offered to guests staying at Disney-owned resorts, as well as at the Swan, Dolphin,

Four Seasons, Shades of Green, Hilton Orlando Bonnet Creek, Waldorf Astoria, and the Disney Springs Area Resort hotels. EMH are periods before official park open or after official park close when only guests staying at these hotels can experience the open Disney World attractions.

There are two varieties of Extra Magic Hours: morning and evening. Morning Extra Magic Hour is typically limited to one hour immediately before a park's regular open. Evening Extra Magic Hours are typically two hours long and begin immediately after a park's regular close. Many popular rides operate during both Morning and Evening Extra Magic, though the selection is usually wider during the evening. For example, at Magic Kingdom, only attractions in Fantasyland and Tomorrowland are typically open during Morning Extra Magic Hour. During Evening EMH, many more attractions stay open, including Frontierland and Adventureland attractions like Big Thunder Mountain Railroad and Pirates of the Caribbean. Evening Extra Magic Hours are typically more popular than morning.

The participating attractions are indicated in Chapter 6. At least one park offers Extra Magic Hours virtually every day. Disney World seems to have settled on the following schedule:

SUNDAY Hollywood Studios morning

MONDAY Animal Kingdom morning

TUESDAY Epcot evening

WEDNESDAY Magic Kingdom evening

THURSDAY Epcot morning

FRIDAY Magic Kingdom morning

SATURDAY Animal Kingdom morning

Seasonal or special events may alter the schedule, so check the park calendars for your dates.

So why don't we endorse visiting the park with Extra Magic Hours more strongly? Over 25,000 rooms on property have the opportunity to "take advantage of EMH" and every guest checking in will receive a Times Guide with the Extra Magic Hours schedule for the week clearly listed. "Up to two exclusive hours inside the park" sounds so overwhelmingly positive that the majority of the 75,000+ resort guests staying on property choose the park with the "extra magic." In turn, the day that a park hosts Extra Magic Hours will typically see at least average crowds for that week.

However, the Extra Magic Hours schedule isn't the dominant driving force that it was before FastPass+ was instituted. Now, guests are more likely to choose which park they plan to visit on which day based on where they were able to book their highest priority FP+, in addition to dining and experience reservations that can be, and often need to be, locked in 180 days in advance.

The key to enjoying Extra Magic Hours is to take full advantage of them. If you're able to arrive before morning EMH begins, then you can have a tremendous amount of success because so few people actually arrive that early. FastPass+ is also not offered during Morning or Evening EMH, so almost all of an attraction's capacity goes to standby, in turn making the line move quicker. Taking advantage of morning EMH will also put you ahead of the curve all morning because you'll already be moving on to less popular attractions once the park opens to everyone, where waits will still be short. For evening EMH, crowds can remain heavy, particularly during the first hour. The second hour is typically much less crowded, and you can get in line for any operating attraction just before the EMH ends. Plan on saving a headliner, like Flight of Passage, Seven Dwarfs Mine Train, or Slinky Dog Dash, for the very end of the night EMH period.

One other thing to keep in mind is how the early mornings and late nights will impact the rest of your vacation and your ability to enjoy it. For example, a late night may make it more difficult to be up for rope drop the following morning, when wait times are guaranteed to be low.

If you're ineligible for Extra Magic Hours or don't intend to take advantage of it, then it makes sense to avoid the parks hosting EMH. On days with morning EMH, there will be a couple thousand people inside the park before you're even able to enter. For evening EMH, crowds swell in the evening as eligible guests park hop over. We typically find that it's easiest to avoid EMH and go about our business on a regular day.

How to Pick Your Disney Resort Hotel

The most important factor is budget. Standard value resort rooms range in price from $112/weeknight at the All-Stars during value season all the way up to $330/night at Art of Animation over Christmas. Standard rooms at the deluxes start at $406 at the Wilderness Lodge in the value season and go up to $1,084/night for a standard view at the Grand Floridian over the holidays. Larger rooms, better locations, and better views cost even more.

There are five different types of Disney resorts:

- **VALUE RESORTS** Lowest prices, smallest rooms, fewest amenities, no table service restaurants. ("Family Suite" rooms, available at Art of Animation and All-Star Music, come in at about twice the size of a standard room, but cost more than twice as much.)

- **MODERATE RESORTS** Middle-of-the-road prices, room sizes, and amenities. Table service restaurants at all but Port Orleans French Quarter.

- **DELUXE RESORTS** Highest prices, largest rooms, most amenities, plentiful dining.

- **DISNEY VACATION CLUB RESORTS** There are multiple deluxe-level room types: Studios are similar to deluxe rooms; Villas, Bungalows at the Polynesian, Cabins at the Wilderness Lodge, and Treehouses at Saratoga Springs are larger and have full kitchens, and, at the two-bedroom and larger sizes, sleep eight people plus.

- **THE CAMPSITES AT DISNEY'S FORT WILDERNESS RESORT** Campgrounds for tent and RV campers (the Cabins at Fort Wilderness are grouped in the moderate class).

What You Can Expect by Price Class

Value Resorts	Moderate Resorts	Deluxe Resorts
Basic, small, ~260 square foot rooms	Good-sized ~314 square foot rooms	Lovely ~344-440 square foot rooms
Cost: $170–$250/night	Cost: $285–$340/night	Cost: $510-$750/night
Two full beds sleeping 4	Most have two queen beds, sleep 4	Most sleep 5 on two queens and a daybed
Split baths	Split baths	Most have split baths
No coffeemakers	Coffeemakers	Coffeemakers
Basic exteriors	Lovely exteriors	Lovely exteriors
Basic landscaping	Lovely landscaping	Lovely landscaping
Basic pools	Nice pools with slides	Great pools with slides
Food court	Food court, plus table service at most	Food court at most; table service at all
Basic dining choices	Better dining at most	Best dining for adults and kids
Hourly luggage service	Bell luggage service	Bell luggage service
Buses to parks	Buses to parks	Room service
Pizza delivery	Pizza delivery	Fun park transport at most, also buses

- All Pop and Movies rooms have queen beds
- All Pop and Movies rooms have coffeemakers

- AKL and WL rooms sleep 4
- AKL has only bus transport to parks

NOTES

Excludes Family Suites, Cabins, DVC
Cost: Average Fall 2020 Price Season
Rooms can hold in addition one more child younger than 3 at check-in

The vast majority of first time visitors stay in one of the first three resort types. The table above shows more detailed distinctions among them. Take heed of the notes at the bottom of the table...none of this is as easy as we'd all wish!

Once you've set your budget, there's no one size fits all answer, but the material in this section, and detailed reviews later in this chapter, should help paint a clearer picture of which resort is the best fit for your group. The reviews focus on the standard room options at each of Disney's resorts, the Disney Vacation Club Studios, and also the popular family suites at Art of Animation and All-Star Music. For a more comprehensive look at the various Disney Vacation Club Villas and updates on the comings and goings of the resorts throughout the year, visit Dave's yourfirstvisit.net.

Dave suggests picking hotels based first on overall kid appeal, mainly visual, and then on transportation convenience in a trip where the Magic Kingdom sees the most visits. Convenience to Epcot is prioritized second.

The chart below is derived from this methodology, with Dave's top picks at the top and on the right. Josh ranks resorts on a wider set of criteria, but largely arrives at the same results.

RESORTS SORTED BY CONVENIENCE AND KID APPEAL

Bold= Value Resort, *Italic* = Moderate Resort, <u>Underline</u> = Deluxe Resort

CONVENIENCE

Very Convenient	<u>Grand Floridian</u>	<u>Contemporary</u>	<u>Polynesian</u>
Convenient	<u>BoardWalk Inn and Villas</u> <u>Beach Club and Villas</u> <u>Yacht Club</u>		<u>Wilderness Lodge and Villas</u> <u>Animal Kingdom Lodge and Villas</u> **Art of Animation** **Pop Century**
Somewhat Convenient	*Port Orleans Riverside* *Port Orleans French Quarter* <u>Old Key West</u> <u>Saratoga Springs</u> *Fort Wilderness*	*Caribbean Beach* *Coronado Springs*	**All-Star Sports** **All-Star Movies** **All-Star Music**
KID APPEAL	Slight Kid Appeal	Some Kid Appeal	Great Kid Appeal

A NEW FACTOR: THE DISNEY SKYLINER

In the fall of 2019, Disney World opened a new transportation option, the Disney Skyliner, that connects Epcot and Hollywood Studios via a gondola system, and includes as part of the system stops at Caribbean Beach, the new DVC offering Riviera, Pop Century, and Art of Animation, with the main hub at Caribbean Beach. The new option promises to make transportation between these parks and these resorts, currently covered by buses, speedier, more fun, and with lower waits. Those picking a value resort have another reason to pick Pop Century or Art of Animation, and those picking a moderate another reason to pick Caribbean Beach.

VALUE RESORTS

Art of Animation and Pop Century are the top two choices, with All-Star Movies the best lower-cost option.

The distinctive features of the value resorts are their tiny 260-square-foot standard rooms, their terrific—but garish to the eyes of many adults—kid appeal, and their short list of resort amenities compared to what you'll find at the moderates and deluxes. For instance, a lot of first-time visitors are surprised that most standard value rooms don't have coffeemakers. You also won't find many leisure activities or any table service restaurants at the values.

Standard value resort rooms sleep four in two full beds. You may also add a child younger than three in a crib. A refurb at Pop Century and All-Star Movies that was completed in July 2018 added rooms with one queen bed, one fold-down queen bed that sleeps two more, and even cof-feemakers. Similar refurbishments are underway at All-Star Music and likely will begin at All-Star Sports later in 2020. These rooms fit the needs of many visitors looking for low prices, as they won't be spending much time in them other than sleeping.

Family Suites at the All-Star Music (520 square feet) and Art of Animation (565 square feet) resorts are much larger, sleep six, and include coffee-makers in every room, but cost more than double the price of standard rooms.

Dave favors Art of Animation with its oversized icons of some of Disney's most popular contemporary properties like *Cars* and *Finding Nemo* that are sure to excite kids. Rooms are bright and cheery, from the deep red clam-shell-themed chairs to the oversize Ariel motif on the shower curtain. Josh loves Animation's detailed theming, but all its standard rooms are located in the Little Mermaid section, which is a five to seven minute walk from the main building. This is less of a concern if you're already planning to stay in one of its more convenient family suites. Pop rooms feature Mickey and Pluto but are blander and more generic looking. Some families and couples may prefer the more subdued room theming at Pop, while others favor the over-the-top décor at Animation. Otherwise, Pop standard rooms average $40 less per night than standard rooms at Art of Animation and have queen beds. Both resorts are newer than the All-Stars, provide dedicated bus service, offer elevated fare at their quick services, and feature more robust Disney-inspired theming.

The other value resorts—All-Star Sports, All-Star Music, and All-Star Movies—average about $40 per night less than Pop and $80 per night less than Art of Animation, but they're also significantly farther away from Magic Kingdom and Epcot. The three All-Stars sometimes share buses and none of their themes (except Movies) are overtly "Disney", though each features smaller character scenes around the resort. Finally, their food courts offer lower quality, less inspired fare.

MODERATE RESORTS

Port Orleans French Quarter, Port Orleans Riverside, Caribbean Beach, and Coronado Springs are all good choices

Standard moderate rooms are found in all moderates except the Cabins at Fort Wilderness. They cost, on average, about $100/night more than the least expensive standard value rooms and about $375/night less than a standard room at the Polynesian Village. Your extra $100/night buys you about 50 more square feet than value rooms, in addition to queen beds (except in Caribbean Beach's "Pirate Rooms"), double sinks, a coffee-maker, a table service restaurant (except at French Quarter), an indoor lounge (except at Caribbean Beach), a pool slide, and hot tubs. The moderates also provide the most cost-effective way to sleep five (in the Alligator Bayou section of Riverside and in many Caribbean Beach rooms) and the most cost-effective way to get a full kitchen in The Cabins at Disney's Fort Wilderness Resort. New rooms in Gran Destino Tower at Coronado Springs represent the first high rise moderate rooms, and the first such with access from interior corridors.

Compared to the deluxes, the moderates (with the exception of Coronado Springs) have limited dining options, no character meals, are less convenient to at least one theme park, and have far fewer services and amenities. Fortunately, living areas are more comparable in size to those in the deluxes than you might expect, especially deluxe resorts with smaller room sizes like those at the Animal Kingdom and Wilderness Lodges.

Of the moderates, all but Port Orleans French Quarter are large and spread out, with dozens of guest buildings spread out over hundreds of acres. All have multiple bus stops (including shared buses at POFQ). All have more amenities than the values, but fewer than the deluxes. Coronado Springs offers the most amenities, including a salon, two gyms, six bars, and the largest hot tub on property. French Quarter offers the fewest, including no quiet pools, and no sit-down restaurant. Luckily, all those amenities and more are a short walk or boat ride away at Port Orleans Riverside.

Moderate resorts favor tranquility and a more sublime atmosphere when compared to the values, but don't offer the lushness and detail of the deluxes. This may translate to less overt kid appeal. There are no 50-foot-tall Mickey Mouse icons at the moderates, and other than some subtle references, nothing about them screams Disney World. Of the moderates, the vast majority of kids prefer Caribbean Beach Resort, with its beautiful white sand beaches, hammocks, and colorful guest houses. It also features a pirate-themed pool and play area that kids adore. Caribbean Beach has become the hub of the new Skyliner gondola system, alleviating its historic transportation issues, we expect, and has also upped its dining options to second best among the moderates.

Each of the moderates, except for Port Orleans Riverside, has both strong pros and strong cons. Port Orleans French Quarter is the most compact and easy to get around, but has the weakest amenities. Caribbean Beach is strong on amenities, and will be stronger with the Skyliner opening, but still has too many bus stops. Coronado Springs has, by far, the best amenities, but business travelers here for conventions or meetings may diminish the mood, and clutter the bars. Port Orleans Riverside has no strong pros, but also no strong cons.

(The Cabins at Fort Wilderness are so different than any other moderate that we refer you to the detailed review later in this chapter. However, we do not recommend them for first-time visitors.)

DELUXE RESORTS

The Wilderness Lodge, Polynesian Village, Contemporary, and Grand Floridian are the best choices.

Compared to other Walt Disney World options, the deluxe resorts are distinguished by having the:

- Most amenities, with the Contemporary and Grand Floridian at the top of this list.
- Nicest views, especially at the Contemporary, Polynesian, Grand Floridian, and Animal Kingdom Lodge.
- Best in-resort and nearby dining options, especially at the four Magic Kingdom-area resorts—the Contemporary, Polynesian, Grand Floridian, and Wilderness Lodge. The Epcot resorts—the BoardWalk Inn, Yacht Club, and Beach Club—have access to many nearby restaurants, but most of them are undistinguished for either kids or parents. The restaurants in the Animal Kingdom Lodge are marvelous, but there's no character dining, and no easy access to more dining at other resorts.
- Best pools, especially at the Beach Club, Yacht Club, Polynesian Village, Wilderness Lodge, and Animal Kingdom Lodge.
- Best transportation, especially at the Contemporary, Polynesian, and Grand Floridian that share the resort monorail to the Magic Kingdom. The Polynesian is most convenient overall. It has resort monorail and boat access to Magic Kingdom, and it's also possible to walk from the Polynesian to the Transportation and Ticket Center (TTC) to catch the Epcot monorail, which eliminates the lengthy monorail ride to the TTC before then having to switch monorails. The Contemporary is just a ten minute walk away from the Magic Kingdom, making it most convenient for a Magic-Kingdom-centric vacation. (A new walkway opening after we go to press will enable walking to Magic Kingdom from the Grand Floridian and—more of a hike—the Polynesian Village as well.) The Beach Club, located just a five minute walk or boat ride away from Epcot's International

Gateway entrance, is the most convenient for an Epcot-centric vacation, particularly during the Food and Wine Festival in the fall.

- Largest standard rooms, with those in the monorail resorts the largest, and those at the Wilderness and Animal Kingdom Lodges the smallest.
- Highest prices for standard rooms, with the monorail resorts the highest, and Wilderness and Animal Kingdom Lodges the lowest.
- Mixed kid appeal, with the Wilderness Lodge and Animal Kingdom Lodge the highest, the Polynesian next, and the Yacht Club and BoardWalk Inn the lowest.

As perhaps is clear by now, there are much bigger differences across the deluxes than in the other price classes. The detailed reviews later in this chapter cover these differences.

In 2018, Disney World made a new perk available to those booking "signature" rooms at the deluxes. Signature rooms are Disney's "club" level rooms—what most others call "concierge" rooms—and also its deluxe-level suites, and the Bungalows at the Polynesian and Cascade Cabins at the Wilderness Lodge. Those booking these already expensive rooms can, for an added $50/person/day (minimum of three days) reserve three additional FastPass+ per day beginning 90 days before their departure date. This new offering will be relevant to only a few, so we won't refer to it much in this book, but for those who can afford it, the ability to get six pre-booked FastPass+ per day, bookable before most others have the chance to book their FastPass+, has the promise of real value.

We particularly recommend the Polynesian which combines kid-and adult-pleasing South Seas theming with large rooms, great dining for both kids and adults, and a terrific pair of pools. It also has the most convenient location for trips particularly focused on Magic Kingdom and Epcot. We also recommend the Wilderness Lodge. The overall architecture—especially the lobby—is stunning. Its location across Bay Lake puts it a fun boat ride or just a short bus ride to Magic Kingdom. It offers one of the most family-friendly restaurants in Whispering Canyon Café. The former Artist Point has been transformed into Storybook Dining, a surprisingly good character meal hosted by Snow White, Evil Queen, Dopey, and Grumpy. Territory Lounge sits adjacent, offering terrific Northwest beer on draft and a menu that should feature past favorites from Artist Point. The main pool is fantastically themed and there's even a geyser that erupts throughout the day near the great new outdoor bar and grill, Geyser Point. The second pool, the newly rebuilt Boulder Ridge Cove, is also delightful. One qualifier—rooms are smaller than at most other deluxes, but prices are in turn lower.

Among the rest, Beach Club is the best choice for an Epcot-focused visit—which most first visits aren't. It's closer to Epcot and less uppity than neighboring Yacht Club. It also shares with the Yacht Club the best pool complex at a Disney-owned resort on property (the pools at the Four Seasons are the best overall on-property pool complex) and is more convenient to the limited Epcot resort quick service dining.

Value Resort Reviews

DISNEY'S ART OF ANIMATION RESORT

Disney's Art of Animation Resort ("AofA") is themed on four wildly popular Disney animated films—*Cars*, *The Lion King*, *Finding Nemo*, and *The Little Mermaid*. Like Disney's other value resorts, this theming is partly achieved with larger-than-life sculptures, but much more than the other values, the theming is also suffused into the landscape and into the rooms themselves. This makes it the most "Disney" of any Disney World hotel, wonderfully so to kids, and unrelentingly and garishly so to some adults. In late 2017, AofA became dog-friendly.

You'll find at AofA four lodging areas, each with two or three buildings framed around one of the movies, and two distinct room types. Family Suites sleeping six are found in the Cars, Lion King, and Finding Nemo areas, and standard rooms similar to those at the other value resorts (except for their much deeper Disney theming) are in the more distant Little Mermaid area. Found in Animation Hall near the entrance to the resort are dining, shops, and guest services. The main "Big Blue" pool, just outside Animation Hall, is the best pool among the values. You'll find two smaller pools as well—a tiny one in the Cars area, and a larger one in the Little Mermaid section.

Transport to theme parks, water parks, and Disney Springs is via bus or gondola. AofA is one of only two resorts at Walt Disney World with one bus stop and no shared buses, making total transit time shorter—nearby Pop Century is the other. In later 2019 the shared AofA/Pop Skyliner station opened, providing gondola access to Epcot and Hollywood Studios. AofA (and Pop) are already the most convenient of the values; the Skyliner will make them even more so. AofA (and Pop Century) are just next to and south of the Epcot Area resort Caribbean Beach, but Disney way-finding identifies them as ESPN Wide World of Sports Area resorts. Regardless, these are the two most centrally located of Disney's value resorts, though neither is particularly close to anything.

Disney's Art of Animation Resort
Little Mermaid Room ~260 Square Feet

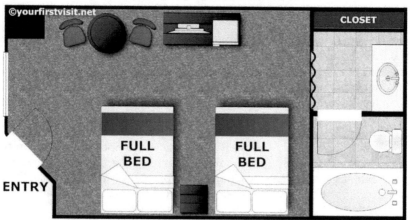

AofA's rich and detailed theming gives it the highest kid appeal, by far, among the values, and perhaps of any Disney World resort—at least for kids into one the movies it showcases. As with all the values, adult appeal is mixed, with some finding it fun, and others garish.

At AofA, there are two very different room types in four very different themed areas.

One room type is standard rooms sleeping four on two full beds (almost identical except in decoration to what you'll find at the other value resorts except for newly refurbed rooms at Pop Century and All-Star Movies). These are all found in the Little Mermaid area, which is also the farthest area from the main pool, Animation Hall, and bus stops. At about 260 square feet, these standard rooms may be the smallest four-person rooms you will ever see in the U.S. outside of historic center-city hotels. Besides the two full beds, you'll find in the sleeping area a table and two chairs, a TV/dresser combo, and a mini-fridge. There are no coffee-makers in these standard rooms. In the divided bath, you'll find a clothes hanging area, hair dryer, and single sink separated from the rest of the room by a fabric curtain. Next to this you'll find the toilet and tub in their own room. Unlike the other value resorts, which have little room theming

Disney's Art of Animation Resort
Family Suite Floor Plan ~565 Square Feet

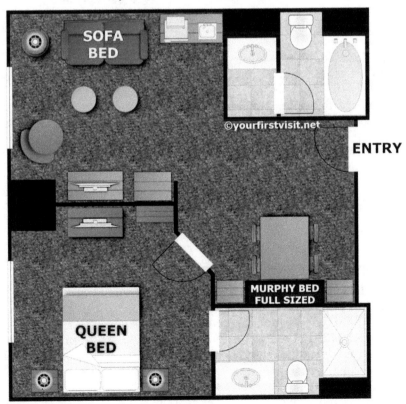

except in refurbed rooms at Pop and All-Star Movies, the *Little Mermaid* gang is quite present in these rooms. No rooms at Art of Animation have balconies. All Little Mermaid rooms are accessed from exterior corridors.

The rest of the rooms at AofA are Family Suites, found in three themed areas—Cars, Finding Nemo, and the Lion King. (No standard rooms are in these three areas, and no family suites are in the Little Mermaid area.) AofA Family Suites sleep six in more than twice the area of standard rooms, and contain a living room with a couch that folds out into a full bed, a dining area with a full bed that folds down, a master bedroom with a queen, two full baths (one connected to the master bedroom) and a kitchenette with a mini-fridge, microwave, and coffee-maker. Each of these rooms is deeply themed to its respective movie. Family Suites are accessed via interior corridors—more comfortable than exterior ones, but potentially more noisy.

Dining is in Animation Hall at the food court, Landscape of Flavors, the most ambitious of Disney's food courts in terms of adventuresome menus and fresh preparation. (Josh finds it unreliable and easily over-pressed by guests—if you do too, the food court at Pop Century is just over the bridge between the two resorts.) There's no indoor bar, but you'll find an outdoor bar by the main pool. There is no table service restaurant at any value, nor any character meals.

Amenities at the resort include movies, jogging trails, playgrounds, and an arcade. Art of Animation and Pop Century are the only value resorts on a lake, but the only water recreation available is gondola and bird-watching.

At AofA there are no upcharges for views, but Finding Nemo suites are more expensive than Cars or Lion King suites, because of their convenience.

Standard four-person rooms average $196/night during the 2020 Value season, $255/night during the Regular season, $272/night during the Summer season, and $251 a night during the Fall season. These prices average about $40 per night than Pop Century, and around $80 more per night than the All-Stars.

Six-person Lion King and Cars family suites average $448/night during the 2020 Value season, $557/night during the Regular season, $572/night during the Summer season, and $554 a night during the Fall season. These prices average about $160 per night more than the only other value resort family suites at All-Star Music. Nemo suites average $30 more per night.

DISNEY'S POP CENTURY RESORT

Disney's Pop Century Resort ("Pop") is themed around the toys, cultural icons, and Disney characters popular in the second half of the twentieth century. Think larger-than-life icons of Roger Rabbit, yo-yos, and a Mickey phone with Mickey, too. Pop has five themed lodging areas, each with one to three buildings framed around one decade—the 50s, 60s, 70s, 80s, and one lonely building representing the 90s. All this is more fun than it sounds, and the icons of characters—Roger Rabbit, Mickey, Mowgli and Baloo, Lady and Tramp—add Disney sparkle. Found in Classic Hall near

Disney's Pop Century Resort
Standard Room Floor Plan ~260 Square Feet

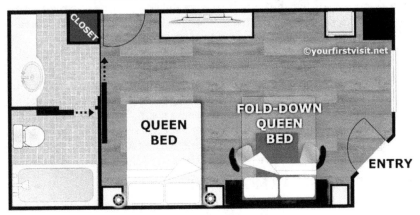

the entrance to the resort are dining, shops, and guest services. The main Hippy Dippy Pool is just outside Classic Hall. You'll find two additional, smaller—but still plenty big—pools, the Bowling Pin pool in the 50s area, and the Computer Pool in the 80s and 90s area. Among these three pools, Pop has the largest area of pool and sunbathing space of any value.

Transport to theme parks, water parks, and Disney Springs is via bus or gondola. Pop is one of only two resorts at Walt Disney World with one bus stop and no shared buses, making total transit time shorter (nearby AofA is the other). In later 2019 the shared Pop/AofA Skyliner station opened, providing gondola access to Epcot and Hollywood Studios. Pop (and AofA) are already the most convenient of the values; the Skyliner will make them even more so. Pop is just next to and south of the Epcot Area resort Caribbean Beach, but Disney way-finding identifies it as an ESPN Wide World of Sports Area resort. Regardless, Pop and AofA are the two most centrally-located of Disney's value resorts, though neither is particularly close to anything.

Not as themed as Art of Animation, especially in the rooms, but more Disney than any of the All-Star resorts except All-Star Movies, Pop has high kid appeal, and is a little less busy to parental eyes than AofA.

Pop completed a room refurb in July 2018. Distinctive features of the refurb include a fixed queen bed, a fold-down queen bed that eliminates the dining table when it is down, a sliding solid door separating the sink area from the living space of the room, and a coffeemaker. At about 260 square feet, these standard rooms may be the smallest four-person rooms you will ever stay in. Besides the two queen beds, you'll find in the sleeping area a table and two chairs, a TV and dresser, a coffee service, and a mini-fridge. In the divided bath, you'll find a closet area, hair dryer, and single sink separated from the rest of the room by a solid sliding door. Next to this you'll find the toilet and tub in their own room. The refurb also includes an upgrade in Disney theming, featuring Mickey and Pluto. No rooms at Pop have balconies, and all are accessed from exterior corridors.

Dining is in Classic Hall at the food court Everything Pop. In terms of size and menu, Everything Pop is well above average among the values. There's no indoor bar, but you'll find an outdoor bar by the main pool. There is no table service restaurant at any value, nor any character meals.

Amenities include movies, jogging trails, playgrounds, and an arcade. Art of Animation and Pop Century are the only value resorts on a lake, but the only water recreation available is bird-watching.

At Pop, you can pay extra for "preferred" rooms closer to Classic Hall and for pool views. Standard view, non-preferred four-person rooms average $171/night during the 2020 Value season, $212/night during the Regular season, $224/night during the Summer season, and $208/night during the Fall season. These prices average about $40 per night less than AofA, and around $40 more per night than the All-Stars.

DISNEY'S ALL-STAR MOVIES RESORT

Disney's All-Star Movies Resort ("Movies") is themed around five movies—*Toy Story*, *The Mighty Ducks*, *Fantasia*, *The Love Bug*, and *101 Dalmatians*—with two accommodation buildings in each theme. These films are represented by much-larger-than-life icons of characters and objects from them. Found in Cinema Hall near the entrance to the resort are dining, shops, and guest services. The main Fantasia Pool is just outside Cinema Hall. You'll find a smaller—but still plenty big—hockey-themed pool in the Mighty Ducks area.

All transport to theme parks, water parks, and Disney Springs is via bus. At lower demand times, Movies shares buses (except to Magic Kingdom) with sister resorts All-Star Music and All-Star Sports. Shared buses stop at Sports first and Movies last—which at times has meant the buses were filled by the time they got to Movies, making this resort the least convenient of the three. The All-Star resorts are Animal Kingdom Area resorts, and are the least conveniently located of the values.

Movies is much more Disney-themed than the other All-Stars, but does not have so rich a set of kid-appealing movies in its themes as AofA, nor

Disney's All-Star Movies Resort
Standard Room Floor Plan ~260 Square Feet

are many of its movies as widely kid appealing as the Disney characters and the toys at Pop. Adults may find the theming garish, or may warm to the represented movies.

A major room refurb was completed at Movies in 2019. Distinctive features of the refurb include a fixed queen bed, a fold-down queen bed that eliminates the dining table when it is down, a sliding solid door separating the sink area from the living space of the room, and a coffeemaker. At about 260 square feet, these standard rooms may be the smallest four-person rooms you will ever stay in. Besides the two queen beds, you'll find in the sleeping area a table and two chairs, a TV and dresser, a coffee service, and a mini-fridge. In the divided bath, you'll find a closet area, hair dryer, and single sink separated from the rest of the room by a solid sliding door. Next to this you'll find the toilet and tub in their own room. The refurb also includes an upgrade in Disney theming, with images of Mickey, Minnie, Donald, and his nephews. No rooms at Movies have balconies, and all are accessed from exterior corridors.

Dining is in Cinema Hall at the World Premiere food court. Movies has the largest food court among the All-Stars, and is average among the values. The bar is set in the exterior wall between the food court and the pool, and serves guests from both areas. There is no table service restaurant at any value, nor any character meals.

Amenities available at the resort include movies, jogging trails, playgrounds, and an arcade.

At Movies, you can pay extra for "preferred" rooms closer to Cinema Hall. Non-preferred rooms average $133/night during the 2020 Value season, $170/night during the Regular season, $186/night during the Summer season, and $171/night during the Fall season. These prices are the same as similar rooms at the other All-Stars, are on average about $80 per night less expensive than AofA, and around $40 less per night than Pop.

DISNEY'S ALL-STAR SPORTS RESORT

Disney's All-Star Sports Resort ("Sports") is themed around five sports—baseball, basketball, tennis, football, surfing—with two accommodation buildings in each theme. These sports are represented by much-larger-than-life icons of sports objects, and by the spaces between the two buildings themed to the playing field of the respective sport. Dining, shops, and guest services are in Stadium Hall near the resort entrance. The main Surf's Up pool is outside Stadium Hall. You'll find a smaller—but still plenty big—baseball field-themed pool in the baseball area.

All transport to theme parks, water parks, and Disney Springs is via bus. At lower demand times, Sports shares buses (except to Magic Kingdom) with sister resorts All-Star Music and All-Star Movies. Shared buses stop at Sports first and Movies last—which means that Sports guests are most likely to get a seat, making Sports the most convenient of the All-Stars, and of average convenience among the values. The All-Star resorts are Animal Kingdom Area resorts, and are the least conveniently located of the values.

Sports appeals to kids interested in its specific themes, but is otherwise thin on general kid appeal. The rooms themselves have only the lightest

Disney's All-Star Sports Resort
Standard Room Floor Plan ~260 Square Feet

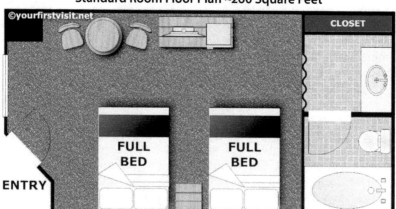

theming related to their area. Adults may find the theming garish, or may warm to the represented sports. All the All-Stars can be overrun with kids competing in events at ESPN Wide World of Sports, and this seems most common at Sports.

Standard rooms at Sports sleep four on two full beds in rooms pretty much identical to what you'll find at the other All-Stars except in newly refurbed Movies rooms. At about 260 square feet, these standard rooms are teeny but adequate for sleeping. Besides the two full beds, you'll find in the sleeping area a table and two chairs, a TV/dresser combo, and a mini-fridge. There are no coffee-makers in these rooms. In the divided bath, you'll find a clothes hanging area, hair dryer, and single sink separated from the rest of the room by a fabric curtain. Next to this you'll find the toilet and tub in their own room. No rooms at Sports have balconies, and all are accessed from exterior corridors.

Dining is in Stadium Hall at the End Zone food court. Recently renovated, this space is still too small for the guests it tries to serve, and is below average among the values. The bar is set in the exterior wall between the food court and the pool, and serves guests from both areas. There is no table service restaurant at any value, nor any character meals.

Amenities available at the resort include movies, jogging trails, playgrounds, and an arcade.

At Sports, you can pay extra for "preferred" rooms closer to Stadium Hall. Non-preferred rooms average $133/night during the 2020 Value season, $170/night during the Regular season, $186/night during the Summer season, and $171/night during the Fall season. These prices are the same as similar rooms at the other All-Stars, are on average about $80 per night less expensive than AofA, and around $40 less per night than Pop.

DISNEY'S ALL-STAR MUSIC RESORT

Disney's All-Star Music Resort ("Music") is themed around five musical genres—calypso, jazz, Broadway, rock, and country, with two accommodation buildings in each theme. These genres are represented by much-larger-than-life icons of musical instruments and other objects related to the theme, e.g., cowboy boots in the country music area, and by a bit of theming here and there of the spaces between the two buildings to the musical genre. Found in Melody Hall near the entrance to the resort are dining, shops, and guest services. The main Guitar pool is just outside Melody Hall. You'll find a smaller—but still plenty big—piano-themed pool deeper in the resort.

All transport to theme parks, water parks, and Disney Springs is via bus. At lower demand times, Music shares buses (except to Magic Kingdom) with sister resorts All-Star Movies and All-Star Sports. Shared buses stop at Sports first and Movies last—which means that Music guest are less likely than Sports guests to get a seat, but more likely than Movies guests. This makes Music of average convenience among the All-Stars, and of below-average convenience among the values. The All-Star resorts are Animal Kingdom Area resorts, and are the least conveniently located of the values.

Music appeals to kids interested in its specific themes, but is otherwise quite thin on general kid appeal. The rooms themselves have only the lightest theming related to their area. Adults will find it the loveliest of the values, and its overall layout the easiest to understand and navigate.

Music has two very different room types: standard four-person rooms found in all its themed areas, and six-person family suites in the Calypso and Jazz areas.

Standard rooms at Music sleep four on two full beds in rooms pretty much identical to what you'll find at the other All-Stars except in newly refurbed Movies rooms. At about 260 square feet, these standard rooms are really small but adequate for sleeping. Besides the two full beds, you'll

**Disney's All-Star Music Resort
Standard Room Floor Plan ~260 Square Feet**

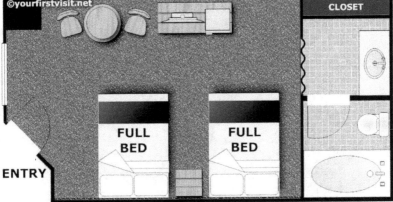

find in the sleeping area a table and two chairs, a TV/dresser combo, and a mini-fridge. There are no coffee-makers in these standard rooms. In the divided bath, you'll find a clothes hanging area, hair dryer, and single sink separated from the rest of the room by a fabric curtain. Next to this you'll find the toilet and tub in their own room. No rooms at Music have balconies, and all are accessed from exterior corridors.

Family Suites at Music sleep six in twice the area of standard rooms, and contain a living room with three furniture items that fold out into beds—a couch that folds out into a full, and a chair and an ottoman that each fold out into twins. It also has a master bedroom with a queen and two full baths, each accessible to anyone in the room, plus a kitchenette with a mini-fridge, microwave, and coffee-maker. These rooms are not nearly as much fun as the suites at AofA, and the fold-out beds are not nearly as comfortable for older/heavier guests. But some families will appreciate the more flexible number of sleeping spots, and others the fact that these suites are on average $160 per night less expensive than those at AofA.

In late 2019, a room refurb project began at Music. We expect standard rooms to be redone to the new two queens/coffeemaker approach we saw at

Disney's All-Star Music Resort
Family Suite Floor Plan ~520 Square Feet

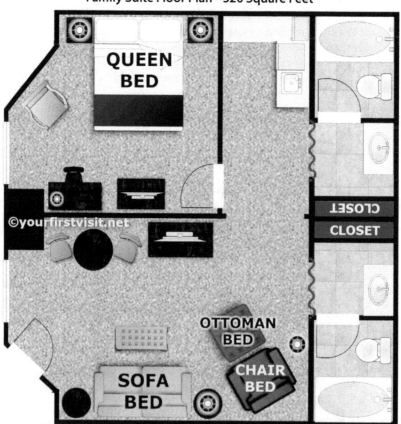

Pop and Movies, but don't yet have a point of view on how the Family Suites might change.

Dining is in Melody Hall at the Intermission food court. In late 2017, Intermission began an experiment in which some menu items are ordered at the cashier stations, rather than at the food prep stations, and when they are ready, signaled for pick-up via a pager. This promising approach, a version of which is common at deluxe counter services, limits congestion in the food-ordering area, at the cost of some members of your party (i.e., those ordering the items available only directly at the prep stations) potentially having their food much earlier than others. The bar is set in the exterior wall between the food court and the pool, and serves guests from both areas. There is no table service restaurant at any value, nor any character meals.

Amenities available at the resort include movies, jogging trails, playgrounds, and an arcade.

At Music, you can pay extra for "preferred" standard rooms closer to Melody Hall. Non-preferred standard rooms average $133/night during the 2020 Value season, $170/night during the Regular season, $186/night during the Summer season, and $171/night during the Fall season. These prices are the same as similar rooms at the other All-Stars, are on average about $80 per night less expensive than AofA, and around $40 less per night than Pop.

Family Suites at Music are all the same cost, whether in Jazz or Calypso. Family Suites average $305/night during the 2020 Value season, $382/night during the Regular season, $415/night during the Summer season, and $379/night during the Fall season. These suites average about $160 less per night than at AofA.

Moderate Resort Reviews

DISNEY'S PORT ORLEANS FRENCH QUARTER RESORT

Disney's Port Orleans French Quarter Resort ("POFQ") is one of two moderates with "Port Orleans" in the name—the other is Port Orleans Riverside Resort. Some mistakenly call these one resort. The only point of commonality most guests will ever notice is that guests at either are welcome to share the other's pools. The confusion comes from Disney shutting down, more than a decade ago, the table service restaurant and bike rentals at what was then known as Port Orleans Resort, and is now POFQ, and then renaming both resorts as Port Orleans—indicating to guests that these amenities weren't really missing, but just more distant, at Port Orleans Riverside, part of the same resort now.

Disney does not much bother with this distinction any more—other than making it clear to guests that they are welcome to partake in everything offered at both. It turns out that despite the missing amenities at Port Orleans French Quarter, it is the most highly valued of the Disney moderates—which is why alone among the moderates it is rarely included in Disney's discounts and other special offers.

POFQ has as its theme New Orleans and Mardi Gras, combining lacy wrought iron, lovely gardens, and cobblestoned streets. Mardi Gras figures and decorations are scattered about, especially near the main pool. POFQ has half as many rooms as Port Orleans Riverside and Coronado Springs, and two-thirds as many as Caribbean Beach, the other traditional moderates, and has—with no lake or river in the middle—a more compact footprint for those rooms. As a result, it is, by far, the easiest moderate to get around. It has no separate areas for its seven accommodations buildings, though you'll see North Quarter and South Quarter signage meant to help you find your building. Near the entrance at the center is dining, shops, and guest services in the Port Orleans Square area. The only pool, the Mardi-Gras themed Doubloon Lagoon, is just steps away, and the sole

Disney's Port Orleans French Quarter Resort
Standard Room Floor Plan ~314 Square Feet

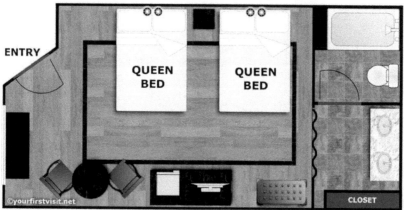

bus stop is right out front. One pool may seem like not enough, but the main pool area at POFQ has 65% of the area of Port Orleans Riverside's main pool, but serves only half as many rooms. A terrific kids splash pool was added in 2016.

All transport to theme parks and water parks is via buses. POFQ sometimes shares buses (except to the Magic Kingdom) with Riverside, but the single bus stop on the MK route makes it the most convenient of the moderates. Disney Springs is accessible by both boat and bus. POFQ, like Riverside, is labeled as a Disney Springs Area Resort in Disney's way-finding material, but is more centrally located than that implies. The Magic Kingdom, Epcot, and Disney's Hollywood Studios are all close.

There's no special kid appeal at POFQ, and in fact the Mardi Gras theming—including, for example, an enormous depiction of a sea serpent at the pool—wigs some kids out. But POFQ is the loveliest and most romantic of the moderates, and that, when combined with the ease of getting around and to the parks, makes it a great favorite of adults and of returning visitors among the moderates.

Rooms at POFQ were refurbed in 2018, gaining wooden floors, added power points, and larger TVs. They sleep four on two queens in about 314 square feet, and all come with a table and two chairs, a dresser/mini-fridge, coffee-maker, hair-dryer, and a divided, family-friendly bath. In the bath, the two sinks and closet/dressing area are shielded from the sleeping part of the room by a curtain, and the tub and toilet have their own room. All buildings have elevators. No rooms have balconies. All rooms are accessed from exterior corridors.

The only dining at POFQ is at the food court Sassagoula Floatworks Food Company, which, after its late 2016 refurb, is well above average among the moderates, and has a nice sprinkling of themed offerings—for example, beignets, Po Boys, jambalaya, and BBQ ribs served with collard greens. (You can, of course, walk to the table service Boatwright's at Riverside.) The indoor bar, the Scat Cats Lounge, expanded in late 2019, is not as rollicking as the River Roost Lounge at Riverside, but one should always have the option to not rollick. There are no character meals.

Amenities are thinner than at the other moderates, although most that are missing are nearby at Riverside. On site, you'll find (besides the pool) an arcade, playground, and movies. (Some nights, movies are at Riverside or POFQ, but not both.)

At POFQ there are no "preferred" rooms—itself an indication of how easy it is to get around for a moderate—but you can still pay extra for king beds, for garden views, for pool views, and for water views. Standard view rooms average $255/night during the 2020 Value season, $302/night during the Regular season, $295/night during the Summer season, and $304 a night during the Fall season. Prices are the same as Port Orleans Riverside and average $5/night more than Caribbean Beach and $20/night more than Coronado Springs.

DISNEY'S PORT ORLEANS RIVERSIDE RESORT

Disney's Port Orleans Riverside Resort ("POR") is one of two moderates with "Port Orleans" in the name—the other is Port Orleans French Quarter. Some mistakenly call these one resort. The only point of commonality most guests will ever notice is that guests at either are welcome to share the other's pools and other amenities.

POR has as its theme the 19th century American South, particularly the bayou and riverine areas of Louisiana and Mississippi. Rooms in the massive resort are in two areas, Magnolia Bend, with four large buildings meant to be reminiscent of plantation mansions, and Alligator Bayou, with many smaller buildings meant to evoke a more rural feel. Found in the Sassagoula Steamboat Company area near the entrance to the resort are dining, shops, and guest services. The main pool, located on a central island, has a bit of saw-mill theming, and is average among moderate pools. Testifying to the sprawl of the resort and the distance of many rooms from Ol' Man Island, you'll find five additional smaller pools around the resort. The resort proper has four bus stops, but sometimes shares buses (except to the Magic Kingdom) with nearby Port Orleans French Quarter, making it less convenient than either Coronado Springs or Port Orleans French Quarter. The overall accommodations footprint of POR is larger than that of Coronado Springs, but, because it has no lake, the main services at POR are more central than those at Coronado Springs. In late 2017, POR became dog-friendly.

All transport to theme parks and water parks is via bus. Disney Springs is accessible by both boat and bus. POR is labeled as a Disney Springs Area Resort in Disney's way-finding material, but is more centrally located than that implies. Before the Animal Kingdom and Blizzard Beach opened, the two Port Orleans Resorts were in fact the most centrally located moderates, and the Magic Kingdom, Epcot, and Disney's Hollywood Studios are still all close—at least after the buses finally get out of the resort. The resort itself is massive, and some rooms are a hike from the main services, and others from the main pool...some from both.

There's no special kid appeal at POR compared to that at Caribbean Beach, and no special adult appeal compared to that at Coronado Springs and POFQ. But even so, POR is likely the best-loved, most frequently recommended, and most loyally defended of all the moderate resorts.

There are three very different room types at POR. All are about the same size as those at the other traditional moderates, about 314 square feet, and all come with a table and two chairs, a dresser/TV/mini-fridge combo, coffee-maker, hair-dryer, and a divided, family-friendly bath. In the bath, the two sinks and closet/dressing area are shielded from the sleeping part of the room by a curtain, and the tub and toilet have their own room. The two story buildings in Alligator Bayou have no elevators, but the taller Magnolia Bend buildings do. No rooms have balconies. All rooms are accessed from exterior corridors. A room refurb project is complete in Alligator Bayou and should be completed across Magnolia Bend in early 2020.

The Alligator Bayou section of POR is one of only two areas at Disney World with traditional moderate rooms that sleep five—two each in two

Disney's Port Orleans Riverside Resort
Refurbed Alligator Bayou Floor Plan ~314 Square Feet

queens, and the fifth in a small murphy bed (about 66 inches long by 31 inches wide, and meant for a kid ten or younger) that folds down beneath the TV. (Caribbean Beach is the other.) These three bed spaces are a separately bookable category—families need not have five people to book them.

Rooms in half the Magnolia Bend section have "Royal" theming, and are more expensive. These rooms sleep four in two queens, and have much prince and (especially) princess detail, including a lovely headboard light show based on the *Princess and the Frog* triggered by an easy-to-miss button on the side.

Rooms in the other half of Magnolia Bend also sleep four in two queens, but do not have the special royal theming—nor its extra cost. They are also largely more convenient than the Royal Rooms, and, if you don't need the fifth sleeping spot, more livable than the Alligator Bend rooms.

Dining is at Sassagoula Steamboat Company, with a food court that's average among the moderates and a table service restaurant, Boatwright's Dining Hall, that's also average. The food court is too small for the crowds it faces, but has some menu items that reflect its theming—e.g., a Swamp burger, a Cajun chicken sandwich, fried green tomatoes, etc. The indoor bar, the River Roost Lounge, has a widely loved family-friendly show from "Ye Haa" Bob Jackson most Wednesday through Saturday evenings. There's also a bar at the main pool. There are no character meals.

Amenities available at the resort include movies, campfires, bike rental, fishing, jogging trails, playgrounds, and an arcade. (Some nights, movies are at Riverside or POFQ, but not both.) The main pool is far too small for the resort, and can't fit everyone who would like to be there.

At POR you can pay more for preferred locations that are a closer walk to the Sassagoula Steamboat Company, for the Royal rooms, for king beds, for garden views, for three bedrooms, and for water views. Four-person, two-bed standard view, non-preferred rooms average $255/night during the 2020 Value season, $302/night during the Regular season, $295/night during the Summer season, and $304/night during the Fall season. Three-bed, five-person rooms average about $13/night more. Prices are the same as POFQ and average $5/night more than Caribbean Beach and $20/night more than Coronado Springs.

DISNEY'S CARIBBEAN BEACH RESORT

Disney's Caribbean Beach Resort ("CB") is themed around Caribbean islands, their beaches, and the pirates who once voyaged among them. Rooms in the resort are found in five "villages" ringing a lake, all named after Caribbean destinations: Barbados (formerly Trinidad North), Trinidad (formerly Trinidad South), Martinique, Aruba, and Jamaica. Each colorful village has palm-tree lined beaches, and each has its own pool and bus stop. The central Centertown area includes another bus stop and the main pool at the resort, the pirate-themed Fuentes del Morro Pool—the best pool of the Disney World moderate resorts.

Six pools and seven bus stops may sound like an abundance of riches. They are not. Rather, there are this many pools and bus stops because of design flaws that make CB large and hard to get around—especially for guests staying at Trinidad. All transport to theme parks, water parks, and Disney Springs is via buses or gondola. The Disney Skyliner gondola has its hub at Caribbean Beach, providing gondola service to Epcot and Hollywood Studios. The hub stop will be particularly convenient to Barbados, Trinidad, and Jamaica. Another stop at the new next-door Riviera Resort is an easy walk from Aruba and will be the best choice for guests there to go to Epcot.

Caribbean Beach completed a refurb of its dining, bar, and shops in October 2018 that largely removed our previous qualms about booking here.

Many rooms at CB have Disney theming—a light touch in most, and deep pirate theming in the distant (and overly expensive) Trinidad area. The combination of Disney-themed rooms, sparkling beaches, bright colors, swaying palms, and the pirate-themed main pool give CB high kid appeal among the moderates. Adults like most of this, too, but can be frustrated by the walking distances and all the bus stops.

There are three types of standard rooms at CB, all about 314 square feet: Pirate-themed rooms that sleep four on two full beds, and two types of non-Pirate rooms—rooms that sleep four on two queens, and rooms that sleep five on two queens and a murphy bed under the TV that's about 30 inches wide by 64 inches long. (The floor plan depicts a five-person room.) These three bed spaces are a separately bookable category—families need not have five people to book them.

Rooms come with a table and two chairs, a dresser/TV/mini-fridge combo, coffee-maker, hair-dryer, a smaller storage chest in four-person rooms, and a divided, family-friendly bath. In the bath, the sinks and closet/dressing area are shielded from the rest of the room by a curtain in the Pirate rooms and sliding solid doors in all other rooms, and the tub and toilet have their own room. The two-story buildings that hold these rooms have no elevators, and no rooms have balconies. All rooms are accessed from exterior corridors.

Disney's Caribbean Beach Resort
Five-Person Room Floor Plan ~314 Square Feet

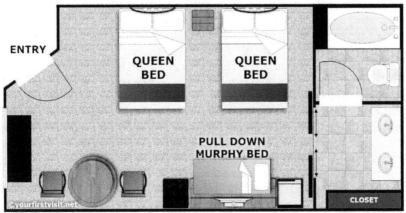

Dining is available in the new table service restaurant Sebastian's Bistro, and new counter service venues in Centertown and Trinidad. Sebastian's Bistro is strong but not worth a special trip, and the Spyglass Grill counter service offering in Trinidad is small but sound. The counter service offerings in Centertown opened with excessive waits and no lunch service, but waits are now down and lunch is available.

Other amenities include movies, campfires, bike rental, fishing, a Pirate Adventure cruise, great jogging trails, and playgrounds. With the elimination in 2017 of more than 550 rooms here, the main pirate-themed pool now more commonly fits everyone who wants to be there.

At CB, you can pay more for preferred locations that are closer to Centertown, for the Pirate rooms that are quite a hike and still have full beds, for king beds, and for water views. Four-person, two-bed standard view, non-preferred rooms average $243/night during the 2020 Value season, $293/night during the Regular season, $289/night during the Summer season, and $305/night during the Fall season. Three-bed, five-person rooms average about $13/night more. This is on average $5/night less than POR and POFQ, and $15/night more than CS.

DISNEY'S CORONADO SPRINGS RESORT

Disney's Coronado Springs Resort's ("CS") theme is based on the American Southwest, Spanish-colonial Mexico, their architectural inspirations in Spain, and the physical remnants of Mesoamerican civilizations. Rooms in the massive resort are found in four areas surrounding a lake: the Casitas, elegant colonnaded three- and four-story buildings; the new Gran Destino fifteen-story tower, with Spanish theming; the Ranchos, a sharply contrasting, desert-inspired area; and the Cabanas, a beach-house themed area with beaches, too—fewer than at Caribbean Beach, but more than at any other moderate. Check-in and guest services are in Gran Destino, as are a fine rooftop restaurant and two bars. The El Centro area, between the Casitas and Cabanas, includes more dining, shopping, and leads to the Coronado

Springs Convention Center. Away from El Centro, and near the actual center of the resort—and most convenient to the Cabanas and Ranchos—is the Mesoamerican-themed main pool, the Lost City of Cibola, in the Dig Site area, the second-best pool among the moderates. Three of the four room areas have their own smaller pool, and each of the four has a bus stop.

All transport to theme parks, water parks, and Disney Springs is via buses (or your rental car). CS is labeled as an Animal Kingdom Area Resort in Disney's way-finding material, but is in fact the most centrally-located of all the moderate resorts. This, combined with its "only" four bus stops, makes it the second most convenient of the moderates—among them, only Port Orleans French Quarter is more convenient for park travel. The resort itself is massive, and some buildings in the Ranchos in particular are quite distant from El Centro and Gran Destino.

Coronado Springs is the only moderate with convention facilities. This has led to much fussing, largely unfair. The same number of rooms occupied by conventioneers rather than families means fewer people in total at the resort (because conventioneers average fewer people per room) and fewer people at the bus stops and pools (as the fewer conventioneers are in meetings, not going to the parks or the pools). Most of the time, except breakfast, there's also fewer people in CS's public dining spaces, as most meetings have meals served as part of the meeting program. However, when a thousand people leave a meeting at once, and all want to go someplace, things clot up quickly.

On the other hand, because of the demands of the business travelers at the convention center, Coronado Springs has a much higher level of services and amenities than at the other moderates. There are the usual movies, campfires, bike rental, fishing, playgrounds, and arcade. In addition, uniquely at CS among the moderates, you'll find not one but two gyms, spa services, a main pool menu with real food, the largest hot tub at Disney World, six bars, four table service restaurants, and a business center. The effect of these extra services is to make Coronado Springs

Disney's Coronado Springs Resort
Standard Room Floor Plan ~314 Square Feet

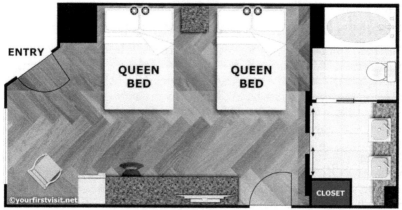

quite attractive to adults and to returning visitors looking for better amenities at moderate prices. Kids like the beach-themed Cabanas, the Dig Site area and main pool, and, if they aren't familiar with the geography, the exotic Southwest theming.

Rooms in Coronado Springs' Casitas, Cabanas, and Ranchos areas completed a refurb in late 2018. Standard refurbed rooms in these three areas at CS hold four people on two queen beds in about 314 square feet. They are similarly sized to those at the other traditional moderates. In a concession to convention travelers, they come with a desk rather than the table and two chairs you'll find in the other traditional moderates, but add a family-friendly easy chair and some Disney art. Most other room amenities are similar—a dresser/TV/mini-fridge combo, coffee-maker, and hair dryer. The bath is divided and family friendly, and after the refurb now has two sinks. Sliding wooden doors separate the bath from the sleeping area, rather than the fabric curtains you'll find in the other traditional moderates except the standard rooms in Caribbean Beach. All buildings have elevators, and no rooms have balconies. All rooms in these three areas are accessed from exterior corridors.

Gran Destino Tower opened in July 2019 and added 545 more rooms, including 50 suites. Accommodations in Gran Destino can have very nice views, and are the only moderate spaces accessed from interior corridors. Standard two-queen rooms, at about 400 square feet, are nominally much larger than those elsewhere at CS, but most of the extra space is in the entry hall, and thus not of much use to most. The bath is larger and nicer than those in the rest of CS, but while divided, is awkwardly laid out. The sinks share a space with a glass-walled shower, and the toilet is in a separate space. This bath would be more livable if the shower was also in the separate space. Other room fittings and fixtures are similar to those in rooms in the rest of the resort—except you won't find any Disney theming in them.

You'll find both more and better dining at Coronado Springs than in any other moderate. Dining is in four areas. Gran Destino Tower has the rooftop Toledo, featuring wonderful views and tapas, seafood and steaks, at a quality level comparable to dining in many deluxe resorts.

Disney's Gran Destino Tower
Standard Room Floor Plan ~400 Square Feet

The bottom-floor Barcelona Lounge serves appetizers and functions as a coffee shop in the morning. In next-door El Centro you'll find El Mercado de Coronado, the counter-service offering; Cafe Rix, a grab and go shop; and two more table-service options, Maya Grill, with a menu suited to the Southwest theming of the resort, and Rix Lounge, the closest thing to a club you'll find in a Disney-owned hotel, which also serves breakfast, lunch, and dinner. The final table service option, Three Bridges Bar and Grill, is on the water between the Casitas and the Dig Site pool, and serves dinner. At the Dig Site itself, uniquely among the moderate pools, you can find even more hot food. There's also six bars—two in Gran Destino, one in El Centro, one on the water outside El Centro, one in Three Bridges, and one at the pool. Of these, we particularly recommend Dahlia Lounge for its Gran Destino rooftop setting and views.

You can pay more for preferred locations that are a closer walk to El Centro, for king beds, for suites, and for water views. Standard view, non-preferred rooms outside of Gran Destino average $235/night during the 2020 Value season, $275/night during the Regular season, $269/night during the Summer season, and $286 a night during the Fall season. Prices average $15/night less than CB, and $20/night less than POR and POFQ. Standard rooms in Gran Destino average $50-$90 more per night than other CS rooms, depending on views.

THE CABINS AT DISNEY'S FORT WILDERNESS RESORT

Disney has had some trouble over the years communicating what's in the Cabins at Disney's Fort Wilderness Resort. Now that there are also starkly different "cabins" at the similarly named Wilderness Lodge, we expect even more confusion. The Fort Wilderness cabins—each its own little building—are distinctive spaces, sleeping six in two rooms, and with full kitchens. There used to be a "home away from home" category which the Cabins were in, but everything else in this group was a "deluxe" class room, and the Cabins didn't match up well with them.

So to eliminate the confusion about amenities, in 2009 Disney re-classed these Cabins as "moderates". This is a fair description of room-level amenities and spaciousness, but there's really few other ways that the Cabins are like the other moderates (inconvenience is one, and thin kid appeal another). As a result, the phrase "traditional moderate" started being used for all the moderates except the Cabins.

The Cabins are one of two lodging options at Fort Wilderness—the other being campsites. Fort Wilderness is one of America's great campgrounds, and the Cabins share in all the wonderful recreational activities available in the rest of this resort. The Cabins are each small, standalone buildings, looking on the outside like a nice small wood-paneled mobile home, and on the inside like a rustic cabin. If driving—and you should have a car to stay in these—you park right in front. Each cabin also has an outdoor barbecue grill and a big deck with picnic table. In late 2017, the Cabins became dog-friendly.

All of the Cabins except those in Loop 2100 completed a refurb in spring 2016 (Loop 2100 Cabins were removed). As you walk in, you'll find first the full kitchen —diminished by the refurb from a range with four burners and a full oven, to a two burner stove and a combined microwave and convection oven. The microwave/oven works better as an oven than you might think, but it is short (with only 6 inches of clearance between the rack and the top of the oven) and can't exceed 450 degrees. Adjacent is a small dining table and small living room. A queen bed folds out from a couch, so this space sleeps two—typically the parents. Further back is a full bath. It's not divided, and is short on hot water, so it doesn't always well suit the six people that these cabins can sleep. Beyond this is the back bedroom, with a tight-fitting queen bed on one side and a pair of bunk beds on the other.

The Cabins are not the least expensive way to get a Disney room for six—a family suite at All-Star Music is that. But they are the least expensive way to get moderate-level fittings and fixtures for six, and are by far the least expensive way to get a (mostly) full kitchen.

The challenge, though, is some crowding, especially around the bath, thin kid appeal—unless your kids love campgrounds—and great inconvenience. If you don't have a car, it takes two transport acts to get off Fort Wilderness and to a park—the first bus gets you to another bus stop or boat dock, from which you go to your final destination. We couldn't imagine staying here if you don't have a car. (Much-loved golf carts are also available for rent. They limit walking or bus waits at the Fort proper, but can't be used off the campground.)

Fort Wilderness has some family-friendly table service dining—the storied Hoop-Dee-Doo Revue, for example. (Mickey's Backyard Barbecue closed at the end of 2018.) There's also Trails End restaurant, with great value for money. Plus you have that kitchen. But there's not much in the way of counter service, and to get to these table service venues from the Cabins, you need to take a bus.

The resort has two pools. One is dull but within walking distance of the Cabins; the other, the main pool, remains the weakest among the

The Cabins at Disney's Fort Wilderness Resort
Cabin Floor Plan ~504 Square Feet

moderates. This pool is farther (a bus trip for most), and is in the same Meadows area as where you'll find many of Fort Wilderness's other amenities. At the Settlement end of Fort Wilderness, you'll find (via bus... you can't drive to these) the beach, marina, boat docks (with boat service both to the Magic Kingdom, and also to the nearby Wilderness Lodge and Contemporary resorts), and the dining noted above.

If you need the lowest-priced kitchen you can find, need to sleep six, and have a car, the Cabins are great options. Otherwise, not so much.

The Cabins have no extra price options for views and such. They average $412/night during the 2020 Value season, $482/night during the Regular season, $477/night during the Summer season, and $483 a night during the Fall season.

Deluxe Resort Reviews

DISNEY'S POLYNESIAN VILLAGE RESORT

Disney's Polynesian Village Resort ("Poly"), a monorail resort, is themed around the Pacific islands of Polynesia. Theming at the Polynesian is pervasive and detailed, but more subtle than that of the jaw-dropping Wilderness Lodge and Animal Kingdom Lodge. Lush landscaping, lovely beaches, flaming torches, and exotically styled and named "longhouses" (where you find the rooms) create a delightful impression. In the Great Ceremonial House ("GCH") near the entrance to the resort are dining, shops, guest services, and, on the second floor, access to the resort monorail with service to the Magic Kingdom, the other monorail resorts, and the Transportation and Ticket Center (TTC). Disney Vacation Club Villas are available for booking in the lagoon and east side of the resort. The main Lava Pool is just outside the GCH, and the smaller Oasis pool is between the main resort and the DVC longhouses.

With travel to the Magic Kingdom available via both monorail and boat, and many rooms at the Polynesian within easy walking distance of the TTC and its Epcot monorail, the Polynesian is the most convenient Disney World resort. Transportation to the other parks and Disney Springs is via buses, typically shared with one or two other Magic Kingdom area resorts. A path that measures about a mile long will connect Magic Kingdom with the Grand Floridian Resort and then the Polynesian Village Resort after it opens in late 2019 or early 2020.

All standard rooms at the Poly sleep five on two queens and a sofa that flips into a twin. Rooms are about 415 square feet, among the largest at Disney World. Besides the two queens and couch, you'll find an easy chair and ottoman, a desk with a small rolling table underneath, desk chair, mini-fridge, TV/dresser combo, two closets, and a coffeemaker. The spacious bath includes two sinks and a hair dryer, but is not divided, making it a little less family friendly than you'll find in more recently built hotels (the Polynesian was built in the early 70s). Second-floor standard rooms don't have balconies; other floors have patios or balconies. Polynesian

Disney's Polynesian Village Resort
Standard Room Floor Plan ~415 Square Feet

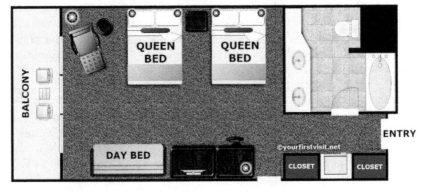

DVC offerings available for rent to the general public include Bungalows and Studios. Studios are most comparable to standard Poly rooms, and sleep five on a queen, fold-out couch, and flip-down 72" x 30" Murphy bed. All studios have balconies. All standard rooms and studios are accessed from interior corridors. Like the other deluxe resorts, you can also reserve concierge-supported rooms (Disney calls these "club" rooms) and suites.

The Poly has three table service restaurants and two quick service options. Dining is in GCH, except for the Oasis Pool and the Luau which has its own building at the northwest edge of the resort. 'Ohana is a great family restaurant that features character breakfasts with Mickey, Lilo, and Stitch. Kona Café has terrific and under-appreciated food. The Luau fills any need you may have for a Polynesian-themed dinner show. The main quick service location is Capt. Cook's, too small for the resort but convenient to the larger pool. A second quick service is at the smaller Oasis pool. While it operates during limited hours, often just from 11am to 5pm, the menu is as unique as it is diverse, offering items like sashimi and grilled sustainable fish tacos that are cumin-spiced with crunchy cabbage and cilantro-lime crema. More great dining is just a monorail ride away at the Grand Floridian and Contemporary. There's a bar outside of 'Ohana, and downstairs you'll find the most distinctive resort bar on property, Trader Sam's.

Amenities available at the resort include beaches, movies, campfires, jogging trails, playgrounds, boat rental, bike rental, fishing, a volleyball court, and an arcade. Poly guests can use the spa and health club Senses on the Poly side of the Grand Floridian. The Poly is one of only three Disney deluxe resorts (the Wilderness and Animal Kingdom Lodges are the others) that are not convention hotels.

At the Poly you can pay extra for views. Standard view five-person rooms average $606/night during the 2020 Value season, $720/night during the Regular season, $659/night during the Summer season, and $684 a night during the Fall season.

DISNEY'S GRAND FLORIDIAN RESORT & SPA

Disney's Grand Floridian Resort & Spa ("GF"), a monorail resort inspired by the Hotel Del Coronado in San Diego, is a lovely mix of gorgeous landscaping, white Victorian shapes and details, and red roofs. It visually enchants adults but does nothing in particular for kids. At opening, it supplanted Disney's Contemporary Resort as Disney World's flagship—and most expensive—hotel, leading some Contemporary Cast Members to refer to GF as the "red roof inn". There are three basic areas at GF: the main building, the outer buildings, and the Disney Vacation Club Villas. The main building has most dining, all shops, guest services, some suites, and several types of "club" rooms (Disney-speak for concierge rooms). The five outer buildings have more club rooms, more suites, all standard rooms, and some smaller but high-ceilinged "dormer" rooms. The Villas are at the southern edge of the resort grounds. From the second floor of the main building, GF guests can access the resort monorail with service to the Magic Kingdom, the other monorail resorts, and the Transportation and Ticket Center (TTC). The uninteresting but large main pool is in a beautifully landscaped area

Disney's Grand Floridian Resort
Standard Room Floor Plan ~440 Square Feet

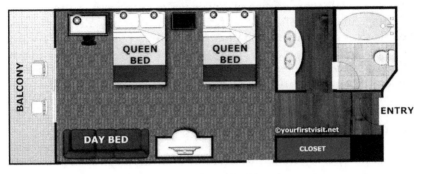

between the main building and the outer buildings, and the smaller but more fun Beach Pool is between the main building and the Villas.

Transportation to the Magic Kingdom is by the resort monorail or a boat shared with the Polynesian. Transportation to Epcot is via the Epcot monorail at TTC, accessible by the resort monorail. Transportation to the other parks and Disney Springs is via buses, typically shared with one or two other Magic Kingdom area resorts. Transportation convenience is above average among the deluxes for a Magic Kingdom focused trip, but not as good as sister monorail resorts the Contemporary and Polynesian. A walking path is being completed from GF to Magic Kingdom, which, when finished, will add another easy way to access that park. From the furthest room the walk will be about three quarters of a mile.

Adults generally love the exterior and grounds of GF, while reactions to interior decorating choices are mixed, with some finding them stuffy. Kids often don't get the theme—a hotel themed as a hotel?—or it fails to delight them.

All standard rooms at GF sleep five on two queens and a sofa that flips into a twin bed. Standard rooms are about 440 square feet—larger than the standard rooms at any other Disney-owned hotel. Besides the two queens and couch, you'll find an easy chair, a desk with a small rolling table underneath, a desk chair, mini-fridge, TV, dresser, closet (with robes!), and a coffee-maker. The spacious divided bath includes two sinks and a hair dryer, and a toilet and tub in a separate room. Rooms in the nearby Villas are also available for rent to the general public. Of the four room types at the Villas, studios are most comparable to standard GF rooms. They sleep five in a smaller overall space, but one with a better bath, on a queen, fold-out couch, and flip-down 72" long murphy bed. All rooms are accessed from interior corridors, and all rooms have balconies or patios.

The Grand Floridian has the best adult dining of any Disney resort, some attractive kid dining, and easy access to other great options at the other monorail resorts. GF has five table service restaurants and one quick service option. Two are on the second floor of the main building. Victoria and Albert's is by far the best and most expensive restaurant at Disney World. Kids under ten are not allowed, and jackets are required. Citricos is a seafood-focused establishment with inspired modern fare. "Resort casual" is the appropriate dress. On the first floor is 1900 Park Fare, with character meals at breakfast and dinner—Mary Poppins and others in the morning, and Cinderella and her family in the evening. Also on the first floor is the unpretentious and unambitious Grand Floridian Café—with no dress code, no characters, and no fancy dining, it's usually the easiest to book, but also the least interesting for kids or adults. The fifth table service restaurant, Narcoossee's, fronts the Seven Seas Lagoon near the boat dock, specializes in steak and seafood, and has a resort casual dress code. The quick service option is in the main building but only accessible from outside, and is one of the best quick service options among the deluxes. Mizner's Lounge on the second floor has been expanded and converted into a Beauty and the Beast themed bar known as Enchanted Rose. There's another bar in Citricos and another at each pool.

The Grand Floridian has an extensive set of amenities, including beaches, movies, campfires, jogging trails, playgrounds, a pirate cruise, boat rental, fishing, a great spa and fitness center, hot tubs, a sports court, and an arcade.

At the Grand, you can pay extra for views. Standard view (Outer Building Garden View) five-person rooms average $729/night during the 2020 Value season, $800/night during the Regular season, $778/night during the Summer season, and $767 a night during the Fall season.

DISNEY'S WILDERNESS LODGE

Disney's Wilderness Lodge ("WL"), near the Magic Kingdom, completed a major refurb in mid-July 2017. Inspired by the great U.S. National Park Lodges, it celebrates them and the mountain West. Its astonishing theming begins with its jaw-dropping lobby and continues with extensive detail everywhere in the resort. Half of the main lodge is the new Disney Vacation Club Copper Creek Villas, and nearby in a separate building is the Disney Vacation Club Boulder Ridge Villas. These villas are also available to all for rent. Guest services, a shop, and most dining are accessed from the lobby. Most rooms and villas are in two wings off the lobby that enclose a mountain-stream-themed courtyard that ends in the delightful main pool. A smaller pool between the WL and the Boulder Ridge Villas re-opened in July 2017.

The Wilderness Lodge is on Bay Lake near Magic Kingdom, a ten-minute boat ride away. Boats also connect the Wilderness Lodge with the nearby Contemporary Resort and Fort Wilderness, giving easy access to the great dining options at those resorts. The other theme parks, water parks, and Disney Springs are accessed via shared buses that can take a while. The Wilderness Lodge is well located for a Magic Kingdom-focused trip. The quality of the exterior architecture, lobby, detailing, and pools make the Wilderness Lodge an astonishingly kid-appealing resort. Adults will enjoy it as well, although they might find its rooms smaller than expected.

Standard guest rooms at WL, with about 340 square feet, are tied with those at Disney's Animal Kingdom Lodge as the smallest deluxe rooms on property (they are also the least expensive such rooms). No five-person rooms are available except in the Boulder Ridge Villas—standard rooms

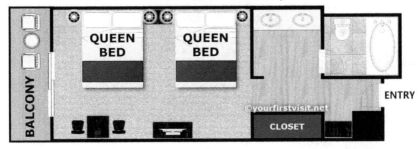

Disney's Wilderness Lodge
Standard Room Floor Plan ~340 Square Feet

sleep four on two queens. Four person rooms with one queen and a set of bunk beds are also available. You'll also find a table and two chairs, mini-fridge, TV, dresser, closet, and a coffee-maker. The divided bath includes two sinks and a hair dryer, and a toilet and tub in a separate room. Of the room types at the two Villas, studios are most comparable to standard WL rooms. Boulder Ridge studios sleep five in a slightly larger space, on a queen, a fold-out couch, and a fold-down smaller bed that's 32 inches by 75 inches. These five-person studio rooms are great choices for five-person families looking for Wilderness Lodge kid appeal who can fit in their beds. Copper Creek studios are the same size as standard Wilderness Lodge rooms, and sleep four on a queen and a fold-out couch. Rooms have balconies or patios, and are accessed from interior corridors. Like the other deluxe resorts, you can also reserve concierge-supported rooms ("club" rooms) and suites, and WL also has larger "deluxe rooms" that sleep six.

Artist Point converted to Storybook Dining at the end of 2018, with Snow White hosting surprisingly good character meals for dinner in a casual, family-friendly atmosphere. Whispering Canyon Café provides fun and family-friendly dining. Other kid and adult-appealing meals are available at the Contemporary and Fort Wilderness—each just a boat ride away. WL has one of the better counter service options among the deluxes, and the best bar of the Magic Kingdom resorts. There's another bar and grill, Geyser Point, between the two pools.

Amenities include movies, campfires, jogging trails, fishing, a spa/fitness center, hot tubs, volleyball, a playground, and boat rental. WL is one of three deluxe resorts (the Polynesian and Animal Kingdom Lodge are the others) that are not convention hotels.

At the Wilderness Lodge you can pay extra for views. Standard view rooms average $416/night during the 2020 Value season, $513/night during the Regular season, $484/night during the Summer season, and $507 a night during the Fall season.

DISNEY'S CONTEMPORARY RESORT

Disney's Contemporary Resort ("Contemporary"), a monorail resort, is essentially un-themed but still iconic, and, on first impression, visually striking. The massive concrete A-frame with monorails passing through the middle is stunning at first view. However, the spare masses and geometric

Disney's Contemporary Resort
Standard Room Floor Plan ~394 Square Feet

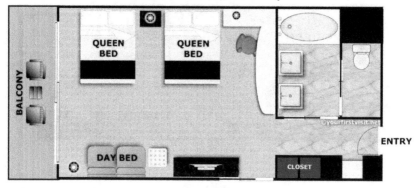

landscaping quickly fade from notice, and there's not much interesting detail earning a second glance. There are three basic areas at the Contemporary—the main Tower, which is what most people mean when they think of it; the South Garden Wing, low-rise rooms mostly without balconies; and Bay Lake Tower, the Disney Vacation Club offering. Found in the main Tower are dining, shops, guest services, and, from a dedicated escalator and elevator on the fourth floor, access to the resort monorail with service to the Magic Kingdom, the other monorail resorts, and the Transportation and Ticket Center (TTC). The dull but large main pool is outside the Tower, and there's a second dull and somewhat smaller pool between the main pool and Bay Lake. At press time, the Contemporary is the only Disney resort from which you can walk to and from the Magic Kingdom, but a walkway connecting the Grand Floridian and Polynesian Village to Magic Kingdom will be opening soon. With travel to the Magic Kingdom available via both monorail and walking, the Contemporary is, by far, the most convenient Disney World resort for trips focused particularly on that park.

Transportation to Epcot is via the Epcot monorail at TTC, accessible by the resort monorail. Transportation to the other parks and Disney Springs is via buses, typically shared with one or two other Magic Kingdom area resorts. There's also boat service among the three Bay Lake resorts—the Contemporary, Wilderness Lodge, and Fort Wilderness.

The Contemporary has nothing of the visual kid appeal of the Polynesian or the Wilderness or Animal Kingdom Lodges, but it does make a strong first impression, and some kids continue to be fascinated by the monorail running through the middle. A rumored re-theming to an Incredibles theme would add kid appeal.

Standard rooms at the Contemporary sleep five on two queens and a sofa that flips into a twin bed. Most rooms are about 400 square feet, among the largest at Disney World. Besides the two queens and couch, you'll find a very large L-shaped desk that is too large to fit gracefully where it is placed, with a small rolling table underneath, a desk chair, mini-fridge, TV, two closets, and a coffee-maker. Clothes storage drawers are in the corner of the desk area, making them a little less usable than those in rooms with more central storage. The spacious bath includes two sinks and a hair dryer, but only the toilet section is divided, making it less family friendly than you'll find in more recently built hotels (the Contemporary was built in the early 70s). Views from the higher main Tower rooms of the Magic Kingdom or Bay Lake are marvelous, and, because it is Disney World's only high-rise hotel, guests in Tower rooms will also find it the most compact Disney hotel to navigate. All Tower rooms have balconies. Garden Wing rooms have similar size and furnishings to Tower rooms, but are much more spread out, and without the views—or balconies—of the Tower rooms. They are also much less expensive. Of the four room types in the Disney Vacation Club at Bay Lake Tower, studios are most comparable to Tower rooms, but sleep only four in a cramped space with a queen and fold-out couch. All rooms are accessed from interior corridors. Like the other deluxe resorts, you can also reserve concierge-supported Tower rooms ("club" rooms), and suites in both the Tower and the Garden Wing.

The Contemporary has three table service restaurants and one quick service option. All dining is in the Tower. The first floor Wave of American Flavors focuses on locally grown and organic offerings. Chef Mickey's on the fourth floor offers a wildly popular buffet attended by Mickey, Minnie, Donald, Goofy, and Pluto. The top-floor California Grill offers fine modern American and sushi dining with a great view of the Magic Kingdom, especially if you are there during the fireworks. The quick service location is the fourth-floor Contempo Café. More great dining is just a monorail ride away at the Grand Floridian and Polynesian, and a boat ride away at the Wilderness Lodge and Fort Wilderness. There's a weak-looking and mis-placed bar on the fourth floor, a fine setting for a bar at the California Grill, and a pool bar.

The fourth floor of the Contemporary is the center of much of its action, and elevators there can be quite crowded. Guests headed from there to the first floor should consider the escalators.

The Contemporary has as broad a set of amenities as you will find at a Disney resort. They include beaches, movies, campfires, jogging trails, playgrounds, boat rental, bike rental, tennis, fishing, a spa and fitness center, hot tubs, a Pirate cruise, a volleyball court, and an arcade.

At the Contemporary, you can pay extra for views. Standard (Bay Lake) view five-person main tower rooms average $708/night during the 2020 Value season, $785/night during the Regular season, $779/night during the Summer season, and $777 a night during the Fall season. Rooms in the low-rise South Garden Wing average $503/night during the 2020 Value season, $590/night during the Regular season, $560/night during the Summer season, and $573 a night during the Fall season.

DISNEY'S BEACH CLUB RESORT

Disney's Beach Club Resort ("BC"), an Epcot resort, is themed to recollect images of Victorian seaside cottages and hotels from Stone Harbor and other Cape May, New Jersey, settings. The exterior architecture is particularly charming, and of high appeal to adults. Kids don't much get its

Disney's Beach Club Resort
Standard Room Floor Plan ~381 Square Feet

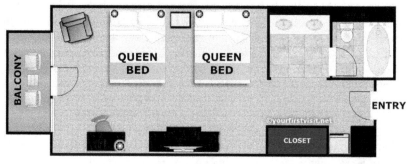

theming until they see the Stormalong Bay pool and its associated beaches and playgrounds. After that, that's all they see... The Beach Club occupies half of an enormous, long-corridored building, with sister resort The Yacht Club taking up the other half. Nearby you'll find the DVC Beach Club Villas. In the center of the building are kitchens and other back-of the house areas, then on either side the table service restaurants of the two resorts, then the guest service areas (one for each) and shops. Near Crescent Lake you'll find Stormalong Bay pool, shared with the Yacht Club—actually three separate pools, each with its own focus: a sand-bottomed shallow pool delightful for little ones; a pool perfect for drifting or tubing; and a pool for swimming. The larger of two fun water slides accessed from a shipwreck on a Crescent Lake beach splashes down at one end of this pool. Some call Stormalong Bay a "mini water park". That's a stretch, yet does capture the difference between it and every other Disney World pool except those at the Four Seasons. There's one smaller pool at the far west end of YC, and two smaller ones near the east end of BC.

The Beach Club is near the back entrance to Epcot, the International Gateway. For Epcot, walk or take a boat. For most BC rooms, the boats are a long walk away, so walking is often the better choice. Hollywood Studios is best accessed by boat, and the other theme parks, water parks, and Disney Springs via shared buses that can take a while. The Beach Club is wonderfully located for trips centered on Epcot or Disney's Hollywood Studios, and a favorite of many returning family visitors. It's not so well located for a Magic Kingdom-focused trip.

Adults generally love the architecture and convenience to Epcot of BC, while kids often don't get the theme—a hotel themed as a cottage?—but just don't care after they see the pool.

Most standard rooms at BC sleep five on two queens and a daybed (some rooms omit the daybed— the floor plan shows such a room). Standard rooms are about 380 square feet—in the middle of the deluxe range, but well-appointed and proportioned. Five-person rooms have beside the beds a desk with a small rolling table underneath, a desk chair, mini-fridge, TV, dresser, closet, and a coffee-maker. The divided bath includes two sinks and a hair dryer, and a toilet and tub in a separate room. Four-person rooms have the same size, omit the daybed, but add an easy chair. Rooms in the nearby Villas are also available for rent to the general public. Of the three room types at the Villas, studios are most comparable to standard BC rooms. They sleep five in a smaller overall space, on a queen, a fold-out couch, and a fold-down bed that was added in a 2016 refurb. All rooms are accessed from interior corridors. Most BC standard rooms have small balconies or patios that seat two, but many BC rooms have tiny balconies with barely room to stand. This choice adds interest and grace to the façade, but impedes livability. Like the other deluxe resorts, you can also reserve concierge-supported rooms (Disney call these "club" rooms) and suites.

BC has two table service restaurants. Cape May Café offers a character breakfast with Goofy, and other characters like Minnie, Chip and Dale, but not Mickey. In the evening, Cape May converts to a no-character "clambake" buffet. Seafood can be good from a buffet—but it can't be great. By the pool is the Beaches and Cream ice cream and burger-focused establishment, with not remotely enough seats. There's no real counter service, just a few options in the back of the gift shop and at Hurricane Hanna's, the pool bar and grill. You can walk to sister resort the Yacht Club and find in the Market nice shelf-stable snacks and a few minor hot options or go to the BoardWalk for sandwiches. Dining in Epcot is also an option, but may be impractical for families without hopper tickets. There's an indoor bar and another at the pool.

Among them, the three Epcot resorts—the Beach and Yacht Clubs, and BoardWalk Inn—provide within walking distance access to almost any amenity, including beaches, movies, campfires, jogging trails, playgrounds, a pirate cruise, boat rental, fishing, a spa/fitness center, tennis, hot tubs, volleyball, a business center, and arcades.

At the Beach Club you can pay extra for views. Standard view rooms average $505/night during the 2020 Value season, $628/night during the Regular season, $586/night during the Summer season, and $624 a night during the Fall season.

DISNEY'S ANIMAL KINGDOM LODGE

Disney's Animal Kingdom Lodge ("AKL"), near the Animal Kingdom theme park, shares with the Wilderness Lodge astonishingly detailed theming and a jaw-dropping lobby, based in its case on African park lodges. It is also near-surrounded with parklands (Disney calls them "savannas") displaying animals. These animals are visible from savanna-view rooms and also from multiple public viewing areas. On several upper floors of the main building (Jambo House) you'll find Disney Vacation Club spaces, the Jambo House Villas, and, a long walk or short bus ride away, even more DVC Villas at Kidani Village, all available for rent. Guest services and a shop are accessed from the main Jambo lobby. Dining is at a lower level. (Kidani has another lobby, shop, and restaurant.) Most Jambo rooms are in two long-corridored semi-circular wings off the lobby that enclose animal savannas. The main pool is as good as any Disney-owned pool except Stormalong Bay at the Yacht and Beach Clubs. A slightly smaller but still wonderful pool serves Kidani.

The Animal Kingdom Lodge is at the far southwest corner of Walt Disney World. Uniquely among the deluxes, all transport to the theme parks, water parks, and Disney Springs is via buses shared with Kidani. Included in this is the Animal Kingdom park—you can't walk there. AKL thus is not particularly well located.

The animals, exterior architecture, lobby, detailing, and pools make AKL an astonishingly kid-appealing resort. Adults enjoy it as well, although they might find its rooms smaller than expected.

Standard guest rooms at AKL, with about 340 square feet, are tied with those at Disney's Wilderness Lodge as the smallest deluxe rooms on property (standard view rooms also are—for a Disney deluxe— inexpensive). Most first-time visitors ought not to pay for views, as they won't be in their rooms enough, but they absolutely should pay for savanna views at AKL. No five-person rooms are available—standard rooms sleep four on two queens. Four-person rooms with one queen and a set of bunk beds are also available. You'll also find a table and two chairs, mini-fridge, TV, dresser, closet, and a coffee-maker. The divided bath includes two sinks and a hair dryer, and a toilet and tub in a separate room. Of the four room types at the Disney Vacation Club Jambo and Kidani Villas, studios are most comparable to standard AKL rooms. They sleep four in a slightly larger space, on a queen and a fold-out couch. Jambo studios are the better choice than Kidani studios, even though smaller, as the Jambo building is much better themed, and dining is much more convenient. Rooms have balconies, and are accessed from interior corridors. Like the other deluxe resorts, you can also reserve concierge-supported rooms ("club" rooms) and suites.

In early 2019, AKL began refurbishing its rooms, generally following recent refurb themes such as wood-laminate floors, bigger TVs, and platform beds with storage underneath. We have not yet stayed in a refurbed room, but from images, they appear to maintain much of the charm of the former spaces. This refurb ought not to affect your enjoyment of the hotel.

There are two table service restaurants at in the main Jambo building, and another at Kidani. In Jambo, Jiko nears the top of many "best Disney dining" lists, has a resort casual dress code, and offers an eclectic African-inspired menu. Next-door Boma is more family friendly, with a wide-ranging buffet. At Kidani, hidden gem Sanaa has an African/Indian

Disney's Animal Kingdom Lodge
Standard Room Floor Plan ~340 Square Feet

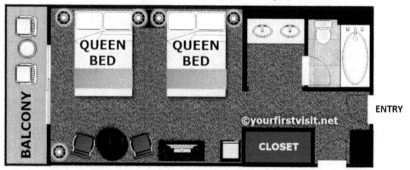

inspired menu. Recently, it began serving a counter-service style breakfast, making mornings much simpler here. AKL also has one of the better
counter service options among the deluxes, and one of Disney World's best
bars. There's another bar at each pool. Unlike the other deluxes, there's no
easy access to more dining at another hotel.

Amenities include movies, campfires, jogging trails, playgrounds, a spa/
fitness center, hot tubs, and arcades. AKL is alone among the Disney deluxe
resorts in not being on water, having no beach, and offering no easy access
to water sports. AKL is one of three deluxe resorts (the Polynesian and
Wilderness Lodge are the others) that are not convention hotels.

At the Animal Kingdom Lodge, you should pay extra for savanna views.
Savanna view rooms average $609/night during the 2020 Value season,
$728/night during the Regular season, $687/night during the Summer
season, and $725 a night during the Fall season. These prices average
about $200/night more than standard view rooms.

DISNEY'S YACHT CLUB RESORT

Disney's Yacht Club Resort ("YC"), an Epcot resort, is themed as a formal
New England yacht club. The dull gray exterior does little to accomplish
this, but there are some nautical decorative elements in the public areas
and rooms. Neither kids nor adults much get its theming, but kids are
delighted by Stormalong Bay pool and its beaches and playgrounds. The
Yacht Club occupies half of a long-corridored building, with sister resort
The Beach Club—warmer, more charming and inviting—taking up the
other half. In the center of the enormous building are kitchens and other
back-of the house areas, then on either side the table service restaurants
of the two resorts, then the guest service areas (one for each) and shops.
Near Crescent Lake you'll find Stormalong Bay pool, shared with the Beach
Club—actually three separate pools, each with its own focus: a sand-bottomed shallow pool delightful for little ones; a pool perfect for drifting or
tubing; and a pool for swimming. The larger of two fun water slides accessed
from a shipwreck on a beach splashes down at one end of this pool. Some
call Stormalong Bay a "mini water park". That's a stretch, yet does capture
the difference between it and every other Disney World pool except those at
the Four Seasons. There's one smaller pool at the far west end of YC, and two
smaller ones near the east end of BC. In late 2017, YC became dog-friendly.

The Yacht Club is near the back entrance to Epcot, the International
Gateway. You can walk or take a boat to Epcot. Hollywood Studios is
accessed by a long walk or by boat, and the other theme parks, water parks,
and Disney Springs via shared buses that can take a while. The Yacht Club
is well located for trips centered on Epcot or Disney's Hollywood Studios,
but not so well located for a Magic Kingdom focused trip.

All of Disney's marketing material stresses the "formality" of the Yacht
Club and the "fun" of the Beach Club. Both points are overstated, but
result in families self-selecting into the prettier Beach Club, and conventioneers (both hotels are convention hotels) into the duller Yacht Club.
This is fine—the Beach Club is the better family choice on any relevant
measure except balconies: all YC rooms have large balconies, while BC

Disney's Yacht Club Resort
Standard Room Floor Plan ~381 Square Feet

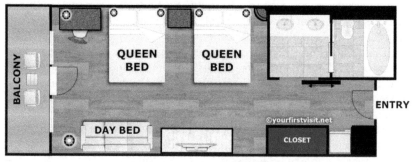

rooms have either small or almost uselessly tiny ones.

Guest rooms completed a much-needed refurb in late 2017. Most standard rooms sleep five on two queens and a daybed (some omit the daybed and sleep four). Standard rooms are about 380 square feet—in the middle of the deluxe range, but well-appointed and proportioned. Five-person rooms have, beside the beds, a desk with a small rolling table underneath, a desk chair, mini-fridge, TV, dresser, closet, and a coffee-maker. The divided bath includes two sinks and a hair dryer, and a toilet and tub in a separate room. Four-person rooms have the same size, omit the daybed, but add an easy chair. All rooms are accessed from interior corridors. Like the other deluxe resorts, you can also reserve concierge-supported rooms (Disney call these "club" rooms) and suites.

YC has two table service restaurants. The Yachtsman Steak House is a top-notch venue with steaks as good as any Disney restaurant. It has a resort casual dress code. The other table service restaurant, Ale & Compass, has little theming and average fare, and because of that is easy to get as a walk-up or last-minute reservation. Minor counter service offerings and nice snacks are available in the Market. You can walk to the nearby Beach Club and find a character breakfast at Cape May Café, burger and ice cream dining at Beaches and Cream, and more weak counter service. The nearby BoardWalk Inn has neither meaningful counter service nor any kid-appealing table service restaurants except for breakfast at Trattoria al Forno featuring Rapunzel, Flynn Rider, Ariel and Prince Eric. Dining in Epcot is also an option, but may be impractical for families without hopper tickets. There's a bar inside and another at the pool.

Among them, the three Epcot resorts—the Beach and Yacht Clubs, and BoardWalk Inn—provide within walking distance access to almost any amenity, including beaches, movies, campfires, jogging trails, playgrounds, a pirate cruise, boat rental, fishing, a spa/fitness center, tennis, hot tubs, volleyball, a business center, and arcades.

At the Yacht Club you can pay extra for views. Standard view rooms average $505/night during the 2020 Value season, $628/night during the Regular season, $586/night during the Summer season, and $624 a night during the Fall season.

DISNEY'S BOARDWALK INN

Disney's BoardWalk Inn ("BWI"), an Epcot resort, has a split visual personality. One part of it, facing Crescent Lake, is themed to recall Atlantic coast boardwalk vacation settings. The rest—including the areas with the most rooms—is themed to recall a quieter and more peaceful Colonial-revival style resort with garden courtyards. The BoardWalk Inn is one of Disney's smallest deluxe resorts, but some corridors are as long as those at sister Epcot resorts the Yacht and Beach Clubs. Cutting across the courtyard can save much walking. Connected through the lobby of the BoardWalk Inn is the enormous Disney Vacation Club property Disney's BoardWalk Villas, also available to all for rent. Guest services and a small shop are in the lobby, and more shopping is downstairs on the BoardWalk. Dining is a little weird—there's next to none "in" the BoardWalk Inn, but several restaurants are accessible just outside on the Boardwalk. In the Villas area you'll find the fun amusement-park themed main pool and a second smaller pool. A third pool, also small, is in an internal courtyard of the Inn.

The BoardWalk Inn is near the back entrance to Epcot, the International Gateway, and is almost as near Epcot as is the Beach Club, and nearer to Disney's Hollywood Studios. You can walk to either park from it, though most take the boat to the Studios. The other theme parks, water parks, and Disney Springs are reached via shared buses that can take a while. The BoardWalk Inn is well located for trips centered on Epcot and the Studios, but not so well located for a Magic Kingdom-focused trip.

From its interior courtyards, the BoardWalk Inn is the loveliest and most compact of the Epcot resorts, and is highly popular with honeymooners. Kids don't get its theme, and the main pool, while fine, isn't at the standard of the pool at the Beach Club, making the Beach Club a better choice for most families. But adults love it, and the resulting demand means BWI is typically as much as $50 a night more expensive than the Beach Club.

Standard guest rooms at BWI, with about 370 square feet, are similar to those in the Yacht Club and Beach Club, mid-sized among the deluxes but well-proportioned and appointed, sleeping four on two queens or five with an added couch. Rooms also have a desk with a small rolling

Disney's BoardWalk Inn
Standard Room Floor Plan ~381 Square Feet

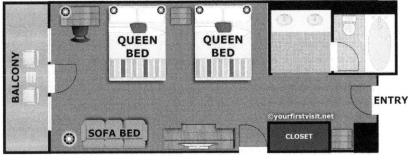

table underneath, a desk chair, mini-fridge, TV, dresser, closet, and a coffee-maker. The divided bath includes two sinks and a hair dryer, and a toilet and tub in a separate room. Four-person rooms have the same size, omit the couch, but add an easy chair. Of the four room types at the Villas, studios are most comparable to standard BWI rooms. After a recent refurb, they sleep five in a similar space on a queen, a fold-out couch, and a fifth fold-down sleeping spot, but can be quite a hike. Rooms have balconies or patios, and are accessed from interior corridors. Like the other deluxe resorts, you can also reserve concierge-supported rooms (Disney call these "club" rooms) and suites, and BW also has larger "deluxe rooms" that sleep six, and Garden Cottages best suited to couples.

The BoardWalk Inn itself has next to no dining, but several restaurants are right outside on the BoardWalk itself. These include the sports-bar style ESPN Club; the Italian restaurant Trattoria al Forno, with a notable character breakfast featuring Rapunzel, Flynn Rider, Ariel, and Prince Eric, that improves the kid appeal of this area quite a bit; high-end, expensive seafood at the Flying Fish Café; and the brew pub Big River Grille. There's no real counter service other than limited offerings at the Bakery and at stalls on the BoardWalk itself. More table service dining is at the Yacht and Beach Clubs, and dining in Epcot is an option, but may be impractical for families without hopper tickets. There's a great bar inside and another at the pool.

Among them, the three Epcot resorts—the Beach and Yacht Clubs, and BoardWalk Inn—provide within walking distance access to almost any amenity, including beaches, movies, campfires, jogging trails, playgrounds, a pirate cruise, boat rental, fishing, a spa/fitness center, tennis, hot tubs, volleyball, a business center, and arcades.

At the BoardWalk Inn you can pay extra for views. Standard view rooms average $542/night during the 2020 Value season, $631/night during the Regular season, $599/night during the Summer season, and $638 a night during the Fall season.

DISNEY'S OLD KEY WEST RESORT

Disney's Old Key West Resort ("OKW") is a Disney Vacation Club Resort, but unlike those discussed so far it is not paired with a deluxe resort, but rather stands on its own. Like all the other DVC offerings, its accommodations are available to Disney Vacation Club members, to others who have rented points from them, and to anyone using cash just like at any other Disney World resort. Except for dining and convenience, its offerings and amenities are comparable to those at Disney deluxe resorts, which is why we discuss it here.

OKW is themed to recall Key West, which it does a bit here and there. But with dozens of three-story buildings winding among water and fairways, it mostly comes across as a pastel-colored example of a vacation condominium community. Neither kids nor adults much get its theming, and there is little to visually signal you are in Disney World.

Old Key West's two- and three-story accommodations buildings—most with no elevators—are scattered across a large expanse, with the central services (dining, shops, check-in, and the main pool) located near the entry

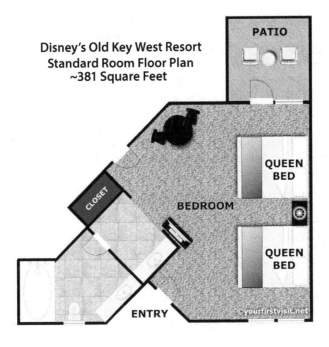

Disney's Old Key West Resort
Standard Room Floor Plan
~381 Square Feet

dard rooms by having a microwave and toaster in addition to the standard coffeemaker and mini-fridge found in both studios and deluxe rooms. Most are also different by having a queen bed and a fold-out couch. Old Key West studios are unique in offering two queens, rather than a queen and sleeper sofa. A sofa creates a more flexible studio; two queens, more comfortable sleeping. OKW studios are about 380 square feet—larger than most other studios—sleep four and have, beside the beds and kitchenette appliances, a table and chairs, TV, dresser, and closet. The bath is not divided, but with a second sink available in the nearby kitchenette the room functions as though it were. Studios here also come with a large patio or balcony.

Larger spaces are also available at OKW. One Bedroom Villas hold five in about twice the space of a studio and Two Bedroom Villas hold nine in about three times the space of a studio. These One and Two Bedroom Villas are among the largest and the most home-like of the DVC offerings. Grand Villas at OKW hold 12 in about five times the space of a studio.

First-timers are often surprised by how thin the dining is at OKW. However, everyone staying here either has a kitchenette, as in the studios, or has the full kitchen that the other OKW accommodations come with. The gift shop is also well-stocked with food. OKW has only one table service restaurant, Olivia's. Much loved among families who return to Old Key West year after year, Olivia's is bright, colorful, and fun, and worth a visit from those staying at OKW—but is by no means destination dining. There's a small counter service venue outside that also serves as the grill for the main pool, and a small bar next to it. Dining in Disney Springs is also an option, but the boats there are slower and less frequent than ideal.

OKW offers most amenities, including movies, campfires, jogging trails, playgrounds, bike rentals, fishing, a spa/fitness center, tennis, basketball, hot tubs, volleyball, and an arcade.

Because of the layout of the accommodations buildings, almost all OKW spaces have nice views, and there are no extra charge options for views or preferred areas. OKW and Saratoga Springs are usually the lowest priced DVC options (other than some not-recommended standard view and "value" studios at the Animal Kingdom Lodge). Studios at OKW average $426/night during the 2020 Value season, $499/night during the Regular season, $480/night during the Summer season, and $494/night during the Fall season.

DISNEY'S SARATOGA SPRINGS RESORT & SPA

Disney's Saratoga Springs Resort & Spa ("SS") is a Disney Vacation Club Resort, but, like Old Key West and the new in December 2019 Disney Riviera Resort, it is not paired with a deluxe resort—it stands on its own. As with all the other DVC offerings, its accommodations are available to Disney Vacation Club members, to others who have rented points from them, and to anyone using cash just like at any other Disney World resort. Except for dining and convenience, its offerings and amenities are comparable to those at Disney deluxe resorts, which is why we discuss it here.

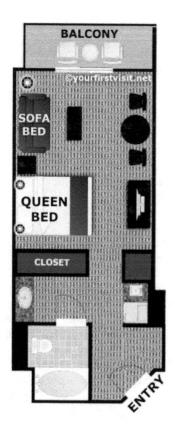

Saratoga Springs is themed to recall the vacation, spa, and horse country around Saratoga Springs, New York, and it does do this a bit here and there. But with large three-story buildings winding among water and fairways, it mostly feels like a golf condominium development. You really could be anywhere.

Saratoga Springs' almost 20 accommodations buildings (all with elevators) are scattered in several named areas across a large expanse, with the main services—dining, shops, check-in, and the main pool—located near the center of the resort, and distant from many accommodations buildings. Uniquely, Saratoga Springs has two full-service pools with slides, bars, food and such: the High Rock Spring pool in the central Springs area, and the Paddock pool in the Paddock area. Another pool, the Grandstand pool, has no slide but is otherwise sound, and two smaller pools with few amenities are in the Treehouse and Congress Park areas.

Disney's Saratoga Springs Resort & Spa Studio Floor Plan ~355 Square Feet

SS is located just east of OKW and is identified in Disney way-finding material as a Disney Springs Area Resort. Often derided for being remote, it's actually not that far from Epcot, Disney's Hollywood Studios, and Magic Kingdom, but is the most isolated resort after the Animal Kingdom Lodge. What makes it particularly inconvenient is the walks to the central services and the five bus stops needed to serve its sprawl (plus two more at the Treehouse Villas—don't even ask). All transportation to the theme parks and water parks is via bus; there's also a boat and a walking path to Disney Springs. A car is handy here— we wouldn't stay at SS without one.

Of the four types of accommodations available at SS, its studios are most comparable to standard rooms at the deluxe resorts, so they are the focus here. All Disney studios are distinguished from deluxe standard rooms by having a microwave and toaster in addition to the standard coffeemaker and mini-fridge found in both studios and deluxe rooms. Most are also different by having a queen bed and a fold-out couch. SS studios are much like most other Disney World studios, except at about 355 square feet are a little smaller. They sleep four and have, beside the bed, sofa bed and kitchenette appliances, a table and chairs, TV, dresser, and a closet. The divided bath has a sink and closet in one part, and toilet and tub in their own room. Studios also come with a patio or balcony.

Disney's Saratoga Springs Resort & Spa
Two-Bedroom Villa Floor Plan ~1075 Square Feet

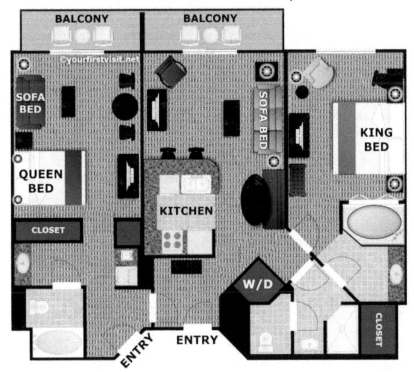

Larger spaces are also available at SS. One Bedroom Villas hold four in about twice the space of a studio and Two Bedroom Villas hold eight in three times the space of a studio. Grand Villas at SS hold 12 in about five times the space of a studio. These are among the smaller of these room types at Disney World, so another DVC venue will be a better choice for most. A unique additional offering at SS is the Treehouse Villas—woefully isolated, with their own buses that go only to Saratoga Springs itself, but a great three-bedroom option for a group of nine with a car or two.

First-timers are often surprised by how thin the dining is at SS. However, everyone staying here either has a kitchenette, as in the studios, or has the full kitchen that the other SS accommodations come with. The gift shop is also well-stocked with food. SS has only one table service restaurant, The Turf Club. Much loved among golfers and romantic for couples, it's less interesting for kids. There's a small counter service venue in the gift shop so that you can apply mustard directly to your stuffed Mickey rather than waiting to stain it by chance, and several of the pools have substantial bar and grill menus. Dining in Disney Springs is also an option, but the boats there are slower and less frequent than ideal, and the walking path is a hike from everywhere except the Congress Park area.

SS offers most amenities, including movies, campfires, jogging trails, playgrounds, bike rentals, fishing, a wonderful spa/fitness center, tennis, basketball, hot tubs, and an arcade. It's also the only Disney resort with a pro shop and golf course start, underneath the Turf Club —and outside the pro shop is another minor dining option, Chips and Slices, with a window serving a limited menu for breakfast and lunch.

Because of the layout of the accommodations buildings, almost all SS spaces have nice views, and there are no extra charge options for views or preferred areas. Saratoga Springs and OKW are usually the lowest priced DVC options (other than some not-recommended standard view and "value" studios at the Animal Kingdom Lodge). SS studios average $426/night during the 2020 Value season, $498/night during the Regular season, $478/night during the Summer season, and $493 a night during the Fall season.

DISNEY'S RIVIERA RESORT

Disney's Riviera Resort ("Riviera"), a new Disney Vacation Club resort, opens December 16, 2019. Like OKW and SS, Riviera is not paired with a deluxe resort, but rather stands on its own. Like all the other DVC offerings, its accommodations are available to Disney Vacation Club members, to others who have rented points from them, and to anyone using cash just like at any other Disney World resort. Its offerings and amenities look to be comparable to those at Disney deluxe resorts, which is why we discuss it here.

According to Disney, Riviera is themed to "European grandeur with fairly tale accents" with "warm and stylish accommodations." Images released so far suggest a perfectly adequate but fairly undistinguished design, so we will take that with a grain of salt until we can see it in person.

The midrise building holds all accommodations and most services and amenities—with the rest just outside—so Riviera will be the most easy

Disney's Riviera Resort
Studio Floor Plan ~423 Square Feet

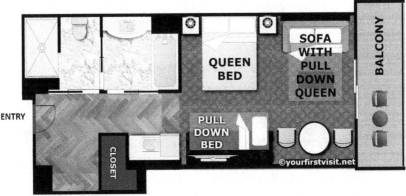

to navigate DVC option. It will offer two pools, one aimed at families and the other for quieter folk, and a water play area for kids.

Riviera is located just south of Epcot, and will have non-stop Skyliner access to Epcot's International Gateway entrance. Disney's Hollywood Studios will also be accessible via Skyliner—with a transfer at next-door Caribbean Beach. Transportation to the other theme parks and water parks will be via bus.

Of the five types of accommodations available at Riviera, its studios (not to be confused with tower studios, discussed below) are most comparable to standard rooms at the deluxe resorts, so they are the focus here. All Disney studios are distinguished from deluxe standard rooms by having a microwave and toaster in addition to the standard coffeemaker and mini-fridge found in both studios and deluxe rooms. Most are also different by having a queen bed and a foldout couch. Riviera studios sleep five on a queen, a sleeper sofa, and a fold-down bed that we expect to be about 72" by 30". These studios will have, besides the beds and kitchenette appliances, a table and chairs, TV, and closet. The bath is divided. Studios at Riviera also come with a large patio or balcony.

Riviera also offers a distinctive new type of accommodation, "Tower Studios." These spaces sleep two on a fold-down queen bed that, when in use, removes the seating from the room. (Balcony chairs can be hauled into the room if needed.) We are interested to see how the livability of these particular spaces turns out.

Larger spaces are also available. One Bedroom Villas hold five in about twice the space of a five person studio and Two Bedroom Villas hold nine or ten (depending on the space) in about three times the space of a studio. From a design point of view, One and Two Bedroom Villas at Riviera appear to have more living area and dining table seating than many older DVC resorts--we will test that in a stay here in early 2020. Grand Villas at Riviera look particularly livable, and sleep 12 in about six times the space of a studio.

Riviera will open with a rooftop restaurant, Topolino's Terrace, that promises delightful views of Epcot's fireworks. A coffee shop/lobby bar, quick service venue, and pool bar and grill will also be available. More dining is a short walk away at Caribbean Beach.

Riviera studios average $630/night during the 2020 Value season, $746/night during the Regular season, $684/night during the Summer season, and $652 a night during the Fall season.

Other Disney World Lodging Options

Besides the Disney-owned value, moderate and deluxe resorts, there are other options as well:

- The Disney-owned multi-room spaces at the DVC resorts.
- The Disney-owned Campsites at Fort Wilderness.
- The on-property, non-Disney-owned hotels: the Swan, Dolphin, Shades of Green, Four Seasons, and the hotels of the Disney Springs Resort Area. Many of these gained access to valuable EMH and 60 day FastPass+ perks through 2020.
- Two just barely off-site hotels, the Hilton Orlando Bonnet Creek and Waldorf Astoria, also recently gained access to EMH and 60 day FastPass+.
- Everything else—the rest of the offsite hotels and vacation homes.

We'll comment briefly on the positive and negatives of each.

MULTI-ROOM VILLAS AT
DISNEY VACATION CLUB RESORTS

The Disney Vacation Club ("DVC") Resorts at Walt Disney World are time-shares with rooms that can also be booked via cash reservations, just like any other Disney World resort hotel room.

Except for the studios, which we've already discussed in the "Deluxe Resorts" section, above, what's distinct about the accommodations in these DVC resorts is the extra space and full kitchens—neither of which will be used much during a first visit, but which can be quite comfortable and convenient for returning visitor.

These villas can also be reserved (usually at a huge cost saving) by privately renting "points" from Disney Vacation Club members.

For most first-time family visitors, the multi-room villas in the DVC resorts are worth considering only under a few circumstances:

- Large families, especially those aimed at a deluxe property, who are not willing to bet on actually getting connecting rooms. (You can request connecting rooms at WDW, but getting them is not guaranteed.) Villas which can sleep 8, 9, 10, and 12 people are available.
- Smaller families looking to spread out into a One or Two-Bedroom Villa, despite the higher price.
- Families aimed at a deluxe hotel, but who can only pull it off through the cost savings of renting DVC points.
- Families who have targeted a resort with which a DVC property is paired, find it is sold out, but can get into the DVC resort.

- People who already are DVC owners.

All of the DVC resorts except Riviera, Saratoga Springs, and Old Key West are paired with a deluxe resort and mostly share the pros and cons of that resort in terms of convenience, kid appeal, dining, amenities, and such.

There are, however, some real variances across the DVC resorts in the livability of their rooms.

STUDIOS add to the routine amenities of a deluxe room a microwave and toaster, and generally sleep four in a queen and a fold out-sofa. Old Key West Studios have two queens. Studios in the Boulder Ridge Villas at the Wilderness Lodge ("BR"), the Polynesian, the BoardWalk Villas, Disney's Riviera Resort ("Riviera"), the Villas at the Grand Floridian ("VGF"), and the Beach Club Villas sleep five—the third sleeping spot is a short fold-down murphy bed that's 72ish inches long and sleeps shorter than that. Studios in Bay Lake Tower at Disney's Contemporary ("BLT") sleep four, but we think the room is too cramped when the fold-out couch is opened. All Studios except those at the Polynesian have one bath. Polynesian Studios have one full bath, and a second bath space with sink and shower.

ONE BEDROOM VILLAS sleep four or five, depending on the resort. They have a king bed bedroom that sleeps two and also a combined full kitchen, dining, and living space that typically sleeps two on a fold-out couch. Old Key West, Bay Lake Tower, and the Villas at the Animal Kingdom Lodge (at Jambo House and Kidani Village, "VAKL") add a third sleeping spot to this area with a fold-out chair; at Riviera and the Villas at the Grand Floridian, this space gets a third spot from a fold-down murphy bed. All One Bedroom Villas except those at Kidani Village and Bay Lake Tower have a single large divided bath; at those two, there's a small bath in the living/dining/kitchen area and another larger one in the king bedroom.

TWO BEDROOM VILLAS come in two flavors:

- One type simply combines a Studio and a One Bedroom through a connecting door, and is known as a "lock-off". These lock-off Two Bedroom Villas combine the capacity and merits of the spaces that make them up. Most sleep eight, but those that combine five-person spaces will sleep nine (BCV, BWV, OKW, BLT, VAKL, BR) or, at the Villas at the Grand Floridian and Riviera, ten.

- A second type, designed as a Two Bedroom Villa from the start, is called in the jargon a "dedicated" villa, sleeps eight or nine, and will have minor variations in the second bedroom compared to a Studio, typically losing the kitchenette, swapping the fold- out couch of the Studio for another queen, and getting another closet instead of an exit to the corridor. At the Grand Floridian, such villas also lose the fold-down bed in the second bedroom and sleep nine.

Two Bedroom Villas don't really have the living or dining space to support the eight or nine people they will hold—a problem particularly acute at the Beach Club Villas, Saratoga Springs, Boulder Ridge Villas at the Wilderness Lodge, and BoardWalk Villas.

Chairs can be moved around to add seats in these smaller spaces, but larger groups will find the Two Bedroom Villas at Riviera, Old Key West, the Villas at Disney's Grand Floridian, Kidani Village, and Bay Lake Tower much more livable.

Bungalows at the Polynesian and Lakeside Cabins at Copper Creek are unlike any other DVC two-bedroom spaces, but also very expensive.

Grand Villas, available at all the DVC resorts except the Beach Club Villas, Boulder Ridge, and the Polynesian Villas and Bungalows, sleep 12 in a king room, two rooms with two beds each, and some sofa beds. They have twice the living/dining/kitchen space of Two Bedroom Villas, and sometimes—at Jambo House, VGF, and most of the BoardWalk Grand Villas—even more.

There's more variation among the Grand Villas than in any other DVC accommodations, so for more on these huge spaces that can go for more than $2,000 a night, see yourfirstvisit.net.

CAMPSITES AT FORT WILDERNESS

Fort Wilderness offers three lodging options—Cabins, group campsites, and individual campsites.

The Cabins were discussed earlier in this chapter, among the Moderates. You'll also find there an overview of the dining, extensive amenities, and inconvenience of Fort Wilderness. Neither of us has enough friends to have rented a group campsite, but they are particularly appropriate for scouts and other youth groups. The individual campsites can be booked for ten people and come in five basic types:

- "Tent or Pop-Up Campsites"
- "Full Hook-Up Campsites"
- "Preferred Campsites"
- "Premium Campsites"
- "Premium Meadow Campsites"

The key distinction is that the two types of Premium Campsites are designed for very large RVs, and have no tent pad. So tent campers, and campers with both an RV and a tent, should avoid them. Full Hook-Up sites have both a large RV spot and also a small tent pad. Tent campers are allowed in the Full Hook-Up campsites, but will find themselves in a sea of rumbling RVs should they choose one, and most commonly will be best served by a Tent or Pop-Up loop. Preferred sites have the same configuration as Full Hook-Up sites, but are closer to Magic Kingdom transportation and Fort Wilderness dining.

Anyone planning for tents at Fort Wilderness should keep three points in mind, all related to the commonly intense weather—heat and storms—in Orlando:

- Bring extra flys to serve as sun shades and rain protection. Your tent, ideally, will have a full coverage fly and a mesh inner body.

- Since the tent pads are sand, few traditional stakes will hold in weather. See the Fort Wilderness review on YOURFIRSTVISIT.NET for suggested alternative stakes. If you can walk comfortably around your site, you don't have enough guy lines out.

- All Fort Wilderness sites, including the Tent or Pop-Up sites, have power. So bring extension cords and multiple fans.

The Campsites at Disney's Fort Wilderness Resort, while wonderful for returning visitors who like to camp or own an RV, are not recommended for typical first-time family visitors to Walt Disney World. The wilderness and backwoodsy theming of this resort, while charming, is so subtle that it will fly over the heads of most kids. Mickey and other Disney themes are almost entirely absent.

Also, the Campsites at Disney's Fort Wilderness Resort are remarkably inconvenient compared to the other Walt Disney World resorts. See the review of the sister Cabins at Fort Wilderness in the Moderates section of this chapter for more details on what Fort Wilderness has to offer.

OTHER ON-PROPERTY HOTELS

There are two groups of resorts operated by third parties on Disney property. First, there's a group of four that are comparable to the Disney deluxe resorts in room size, quality, amenities, and location. These are Shades of Green, the Swan, the Dolphin, and the Four Seasons. Full reviews follow, but here's the key points:

- **SHADES OF GREEN** is an inexpensive deluxe-level resort near the Polynesian for U.S. service members, career military retirees, other eligible guests, and their families and sponsored friends. Shades of Green guests are eligible for EMH and FP+ at 60 days.

- **THE SWAN AND DOLPHIN** are deluxe hotels near the Epcot resorts—a little closer to Hollywood Studios than Epcot, compared to the other Epcot resorts. Guests at the Swan and Dolphin are eligible for EMH and for FastPass+ at 60 days. Both resorts are competitively priced, but suffer from a daily $30 resort fee. A third resort, the Cove, is expected to join this Marriott Bonvoy group later in 2020.

- **THE FOUR SEASONS RESORT ORLANDO** opened in 2014 as the first five-star resort at Walt Disney World. It has the largest standard rooms on property, great dining for adults, a character breakfast a couple of times a week with Goofy, and the best pool complex at Walt Disney World. In 2018, Four Seasons added access to EMH and FastPass+ at 60 days.

Second, there's a group of seven hotels in the Disney Springs Resort Area. While their prices may initially seem attractive, high resort fees typically push the price up. The Disney Springs Resort Area isn't convenient to anything but shopping and dining, and these hotels have their own, often disappointing, park transportation. Guests at these seven hotels are eligible for EMH, and for FastPass+ at 60 days. These new perks have been extended through at least 2020 at these hotels.

THE DISNEY WORLD SWAN AND DOLPHIN

The Disney World Swan and Disney World Dolphin ("Swan and Dolphin") are paired, connected Marriott (formerly Starwood) convention resorts that share all amenities and have easy access to Epcot and Disney's Hollywood Studios. The two resorts have unusual exterior decorations—off-putting to some and delightful to others—and lovely but un-themed interiors. The larger Dolphin has more amenities just an elevator ride away, but offers full beds in its standard rooms. The smaller Swan is more of a walk to some amenities, but has queen beds in its standard rooms.

The Swan and Dolphin are not owned by Disney, but even so share in the most valuable perk available to guests staying at a Disney-owned resort: they can book FastPass+ at 60 days. Swan and Dolphin guests also are eligible to attend Extra Magic Hours, and the two hotels are fully integrated into the same transportation system that serves Disney's own Epcot resorts—the Yacht Club, Beach Club, and BoardWalk Inn. Guests here get free parking at the parks, but can't use the Dining Plan, and can't use Disney's Magical Express.

The Swan is a long mid-rise building with a curved roof that has enormous statues of swans on top. The Dolphin is larger and taller, rising to a pyramid flanked by enormous statues of a curious nondescript fish. Each hotel has its own amenities which guests at either can use, and the two are connected centrally by a covered walkway, and are connected at the side by a sweep of pool after pool after beach after pool that collectively are the third best pool complex at Disney World.

The Swan and Dolphin are just beyond the BoardWalk Villas and Yacht Club. Guests can use either Disney boats or a walking path to get to Hollywood Studios and Epcot. The other parks and Disney Springs are served by shared buses which can take awhile. This location makes them a fine choice for a visit centered on Epcot, but not so much for a trip focused especially on the Magic Kingdom—as most first visits are.

Standard rooms at the Swan were refurbed in 2015, and a refurb of Dolphin rooms was completed in 2017. Swan rooms offer two queen beds and a divided bath with two sinks, and the slightly larger (360 vs. 340 square

Walt Disney World Dolphin
Standard Room Floor Plan ~360 Square Feet

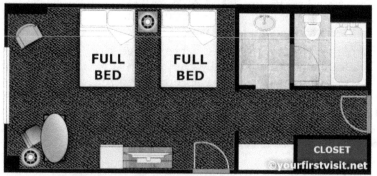

feet) Dolphin rooms offer two full beds and a divided bath with a single sink. The queens and extra sink make Swan rooms better for most families.

Other amenities are similar. These rooms have beside the beds and bath a dresser, desk, mini-fridge, TV, closet, and a coffee-maker. All rooms are accessed from interior corridors, and only some have balconies. As is typical of convention hotels, many suites are also available in addition to the standard rooms.

The Swan and Dolphin have great adult dining at Kimonos, Shula's Steak House, and Todd English's bluezoo, and some OK kid dining including a character meal at Garden Grove. Casual dining is much better than that at Disney's Epcot resorts, and two more casual venues (at the Swan) should open soon. More dining is easily accessible in the Disney hotels, along the nearby BoardWalk, and, for those with hoppers, in Epcot itself.

Amenities at the Swan and Dolphin are comparable to those at Disney deluxe resorts, missing only water sports. Besides the great pool complex, they include playgrounds, spas, fitness centers, tennis, hot tubs, and arcades.

The lack of Disney theming and relative inconvenience to the Magic Kingdom makes us less than keen on the Swan and Dolphin for first-time visitors, and the masses of conventioneers can make them even less fun. (Disney's Epcot resorts are all convention hotels as well, but at a much smaller scale.) But the Swan in particular can be a great choice for a later, more Epcot-focused trip. Dining is better than at Disney's Epcot resorts, the pools are better than those at the BoardWalk Inn (though not as good as those shared by the Yacht and Beach Club), and standard rooms prices are typically lower than what you'd pay for Disney Epcot resort standard rooms.

Prices at the Swan and Dolphin are less transparent than those at the Disney resorts, and sometimes obscure that fact that unlike at the Disney-owned hotels you pay a required resort fee. But even with these extra costs, rooms are often less than the Disney-owned Epcot resorts.

Walt Disney World Swan
Standard Room Floor Plan ~340 Square Feet

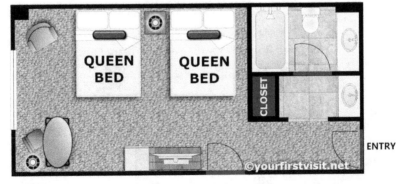

SHADES OF GREEN

Shades of Green Resort ("Shades") is a military-owned Armed Forces Recreation Center in the heart of Walt Disney World. The resort overall is un-themed and bland—it could be anywhere—but eligible guests who stay here will find some of the nicest rooms at Disney World at very low prices—prices here vary by rate/rank, but generally are competitive most of the year with Disney's least expensive resorts. Eligibility is complicated, but its rooms can be booked by eligible "sponsors" who are currently serving or career retired, or the spouses of such folk, plus a host of other classes detailed on Steve Bell's site militarydisneytips.com. (Veterans who are not career retired can stay in September and January.) Sponsors can book a room for themselves as well as 2–5 additional rooms (depending on the time of year and whether a spouse is involved) for their family and friends at the same low rates.

While Shades is not owned by Disney, its guests do have access to the most valued Disney World perks—Extra Magic Hours and, new beginning late 2017, access to FastPass+ at 60 days. They don't get free parking at the parks ($25/day), aren't eligible for Disney's Magical Express airport transportation, and can't use the Dining Plan.

Shades has a large wood and stone lobby building where guest services, the bus stop, and most dining are located. Guest rooms are in two wings off the lobby. The Palm wing is newer, prettier, and closer to parking. The less attractive Magnolia Wing is closer to the two pools at the resort, one near the lobby and another at the far end of the Magnolia wing that has a kids play area, water slides, and easy access to a sports bar and grill.

Shades is nestled between two golf courses in the Magic Kingdom area, across the street from Disney's Polynesian Village Resort. Park transport is via its own bus system that is not as good as the buses serving the Disney-owned resorts. Buses commonly start too late, run too infrequently, and don't directly serve the Magic Kingdom or Epcot, instead dropping guests headed to those parks off at the Transportation and Ticket Center. Many Shades guests walk to the Polynesian to take advantage of its transportation—it's about half a mile from the lobby at Shades to the Poly's monorail stop.

Shades of Green Resort
Standard Room Floor Plan ~480 Square Feet

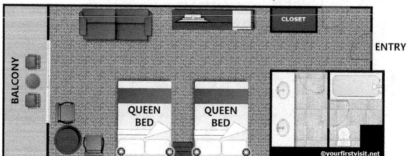

Standard rooms at Shades sleep five on two queens and a couch that converts into a single bed. These rooms are about 480 square feet—larger than those in any Disney-owned resort. Rooms have beside the beds and couch a large table with two chairs, mini-fridge, TV, dresser, closet, and a coffee-maker. The divided bath includes two sinks and a hair dryer, and a toilet and tub in a separate room. All rooms are accessed from interior corridors, and all have large balconies. A few suites are also available.

Shades has multiple dining options, none of them particularly fun, distinctive or memorable compared to Disney alternatives, but all providing good value for the money. Additional dining is easily accessible at the Polynesian, and from the monorail stop there at other resorts.

Amenities at Shades are a little thin compared to those at the more expensive Disney-owned resorts, but stronger than those in Disney's less expensive resorts, and include playgrounds, a spa, a fitness center, tennis, hot tubs, and an arcade.

You won't find a better room for the money anywhere else at Disney World, making Shades a great choice for returning visitors, especially with its new access to FastPass+ at 60 days, but the combination of bland theming and not-so-convenient transport makes us hesitant to recommend it for first-time visitors. Many eligible first-timers will be better served by staying at a Disney-owned resort using Disney's Armed Forces Salute discount.

Prices at Shades are based on rank/rate. At press time, standard rooms range from $124/night to $154/night. Unlike the Disney resorts, Shades prices don't vary over the course of the U.S. government fiscal year. Discounts are often available. For more on these and everything Shades or military, see militarydisneytips.com

FOUR SEASONS RESORT

The Four Seasons Resort Orlando at Walt Disney World Resort ("Four Seasons") opened in 2014 as Walt Disney World's first five star resort. Lovely but essentially un-themed (it could be anywhere), the 17-story hotel has elements of Spanish Colonial Revival architecture, with inadvertent references to the Tower of Terror. A wonderful respite for returning visitors who plan extensive hotel or pool time, Four Seasons has the nicest standard rooms on property, the best pool complex at

Four Season Resort Orlando
Standard King Bedroom Floor Plan ~500 Square Feet

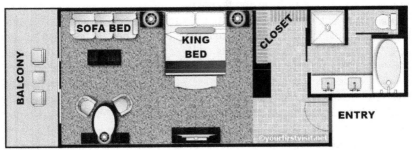

Disney World, and fine dining for adults (and a bit of playful dining for kids). But transportation and theming issues make it perhaps not the best choice for first-timers.

Four Seasons is not owned by Disney, but in 2018 its guests gained access to the most valuable perks that those staying in Disney-owned resorts receive: Extra Magic Hours and FastPass+ at 60 days. They don't get free parking at the parks, can't use the Dining Plan, and can't use Disney's Magical Express.

Four Seasons is a mid-sized high rise with guest services on the lower floors and rooms and suites on the upper floors. One of its long sides overlooks its parking lots, and the other has distant vistas of the Magic Kingdom and Epcot, and near views of its wonderful pool complex—the best at Disney World—which includes an adult-only pool, large lazy river pool, pool slide complex, and family pool.

Four Seasons is deep in the Golden Oak residential area, between Fort Wilderness and Port Orleans Riverside. Park transport is via its own motor coach system that is more comfortable but less convenient than the buses serving the Disney-owned resorts. Coaches run too infrequently, and (as of Dave's last stay) begin their schedules too late and end too early.

There's two flavors of standard rooms at Four Seasons, identical except on their bed side, where one offers two full beds and an easy chair, and the other a king bed and a couch that converts into a queen sized bed that is, by far, the most comfortable sofa bed Dave's ever slept on. (The floor plan is of the king bed variant.) All but the shortest and most slender of families seeking one room should choose the king/sleeper sofa floor plan over the full beds. The most common layout pairs one of each of these room types with connecting doors and a deep entry alcove that can also be closed off at the corridor end—making for an easy, albeit expensive, set-up for families seeking more than one room's worth of space or beds.

These standard rooms are about 500 square feet—the largest on property—and have beside the beds and chair or couch, a large table with two chairs that can serve as a desk as well, TV, dresser, enormous closet with more drawers, and a coffee-maker/mini-fridge set up all ready for you to order in a full bar. The overly open bath includes two sinks, a hair dryer, a tub and a separate shower, and a toilet in a separate glass-walled room. All rooms are accessed from interior corridors, and all have large balconies. Suites of all flavors are also available, including a nine-bedroom option going for more than $10,000 a night—add taxes and tips, and pretty soon you are talking about real money.

Four Seasons has multiple dining options, including Capa, a distinctive rooftop Spanish steakhouse with distant views of the Magic Kingdom and Epcot fireworks; Ravello, a more casual lower level Italian option; character meals with Goofy certain mornings; and other pool-side and casual options. Unlike at the Disney deluxe resorts (except the Animal Kingdom Lodge), there's no easily accessible nearby hotels offering additional dining venues.

Four Seasons offers all the amenities you'll find at any other Disney World hotel except for beaches and water sports. You won't find a more relaxing, delightful, or peaceful resort anywhere else at Disney World, but the combination of bland theming and not-so-convenient transport makes us hesitant to recommend it for first-time visitors. Most first-timers who could afford Four Seasons will be better served by staying at one of the monorail resorts (Contemporary, Grand Floridian, or Polynesian), and saving Four Seasons for a return trip when relaxing at the hotel is as important a priority as is visiting the parks.

Future pricing at Four Seasons is not so easy to uncover as it is at the Disney-owned resorts, but the least expensive rooms at Four Seasons are easily competitive with the Disney monorail resorts, especially if your dates are flexible.

THE DISNEY SPRINGS RESORT HOTELS

The seven hotels of the Disney Springs Resort Area are on Disney World property but owned and operated by third parties. These are a mix of small and larger hotels (though none is as large as the largest Disney hotels), some aimed at conventioneers, others at families, others at couples, and some all suites. In 2018, perhaps as a time-limited experiment but one that will be extended at least through 2020, guests at all of these gained access to the two most valued Disney World perks: Extra Magic Hours and FastPass+ at 60 days.

The best among these are the Hilton Buena Vista Palace, the Hilton Orlando Lake Buena Vista, and the tower side of the Wyndham Lake Buena Vista. Among the lower-priced options, the other side of the Wyndham, the Wyndham Garden, is the best choice. For more on these hotels, including reviews, floor plans, and hundreds of images, see the material that begins at yourfirstvisit.net/dsra.

To book them through the Walt Disney World Travel Company, start on your My Disney Experience account on the Disney World website, click at the top "Places to Stay," and then under "More Great Accommodations" click "Disney Springs Resort Area Hotels."

THE BONNET CREEK RESORT HOTELS

The Bonnet Creek Resort is a private enclave with four—soon to be five—hotels, surrounded by Disney World but not on Disney property. Located right next to Caribbean Beach, these hotels are, by far, the most convenient "off-site" hotels for Disney World visitors.

In spring 2019, guests staying at two of the Bonnet Creek hotels—the Hilton Orlando Bonnet Creek and the Waldorf Astoria Orlando—gained access to the two most prized Disney World perks, access to FastPass+ booking 60 days before arrival, and eligibility to use Extra Magic Hours. We've stayed in each since they gained these perks, and think the Hilton is a fine choice and the better choice of the two for families. Full reviews are on yourfirstvisit.net.

OFF-PROPERTY HOTELS AND VACATION HOMES

We think first-timers should stay at a Disney-owned resort, and that returning visitors—especially if their last visit was before

FastPass+—should strongly consider doing so. However, an off-site stay may remain attractive due to significantly lower prices, especially when considering the cost for a family of five to stay on property. While it's theoretically possible for a family of five to stay in the Murphy bed rooms at Caribbean Beach or Riverside, we're still talking about five people sharing a single bathroom and 314 square feet of total space. Disney's idea of a value-priced family suite at Art of Animation starts at $338 per night and skyrockets up to $570/night over the holidays.

However, staying off-site presents another set of costs and challenges. First, any scheduled shuttle transportation from most off-site resorts can be as weak as one bus in the morning and one bus at night. These times are often rigid and inconvenient, whether the bus arrives after park opening or departs long before the nighttime entertainment or the park closes. Miss the bus and it's an expensive cab ride. Off-site guests often rent cars, but that reduces convenience and increases costs. Parking at the theme parks is $25 per day (due only *once* per day, if you keep your receipt). Second, resort fees that typically cost $15-$30 per night are another concern. For some families, the price discount may be too much to overlook this trip, and there's nothing wrong with that. But be sure to consider all the costs associated with a stay that may not be included in the initial price.

There are literally thousands of off-site hotels, motels, campgrounds, vacation homes, condos, etc., in and around Orlando. Returning visitors who know their way around can stay anywhere, but we suggest that first timers target their search to the Highway 192/West Irlo Bronson Highway and/or the Disney Springs Resort Area. The value of honing in on these two areas is simple: from almost any place in Walt Disney World, you can find directional signage to 192, and directional signage to Disney Springs.

Walt Disney World is much more complicated than many first-time visitors imagine, and your first few days of finding your way around will be made simpler by this signage.

- The street address of hotels on 192 will include either "Highway 192" and/or the words "Irlo Bronson Highway".

- The street address of hotels in the Disney Springs Resort Area will include "Hotel Plaza Boulevard" (or, in the case of the Hilton Orlando Buena Vista Palace, "Buena Vista Drive").

It's possible to find multiple-bedroom vacation homes available for short-term rentals in the Orlando area for a fraction of the price you'd pay to stay in some of the deluxe large family options at Walt Disney World, even counting your rental car costs. Airbnb is also becoming more accepted in Orlando.

First-time visitors benefit most from staying on property at a Disney owned and operated resort. While more expensive than their off-site counterparts, it's hard to put a price on the convenience and peace of mind that an on-site stay in a Disney resort offers.

CHAPTER SIX

How to Spend Your Time

This chapter:

- Provides example, pre-made itineraries for guests arriving on a Saturday and planning to spend nine days in Orlando.
- Presents introductions to touring each of the major theme parks, with reviews and insight into every single theme park attraction.
- Follows with Cheat Sheets that cover everything you need to bring with you to the theme parks. These include what to expect at park open, detailed touring plans including when you can expect to arrive and depart each attraction, FastPass+ priority so you know which experiences will save you the most time, and advice on how to see the nighttime spectaculars with the least hassle. Color copies of the newest versions of these Cheat Sheets are available at yourfirstvisit.net/easy-guide-2020-changes.

We open with a discussion of one of Disney's newest innovations, FastPass+, and how it has transformed the theme park experience in positive and negative ways. Maximizing FastPass+ is an important strategic advantage and we'll cover the best methods to save you hours in line every day.

Next, we focus on itinerary planning, including:

- Deciding how many days to visit each park.
- Picking the best park to visit each day based on crowds and entertainment offerings.
- Creating a daily touring plan that blends easy morning touring, strategically chosen FastPass+ experiences, and the best dining choices.

Example itineraries are provided to give you an idea about how best to plan your vacation in its entirety. Modifications can easily be made depending on where you want to go and what you want to do.

This is the lengthiest chapter because the theme parks are what a Walt Disney World vacation is all about. Plan to digest it over several sessions.

FastPass+ at Walt Disney World

Disney's digital FastPass+ system replaced legacy paper FASTPASS in early 2014. More attractions than ever before offer FastPass+, including nighttime spectaculars like Fantasmic! at Hollywood Studios and character meet and greets like Rapunzel and Cinderella at Magic Kingdom.

Each attraction has one or two entrances. At attractions that do not offer FastPass+, there is a single line called the "standby queue". Here, guests simply get in line and wait their turn. At FastPass+ enabled attractions, there are two separate lines—the standby queue and the FastPass+ return queue.

At attractions with both types of entrances, guests with a FastPass+ can experience an attraction with priority boarding. Attractions like Tower of Terror and Toy Story Mania admit as many as seven FastPass+ riders for every one standby rider. Thus, those with FastPass+ wait much less than those in standby lines, and push up standby waits because they receive priority boarding, even if they arrive long after a standby rider.

Disney bills FastPass+ as an "easy way to reserve some of your must-do fun before you leave home". Indeed, all guests with tickets may book up to three FastPass+ experiences in advance for each day the ticket is valid. Guests staying at Disney-operated resorts, in addition to the Swan and Dolphin resorts, may book up to 60 days in advance of a given date. New in 2018 and continuing through 2020, guests staying in Shades of Green, Hilton Bonnet Creek, Waldorf Astoria, Four Seasons, or in a Disney Springs Resort Area hotel may also book up to 60 days in advance. Guests staying in all other accommodations may book up to 30 days in advance. This is one of the most positive features of the program—guests may schedule headlining attractions like Toy Story Mania, Test Track, Space Mountain, and the Princess Fairytale Hall Meet and Greets from the comfort of their home long before they arrive in Orlando, or even the day of a visit to the theme park from their smartphone or in-park kiosk. But there are two major negatives:

- Guests must select a specific one-hour window on a specific day. Based on the attraction reviews that follow, you may decide that the group wants to meet Ariel at Ariel's Grotto in Magic Kingdom. But you'll need to pick a specific date and time—August 27 from 2:15–3:15pm, for example. (The rest of this chapter helps with all these choices—which days, which rides, which FastPass+, and which times.)

- Some attractions distribute a very limited number of FastPass+ opportunities, making booking 30–60 days in advance necessary.

Later in this chapter, we'll discuss the importance of choosing which theme park to visit based on crowds and entertainment. This goes hand in hand with Chapter 7, which discusses restaurant reservations, some of which must be booked a whopping six months in advance. Combined with the FastPass+ priority discussion next, picking attractions and theme parks is easy, but being forced to select specific hour-long windows for each ride can feel like too much micro-managing and reduce spontaneity.

There is no such thing as legacy FASTPASS inside the theme parks anymore, which—for those who have visited before—means no more paper FASTPASS tickets. Legacy FASTPASS tickets were generally distributed at each attraction that offered it, necessitating backtracking and long walks to collect FASTPASSes over the course of the day. The good news is that FastPass+ eliminates the need to visit each attraction for which you'd like a FastPass+. Gone are the days of sending Dad to Splash Mountain with everyone's park tickets while the rest of the group rides Buzz Lightyear's Space Ranger Spin 20 minutes away.

The introductions to each theme park below, along with the Cheat Sheets, include a list of the attractions that offer FastPass+. Attractions are ranked based on how much time and hassle using FastPass+ will save. For example, Slinky Dog Dash, Rock 'n' Roller Coaster, and Tower of Terror are the top priorities at Hollywood Studios because using FastPass+ at each will save 60 or more minutes in line most of the day. Muppet*Vision 3D is ranked near the bottom because using FastPass+ won't save any time since everyone that shows up for the next show will be admitted. There are a few other considerations also taken into account. For example, the queue for Tomorrowland Speedway at Magic Kingdom is outdoors and exhaust from the cars permeates through the entire area. Speedway is prioritized over several other attractions because it will not only save 20 or more minutes in line, but also bypass much of the stench.

Because FastPass+ experiences can be booked in advance, the new program adds certainty to your schedules and also makes arriving late at a theme park much easier than with the legacy FASTPASS system. Prior to FastPass+, Toy Story Mania legacy FASTPASSes would typically be gone before 11am, with return times well into the evening by 9:45am. This meant guests needed to arrive early to secure FASTPASSes with an unknown return time, or find themselves in a 75+ minute standby line at some point later in the day. Now you can leave home knowing you have Toy Story Mania booked in the afternoon, and no longer need to arrive at the park early to assure you can enjoy it.

Unfortunately, Disney has instituted a tiering system at Animal Kingdom, Epcot and Hollywood Studios, which means guests at those parks can initially reserve only one high priority ("Tier 1") attraction per day in advance. At Animal Kingdom, guests can pick only one of the two Pandora rides. At Epcot, guests choose between Frozen Ever After, Test Track, Soarin', and the nighttime spectacular. At Hollywood Studios, Millennium Falcon: Smugglers Run and Star Wars: Rise of the Resistance do not currently offer FastPass+, though both rides are set up to use the system. We expect this to change at some point in 2020, at which time Rise of the Resistance will be the clear FastPass+ priority of the two. Currently, the Studios' five most popular rides, Slinky Dog Dash, Rock 'n' Roller Coaster, Tower of Terror, Toy Story Mania, and Alien Swirling Saucers all comprise Tier 1, and guests may initially select only one of these. Star Tours and the various shows comprise Tier 2, with guests able to initially make two selections. Regardless of what Disney does to the FastPass+ tiers in the future, the list of priority attractions shouldn't change with Rise of the Resistance and Slinky Dog Dash being the two highest priorities, followed by Smugglers Run, Rock 'n' Roller Coaster, and Tower of Terror. Because guests may only choose one priority ride in advance, it does increase the availability of those attractions as 4th and subsequent FastPass+ selections later in the day. Refresh availability on the app or website throughout the day looking for higher priority attractions and better return times.

Choosing the Best FastPass+ Time Slots

When considering when to schedule your FastPass+ experiences, there are two main schools of thought. The first is to schedule FastPass+ beginning right at park opening, with the goal of scheduling a 4th FastPass+ as early as possible. To book a 4th FastPass+, you must use the initial three or the window on the third must pass. So if you book Space Mountain for 9–10am, Buzz Lightyear's Space Ranger Spin for 10–11am, and Peter Pan's Flight for 11am–12pm, you would be eligible to schedule a 4th FastPass+ immediately after you use the 3rd or any time after 12pm should you not use the Peter Pan FastPass+.

Initially, Disney required all guests to book three FastPass+ in advance, but now guests may pre-book one FastPass+ experience at a time, up to three total experiences, so long as each is at the same theme park. Most guests visiting just one park each day will want to select the maximum number of three in advance for the best selection.

Also, keep in mind that at Animal Kingdom, Epcot, and Hollywood Studios, guests must use or let expire all three of their initial FastPass+ selections in order to book a second Tier 1 FP+. So you can't book just Toy Story Mania from 9–10am, use it right at 9am, and then try to book a 2nd FP+ for Toy Story Mania or another Tier 1 attraction like Slinky Dog Dash. You would be able to book either after using your two Tier 2 selections. Guests planning to park hop could schedule and use just one FastPass+ at one park and then immediately schedule their second FastPass+ at another park, regardless of tier, but based on availability. So you could book and use Toy Story Mania in advance and after using it, immediately book Soarin' at Epcot if times are available.

The benefit to booking earlier times is that each additional FastPass+ selection is based on availability, and availability is better earlier in the day when fewer people have had the opportunity to select additional FastPass+. The downside is that on busier days, there may be very little availability for the priority attractions even at 11am.

Another downside is that using FastPass+ earlier in the day, when standby waits are shorter, will save less time than using the same FastPass+ later. For example, a Space Mountain FastPass+ used at 9:30am might save 15 minutes in line. A Space Mountain FastPass+ used at 12:30pm might save 60 or more minutes in line because afternoon crowds are so much heavier.

The second school of thought is to schedule FastPass+ in the late morning and afternoon when it will save the most time and take advantage of short standby waits at most attractions in the early morning. Our advice is to begin scheduling FastPass+ as early as 10:30am at a high priority attraction like Test Track or Seven Dwarfs Mine Train. While availability for a 4th FastPass+ will be worse later in the afternoon, it's likely that the same attractions that were available at 11:30am will be available at 1:30pm.

If you're planning to schedule your first FastPass+ for 9–10am, plan to use it as close to 10am as possible to save the most time and take advantage of short standby waits elsewhere before then.

Also note that scheduling a nighttime spectacular in advance inhibits your ability to make additional FastPass+ selections earlier in the day. For example, if you select Slinky Dog Dash, Star Tours, and Fantasmic! as your initial three selections, you won't be able to select a 4th FastPass+ choice because you won't use your third selection until the very end of the night. So there are some tradeoffs should you wish to take advantage of the reserved FastPass+ viewing areas at the nighttime entertainment.

When searching for additional FastPass+ opportunities, it's important to remember that experiences that other people change or cancel become available for anyone to book. While there may not initially be any availability for Rock 'n' Roller Coaster the first time you check, there may be if you refresh the inventory by pressing a new time at the top of the FastPass+ selection screen. Continue clicking different times until a desired FastPass+ selection becomes available, keeping in mind that the most-sought-after experiences are the ones that become available the least often. A rare Flight of Passage FastPass+ may not show up the first hundred times the screen is refreshed, but most attractions will eventually become available as there are thousands of FastPass+ experiences distributed each day for most rides and shows. Also consider refreshing availability for a better return time. Rock 'n' Roller Coaster may initially show availability for several hours in the future. Refresh and a more convenient return time may show up. The earlier in the day you use your third FastPass+ and begin refreshing for a 4th, the more likely it is that a rare FastPass+ experience will become available. This process can be duplicated as long as your patience and the operating hours of the park allow.

Finally, keep in mind that FastPass+ does not operate during morning or evening Extra Magic Hours. That's mostly good news for those visiting during the extra time because it means FastPass+ returners won't bog down standby queues unnecessarily, in effect leveling the playing field for all on-site guests in attendance.

Designing Your Own Walt Disney World Itinerary

The art of itinerary design has three parts: dividing your time among the parks, picking the best days to visit each park, and shaping what you do each day to minimize time spent waiting in line.

ALLOCATING YOUR TIME AMONG THE PARKS

Chapter 3 covered in-depth how to divide your time depending on party size, makeup, and length of vacation. As a refresher, most guests will spend the most time at Magic Kingdom, with Epcot being a close second, except for those traveling with the youngest children. Most guests spend about a day each at Hollywood Studios and Animal Kingdom, though the Star Wars addition at Studios may cause enthusiasts to spend more time there, and visiting Pandora at Animal Kingdom may necessitate devoting more time at that park. Guests on shorter vacations will need to prioritize which experiences are most important and either use the park hopper upgrade to visit more than one park per day or potentially skip a park altogether.

PICKING THE BEST DAYS TO VISIT THE PARKS

There are several factors that contribute to the decision on which theme park to visit each day, including expected crowds and nighttime entertainment. We used to offer daily advice about six-and-a-half months ahead, but Disney has so limited the information it publishes that far in advance that we can no longer be precise in this advice. For imprecise guidance for your dates, leave a comment on any page of Dave's yourfirstvisit.net.

In general, the longer a theme park is open and the more nightly entertainment it offers compared to the other parks, the busier it will be. This is especially true at Magic Kingdom, which can see wildly different operating hours and entertainment offerings, particularly during Mickey's Party Season from the middle of August through the third week in December. During that time, it's not uncommon for Magic Kingdom to be open to regular ticketholders only from 8am or 9am to 6pm and offer no evening fireworks three or four days per week, while the other days it's open as late as 1am with fireworks. The days with longer hours are significantly more crowded because people equate longer hours with more bang for their buck. This isn't necessarily true. While a longer day does offer more time in the park, it also brings with it longer lines, increased congestion in common areas, and a more stressful overall experience. With two days at Magic Kingdom, most guests will want to visit on one less crowded day to hammer out the priority attractions and also visit on a day that they can enjoy the nighttime entertainment. During other times of the year, Magic Kingdom typically offers fireworks nightly, making it easier to see the show.

- Animal Kingdom is typically least busy on Sundays, Tuesdays, and Wednesdays. It's busiest on Mondays, Thursdays, and Saturdays.
- Epcot is generally least busy on Wednesdays, Thursdays, and Fridays. Saturdays are typically busiest.
- Tuesdays, Wednesdays, and Thursdays are usually best for Hollywood Studios. Saturdays and Sundays typically see higher attendance.
- Magic Kingdom is typically least busy on Sundays and Wednesdays with the highest attendance on Saturdays.

One reason why Magic Kingdom tends to be busiest on Saturdays is the number of people who want to visit The Most Magical Place on Earth before heading home on Sunday, in addition to the number of local passholders that prefer to visit on the weekend. Josh's recent work has suggested much less day-to-day variation in crowds at Magic Kingdom than in the past, except during the party season, when days with late closes continue to be brutally crowded.

With the popularity of Galaxy's Edge, we expect weekends at Disney's Hollywood Studios to also see much higher crowds than most weekdays.

You might consider roughly following this schedule:
- Sunday: Magic Kingdom
- Monday: Epcot
- Tuesday: Animal Kingdom
- Wednesday: Magic Kingdom

- Thursday: Hollywood Studios
- Friday: Epcot
- Saturday: Half day – either rope drop to lunch or a late arrival through Park close at your choice of Park, or a day off

That gets you to each park on one of its best days of the week, on average, and to Magic Kingdom on its two best days of the week. With Galaxy's Edge open, visiting the Studios on a weekday later in the week should continue to be an intelligent choice. From August through December, double check the Mickey's Party dates and note early closes at Magic Kingdom. Those days will be less crowded.

Once you've sorted out which parks you will visit on which days, begin entering the details in the planning sheet, on the next couple of pages. (There's room in it for dining as well, which is coming in Chapter 7.)

DESIGNING YOUR PARK APPROACH FOR EACH DAY

After you've divided your days among the parks, and picked days to visit each park, your final step is designing your approach for each day.

There are two easy ways to go about this:

- Model your visit around the daily agendas you'll find linked to from the itineraries on yourfirstvisit.net/itineraries. We give an example of these itineraries after the worksheet.
- Use the park overviews and ride reviews that come just after the example itineraries, to tailor the easyWDW Cheat Sheets at the end of this chapter to a trip that's perfectly adapted to your group and the length of your trip!

Example Itineraries for Disney World

If you have chosen to do an eight-night, nine-day trip with a Saturday arrival, and your kids are at least 8 years old and 48 inches tall, then you'll find an itinerary for dates within the next six or so months (they are released as Disney releases its operating calendar) at yourfirstvisit.net/itineraries. Scan down the dates at that link and click to the itinerary suggested for that date—taking special note of words like "but see this for required changes…".

When you do so, you'll find an itinerary like the example, and with it links to daily touring plans based on that itinerary and a tailored To-Do List with suggested FastPass+. While the example will give you an idea about what we're looking at, they do change based on different weekly schedules. The list at yourfirstvisit.net/itineraries will be updated with itineraries for each specific week.

Disney World Itinerary Planning Worksheet

Underline =
Counter/Quick Service

Bold =
Table Service

Italic =
Cash, not Dining Plan

Red =
Character Meal

Meals:	_____ day	_____ day	_____ day	_____ day
Breakfast				
Lunch				
Dinner				
Parks, Etc:				
Early Morning				
Late Morning				
Early Afternoon				
Late Afternoon				
Evening				
Late Evening				
Notes:				
Parade				
Fireworks				
Park-Open Target				
FastPass+ Target				

Meals:	_____ day	_____ day	_____ day	_____ day
Breakfast				
Lunch				
Dinner				
Parks, Etc:				
Early Morning				
Late Morning				
Early Afternoon				
Late Afternoon				
Evening				
Late Evening				
Notes:				
Parade				
Fireworks				
Park-Open Target				
FastPass+ Target				

"FastPass+ Target" is the Tier One Fastpass+ to aim for; at time of writing, only Epcot and Hollywood Studios have tiered FastPass+

Example Disney World Itinerary

This itinerary does not work for all dates! See yourfirstvisit.net/itineraries

	Saturday	Sunday	Monday	Tuesday
Meals:				
Breakfast	*Travel*	*Hotel Room*	*Hotel Room*	*Hotel Room*
Lunch	*Travel*	Flame Tree Barbecue or Hotel	Hollywood Studios or Hotel Counter	**11a Chef Mickey's****
Dinner	**6p Akershus or San Angel Inn**	**5.30p Tusker House ROL Dining***	Hollywood Studios or Hotel Counter	**6.15p Hoop-Dee-Doo Revue****
Parks, Etc.:				
Very Early Morning			Hollywood Studios—see text for time	
Early Morning	*Travel*	At Animal Kingdom by 8.15a	Hollywood Studios	At Magic Kingdom by 8.15a
Late Morning	*Travel*	Animal Kingdom	Optional Hollywood Studios	Magic Kingdom
Early Afternoon	At Epcot ASAP	Off	Optional Hollywood Studios	Magic Kingdom
Late Afternoon	Epcot	Off	Hollywood Studios	Magic Kingdom
Evening	Epcot	Animal Kingdom	Hollywood Studios	
Late Evening			Hollywood Studios	
Notes:				
Parade				
Evening Show	Epcot Forever	Rivers of Light	Fantasmic; Star Wars or Jingle Bell	
Park-Open Target	n/a	Kilimanjaro Safaris	Star Wars; Toy Story Mania	Buzz Lightyear
FastPass+ to pre-schedule	Frozen Ever After, Spaceship Earth	Na'vi River Journey, Finding Nemo, Kali River Rapids	Tower of Terror, Indiana Jones, Frozen Sing-Along	Space Mountain, Tomorrowland Speedway, Jungle Cruise

Underline = Counter/Quick Service
Bold = Table Service
Italic = Cash, not Dining Plan
Red = Character Meal

	Wednesday	Thursday	Friday	Saturday	Sunday
Meals:					
Breakfast	*Hotel Room*	*Hotel Room*	*Hotel Room*	*Hotel Room*	*Hotel Room*
Lunch	Hollywood Studios Counter	**TBD Cinderella's Royal Table****	Sunshine Seasons	Magic Kingdom or Hotel Counter	Animal Kingdom Counter or Travel
Dinner	Sunset Ranch Market	Magic Kingdom or Hotel Counter	Epcot or Hotel Counter	**6p Crystal Palace**	*Travel*
Parks, Etc.:					
Very Early Morning	Optional Hollywood Studios—see text				
Early Morning	Optional Hollywood Studios	At Magic Kingdom by 8.15a	At Epcot by 8.15a	At Magic Kingdom by 8.15a	At Animal Kingdom by 8.15a
Late Morning	Optional Hollywood Studios	Magic Kingdom	Epcot	Magic Kingdom	Animal Kingdom
Early Afternoon	Hollywood Studios	Magic Kingdom	Epcot	Off	Animal Kingdom
Late Afternoon	Hollywood Studios	Magic Kingdom	Epcot	Off	*Travel*
Evening	Hollywood Studios	Magic Kingdom		At Magic Kingdom by 5.30p	*Travel*
Late Evening	Optional Hollywood Studios			Magic Kingdom	
Notes:					
Parade				Afternoon Parade	
Evening Show	Anything missed Monday			Happily Ever After	
Park-Open Target	Star Wars; Rock 'n' Roller Coaster, Slinky Dog Dash, Star Tours, Beauty and the Beast	Peter Pan, Seven Dwarfs Mine Train, Haunted Mansion, Enchanted Tales with Belle	Soarin' Around the World, Test Track, Turtle Talk with Crush, Mission: SPACE	Splash Mountain, Big Thunder Mountain, Pirates of the Caribbean, and a third	Expedition Everest, Avatar Flight of Passage; Festival of the Lion King

*As Rivers of Light Dining Package   **Two table-service credits

Disney's Animal Kingdom

With the opening of Pandora: The World of Avatar on May 27, 2017, along with the addition of plentiful nighttime entertainment, touring Animal Kingdom is now more complicated. First, the new land brings two new rides in Avatar Flight of Passage and Na'vi River Journey. Flight of Passage is easily one of Walt Disney World's most popular rides with an average wait time that exceeds two hours and incredibly limited FastPass+ availability. Guests able to book FastPass+ for Flight of Passage will have the easiest time as Na'vi River Journey is easy to ride with a short wait first thing in the morning, or last thing at night, and the average wait is closer to an hour.

Furthermore, the addition of the Rivers of Light nighttime spectacular, Tree of Life Awakenings projection show, and the novelty of experiencing Kilimanjaro Safaris, Expedition Everest, and Pandora after dark, may be cause to stay later into the evening than past visits. With regular summer hours being as long as 8am–11pm, it would be difficult or impossible to spend all 15 hours in the park with the heat and the crowds. Guests with longer trips may elect to spend parts of two days at Animal Kingdom or otherwise plan a lengthy afternoon break over the course of a single day. Some guests with a limited number of attractions that they would like to experience may also be able to make a late arrival work.

Overall, it's possible to enjoy the majority of Animal Kingdom's best attractions in a single day, but those who would like to see all of the shows, walk the nature trails, and slow down a bit to take in all of the sights and sounds should consider spending two days. That's particularly true much of the year when seeing Rivers of Light and experiencing the other nighttime attractions is difficult due to operating hour constraints. The introductions, reviews, and cheat sheets that follow will help guide you through the planning process.

FASTPASS+ PRIORITY

FastPass+ at Animal Kingdom is divided into two groups. One group includes the two rides that opened with the new Pandora: World of Avatar land. From these two you can pick just one. The other group includes all other Animal Kingdom FastPass+ attractions, and from these, you can pick two more.

Pandora (choose one):

1. Avatar Flight of Passage
2. Na'vi River Journey

Everything else (choose two):

1. Kilimanjaro Safaris
2. Expedition Everest
3. Animation Experience at Rafiki's Planet Watch (due to very few experiences available)
4. Kali River Rapids (when highs are 80+ degrees)
5. Adventurers Outpost Mickey and Minnie (due to few experiences available)

6. DINOSAUR
7. Rivers of Light (primarily first show; last show is easier to see in standby)
8. Kali River Rapids (when highs are under 80 degrees)
9. Festival of the Lion King
10. Finding Nemo the Musical
11. Up! A Great Bird Adventure
12. Primeval Whirl
13. It's Tough to Be a Bug

Guests may initially select only one Pandora ride in advance. Avatar Flight of Passage wait times average 125+ minutes, while Na'vi River Journey's average wait is closer to 70 minutes, making the choice of which to select obvious when both are available 60+ days in advance. From among the other choices, Kilimanjaro Safaris and Expedition Everest typically save the most time and have relatively limited availability most afternoons. If you'd like to do the Animation Experience, book it in advance or as your 4th FastPass+ earlier in the day, as there are few seats available for each experience and it ends earlier in the day than the rides and character meets. Kali River Rapids and DINOSAUR in the afternoon also save 30-60 minutes most days, but availability as a 4th or subsequent FastPass+ is usually higher.

Rivers of Light may be a good choice for those arriving later in the day, but choosing the nighttime show will result in the inability to make other FastPass+ selections until after the show, thus limiting the day's FastPass+ opportunities to just three. The Adventurers Outpost Mickey and Minnie Meet has limited availability, but wait times are usually under 30 minutes, which is less time savings than the major rides. During cooler days, there is far less demand for Kali River Rapids because fewer people are interested in getting wet.

Time savings at Festival of the Lion King and Finding Nemo the Musical is negligible with FastPass+ since it requires the user to arrive at the shows early enough that a similar seat in standby should be available. On the plus side, using FP+ guarantees a seat, which makes an arrival closer to show time possible, even if the seat is unlikely to have a great view. Using FastPass+ at Up! A Great Bird Adventure is unlikely to save time, but it does guarantee the seat and because show times are limited, availability is lower than the last two attractions on the list. Finally, Primeval Whirl and It's Tough to Be a Bug have availability almost all day, making it easy to secure FastPass+ for these experiences after using the day's initial allotment.

ARRIVING AT ANIMAL KINGDOM

Guests headed to Avatar Flight of Passage first want to arrive at least one hour before official park open to be among the first couple of hundred people to arrive at the attraction. Posted waits will hit 100+ minutes within 15 minutes of opening. Those headed anywhere else, including Na'vi River Journey, can safely arrive 30 minutes before open and find short waits at any other attraction.

Almost all guests arrive by Disney bus or their own transportation. Guests parking early can easily walk to the main entrance. Guests arriving later and parking farther out have the option of walking or taking a tram. Those arriving via Disney bus will be dropped off just a minute or two walk away from the main entrance.

Bag check precedes the ticket windows. Since Pandora opened, Animal Kingdom ticket windows have seen longer lines, but they're still typically shorter than Magic Kingdom or Epcot. Guest Services is located on the far left both inside and outside the main entrance. Stroller and wheelchair rentals are located on the right just inside the main entrance.

Rainforest Café sits on the left with an entrance/exit both inside and outside the park. Theme park admission is thus not required to dine at the restaurant, which is only convenient as you enter or exit the park.

THE OASIS

Unlike the entry into any other Disney theme park, The Oasis is nearly devoid of shops, restaurants, and loud stimuli. Instead, the area works to transition visitors into the lush, tropical, animal-filled surroundings that set the tone for the rest of the park. Expansive animal habitats display iguanas, anteaters, macaws, ducks, and a variety of other animals amidst rushing waterfalls, dense vegetation, and a burgeoning canopy. Guests arriving prior to park opening will want to breeze through the Oasis with plans to return either in the afternoon or on the way out. Time spent here at open will only result in thousands of people passing you and filling the queues for the major attractions, in turn pushing up wait times. With an afternoon arrival, plan to slowly meander around the winding pathways, taking in the various exhibits for 15–30 minutes.

DISCOVERY ISLAND

After The Oasis, guests cross a bridge to Discovery Island, the central hub for the entire park. Discovery Island circles the 14-story hand-carved Tree of Life, the park's central icon, and an easy marker for guests trying to make their way back to the main drag from one of the peripheral lands. DinoLand and Asia are off to the right, in addition to the Adventurers Outpost Mickey and Minnie meet and greet, It's Tough to Be a Bug 4D show, and Flame Tree Barbecue, one of the park's best quick services. Off to the left is Pizzafari, another quick service option offering pizzas and garlic knots in a bright, air-conditioned space. Attached to Pizzafari is a new signature restaurant called Tiffins, which specializes in African, Asian, and South American flavors in an atmosphere that celebrates Disney Imagineers' exploration of those continents as they planned and conceptualized the construction of the park. Nomad Lounge, located inside Tiffins, offers what is probably the most relaxing air-conditioned respite for a drink in any Disney theme park. Past Pizzafari is the park's Starbucks location, followed by Africa, one of the three major lands. Pandora: The World of Avatar replaced Camp-Minnie Mickey in May 2017. The land's main entrance is down the path to the left of Pizzafari and Tiffins.

Discovery Island is where you'll find the bulk of the shopping opportunities, with Island Mercantile and Discovery Trading Company supplying the widest selection. Virtually anything you would find in any of the smaller stores can be found here. Plan to return in the afternoon for some air-conditioned perusing when few people are shopping and the waits at the attractions are longer. Like the major stores at the other theme parks, Island Mercantile and Discovery Trading Company remain open for at least 30 minutes after close, allowing for last-minute impulse buys.

Adventurers Outpost

RANKING Don't miss for those that want to meet Mickey and Minnie together; skippable otherwise. **EMH** No. **FP+** Yes. High priority for guests wanting to meet the characters. **TYPE** Meet-and-greet. **REQUIREMENTS** None.

WHAT TO EXPECT Guests line up outside the winding queue before entering a small air-conditioned room prior to the meet and greet. Mickey and Minnie greet together in their safari outfits with a fun adventurer's background. This is the only regular meet-and-greet where both Mickey and Minnie greet and take pictures together. **SCARY FACTOR** None.

WHEN TO GO Before 9:45am, during the last hour they meet, or with Fast-Pass+. **EXPECT TO WAIT** Peak afternoon waits are typically 25 to 40 minutes. **LENGTH** About two minutes of signing, mingling, and picture taking.

It's Tough to Be a Bug

RANKING Minor attraction. **EMH** Morning. **FP+** Yes. Low priority. **TYPE** 4D Show. **REQUIREMENTS** None.

WHAT TO EXPECT The theater is dark, loud, and there are a number of effects that "add" to the experience. Otherwise, It's Tough to Be a Bug is a fun 3D theater show (in-theater special effects make it "4D") based on *It's a Bugs Life* that most guests enjoy. **SCARY FACTOR (WITH MINOR SPOILERS)** Low for those 12 and older, but it may frighten younger kids. Animatronic spiders, termites, beetles, hornets, and more make appearances; several effects add to the anxiety: smoke, a "sting" from the back of the seat, insects dropping from the ceiling, and the sensation that bugs are running under your feet. If you're scared of bugs, this show may not be for you. At the same time, all of the bugs are "cartoony" like in the movie and not particularly realistic.

WHEN TO GO Afternoon when waits have peaked elsewhere. **EXPECT TO WAIT** Only as long as it takes for the next show to start. **LENGTH** 8 minutes. **WHERE TO SIT** Target the back few rows and let guests fill about half the row before entering. With apprehensive kids, instead sit at the end of a row for an easy exit.

Rivers of Light: We Are One

Rivers of Light is the park's nighttime spectacular that's scheduled at least once most nights with the first show after dark and the last show typically scheduled at or just past park close. If a show is scheduled after official close, anyone is welcome to stay and see it. It takes place on Discovery River with stadium seating in Asia (FastPass+) and DinoLand (dining package and standby).

RANKING Debatable. The avant-garde show relies heavily on unconventional visuals and whimsical music without fireworks or, arguably, a coherent storyline or anything resembling a true climax. See it and decide for yourself. It's several years in the making. **EMH** No. **FP+** Yes. It's a high priority for those who need to see the first show and don't want to use a dining package. Those able to use a dining package or see a later show in standby will probably want to make their initial three FastPass+ selections elsewhere. **TYPE** Outdoor theatrical production. **REQUIREMENTS** None.

WHAT TO EXPECT The 15-minute show features music, special effects, floats, and animal folklore to tell a story about how everything in nature is connected. Originally, a pair of shamans and their acolytes appeared on the two boats and helped move the story along, but Disney removed them in September 2018, ostensibly for budgetary reasons. The show's energy suffers because of it. Disney refreshed the original offering in May 2019, adding scenes from Disney animated movies and their *Nature* series. This didn't do much to improve the quality of the production. For the first show, plan to arrive with FastPass+ or dining package reserved seating at least 25 minutes before show time. To see the first show in standby, arrive at least 45 minutes before show time as there's only room for about 1,000 people in that section. For the second show, arrive 15 minutes early with FastPass+ or 15–30 minutes before show time in standby. **SCARY FACTOR** Just the standby wait. While dark, the show doesn't feature overtly scary visuals.

WHEN TO GO Usually one show shortly after dark and, if offered, a second show scheduled 75–90 minutes later. **LENGTH** 15 minutes.

PANDORA

Animal Kingdom's newest land, with a reported price tag north of $500 million, is a breathtaking sight to behold. Towering mountains that appear to float in midair greet guests with bright flora, cascading waterfalls, and thousands of details spread out around the 12-acre expanse. It's one of the most immersive areas in any theme park worldwide. Avatar Flight of Passage is the marquee attraction. A state-of-the-art motion simulator, riders actually feel like they've mounted a banshee before taking a ride through the lush landscape of Pandora. Na'vi River Journey is its much tamer cousin, featuring a scenic, slow-moving boat ride through a dark, bioluminescent rainforest.

Windtraders, Pandora's principal retail store, offers interactive experiences in addition to the thousands of items available for sale. Visitors have the opportunity to "adopt" a banshee that sits playfully on the owner's shoulder, complete with a remote control that moves the limbs of the bird-like predator. Guests may also elect to have their own Avatar action figure made based on their likeness. After being scanned by a technician, the figure will be available to take home shortly after.

Satu'li Canteen, the land's major quick service, offers some of the best and most unique fast food at Walt Disney World. Best are the various bowls filled with steak, chicken, shrimp, or tofu on top of several different base choices, including quinoa and vegetable salad or red and sweet potatoes. Kids can choose from a smaller version of the bowl, in addition to a hot dog or cheese quesadilla. Pay special attention to the blueberry cheesecake dessert.

A takeaway bar named Pongu Pongu sits next to Windtraders, offering alcoholic and non-alcoholic frozen beverages, in addition to pineapple-filled cream cheese lumpia, which are like spring rolls with a sweet, tropical flavor.

Unsurprisingly, virtually none of the merchandise or anything else you see in Pandora focuses on the characters or plot of the first Avatar film. Seeing the movie will enhance your experience a bit, but the rides are perfectly enjoyable with virtually no previous knowledge of James Cameron's alien world.

Avatar Flight of Passage

RANKING Don't miss. **EMH** Morning, Evening. **FP+** Yes, highest priority. **TYPE** 3D flight simulator. **REQUIREMENTS** 44" or taller.

WHAT TO EXPECT The lengthy standby queue is a spectacle in its own right, winding around a mountain outdoors before arriving at the laboratory inside. Guests enter the first of two pre-show rooms, where riders are introduced to the Avatar link process. Next, guests are instructed on how to mount the ride vehicle, which is similar to getting on a bicycle. Some larger and/or taller guests have had trouble fitting on the seat. There is a test seat in front of the entrance that you can try if there's any concern. The trick is to sit as far forward as possible with your legs against the front restraints. The theater where the ride takes place is split into two rooms on each floor with three floors per theater. Eight riders in a single file line will board in each room, for a total of 16 people per floor or 48 people per theater. Unlike Soarin', the ride vehicles aren't lifted into the air in dramatic fashion—each row is already situated where it needs to be. After takeoff, the theater and ride vehicles move to simulate flight to great effect with the 3D images working in tandem with physical effects to create a real feeling of soaring through the world of Pandora. Even those who suffer from motion sickness typically report few problems. It's a tremendous move forward in flight simulation and a don't miss. **SCARY FACTOR** The ride vehicle restraints are a bit strange and some of the effects are surprising, but most riders should be at ease upon takeoff. Only those extremely scared of heights should be put off. The theater drops a few feet from time to time to simulate a mild plunge, but there is nothing overtly scary about the experience. Almost everyone leaves proclaiming it as one of their favorite rides, making it worth any initial unease. Motion sickness is much less of a problem than at imulators like Star Tours due to the smoothness of the ride and the high frame rate of the film.

WHEN TO GO Absolutely first thing in the morning if you arrive at least an hour before open. Standby waits are shortest during the day between 1:30–4pm and riding last thing at night is a viable alternative with actual waits that should be 45–70 minutes. Use FP+ if possible. **EXPECT TO WAIT** Posted waits are typically 150+ minutes within 15 minutes of opening. Other than absolutely first thing in the morning, expect to wait between 75–120 minutes in the afternoon and 50–75 at park close. Peak waits are typically in the vicinity of three hours. **LENGTH** 5 minutes. **WHERE TO**

SIT Seats in the middle of each row (seats 6–10) have a more straight-on view with the middle row experiencing the most movement.

Na'vi River Journey

RANKING Major attraction. **EMH** Morning, Evening. **FP+** Yes, but it's a much lower priority than Avatar Flight of Passage and guests may select only one or the other. If Flight of Passage isn't available, Na'vi River Journey is a better choice than any other Animal Kingdom attraction. **TYPE** Boat ride. **REQUIREMENTS** None.

WHAT TO EXPECT Na'vi River Journey is a scenic, indoor boat ride with an intensity similar to it's a small world or Living with the Land. The queue is all outdoors, though at least half is covered. Riders board small boats with just two rows each. Each row seats a maximum of four people. The ride is dark, but never ominous, with bright bioluminescent flora lighting the path and an incredibly detailed, 8-foot tall animatronic Na'vi Shaman of Songs at the end. The ride is pleasant enough, but it's sparse on story and at under five minutes, feels short. **SCARY FACTOR** Only for the intensely scared of the dark. Nothing pops up or is intended to startle.

WHEN TO GO Within 45 minutes of the park opening, during the last hour of operation, or with FastPass+. **EXPECT TO WAIT** Waits are typically under 15 minutes during the first and last half hour of operation, but should hit 45 minutes within an hour of open and typically peak between 70 and 100 minutes. **LENGTH** 5 minutes. **WHERE TO SIT** Request the front row for the best view.

AFRICA

Home to Kilimanjaro Safaris, Festival of the Lion King, Gorilla Falls Exploration Trail, and the Wildlife Express Train to Rafiki's Planet Watch, Africa is Animal Kingdom's largest land. Guests enter through Harambe, a rural African marketplace surrounded by buildings inspired by the ones Disney Imagineers saw during their travels across the continent. You'll see everything from a fortress reminiscent of Zanzibar to thatched huts built by the Zulu in South Africa.

Tusker House Restaurant (a Mickey-hosted character meal), Mahindi Popcorn, Dawa Bar, and Tamu Tamu Refreshments are the first buildings guests see as they cross the bridge over to Africa. Farther back, Mombasa Marketplace is the large store on the right, offering authentic African crafts, Animal Kingdom merchandise, and African wines. Kusafiri Bakery is on the left, serving baked treats and beverages. The entrance to Kilimanjaro Safaris is straight back with the entrance to Gorilla Falls Exploration Trail to the right near the Wildlife Express Train station. Harambe Market is the area's principal, open-air quick-service venue. Here, you'll find a nice variety of tasty entrees like a beef and lamb gyro, pork sausage on naan bread, and and rice bowls featuring chicken, ribs, or vegetables. The area is most pleasant in cool weather, as there is little to protect guests in line from the elements, and all seating is outdoors.

Festival of the Lion King

RANKING Major attraction. **EMH** No. **FP+** Yes. Low priority. FastPass+ users enter the theater before standby if they arrive 20+ minutes early and have their choice of seats. **TYPE** Musical theater show. **REQUIREMENTS** None.

WHAT TO EXPECT Lion King reopened in a new theater on June 1, 2014, though few things changed from its original run in Camp Minnie-Mickey. The show reprises songs and characters from the movie and features acrobatics, Animatronics, singing, dancing, fire, theater, and the most elaborate costumes and sets you'll find at Disney World. With more than 50 performers, there is almost too much to take in. **SCARY FACTOR** Low, the theater is dark and sometimes loud, but there is little to frighten youngsters.

WHEN TO GO First and last shows are least crowded. **EXPECT TO WAIT** Arrive 10 to 20 minutes early. **LENGTH** 30 minutes. **WHERE TO SIT** The section you choose isn't as important as the row you select. Higher than the eighth row provides a better view of the various floats and sets.

Kilimanjaro Safaris

RANKING Don't miss. **EMH** Morning. **FP+** Yes. High priority. **TYPE** Safari ride. **REQUIREMENTS** None.

WHAT TO EXPECT Riders board a 32-passenger open-air safari truck and take a mildly bumpy, fully narrated trip through the 100-acre Harambe Wildlife Reserve. It's basically a simulated, shortened safari through lifelike savannas populated with rare animals, including black and white rhinoceroses, cheetahs, flamingos, lions, giraffes, warthogs, zebras, wildebeests, ostriches, crocodiles, antelopes, and more. The animals aren't always "out" and your viewing may be limited by the time of day and simple luck of the draw. Disney extended the Safaris' hours through park close in May 2016 to mixed results. More recently, guests may enter the queue and ride up to an hour before park close. We recommend a ride that begins a few minutes after sunset when the animals are still active and the savannas are dimly lit. Once the sun goes down, it's difficult to see the few animals that remain and the storyline does little to keep the ride engaging. **SCARY FACTOR** None during the day and it's not much darker than other areas at night. **CAN WE HANDLE IT?** Mild jostling. If you have back or neck problems, request a front row where it's less bumpy.

WHEN TO GO During the first hour of operation, around sunset, or with FastPass+. Try to ride during the day and later at night for the best of both experiences. **EXPECT TO WAIT** 30–75 minutes in the afternoon. **LENGTH** 20 minutes. **WHERE TO SIT** Those sitting on the ends of the rows have the most unobstructed views. Otherwise, the driver's side has the best view.

Gorilla Falls Exploration Trail

RANKING Minor attraction. **EMH** Morning. **FP+** No. **TYPE** Self-guided walking tour, zoo exhibit. **REQUIREMENTS** None.

WHAT TO EXPECT Visitors walk along the path and enter various enclosures and exhibits that show off the animals in their native habitats. Expect to see hippopotamuses, meerkats, naked mole rats, gorillas, okapi (the only known relative of the giraffe), and an extensive number of rare African bird species. **SCARY FACTOR** Zero.

WHEN TO GO Anytime, but the gorillas are out more consistently in the late afternoon and the trail closes before dusk. **EXPECT TO WAIT** No waits. **LENGTH** Gorilla Falls is a little less than a half mile long. Most visitors spend about 30 minutes moving through the trail and the various exhibits.

Rafiki's Planet Watch

RANKING Fun but skippable. **EMH** No. **FP+** Yes, for the animation academy. Low priority. **TYPE** Zoological exhibits and interactive experiences. **REQUIREMENTS** None.

WHAT TO EXPECT Rafiki's Planet Watch is a collection of nicely air-conditioned diversions from long waits in the hot sun. You'll find a variety of exhibits that you'll need to take some time with if you want to get anything out of them. There are no rides or thrills at Planet Watch—just educational exhibits. Here's what's available:

- *Affection Section*, a petting zoo. The animals here are mostly species that are endangered or otherwise at risk.

- *The Animation Experience,* where guests have an opportunity to follow along with an artist as they draw their own character from a Disney animated feature over the course of a 20-minute class.

- *Conservation Station*, the main building at Rafiki's Planet Watch housing the majority of the live and hands-on exhibits. Veterinarians and wildlife experts will answer questions and give insight into how the Animal Kingdom operates. You can view live-camera feeds of backstage areas where the animals are kept, as well as a variety of other exhibits featuring a wealth of information on conservation efforts around the globe. Exhibits and activities can change on a daily basis because the area is actually used for live preparation and animal surgeries, so you never know what you'll see.

SCARY FACTOR Minimal. There is a snake or two and the mornings may feature intensive veterinary procedures on the wildlife, but both can be avoided.

WHEN TO GO Between 11am and 3pm when crowds and temperatures peak elsewhere. There are no waits and the main building offers plentiful air conditioning. Closes shortly before dusk. **EXPECT TO WAIT** Riders must board the Wildlife Express in the back right corner of Africa. Expect to wait up to ten minutes to board the train and another seven minutes to ride over. **LENGTH** As little or as long as you want. Most guests spend about 30 minutes.

Wildlife Express Train

RANKING Fun but skippable. **EMH** No. **FP+** No. **TYPE** Slow-moving transportation. **REQUIREMENTS** None.

WHAT TO EXPECT Guests wait at the station for the slow-moving, open-air train that arrives every eight-or-so minutes. All guests seated on the train sit facing the sights as it slowly travels through backstage areas where riders have an opportunity to see where the elephants sleep, among other things. This is the only way to travel to and from Rafiki's Planet Watch. **SCARY FACTOR** Zero.

WHEN TO GO Between 11am and 3pm when crowds and temperatures peak elsewhere is best. Begins operation 30 minutes after regular park open and closes shortly before dusk. **EXPECT TO WAIT** Between two and ten minutes. **LENGTH** The trip lasts about seven minutes.

ASIA

Home to perhaps Disney's best roller coaster, in addition to a white water rafting ride, jungle trek, and UP! A Great Bird Adventure, Asia has a lot to offer underneath its dense vegetation and gorgeously detailed theming. Asia is accessible via Discovery Island, a path from Africa, or DinoLand. Guests arriving from Africa or Discovery Island will first happen upon UP! A Great Bird Adventure. Continuing on, Yak & Yeti Restaurant and quick service are located on the left. The table service restaurant, which is operated by the same parent company as Rainforest Café, serves very good pan-Asian food at relatively reasonable prices, but the quick service arm has reduced offerings and the quality has come down considerably in recent memory. Still, the honey chicken, chicken fried rice, and egg rolls are all very good, though the all-outdoor seating can be uncomfortably hot and humid during the summer months. Just past Yak & Yeti on the left is the walkway to Kali River Rapids and Maharajah Jungle Trek. Free lockers are available near Kali River Rapids to keep belongings dry while enjoying the ride. Continue ahead and Expedition Everest is unmistakable in the distance. The ride entrance is again on the left. Passing Everest will take you to The Theater in the Wild, home of *Finding Nemo–The Musical.*

Shopping is thin through Asia, though you don't want to miss the clever Yak & Yeti-themed merchandise to the right of the quick service, or all the Expedition Everest-themed merchandise at the attraction's exit.

Expedition Everest

RANKING Don't miss. **EMH** Morning. **FP+** Yes. High priority. **TYPE** Roller coaster. **REQUIREMENTS** 44" or taller.

WHAT TO EXPECT Interesting artifacts in the queue create the back story of a mysterious beast that resides in the sacred mountains. Riders board (two per row) a train that traverses high speed twists, turns, and drops before a final confrontation with the Yeti. **SCARY FACTOR** Medium-High. Guests plummet down an 80-foot drop at speeds up to 50 miles per hour in the dark, but it could be worse. **CAN WE HANDLE IT?** If you enjoyed Rock 'n'

Roller Coaster, or any other "big coaster", you shouldn't have a problem. It is more intense than Space Mountain, but not so intense that the younger crowd won't be jumping up and down begging to ride. Some motion sickness risk, but no loops or inversions. Little jostling or jerkiness.

WHEN TO GO At park open, after dark, or with FastPass+. **EXPECT TO WAIT** 25 to 50 minutes in the afternoon. **LENGTH** 3 minutes. **WHERE TO SIT** The first row provides the best view, but the last provides the wildest ride. There really isn't a bad seat on the train. **SINGLE RIDER LINE:** Yes, to the right of standby entrance. Waits are typically under ten minutes.

Kali River Rapids

RANKING Major attraction. **EMH** Morning. **FP+** Yes. High priority when temperatures are 80+. **TYPE** Flume ride. **REQUIREMENTS** 38" or taller.

WHAT TO EXPECT Expect to get drenched on Kali, which follows a story about the destruction caused by illegal forestry. Riders board large rafts that seat 12 people in a circle around the outside perimeter of the raft. Your raft will be pulled up a 90 foot hill and then be released to freely but briefly float down the rapids, passing through geysers, waterfalls, and beautiful tropical jungles before plummeting down a 30-foot waterfall. The drop isn't fast or particularly thrilling, but it is still fun. Our opinion is that it's not worth the wait or the possible discomfort of wet socks and clothes. Complimentary lockers are located across from the entrance. Put everything you don't want getting wet inside before riding. **SCARY FACTOR** The ride starts off with a 90 foot uphill ascent, but there are no steep drops.

WHEN TO GO When it's hot, ride in standby before 10am or after dark. FastPass+ is useful in the afternoon. In cooler temperatures, anytime. **EXPECT TO WAIT** 35 to 70 minutes in the afternoon when it's hot; 15 to 20 minutes when temperatures are under 70. **LENGTH** 5 minutes total, 2 of which are spent on the initial lift. **WHERE TO SIT** Anywhere.

Maharajah Jungle Trek

RANKING Minor attraction. **EMH** No. **FP+** No. **TYPE** Self-guided walking tour, zoo exhibit. **REQUIREMENTS** None.

WHAT TO EXPECT Like Gorilla Falls in Africa, Maharajah is a trail that takes visitors through several zoo-like exhibits and enclosures. You'll (hopefully) see tigers, gibbons, water buffalo, a komodo dragon, and hundreds of exotic birds in lush habitats. Bats are located in a separate house that's easy to skip if you prefer. **SCARY FACTOR** None.

WHEN TO GO Much of the Trek is shaded and cooler than other areas in the Animal Kingdom, which makes it a good choice during the afternoon heat when attraction lines elsewhere are longest. Closes shortly before dusk. **EXPECT TO WAIT** No waits. **LENGTH** Maharajah is a little longer than a third of a mile and most visitors spend about 20 minutes walking through it.

UP! A Great Bird Adventure

RANKING Minor attraction. **EMH** No. **FP+** Yes. Low priority. **TYPE** Stage show. **REQUIREMENTS** None.

WHAT TO EXPECT A Great Bird Adventure is similar to Flights of Wonder, the show it replaced, with a couple of key changes. First, Russell and Dug appear on stage, which increases the interest levels of most kids. But the characters don't add much to the educational aspect of the show and because their dialogue is all pre-recorded, the dynamic sometimes feels forced and unnatural. Still, the birds continue to steal the show, performing some great tricks. Many guests report enjoying the show much less than Flights of Wonder, but the fact that it's easy to see may make a stop worthwhile, especially for those who enjoy *Up*. **SCARY FACTOR** Low for anyone without ornithophobia.

WHEN TO GO An afternoon show is best when waits are high elsewhere. **EXPECT TO WAIT** Arrive 10-20 minutes early depending on how close to the stage you'd like to sit. **LENGTH** 25 minutes. **WHERE TO SIT** The bleachers towards the back offer a higher rise between rows, but are farther back from the stage. Consider sitting off to the side where it's less likely someone's head will be blocking the view.

DINOLAND USA

By far the least appreciated land in any domestic Disney theme park, DinoLand follows the story of the Dino Institute and their Time Rover Tours. The fictitious backstory is that, in 1947, researchers found dinosaur fossils in Diggs County and "Dino fever" took hold of the area, bringing in thousands of tourists. A local entrepreneurial couple, Chester and Hester, took advantage of the influx by building Chester and Hester's Dino-Rama, a collection of cheap carnival games, gaudy colors, and off-the-shelf rides.

Indeed, much of DinoLand is themed to a cheap carnival built on top of a parking lot—on purpose. Whether it works is another debate, but the Imagineers that designed the park would tell you it took more time and energy to make the parking lot look old and decrepit than it did to install much of the vegetation around the park.

Guests walking from Asia will first see The Theater in the Wild on their left. This houses one of Disney's most elaborate stage shows, *Finding Nemo–The Musical*. In the center of DinoLand sits Primeval Whirl and TriceraTop Spin. TriceraTop Spin is a spinner similar to Dumbo and The Magic Carpets of Aladdin, while Primeval Whirl is an off-the-shelf wild-mouse-style coaster. Farther back to the left of Restaurantosaurus is DINOSAUR, the land's major attraction and a fun dark ride that transports lucky riders back to the end of the late Cretaceous period. A number of characters meet in DinoLand, including Goofy, Pluto, Chip, and Dale. Restaurantosaurus itself is a burger-and-nugget quick service option with fun theming, plentiful air conditioning, and refillable fountain beverages.

Chester & Hester's Dinosaur Treasures shop is located near TriceraTop Spin's exit. There's nothing here that isn't available elsewhere. Another small store is located at DINOSAUR's exit. Here, you'll find some fun dinosaur-themed merchandise.

DINOSAUR

RANKING Don't miss. **EMH** Morning. **FP+** Yes. Medium priority. **TYPE** Dark ride. **REQUIREMENTS** 40" or taller.

WHAT TO EXPECT DINOSAUR is located in the Dino Institute, an elaborately themed queue area with authentic dinosaur fossils. After you move through the queue, you will be taken to watch a short video where the storyline is explained. Once the pre-show concludes, you will move to the next area where you board a 12-person (three rows with four people in each row) Time Rover vehicle. Once strapped in, you will embark on your wild ride through time and space. **SCARY FACTOR** High. DINOSAUR is one dark, loud, bumpy ride. Although there are no drops more than a few feet and the vehicles don't move particularly fast, this may still prove to be the scariest ride at Animal Kingdom. **CAN WE HANDLE IT?** Besides being scary and bumpy, DINOSAUR is rough on those with even moderate motion sickness.

WHEN TO GO Before 10:30am or two hours before park close. Disney has been closing the ride an hour before the rest of the park and may sometimes open it 30 minutes after the rest of the park. Double check the Times Guide if you're planning on riding first or last thing. **EXPECT TO WAIT** 25 to 40 minutes in the afternoon. **LENGTH** 4 minutes. **WHERE TO SIT** Put apprehensive kids in the middle seats. The front row affords the best view.

Finding Nemo: The Musical

RANKING Major attraction. **EMH** No. **FP+** Yes. Low priority. **TYPE** Musical theater show. **REQUIREMENTS** None.

WHAT TO EXPECT Featuring the *Finding Nemo* characters, the show is housed in an air-conditioned theater with fairly comfortable bench seats with backs. Tony Award-winner Robert Lopez and his wife Kristen Anderson-Lopez (now of "Let It Go" fame) penned 16 original songs for the show, and Michael Curry, who helped design the wildly successful *Lion King* Broadway show, served as lead designer. The actors and puppeteers wear costumes and are just as much a part of the show as the puppets themselves. Don't be put off by this being "just a puppet show" because it's much, much more than that. Note that this is one of Disney World's longest shows and you'll need to be prepared to budget about an hour to experience it, at least 40 minutes of which will be seated on relatively uncomfortable benches. **SCARY FACTOR** Low. Nemo gets into some trouble with a shark puppet, but that's about it.

WHEN TO GO First and last shows are least crowded. **EXPECT TO WAIT** You'll want to be lined up about 20 minutes before it begins. **LENGTH** 40 minutes. **WHERE TO SIT** Plan to sit at least half way up in the middle seating section. Sitting any closer may result in a cropped view of the stage that requires a lot of head turning to see the action. FastPass+ users who arrive 20+ minutes early file into the theater before standby guests.

Primeval Whirl

RANKING Fun but skippable. **EMH** Morning. **FP+** Yes. Low priority. **TYPE** Wild mouse coaster. **REQUIREMENTS** 48" or taller.

WHAT TO EXPECT Riders board four-person spinning ride vehicles reminiscent of Mad Tea Party. The vehicles travel up a steep incline before being unleashed on a track that features no serious drops or g-forces. It is a herky-jerky ride with the occasional neck-snapping stop. **SCARY FACTOR** Medium. While technically less intense than other coasters, the spinning can be disconcerting and it "feels" like you're higher up than you are. **CAN WE HANDLE IT?** The ride can be incredibly hard on necks and backs. Anyone with pain should skip the ride.

WHEN TO GO Before 10:30am or two hours before park close. The ride recently shifted to seasonal status, so it may only be operating on the busiest days of the year. **EXPECT TO WAIT** 15 to 30 minutes in the afternoon. **LENGTH** 3 minutes. **WHERE TO SIT** The common advice is to evenly distribute weight on each side of the vehicle for less spinning. Or conversely, stick two heavier people on one side and two lighter people on the other for more spinning. Does it have an effect? Probably not, but it might make you feel better.

The Boneyard

RANKING Fun for kids, skippable for everyone else. **EMH** No. **FP+** No. **TYPE** Playground. **REQUIREMENTS** None.

WHAT TO EXPECT The Boneyard is an elaborately themed playground aimed at young kids and has several stories of sand pits, swings, and things to climb on. **SCARY FACTOR** None.

WHEN TO GO Visit with youngsters when the bigger kids are riding Primeval Whirl and DINOSAUR. Otherwise, visit in the late morning or afternoon when waits elsewhere peak. The Boneyard does get hot, so save it for the end of the day during the summer. **EXPECT TO WAIT** Very rarely any wait. **LENGTH** As long as it takes to pry Junior away.

TriceraTop Spin

RANKING Fun diversion, especially with kids. **EMH** Morning. **FP+** No. **TYPE** Spinning ride. **REQUIREMENTS** None.

WHAT TO EXPECT Riders enter four-person dinosaur-themed vehicles with two rows of two people. Each row has a joystick that can slightly alter the way the vehicle moves: either up and down or back and forth. The ride vehicles slowly move around the base of the ride in a circle. **SCARY FACTOR** Minimal. Although the ride does move up, down, and side to side, it's geared towards young children and it shouldn't frighten anyone.

WHEN TO GO Before 11am or about two hours before park close. **EXPECT TO WAIT** Peak waits of 10 to 15 minutes are common. It's a walk-on, early and late. **LENGTH** 90 seconds. **WHERE TO SIT** Your choice, though young kids will be asked to sit on the inside so they won't accidentally fall out. Riders in the front can reach behind and use the joystick in the back row if there's nobody back there.

Epcot

Epcot, which is unlike any other theme park in the world, is a quintessential part of any theme park vacation. With an emphasis on education and understanding the world around us, many of its attractions take time and a little effort to enjoy.

Epcot consists of two very different pieces: Future World and World Showcase. Future World is where you'll find two of the park's three headlining rides, Soarin' and Test Track, in addition to the bulk of the secondary attractions. It's the area located just inside the main entrance and consumes the north half of the park. In the next year or two, Future World will be rebranded as three Neighborhoods – World Celebration, World Discovery, and World Nature. World Showcase is home to most of the dining and shopping experiences, in addition to the emphasis on the cultures of the world that the park is so famous for providing. Frozen Ever After, which replaced Maelstrom in the Norway Pavilion in June 2016, is also found here. Peak waits are typically 75 minutes. Remy's Ratatouille Adventure, a clone of the trackless dark ride from Disneyland Paris, will open in the back of the France Pavilion in Summer 2020. We expect peak waits to be in the 60 to 75 minute range. A restaurant, primarily serving crepes, will also open in France around the same time.

Future World usually operates from 9am (rarely, from 8am) through regular park close, although the Imagination Pavilion usually closes at 7pm, along with Living with the Land and select other attractions.

Most of World Showcase opens at 11am, with a few exceptions. The bakery in France opens daily at park open, though most guests will want to visit later in the day and focus first on attraction priorities. Remy's Ratatouille Adventure should also open with the park upon its summer 2020 debut. The Norway Pavilion, including the Frozen Ever After ride and Royal Sommerhus Anna/Elsa Meet and Greet, also opens with the park. While waits to meet Anna and Elsa typically peak under 30 minutes thanks to a healthy hourly capacity, Frozen Ever After is a major priority. We recommend riding with FastPass+ later in the day to avoid the morning rush.

FASTPASS+ PRIORITY

FastPass+ at Epcot is divided into two tiers. In Tier 1 are Frozen Ever After, Soarin', Test Track, and the nighttime spectacular. Seven selections comprise Tier 2 with only a few offering much value in most situations..

Tier 1 *(choose one)*

1. Test Track
2. Frozen Ever After
3. Soarin'
4. Epcot Forever / HarmonioUS

Tier 2 *(choose two)*

1. Mission: SPACE
2. Spaceship Earth
3. Living with the Land

4.   Journey into Imagination with Figment

5.   The Seas with Nemo and Friends

6.   Turtle Talk with Crush

7.   Pixar Short Film Festival

ARRIVING AT EPCOT

Guests aiming to take advantage of shorter morning waits should arrive at the main entrance at least 45 minutes before open, or at the International Gateway at least 30 minutes before open.

Most guests arrive at the main entrance via Disney bus, the monorail, or their own automobile. Guests staying at the Beach Club, Yacht Club, Board-Walk Inn, Swan, and Dolphin may walk from their resort or take the boat to the International Gateway entrance in the World Showcase between the United Kingdom and France pavilions. The Disney Skyliner gondola system also stops at the International Gateway, connecting guests from Pop Century, Art of Animation, Caribbean Beach, Riviera, and Hollywood Studios. Guests visiting Epcot from those locations may also elect to take a bus to the main entrance. Guests transferring from Magic Kingdom or the Magic Kingdom parking lot (TTC) arrive at the main entrance via the monorail.

Guest Services outside the main entrance is on the far right, while Guest Services inside is on the far left past Spaceship Earth. Wheelchair and ECV rental are on the left just inside the entrance. At the International Gateway, Guest Services is located outside the entrance. Wheelchairs and ECVs are available for rental inside on the left.

FUTURE WORLD EAST

Future World East is where you'll find two of Future World's three top priority attractions: Test Track and Mission: SPACE. Most guests visiting only for one day will want to start on this side, and guests spending two or more days will also want to plan a morning starting with Test Track or a late arrival with Test Track as a FastPass+ selection.

Bypass Spaceship Earth, the park's icon, first thing in the morning. The iconic structure that looks like a giant golf ball enjoys lower peak waits than the headliners and sees shorter waits after 6pm. Many uninformed guests ride Spaceship Earth first thing, putting them at a great disadvantage as they won't arrive at Test Track until at least 9:30am, when waits will already be hitting 30+ minutes. Spaceship Earth is expected to close in early 2020 for a major refurbishment that should continue through the end of the year.

Quick service dining choices are slim—Electric Umbrella is really it, and it serves a limited menu featuring Disney's standard burgers, chicken nuggets, and sandwiches. Electric Umbrella is also scheduled to close for extensive refurbishment in early 2020. Various stands serve snacks like pretzels, churros, and beer.

Space 220 is a new restaurant expected to open in early 2020 in between Test Tack and Mission: SPACE. Guests will ride a special elevator up to the restaurant, which is themed to a space station with panoramic views of Earth below. Patina, the same restaurant group that runs dining in the Italy Pavilion, will operate the venue with cuisine that's expected to focus on international flair. The concept is one that we're looking forward to experiencing.

Mouse Gear is the largest store in Epcot, offering the widest assortment of theme park merchandise outside of World of Disney at Disney Springs. It will also close in early 2020 for an extensive refurbishment.

Mission: SPACE

RANKING Major attraction. **EMH** Morning, Evening. **FP+** Yes. High priority. **TYPE** Simulator. **REQUIREMENTS** Must be 44" tall to ride the Mars mission; 40" for Earth. Mission: SPACE has more warnings than any other ride at Disney World. Consider skipping if you have suffered motion sickness on any other ride, or are claustrophobic.

WHAT TO EXPECT Mission: SPACE is a space flight simulator, where riders board small four-person capsules that are intended to mimic the inside of a space shuttle. There are two versions of this ride. Mars features a spinning takeoff with G-forces up to 2.5, and is much more thrilling and much more risky for those with physical or motion sickness issues. The Earth version debuted in August 2017 with a storyline that revolves around circling the green planet. There is no spinning takeoff, and thus, no G-forces to worry about. After the initial takeoff, the rest of the ride is rather tame with only slight movements by the simulator while you watch a small screen in front of you. During the Mars mission, the intense aspects last for about 15 seconds at takeoff and again for a short amount of time when the spacecraft travels through an asteroid field. Those that have previously experienced Mission: SPACE Orange may want to try Earth for a new experience. **SCARY FACTOR** Medium. The ride itself is not particularly scary, but there are some iffy moments. Mission: SPACE does induce anxiety due to negative hype over people getting sick from the spinning. **CAN WE HANDLE IT?** Apprehensive riders should begin with the Earth mission.

WHEN TO GO Before 10:30am, after 7pm, or with FastPass+. **EXPECT TO WAIT** Peak waits of 30-45 minutes are common. **LENGTH** 5 minutes. **WHERE TO SIT** Experience is the same from any of the four seats.

Spaceship Earth

RANKING Don't miss. **EMH** Morning, Evening. **FP+** Yes. High Tier 2 priority. **TYPE** Dark ride. **REQUIREMENTS** None.

WHAT TO EXPECT Spaceship Earth is a slow moving, dark omnimover ride that takes guests as high as 16 stories inside Epcot's famous geodesic sphere. Visitors ride past more than 20 Animatronic displays featuring scenes from the past 40,000 years that depict how communication techniques have changed with time. A classic. **SCARY FACTOR** Low. The ride is dark, but there are no startling elements.

WHEN TO GO After 6pm or with FastPass+. **EXPECT TO WAIT** Peak waits of 30 minutes are common. Expect to wait less than 10 minutes after 6pm. **LENGTH** 15 minutes. **WHERE TO SIT** Each row seats two to three people. The view from the left is arguably better.

Test Track

RANKING Don't miss. **EMH** Morning, Evening. **FP+** Yes, high Tier 1 priority. **TYPE** Dark/thrill ride. **REQUIREMENTS** 40" or taller.

WHAT TO EXPECT After a 2012 renovation, riders are to imagine themselves to be "inside" a computer simulation of a car being tested. Guests first design their own prototype automobile at a kiosk. The design process takes about three minutes and riders choose what they want their automobile to look like and whether they want to favor capability, efficiency, responsiveness, or power. In a surprise to many, this design step does not affect the ride in any way. Riders then board six-person vehicles with two rows of three seats each and embark on their journey with several sharp turns and increases and decreases in speed before launching outside at speeds up to 65 miles per hour. **SINGLE RIDER:** Test Track offers a single-rider line with the entrance to the left of standby. Waits are usually shorter than standby or FastPass+ because single riders don't go through the design process and the seating arrangement creates more openings. **SCARY FACTOR** Medium. Test Track is just a little more intense than normal driving, but there are some herky-jerky movements and sudden starts and stops. Most people fare fine.

WHEN TO GO Immediately after park opening, in the final hour, or with FastPass+. **EXPECT TO WAIT** 60–100 minutes in the afternoon. **LENGTH** 5 minutes. **WHERE TO SIT** Request the front row for the best view.

FUTURE WORLD WEST

Three large pavilions make up the bulk of Future World West. Soarin' on the lower level of the Land Pavilion is its headlining attraction that remains a high morning priority after receiving a new film and the addition of a third theater in June 2016. Most other attractions can safely be saved for the afternoon or early evening. Character Spot, as it operated prior to September 2019, is no more. Mickey, Minnie, and Goofy moved to a temporary location in the building opposite of the old entrance and the experience no longer offers FastPass+. Visit in the first or last hour of operation if possible. The characters will move to different locations at some point in 2020, with Mickey headed to the Disney & Pixar Short Film Festival lobby area and Minnie going to the World Showcase Gazebo. Joy and Sadness from "Inside Out" continue to meet in Character Spot, but will move to a new location in Imageworks, which doubles as the exit from Journey into Imagination with Figment inside the Imagination Pavilion, in early 2020. Wreck-It Ralph and Vanellope also meet in Imageworks and should continue to do so.

Sunshine Seasons is one of the best quick services in any theme park. You'll find it in between Soarin' and Living with the Land in the Land Pavilion. Coral Reef and Garden Grill are the two table service restaurants. Coral Reef receives mixed reviews, but the view of The Seas aquarium is intriguing. Garden Grill is a fun family-style character meal hosted by farmers Mickey, Pluto, Chip, and Dale inside the Land Pavilion. Starbucks and Club Cool both closed in September 2019, with the expectation that both will reopen in new locations sometime in late 2020 or 2021.

Retail is light, with small stores and kiosks popping up at most attraction exits.

Awesome Planet (opening January 17, 2020)

RANKING Sublime, skippable. **EMH** Potentially Evening. **FP+** Unlikely. **TYPE** Film with in-theater effects. **REQUIREMENTS** None.

WHAT TO EXPECT Disney promises "spectacular nature photography, immersive in-theater effects, and space sequences [that] will stir Epcot guests and deliver an environmental message that will resonate far beyond its final scenes." We expect a beautifully-shot film that probably won't make or break your visit to Epcot, but should serve as a relaxing diversion. **SCARY FACTOR** None.

WHEN TO GO In the afternoon when waits are longer elsewhere. **EXPECT TO WAIT** Up to 15 minutes for the next show to begin. **LENGTH** 15 minutes. **WHERE TO SIT** Like any movie theater, the middle is a good choice Also consider sitting away from everyone else for a quieter, more intimate experience.

Baymax and Joy/Sadness

RANKING Don't miss for those who wish to meet the characters; skippable for others. **EMH** Currently Morning and Evening, but that's likely to change when the characters move to the Imagination Pavilion in 2020. **FP+** No. **TYPE** Meet and greet. **REQUIREMENTS** None.

WHAT TO EXPECT Baymax currently meets separately from Joy & Sadness with a fun workshop backdrop. Because he isn't able to interact much with guests, waits are typically under 20 minutes, and the meet and greet isn't necessarily a high priority. Joy & Sadness, on the other hand, spend a lot of time with each group and wait times rise to 30+ minutes almost immediately after park open. If this is a must-do for your group, you'll either need to visit first thing at park open, right before park close, or be prepared to wait 45+ minutes at some other point in the day. Both queues are completely indoors and air-conditioned. At least Joy is expected to move to the Imageworks building in the Imagination Pavilion in 2020, with the potential that Sadness will join her. Baymax may complete his run after Character Spot closes in 2020. **SCARY FACTOR** None.

Character Spot

RANKING Don't miss for those who wish to meet the characters; skippable for others. **EMH** No. **FP+** No. The original Character Spot did offer FastPass+, but the current location does not. **TYPE** Meet and greet. **REQUIREMENTS** None.

WHAT TO EXPECT Guests meet Mickey, Minnie, and Goofy, individually, one after the other, in their classic outfits. Character Spot will close in 2020 with the characters meeting elsewhere. Mickey is expected to move to a new location inside of the Disney & Pixar Short Film Festival lobby, with Minnie headed to the World Showcase Gazebo, which is located on the left as you walk towards the Mexico Pavilion in World Showcase. Goofy may meet outside, or move to a different indoor location. **SCARY FACTOR** None.

WHEN TO GO Late in the evening—ideally after 7pm. Waits are also short before 10am. **EXPECT TO WAIT** Peak waits are typically 30 minutes. **LENGTH** About five minutes of signing, mingling, and picture taking.

Disney and Pixar Short Film Festival

RANKING Relaxing, but skippable. **EMH** Evening. **FP+** Yes, lowest priority. **TYPE** 4D film. **REQUIREMENTS** None.

WHAT TO EXPECT Located in the Imagination Pavilion alongside Journey into Imagination with Figment, this is a straightforward set of three shorts from Disney and Pixar projected in 3D with a couple of in-theater effects. The shorts are available on YouTube and a variety of other media, but the theater is air-conditioned with comfortable seating, making it a good choice if you have 20 minutes to burn during a hot afternoon. In early 2020, Mickey Mouse will begin greeting in the same building's lobby. This will likely increase the number of people in the area, and potentially the number of people watching each show, but there will still be plenty of seats available. **SCARY FACTOR** None.

WHEN TO GO Go in the afternoon when waits are longer elsewhere. **EXPECT TO WAIT** Up to 15 minutes for the next show to begin. **LENGTH** 15 minutes. **WHERE TO SIT** Like any movie theater, the middle is a good choice.

Journey into Imagination with Figment

RANKING Minor attraction. **EMH** Evening. **FP+** Yes. Low priority. **TYPE** Dark ride. **REQUIREMENTS** None.

WHAT TO EXPECT Narrated by Dr. Nigel Channing with frequent interruptions by Figment the purple dragon, Journey takes riders slowly through a variety of rooms, each designed to stimulate the senses. **SCARY FACTOR** Low. This will only startle the young that are prone to attraction anxiety.

WHEN TO GO In the afternoon or with a shorter child while the rest of the group rides the thrill rides. Usually closes at 7pm. **EXPECT TO WAIT** Peak waits of 20 to 30 minutes. **LENGTH** 5 minutes. **WHERE TO SIT** Any row.

Living with the Land

RANKING Minor attraction. **EMH** Morning, Evening. **FP+** Yes. Low priority. **TYPE** Slow boat ride. **REQUIREMENTS** None.

WHAT TO EXPECT Living with the Land is a meandering, educational boat ride about crop cultivation. It's more fun than it sounds! **SCARY FACTOR** Low, unless you have a fear of genetically modified organisms.

WHEN TO GO By 10:30am or after 5pm is best. Usually closes at 7pm. **EXPECT TO WAIT** 20-30 minutes in the afternoon. **LENGTH** 15 minutes. **WHERE TO SIT** Request the first row for the best view.

Soarin' Around the World

RANKING Don't miss. **EMH** Morning, Evening. **FP+** Yes. High priority. **TYPE** Simulator. **REQUIREMENTS** Must be 40" tall to ride.

WHAT TO EXPECT Disney added a third theater in June 2016, in addition to installing a new film featuring scenes from around the world, including flyovers of the Eiffel Tower and Taj Mahal. Now known as Soarin' Around the World, the ride system and overall experience are largely the same, though the new film demands a re-ride for anyone who enjoyed the California version and is a favorite of many first-time visitors. Riders are led into a large room with an 80-foot-tall concave movie screen and three ride vehicles, each of which has three rows. Once all riders are seated, the vehicles are lifted into the air so that each row is above the row below it. A series of scenes are projected onto the screen and the ride vehicles move with the scenes to simulate a hang-gliding flight. **SCARY FACTOR** Minimal. The ride takes visitors 40 feet in the air, which may be frightening for those intensely scared of heights. Motion sickness is much less of a problem than "hang glider" might imply. The ride is gentle and there are no significant drops or sharp turns.

WHEN TO GO Immediately after park open, in the final hour of operation, or with FastPass+. **EXPECT TO WAIT** Afternoon waits are typically in the 40–60 minute range and peak around 75 minutes most days. **LENGTH** 5 minutes. **WHERE TO SIT** The best seats are in the front row of the middle vehicle because other people's feet won't be dangling in front of your face. This is one of the rare rides where your request will actually make a major difference in how much you enjoy it. Strongly consider requesting the first row.

The Seas with Nemo and Friends

RANKING Minor attraction. **EMH** Evening. **FP+** Yes. Low priority. **TYPE** Dark ride. **REQUIREMENTS** None.

WHAT TO EXPECT Nemo & Friends is a slow "clam-mobile" ride through a long *Finding Nemo* themed tunnel. The neatest part of the attraction is when the characters from *Finding Nemo* are shown swimming with real fish inside of the 5.7 million gallon salt-water tank. The ride lets visitors out at The Seas Pavilion, which is full of hands-on activities and places to view the 6,000+ underwater animals that live within one of the largest undersea environments in the world. **SCARY FACTOR** Low. There is a friendly shark Animatronic and it's dark, but that's about it.

WHEN TO GO Before 11am or after 7pm. **EXPECT TO WAIT** Peak waits of 30 minutes are common. Expect to wait less than 15 minutes before 10:30am and after 7pm. **LENGTH** 5 minutes. **WHERE TO SIT** Each clam-mobile seats three across a single row.

Turtle Talk with Crush

RANKING Don't miss for those with young kids, major attraction for everyone else. **EMH** Evening. **FP+** Yes. Medium priority. There are no reserved seats, but FastPass+ guarantees admittance to the next show. **TYPE** Interactive show. **REQUIREMENTS** None.

WHAT TO EXPECT Turtle Talk is a live, interactive show featuring Crush, the turtle from *Finding Nemo* and in a summer 2016 update, characters from *Finding Dory* as well. The theater is small and the kids are asked to sit up front. Crush moves, chats, and fields audience questions in real time, and every show is unique and drop-dead cute. **SCARY FACTOR** Zero.

WHEN TO GO Shows usually begin at 9:40am and run until 8:40pm. Visit before 10:30am or after 7pm. **EXPECT TO WAIT** Up to 30 minutes in the afternoon, but usually just as long as it takes for the next show to begin. **LENGTH** 15 minutes. **WHERE TO SIT** Kids should sit on the floor up front. Adults file into the bleacher-style seating in back.

WORLD SHOWCASE

World Showcase is a collection of 11 pavilions, each themed to a country or collection of countries. The emphasis is on eating, drinking, and shopping, but each pavilion offers authentic entertainment and shows, in addition to the occasional ride. International cast members brought in to fill most roles help introduce guests to their respective cultures and add an additional layer of authenticity. It's truly a world's fair.

With the Frozen Ever After ride now open in place of Maelstrom, the Norway Pavilion should play a major part in most visitors' day(s) at the park. Because of its limited capacity and the popularity of Anna and Elsa, afternoon waits often peak at 75+ minutes. We recommend using FastPass+ when possible, which usually cuts actual waits down to fewer than 15 minutes. Norway is also home to the Royal Sommerhus meet and greet where guests have an opportunity to meet Anna and Elsa inside their air-conditioned summer home. While waits used to exceed two or three hours, thanks to increased capacity, waits for the Sommerhus rarely peak over 30 minutes and should be under 20 minutes most afternoons.

France will also play a bigger role in most guests' visits after the Remy's Ratatouille Adventure ride opens in summer 2020. We expect waits to hover around an hour most of the day, but they should rise slower in the morning due to the long distance from the main entrance keeping a lot of guests from visiting early. Guests entering from the International Gateway may elect to begin their day at the Ratatouille Adventure because of its close proximity to that area.

In addition to new attractions in Norway and France, Disney has installed a variety of interactive experiences designed to make kids more excited about visiting World Showcase. The most popular is Agent P's World Showcase Adventure themed to the popular Phineas and Ferb television show. Guests have an opportunity to embark on a kind of scavenger hunt throughout World Showcase by signing up at agentpwsa.com while at Epcot or by opening up the My Disney Experience app and following the prompts to the signup website there. A new game featuring characters from *DuckTales* is expected to replace the World Showcase Adventure on the Play Disney Parks app in 2020. Kids also have the opportunity to sit down with Cast Members in each pavilion and collect free postcards. Even if you're not interested in any of the attractions that open early, moving up to World Showcase as close to 11am as possible guarantees low crowds at the various stores, exhibits, entertainment, and food outlets, and the least amount of hassle overall.

Epcot Forever (replaced with HarmonioUS in 2020)

Epcot Forever is currently the park's nighttime spectacular, scheduled every night at regular park close, and lasting for about 12 minutes. It takes place on World Showcase Lagoon with viewing available from around World Showcase. Detailed advice on where to see the show is in the Epcot Cheat Sheet at the end of the chapter. Despite the name, Epcot Forever is a temporary show in front of the arrival of HarmonioUS at some point in 2020.

RANKING Don't miss. **EMH** No. **FP+** Yes. Low Tier 1 priority. The FastPass+ viewing location is at the base of World Showcase across from the United States Pavilion in an area called Showcase Plaza. It's a low priority because the show is easy enough to see outside the viewing area and using FastPass+ elsewhere will save more time. Note that the view is excellent and using FP+ eliminates much of the wait required for one of the prime viewing locations. Those skipping the priority rides or planning to arrive late for dinner and the show may find use in selecting it. The show may also be available as a 4th FastPass+. **TYPE** Fireworks show. **REQUIREMENTS** None.

WHAT TO EXPECT Guests begin to fill in along the railing as much as two hours in advance, but most guests will find satisfying viewing locations as few as 15 minutes before show time. The action takes place on World Showcase Lagoon as fireworks explode above. **SCARY FACTOR** Low. The fireworks are occasionally loud, particularly at the end.

TYPICAL SCHEDULE: Begins at regular park close. **LENGTH** 12 minutes.

Our World Showcase reviews begin in Mexico and run clockwise around World Showcase Lagoon.

Mexico Pavilion

Framed by a giant Mesoamerican pyramid, Mexico is home to a boat ride, two sit-down restaurants, a quick service outlet, a tequila bar, a margarita stand, a Donald Duck meet and greet, and a mariachi band. Most of what Mexico offers is located inside the dark, air-conditioned pyramid that acts as a cool respite from the heat. Grab a margarita and enjoy the heritage exhibits, stores, ambiance, and music.

San Angel Inn, nestled along the water and immersed under the perpetual twilight inside the pyramid, is one of our favorite restaurant experiences. While the menu descriptions may seem a bit exotic at first, the flavors should be familiar. La Cantina de San Angel is the pavilion's quick service, offering an array of tacos, empanadas, and salads for lunch and dinner. We like the very shareable nachos, but more unique food can be found in other pavilions and outdoor seating is inadequate after 4pm. La Hacienda de San Angel, a second table service restaurant that's open for dinner at 4pm, is located on the lagoon and offers picturesque views to those who request window seats. The menu is limited and on the expensive side, but some guests may prefer the air-conditioned, homey atmosphere. Margaritas are best inside the pyramid at La Cava del Tequila, which also serves small bites and chips and salsa. Overall, most guests that stop for food and drinks should leave satisfied, but our preference is to search out something more unique.

Minor attraction: Gran Fiesta Tour is a relaxing, slow-moving boat ride through the world of *The Three Caballeros*. The ride lasts about seven minutes and follows Jose Carioca and Panchito as they hunt down Donald before a big gig. Waits are under five minutes most of the time. On busier days, visit before 12:30pm or after 7pm.

Norway Pavilion

Themed to a Viking-era village, Norway features a replica of the 14th century Akershus Fortress, originally built to protect Oslo from attack. In Disney's version, you'll find a princess-hosted character meal inside. The detailed stave church features an interesting exhibit inside that explains how Norse mythology guided the Viking way of life through artifacts, statues, and artwork. Kringla Bakeri, the pavilion's quick service, offers excellent, inexpensive treats. At the Puffin's Roost, guests can peruse fun Norway-themed merchandise alongside authentic (and expensive) hand-knit apparel, perfume, and toys.

Norway is also home to one of the highest FastPass+ priorities in Epcot: Frozen Ever After. While the attraction faced an uphill battle with a lot of fans due to the intellectual property it introduced to World Showcase and love for the ride that it replaced, reviews are largely positive. That's good news because it means that it's a fun ride that most guests will enjoy, but it also means that you're going to want to ride it, which can be a hassle for those with only one day to visit or for those unable to secure FastPass+.

Frozen Ever After

RANKING Don't miss for anyone able to secure FastPass+ or willing to wait in line. **EMH** Morning, Evening. **FP+** Yes. High Tier 1 priority. **TYPE** Boat ride. **REQUIREMENTS** None.

WHAT TO EXPECT Once inside, the queue walks guests throughout the port town of Arendelle during its summer season celebration before a quick visit inside Oaken's Tokens and then onto the boat that will whisk riders through scenes that include the frozen Willow Forest, Troll Valley, and Queen Elsa's Ice Palace high atop the North Mountain. Olaf, Elsa, Anna, Kristoff, and Sven make multiple appearances as they sing a variety of everyone's "favorite" songs from the movie. The animatronics should impress even the most cynical and kids eat it up. **SCARY FACTOR** Low. It's dark at times and there are a couple of small drops, but anyone who made it through Pirates of the Caribbean or any similar ride will be just fine.

WHEN TO GO With FastPass+ if at all possible, which will reduce 60+ minute actual waits to fewer than 15. Otherwise, those able to get in line right before park close should do so, when actual waits of fewer than 30 minutes are common. Getting to the ride first thing in the morning is a chore, but those who arrive at least 45 minutes before park open and walk quickly should find short waits first thing. **EXPECT TO WAIT** Peak waits are typically 75 minutes. Ride during a recommended time or with FastPass+. **LENGTH** 5 minutes. **WHERE TO SIT** Boats have four rows with up to three adults fitting in each. The view from the far left seats is arguably better.

Royal Summerhus

RANKING The best opportunity to meet Anna and Elsa up close. **EMH** Morning, Evening. **FP+** No. **TYPE** Meet and greet. **REQUIREMENTS** Just the inclination to get in line.

WHAT TO EXPECT Those familiar with Maurice's Cottage at Enchanted Tales with Belle inside Magic Kingdom will recognize the quaint aesthetics of Anna and Elsa's summertime home. Guests have a lot to look at as they wait for their turn to meet Anna and Elsa. While the sisters meet separately, there is just one line for both. **SCARY FACTOR** None, unless you are a Disney World guidebook author that has to go through the line over and over in the name of "research."

WHEN TO GO Surprisingly, this is a good choice in the afternoon or evening. Waits typically peak early as guests hurry to the ride and then over to the meet and greet. Try after 11am. **EXPECT TO WAIT** 15–20 minute waits are common. **LENGTH** The sisters are among the most personable of the princess characters. Expect to spend a minute or two with each.

China Pavilion

An intricately detailed triple-arched ceremonial gate welcomes visitors to China. Immediately past the gate is a replica of the Temple of Heaven, inside of which guests have the opportunity to view a 15-minute Circle-Vision 360 film. While you wait for the next film to begin, check out the Shanghai Disneyland exhibit through the door on the left. Chinese acrobats perform most days either in the courtyard or inside the Temple of Heaven in the Hall of Prayer for Good Harvests.

Nine Dragons is the pavilion's table service restaurant, serving up traditional and contemporary Chinese food. It has a lousy reputation, but the food has improved in recent memory and the portions are large. Lotus Blossom is the quick service arm, serving some of the fastest, no-fuss food in World Showcase. With so many other options, it's difficult to recommend it strongly, but portions are typically large with prices lower than a lot of other restaurants. The Joy of Tea stand on the water is a surprisingly good spot to pick up a strong drink or fruity cocktail depending on the group's mood at the time.

Shopping in China is above average at the expansive House of Good Fortune on the left side of the pavilion. You'll find silk robes, traditional fans, tea sets, jewelry, puppets, and more.

Germany Pavilion

Featuring a statue of Saint George slaying a dragon, and a clock tower with a glockenspiel that chimes on the hour, the architecture in Germany is interesting and varied. A rotating musical act plays on a stage to the left of the pavilion most days. Also, take a moment to peruse Karamell-Kuche (Caramel Kitchen), in addition to the stores that offer made-in-Germany toys, cuckoo clocks, beer steins, toys, apparel, and other fun items. As you walk toward Italy, pay special attention to the outdoor model train set on the left.

Biergarten is the table service restaurant, featuring a smorgasbord of traditional German salads, roasted meats, pretzel bread, soups, and more. A traditional oompah band plays intermittently throughout the day inside the restaurant. Sommerfest is the pavilion's quick service, offering bratwurst, frankfurters, and other traditional German foods. Seating is scarce.

Italy Pavilion

The focal point of the Italy Pavilion is the 105-foot-tall functioning replica of St Mark's Campanile, the bell tower that looks out over the World Showcase Lagoon. Also prominently featured is a replica of the Doge's Palace, originally built by the Venetians in the early 14th century. In typical Disney fashion, the Palace is full of fine Italian perfume, handmade masks, soccer jerseys, pasta, and other items Italia. Italy is otherwise mostly restaurants and bars. Best is Via Napoli in the back of the pavilion, serving authentic Neapolitan pizzas. Without a reservation, try Tutto Gusto, the wine bar attached to the Tutto Italia restaurant with hundreds of Italian wines, Italian beer on draft, and an appetizer and dessert menu that's hard to beat. Tutto Italia is more formal, but still perfect for families and couples, serving regional Italian fare. A mime entertains guests most days.

United States Pavilion

The United States Pavilion is mostly housed inside of a single Colonial-style mansion that was built using 110,000 hand-made Georgian clay bricks.

Major attraction: *The American Adventure*, a 30-minute theater show blending film and Animatronics, is the principal attraction. The patriotic show briefly retells the history of America and runs on a set schedule with the next show listed on posters outside the pavilion. The theater seats over a thousand in comfortable air-conditioning, making it a perfect respite from the afternoon heat. The show is often preceded in the afternoon by the Voices of Liberty a cappella group inside the mansion.

Outside, the America Gardens Theater is home to various free concerts throughout the year with space-available seating, including Garden Rocks, Sounds like Summer, Eat to the Beat, and the Candlelight Processional.

Liberty Inn, the previous quick service, closed in July 2019 to make way for The Regal Eagle, a new fast food outlet serving barbecue. It's slated for an early 2020 open. Fife & Drum Tavern outside serves beer, pretzels, turkey legs, popcorn, and other snack items.

Japan Pavilion

The red torii gate and the 85-foot-tall Goju-no-to pagoda welcome guests to the Japan Pavilion. These and other buildings are surrounded by beautiful gardens made up of native Japanese plants, bamboo, and evergreen, maple, and monkey puzzle trees. The large courtyard in the middle of the pavilion makes Japan feel more open, relaxed, and less cluttered than other pavilions. Be sure to cross the bridge leading to the White Heron Castle and check out the koi fish below.

There are no rides or theater shows in Japan, but it is rich with entertainment and culture. Enjoy the athletic Taiko drummers on the pagoda steps and the cultural exhibits inside the castle. The Mitsukoshi Department Store on the right side of the pavilion is among the best in Disney World, offering more than 50,000 unique products. Kimonos, Samurai swords, Bonsai trees, chopstick sets, calligraphy brushes, toys, and everything in between are available. Check out the popular Pick-a-Pearl where guests can pick an oyster and discover what's inside. Hundreds of relatively inexpensive food and drink items are offered in the final room, in addition to a sake bar with samples available by the glass.

Dining options are even more plentiful. Teppan Edo, a traditional hibachi-grill experience similar to Benihana, is one of the more consistent restaurants on property, offering grilled meat, fish, and vegetables. Tokyo Dining focuses on sushi and tempura in a contemporary setting. Takumi-Tei is the newest and most expensive option, offering a high-end signature experience that includes a $130+ Omakase meal, in addition to the finest cuts of Japanese beef, among other choices. Outside, Katsura Grill serves quick service sushi, teriyaki, and other traditional food. Indoor air-conditioned seating is available, in addition to the beautiful outdoor garden setting. Food at Katsura is merely okay, but it's a relaxing location. A sake bar, also serving cocktails and beer, is located outside across from Mitsukoshi Department Store. Also outside, Kabuki Café serves kaki gori (snow cones) with traditional toppings, in addition to smoothies, beer, and other snacks.

Morocco Pavilion

Morocco is represented by architecture and monuments from three famous Moroccan cities: Casablanca, Fez, and Marrakesh. Koutoubia Minaret, the focal point of the pavilion, is a replica of the 12th century Marrakesh prayer tower. Morocco is the only state-sponsored World Showcase pavilion, and the country played an integral part in the design and construction of the buildings, gardens, and Bab Boujeloud arch. The King of Morocco actually sent his personal craftsmen to construct and lay tile in much of the pavilion, making this one of the most authentic areas in Epcot. Because of the religious significance of many of Morocco's buildings, lights are not shined on the pavilion during IllumiNations.

Morocco is the most-passed-over pavilion, which is unfortunate because there is a lot to see and do, despite it not offering a major show or ride. An authentic musical act entertains guests with live music and dancing most days on the outdoor stage. We highly recommend taking 20–30 minutes to explore the marketplace, museum, and art gallery. Restaurant Marrakesh is the under-rated Moroccan restaurant in the pavilion, specializing in couscous and anything with a shank. A belly dancer appears inside the restaurant throughout the day. Spice Road Table opened in late 2013, offering small Mediterranean tapas, wines, cocktails, and desserts, and adding more sizable entrees in 2015. It's a beautiful restaurant that overlooks the picturesque lagoon. While reservations are offered, it's virtually never necessary to book one in advance.

Tangierine Café is the quick service, featuring shawarma and falafel. While the food is a bit more expensive, portions are large and the food is freshly prepared. It's our favorite World Showcase quick service.

France Pavilion

The replica of the Eiffel Tower is the most recognizable feature of the France Pavilion. The buildings are themed like those found in Paris between 1870 and 1910, otherwise known as La Belle Epoque, or The Beautiful Time. France features a gorgeous courtyard area with a fountain and immaculately maintained gardens.

Historically, France's main attraction has been an 18-minute film titled Impressions de France. Projected onto five large screens, Impressions provides a 200-degree panoramic view of France, its people, and its culture. You'll experience many of France's most popular destinations, including the gardens at Versailles, the Eiffel Tower, and the breathtaking French Alps. Unlike the films at China or Canada, you'll be able to sit and relax during the air-conditioned show. Beginning on January 17, 2020, Beauty and the Beast Sing-Along will play on the same screen as Impressions. The two shows are expected to alternate throughout the day. In addition, the fun Serveur Amusant comedy/acrobat show is scheduled most days with several afternoon shows.

Remy's Ratatouille Adventure, a 3D dark ride based on a similar attraction in Disneyland Paris, is expected to open in summer 2020. Reviews of the original ride are mixed, but at a minimum, it should be a fun diversion in World Showcase, even if it's not a complete showstopper. We expect waits to hover around an hour from 11am onward, with shorter waits early in the morning, and late at night.

France is home to two sit-down restaurants, a quick service boulangerie patisserie (bakery), and an ice cream parlor, in addition to the crepe restaurant that is expected to open alongside the Ratatouille ride in the summer of 2020. Chefs de France downstairs is themed to a casual Parisian bistro, and while the charm remains, the more-expensive, single all-day menu may be more money than you want to spend for lunch. If you do visit, consider a meal around sunset when $30+ salmon and steak dishes are comparable to other options. Upstairs is the ritzier Monsieur Paul, serving a more expensive dinner-only menu catered toward adults. Les Halles Boulangerie Patisserie, located in the back of the pavilion, serves sandwiches, quiche, salads, desserts, and other French specialties. It's an excellent spot to pick up a snack or a meal. Finally, L'Artisan des Glaces serves freshly prepared sorbet and ice cream with the option of a shot of liquor poured on top.

Shopping includes wine, perfume, and fun French-themed Disney merchandise.

Remy's Ratatouille Adventure (opening summer 2020)

RANKING Major attraction. **EMH** Likely Morning, Evening. **FP+** Likely a moderate priority. **TYPE** Dark ride. **REQUIREMENTS** None.

WHAT TO EXPECT Shrink down to the size of a rat and join Remy on a wild ride through a gigantic kitchen as you avoid Chef Skinner inside

Gusteau's famous Parisian restaurant. The experience probably relies too much on screens instead of animatronics and physical sets, but it's a fun little addition to World Showcase and a ride worth experiencing. **SCARY FACTOR** Low, at least as long as you don't see a 4D cat. Some of the imagery is meant to startle and excite, but even the youngest guests should feel safe. Motion sickness may be an issue for those incredibly prone to nausea.

WHEN TO GO During the first or last 90 minutes of operation or with Fast-Pass+. **EXPECT TO WAIT** Waits should hover between 45 and 75 minutes most of the day. **WHERE TO SIT** The Sit in front for a better view.

United Kingdom Pavilion

The United Kingdom Pavilion is one of the more architecturally diverse World Showcase pavilions, with the Hampton Court Palace, Anne Hathaway's (William Shakespeare's wife) thatched roof cottage, two castles, and a miniature version of Hyde Park represented. You'll see replicas of the red phone booths England is so famous for, as well as a variety of beautiful garden areas.

The British Revolution, playing hits from The Who, Beatles, Led Zeppelin, and others, is the entertainment here. Several shops carry a range of British goods, including tea, perfume and makeup, apparel, and a lot of Guinness- and Beatles-related merchandise.

Rose & Crown Dining Room is the pavilion's table service restaurant. It's casual, low key, and your best opportunity to watch the nighttime spectacular from a restaurant while you dine. The Pub next door is an excellent spot to grab a pint. Yorkshire County Fish Co. outside serves excellent fast food fish and chips with limited picturesque seating along the lagoon.

Disney announced a Mary Poppins overlay and a new attraction coming to the Pavilion with very few details. We don't expect the transformation to have a significant effect on visits in 2020, but construction may begin at some point during the year.

Canada Pavilion

Gorgeous Victoria Gardens and a replica of the Canadian Rockies, complete with a 30-foot waterfall, lead guests into the Canada Pavilion. The Hotel du Canada, modeled after Ottawa's Fairmont Chateau Laurier, is the pavilion's largest and most magnificently detailed building. "O'Canada!" was the name of the Circle-Vision 360 film that closed in July 2019 to make way for "Canada Far and Wide," which debuts on January 17th, 2020. We look forward to its air-conditioned return. A 15-minute Canadian musical act is scheduled most days at the outdoor stage.

Le Cellier is the pavilion's table service restaurant, primarily offering steak. Like Monsieur Paul in France, it's a signature restaurant, which means it will set you back two Dining Plan credits and is more expensive out of pocket than most restaurants.

Shopping is limited to stuffed animals and other toys, along with apparel items and some food and beverages.

Disney's Hollywood Studios

Disney's Hollywood Studios opened as a combined theme park and working production studio under the name Disney-MGM Studios on May 1, 1989. The name changed to Disney's Hollywood Studios in 2008. While several famous shows and movies were filmed or animated on site, it's been more than fifteen years since any serious studio work has happened here. It's now "just" a Disney theme park, but several of Hollywood Studios' rides and shows are among the best in Walt Disney World and there's plenty here to fill an entire day.

Touring the Studios is more complicated than one might expect due to long lines at the headliners and several lengthy stage shows that run on a limited schedule. The layout is also a bit confusing for first-time visitors. The Cheat Sheet map at the end of the chapter will make traversing the park significantly easier.

STAR WARS: GALAXY'S EDGE AND THE FUTURE OF DISNEY'S HOLLYWOOD STUDIOS

Star Wars: Galaxy's Edge is a new, 14-acre land based on the world's most popular science-fiction franchise, the majority of which opened on August 29, 2019. At that time, Millennium Falcon: Smugglers Run came online, along with the stores, kiosks, eateries, and other experiences that make up the bulk of the land's offerings. Star Wars: Rise of the Resistance, the other new ride, opened on December 5, 2019.

In Galaxy's Edge, guests are transported to the planet of Batuu, just after "Return of the Jedi," as the First Order is rising to prominence. While the area that you'll visit was once a bustling frontier outpost, it's now home to an assortment of smugglers, bounty hunters, and other cutthroats trying to keep a low profile away from watchful eyes.

The first attraction to open, Smugglers Run, is a simulator ride that allows guests to board and pilot the Millennium Falcon with engineers and gunners providing support. Your execution, along with the performances of the other crew members on your team, will affect what happens during the ride in real time.

Rise of the Resistance is the second major attraction, and one that thrusts guests into the middle of an epic battle between the Resistance and First Order. Riders board eight-person transport ships and go toe-to-toe with Star Destroyers. Both of the rides, and the land itself, push the boundaries of what theme parks have traditionally been able to offer, both in terms of technological advancements and storytelling.

Galaxy's Edge is home to five main food and drink outlets. Oga's Cantina offers a wide assortment of concoctions, both alcoholic and non-alcoholic, all served in unique vessels. Unlike most lounges on property, Oga's accepts reservations with the same rules as other Disney restaurants. It's very popular, so book a reservation as soon as you're eligible. Since opening, Oga's has carried a strict two-drink/45-minute maximum, so don't expect to dwell here long. 45 minutes is plenty to take in all that there is to see and we recommend any Star Wars fan to visit.

The Milk Stand serves the Blue and Green Milk that Luke Skywalker made famous. Both beverages are plant-based, non-dairy drinks that are largely sugar, coconut oil, and rice milk. Reviews of the drinks are mixed and we recommend ordering one of each for the group to share before committing more money. Even if you love them, the $8 ask for a small cup is expensive. Both flavors are also available with a splash of alcohol.

Docking Bay 7 Food and Cargo is the main quick service, offering a bounty of upscale fast food selections that include ribs served with a blueberry corn muffin, a plant-based kefta "meatball" dish with herb hummus, a chilled shrimp noodle salad, and much more. Prices are on the high side with the pot roast coming in at $19 and the ribs priced at $17 to start, but quality is high.

Ronto Roasters uses an old podracer engine to roast meats for a variety of wraps. Spicy and sweet turkey jerky are also available. At $13 for the Ronto Wrap with grilled pork sausage, peppercorn sauce, and tangy slaw wrapped in pita bread, it's another expensive endeavor, but they sure are tasty.

Rounding out the major options, Kat Saka's Kettle serves popcorn.

More than a half dozen Black Spire Outpost Shops can be found around Batuu. At Toydarian Toymaker, guests have the opportunity to peruse and buy "artisanal playthings and collectibles handmade by the busy toymaker, Zabaka the Toydarian." At Dok-Ondar's Den of Antiquities, you'll find "unique items that include everything from jewelry, to ancient tools, to rare kyber crystals, to statues, to a collection of famous lightsabers." The exotic Creature Stall offers an assortment of toys and plush from all around the galaxy. Black Spire Outfitters stocks apparel and accessories, while Resistance Supply sells pins, hats, badges, and more for those looking to stand up to the First Order. First Order Cargo, on the other hand, stocks merchandise in support of Kylo Ren.

Guests also have the opportunity to take the Build Your Own Lightsaber experience to the next level at Savi's Workshop, where interested patrons will enter the Chamber of the Guardians and embark on an intimate, 25-minute experience customizing their new space sword. Lightsabers start at $199.

Droid Depot is another interactive experience where builders are able to construct droids from an incredible assortment of parts with prices starting at $99. The finished product will be charged on-site and work with a provided set of remote controls as the droid interacts with other machines throughout Batuu.

Given the worldwide popularity of Star Wars, coupled with the marketing might of the Walt Disney Company, many expected Galaxy's Edge to be completely overrun with excited guests for its first few months of operation. The Galaxy's Edge opening in California largely underwhelmed, with the resort experiencing some of the lowest crowds in years, and few turned up to visit the new land in Florida after opening weekend in August 2019. We expect that Galaxy's Edge will help push people towards visiting the resort over the next couple of years, but it evidently isn't a huge driver. With all of Galaxy's Edge being open in 2020, more people may elect to visit with the land completely open.

FastPass+ was not offered at Smugglers Run when it opened, and it won't be offered at Rise of the Resistance to start, either. Both rides are set up to offer FastPass+ with the familiar MagicBand/ticket scanners in front of the entrances to both attractions with dedicated lines for priority boarding. We expect FastPass+ to be offered at some point in 2020. When and if FP+ is offered, Rise of the Resistance should be the clear priority.

While Galaxy's Edge didn't initially drive attendance higher after its partial opening in August 2019, the opening of Rise of the Resistance, arguably Walt Disney World's best overall attraction, is beginning to push up interest in the new Star Wars Land. As the attractions and the land's offerings continue to mature, we expect Disney's investment in the park to pay off, and attendance to steadily increase throughout 2020.

Outside of Galaxy's Edge, Mickey and Minnie's Runaway Railway is the other new ride coming to Hollywood Studios, now slated for a March 4th, 2020 opening. Housed inside of the Chinese Theater, where Great Movie Ride used to reside, guests have the opportunity to Join Mickey and Minnie as they embark on a relaxing picnic, only to be pulled into a cartoon aboard Goofy's crazy train in a ride that Disney is describing as a "zippy, zany, out-of-control adventure." We have high hopes for the new attraction, which may actually stand out against the Galaxy's Edge offerings.

FASTPASS+ PRIORITY

Tier 1 (choose one)

1. Slinky Dog Dash
2. Rock 'n' Roller Coaster
3. Tower of Terror
4. Toy Story Mania
5. Alien Swirling Saucers

Tier 2 (choose two)

1. Star Tours
2. Frozen Sing-Along
3. Beauty and the Beast Live on Stage
4. Indiana Jones Epic Stunt Spectacular
5. Disney Junior Dance Party
6. Voyage of the Little Mermaid
7. Fantasmic
8. Muppet Vision 3D

Guests may initially select in advance only one attraction from Tier 1, which includes all five of the most popular rides in the park outside of Galaxy's Edge. This complicates touring quite a bit. Previously, guests were able to book in advance one of the Toy Story Land rides, like Slinky Dog Dash, in addition to two more priority rides outside of it, like Rock 'n' Roller Coaster and Tower of Terror. Now, only one of these high priority attractions may be selected.

One potential piece of good news is that everyone else is in the same boat and day-of FastPass+ availability is a little better for priority attractions. At Epcot, the tier system makes it easier to secure Tier 1 attractions as 4th FastPass+ selections because guests may only select one attraction in advance from Tier 1, which includes Frozen Ever After, Soarin', and Test Track. If people were able to select two or three of these in advance, then there would be far less availability as most people would pick three priority experiences from the available inventory as soon as they're able. With most guests visiting the Studios selecting one of the top three priority rides from Tier 1 in advance, there is more availability for Toy Story Mania and Alien Swirling Saucers, along with the others, later in the day.

ARRIVING AT THE STUDIOS

Most guests arrive via Disney bus or their own automobile. The bus stops are just minutes away from the main entrance, while guests driving have the option of walking or taking a tram from the parking lot. Guests staying at the BoardWalk Inn, Yacht Club, Beach Club, Swan, or Dolphin either walk or take the boat that typically begins service one hour before regular open. Walking or taking the boat both take about 25 minutes, but walking cuts down on the wait for the first boat and allows you to arrive much earlier in the morning. Guests staying at Pop Century, Art of Animation, Caribbean Beach, Riviera, or transferring from Epcot's International Gateway have the option of using the Disney Skyliner gondola system, with the station incredibly close to the Studios' main entrance. Guests coming from those locations may also take a Disney bus.

Guest Services is located on the left inside and outside of the main entrance. Ticket booths in front of the entrance can handle any purchases or upgrades. Wheelchair and stroller rental are just inside on the right.

HOLLYWOOD BOULEVARD

Hollywood Boulevard, the Studios' main drag, is similar to Main Street, U.S.A. at Magic Kingdom. The left side consists almost entirely of retail with Mickey's of Hollywood and Keystone Clothiers carrying the widest selection of merchandise in the park. PhotoPass and a couple smaller stores are on the right, followed by Trolley Car Café, the park's sizable Starbucks location. Hollywood Brown Derby, a pricey signature restaurant that costs two credits on the Dining Plan, serves the best food in the park on the right near the end of the Boulevard. Starring Rolls, the popular quick service eatery specializing in sandwiches, cupcakes, and other baked goods, closed unceremoniously in early 2017. An assortment of similar pastries and other treats is available across the street at Trolley Car Café. Grauman's Chinese Theater, which used to house the Great Movie Ride and will soon contain Mickey and Minnie's Runaway Railway, stands tall at the end of the street.

Mickey and Minnie's Runaway Railway
(opening March 4, 2020)

RANKING Major attraction. EMH Likely Morning, Evening. FP+ Likely a moderate priority. TYPE Dark ride. REQUIREMENTS None.

WHAT TO EXPECT Marketed as the first 2 1/2-D movie-themed attraction, guests will board a zany train engineered by Goofy as it passes by bright animated landscapes. **SCARY FACTOR** With no height requirement, the ride is unlikely to be too intense for younger riders.

WHEN TO GO During the first or last 90 minutes of operation or with FastPass+. **EXPECT TO WAIT** 60-minute peak waits should be the norm. **WHERE TO SEE IT** We expect the back row to provide the most movement and the front row to provide the clearest views.

Star Wars: A Galaxy Far, Far Away

RANKING Star Wars fans may enjoy seeing the characters on stage. **EMH** No. **FP+** No. **TYPE** Stage show. **REQUIREMENTS** None.

WHAT TO EXPECT On the stage in front of Grauman's Chinese Theatre, Kylo Ren, Darth Vader, Darth Maul, Boba Fett, BB-8, C-3PO, R2D2, and others appear on stage in what may seem more like a fashion show than anything else. But this is the only time several of these characters appear. **SCARY FACTOR** Low. Some of the characters are purposefully intimidating, but there's little danger involved. A few fireworks go off toward the end.

WHEN TO GO There are typically six or seven shows scheduled daily on the half hour beginning in the morning and ending in the late afternoon with a break in the middle of the day. See whichever show is convenient. **EXPECT TO WAIT** For front row spots, arrive at least 20 minutes early. Arrive a minute or two before show time to see it from further back. **LENGTH** 15 minutes. **WHERE TO SEE IT** The main problem is the low height of the stage and the number of kids that will be hoisted on shoulders ahead of you. We like to see the show from further back off to the side where there are typically fewer of these shoulder kids. For a more intimate experience, stand near the ramp on the left side of the stage where the characters enter and exit the stage. You'll get a much better look, but will miss most of what happens on stage. Big fans may want to see a show from both vantage points.

ECHO LAKE

Star Tours is the standout in this land, which is also home to Indiana Jones Epic Stunt Spectacular, Frozen Sing Along, and Jedi Training Academy. The Mickey Shorts Theater will also join the ranks in March 2020, replacing The Path of the Jedi in the theater to the left of the Hyperion Theater, where the Frozen Sing Along is performed. Here, guests can watch several animated shorts featuring Mickey Mouse, including an exclusive cartoon. 50's Prime Time Café, with its comfort food and fun atmosphere, is Dave's favorite Studios restaurant. Hollywood & Vine next door is a buffet featuring Disney Junior characters during breakfast hours. A seasonal meal hosted by Minnie and featuring Mickey, Goofy, Donald, and Daisy follows for lunch and dinner. Backlot Express is the fast food eatery, now sporting a menu that has improved a bit. The Cuban sandwich stands out and the Southwest Salad with crisp wontons, black bean relish, and avocado is also above average. Add plentiful seating, indoors and out, along with the ability to refill your own fountain beverage, and you come away with one of the better, more comfortable quick service experiences in the park. Dockside Diner on Echo Lake serves hot dogs and a rotating selection of other entrees, in addition to beer and boozy lemonades. Tatooine Traders sits adjacent to Star Tours and is a good location for Star Wars merchandise. Indiana Jones merchandise is available at the show's exit and to the right of 50's Prime Time.

Celebrity Spotlight Olaf Meet and Greet

Olaf meets all day across from Backlot Express to waits that often peak no higher than 20 minutes, making it a good stop before or after lunch.

Frozen Sing-Along

RANKING A must for fans of Frozen, surprisingly enjoyable for everyone else. **EMH** No. **FP+** Yes. FastPass+ guarantees the user a seat at a specific show, but there is no reserved section for FastPass+ users. Because all guests are allowed into the theater about 15 minutes before show time, FP+ users need to arrive at least 20 minutes before the show starts to see any advantage, which is usually early enough that there would be plenty of availability in standby. In other words, using FP+ here is only beneficial if you plan to arrive about five minutes before show time and don't care where you sit—only that you'll be able to. **TYPE** Stage show. **REQUIREMENTS** Nothing more than your patience.

WHAT TO EXPECT Guests enter a comfortable, air-conditioned theater for an engaging stage show featuring Anna, Elsa, and the newly-appointed "Royal Historians" of Arendelle. Anna appears briefly at the beginning and Elsa joins her for a powerful number at the end of the show, but the bulk of the time is spent enjoying the genuinely funny banter between the historians with a crowd that intermittently bursts out into song. **SCARY FACTOR** Only your neighbor's singing voice.

WHEN TO GO Most guests will want to see an afternoon show to enjoy some air conditioning and a comfortable seat, perhaps as a 4th or 5th Fast-Pass+ selection. Those already planning a short day may elect to see the first and least crowded show of the day. **EXPECT TO WAIT** Arrive 20–30 minutes before show time. **LENGTH** 25 minutes. **WHERE TO SIT** In the middle section about halfway up.

Indiana Jones Epic Stunt Spectacular Show

RANKING Major attraction. **EMH** No. **FP+** Yes. Low priority. **TYPE** Show. **REQUIREMENTS** None.

WHAT TO EXPECT A large theater seats about 2,000 people on bleach-er-style seating. In the show, actors perform a series of stunts that mirror those from the movie *Raiders of the Lost Ark*, and the director explains how they are executed so they are safe and seem real. You'll see large explosions, sword fights, car chases, gun battles, and a number of other exciting stunts. **SCARY FACTOR** Low. While there are some thrilling moments on stage, the audience is never in any danger, real or imagined.

WHEN TO GO The first and last shows of the day are typically least crowded. **EXPECT TO WAIT** Arrive at least 20 minutes early. **LENGTH** 30 minutes. **WHERE TO SIT** At least half way up, in the center section.

Star Tours

RANKING Major attraction. **EMH** Morning, Evening. **FP+** Yes. Moderate priority. **TYPE** Motion simulator ride. **REQUIREMENTS** 40" or taller.

WHAT TO EXPECT Riders sit in a large 40-person simulator themed like the inside of a StarSpeeder 1000 spaceship. A 3D movie plays in the front and the ride vehicle tilts, bumps, vibrates, sways, etc., so it feels like you're actually inside of the StarSpeeder making the journey that you see in front of you. Disney advertises that the attraction has "more than 50 story combinations" because there are four scenes during the ride, each of which has a few different character or destination possibilities. For example, you might visit Chewbacca's home planet of Kashyyyk or the icy planet of Hoth after being directed by Yoda, Admiral Ackbar, or Princess Leia. Star Wars fans may wish to ride two or three times over the course of the day to see as many of the scenes as possible. In addition, Disney added a scene from the planet Jakku and a transmission from BB-8 in late 2015, followed by another new scene from the salty mineral planet Crait in late 2017. Scenes from "Rise of the Skywalker" were also added in December 2019. **SCARY FACTOR** Low. There is a moderate amount of danger involved, but it isn't realistic enough to be scary. **CAN WE HANDLE IT?** The biggest problems are motion sickness and the jerkiness of the ride. Avoid if similar attractions have caused problems. Request the middle of row three for the least amount of jostle and avoid the corner seats in the front and back if motion sickness may be an issue.

WHEN TO GO After the priority attractions, in the last two hours of operation, or with FastPass+. **EXPECT TO WAIT** 20–40 minute afternoon waits are common. **LENGTH** 5 minutes. **WHERE TO SIT** Views are similar from most seats. You'll experience the most motion in the far left or right seat in the back row.

GRAND AVENUE

Once part of the now defunct Streets of America, Grand Avenue is home to Muppet Vision 3D, PizzeRizzo, BaseLine Tap House, and Mama Melrose's Ristorante Italiano, in addition to a few stores. Muppet Vision is the epitome of an anytime attraction and a fantastic opportunity to get off your feet in the afternoon heat. PizzeRizzo replaces Toy Story Pizza Planet with a menu that still focuses on reheated pizzas, in addition to salads and meatball subs. Mama Melrose is not Disney's best Italian restaurant, but it still offers serviceable pizzas in a calmer setting than next door for not a whole lot more money. The pricier pasta and meat options are inconsistent and best skipped unless Disney Dining Plan credits are being used. BaseLine Tap House opened in the middle of 2017, offering a menu of draft beers hailing from the great state of California, in addition to a couple of wines and cocktails on tap. The charcuterie board is surprisingly good and we like to stop from time to time for a snack and a customizable beer flight.

Muppet Vision 3D

RANKING Don't miss. **EMH** No. **FP+** Yes. Low priority. **TYPE** 4D show. **REQUIREMENTS** None.

WHAT TO EXPECT A 12-minute pre-show video in a room full of Muppet gags welcomes viewers. The theater is large, air-conditioned, and comfortable. The 4D film follows the Muppets as they prepare for a show and features a live-action Sweetums character at the end. **SCARY FACTOR** Low. At times the show is loud.

WHEN TO GO Afternoon when crowds have peaked elsewhere. The show is typically open from just 10am to 6pm, so double check the Times Guide if you're planning on seeing it later in the day. **EXPECT TO WAIT** Only as long as it takes for the next show to start. **LENGTH** 12-minute pre-show, 17-minute show. **WHERE TO SIT** Let guests stream in and fill about half of a row at least half way back from the front before entering in order to sit in the middle.

STAR WARS: GALAXY'S EDGE

Galaxy's Edge is home to an assortment of shopping and dining opportunities, in addition to two rides. The Millennium Falcon: Smugglers Run simulator ride opened on August 29, 2019, along with all of the eateries and shopping. Savi's Workshop, where aspiring Jedi can build $199+ custom lightsabers during an intimate, 25-minute experience, impresses in its immersion. The Droid Depot, where guests can build their own remote-control droid, is another interactive option amid numerous stalls and stores selling all kinds of Rebel and First Order wares. Reservations up to 180 days in advance are available for both Savi's Workshop and the Droid Depot, with the lightsaber experience proving to be more popular. Definitely make a reservation for Savi's if you're interested in participating.

Docking Bay 7 Food and Cargo is the principal quick service, offering up an assortment of higher-priced, higher-quality fast food than most other eateries at the Studios. It's backed up by Oga's Cantina, a popular lounge offering alcoholic and non-alcoholic drinks. Kat Saka's Kettle serves popcorn and The Milk Stand is where you'll find Blue and Green Milk, both of which are non-dairy.

Star Wars: Rise of the Resistance is slated to open December 5, 2019. We expect it to impress even more than Smugglers Run.

Millennium Falcon: Smugglers Run

RANKING Major attraction. **EMH** Morning, Evening. **FP+** Not yet. **TYPE** Motion simulator ride. **REQUIREMENTS** 38" or taller.

WHAT TO EXPECT Smugglers Run is similar to an interactive version of Star Tours. Like Avatar Flight of Passage at Animal Kingdom, the queue sets the stage for everything that follows, as guests walk through Ohnaka Transport Solutions before receiving their mission from Hondo Ohnaka himself. Guests then board the cockpit of the Millennium Falcon and are assigned one of three jobs in pairs: Engineer, Gunner, or Pilot. Unlike Mission: SPACE at Epcot, where your ability to press the buttons does not alter the ride experience in any way, the quality of your performance dictates how well your mission goes, as well as what you see on-screen. Because of this, your experience will be significantly different depending on the competence of your crew and how well you do. The pilot is the most difficult position, particularly for first-time riders as you'll need to guide the stubborn ship using unfamiliar, sensitive controls. The other two positions rely largely on the rider's ability to press a button when it lights up. If you're planning on riding twice, you might enjoy whichever position you're assigned, but we'd recommend adventurous riders giving the pilot chair a shot. It's the most rewarding. Reviews of the ride are mixed, but the package as a whole is worth experiencing, even if the actual ride portion can be a bit underwhelming. **SCARY FACTOR** Mostly the wrath of your crew if you do a poor job. Smugglers Run isn't particularly intense, but the cockpit does get dark and change colors throughout the experience with bright reds and greens before returning to neutral blacks and greys. Very young guests may be startled and the incredibly claustrophobic may not appreciate the relatively tight quarters once onboard the ship.

WHEN TO GO First thing or last thing at night. **EXPECT TO WAIT** Afternoon waits are typically in the 60 to 90 minute range, but will go up if FastPass+ is introduced. Single rider is also an option. The line bypasses the pre-show and you won't be able to choose your position, but waits are typically just five to ten minutes, even when the posted wait is much longer. **LENGTH** 5 minutes. **WHERE TO SIT** Request one of the two pilot seats for the most control, or the Engineer position if you'd like to sit back and relax.

Star Wars: Rise of the Resistance

RANKING Don't miss. **EMH** Not available when the ride opened, but should eventually be added to Morning and Evening. **FP+** Not yet, but should be added at some point in 2020. **TYPE** Mixed experience dark ride on a level never before seen. **REQUIREMENTS** 40" or taller.

WHAT TO EXPECT Rise of the Resistance is the grandest and most innovative experience that Walt Disney Imagineering has ever created. The attraction includes walkthrough, simulator, and dark ride elements over the course of a nearly 20-minute experience. We don't want to give away what happens, but we can virtually guarantee that you'll leave impressed. **SCARY FACTOR** Rise of the Resistance is intense at times, but it's not overtly scary. The main ride vehicle is similar to the one that you'll board on DINOSAUR, making for a relatively comfortable overall trip. There is a brief, short vertical drop that's more surprising than unsettling. The ride is packed with action, but most guests who meet the 40" height requirement should be just fine.

WHEN TO GO Disney has been using a virtual queue boarding group system as the only means for guests to gain access to the attraction. Once a guest scans their ticket/MagicBand and enters the Studios, they're eligible to join a boarding group via the My Disney Experience app or via Guest Experience Team Cast Members stationed around the Park. It's essential to join a boarding group as early as possible, as all boarding groups are routinely filled before 8am, and inventory could run out before 7:15am, even with the Studios scheduled to open at 8am or 9am. Join a boarding group immediately after entering the park. The boarding group signup process is similar to booking a FastPass+, with the signup screen looking nearly identical. One member of the group may sign up anyone who is connected to their My Disney Experience account, and eligible to join a boarding group by entering Hollywood Studios that day. If you see the members of your party when you go to book FastPass+ on the app or DisneyWorld.com, then you'll also see them on the boarding group signup screen. Keep in mind that everyone must have entered the Studios in order to be assigned a boarding group. One member of the party can't go early and sign those up who are still in bed or still on their way to the park. Lower-number boarding groups will be called over to ride first, which is another benefit of joining a boarding group early. When your group is called, you should receive a notification on the My Disney Experience app, but continue checking your phone to see which boarding groups are eligible to ride, as the notification may not come. Once your boarding group is eligible to ride, you have up to two hours to make it over and scan in. So even if you're eating lunch or on another attraction, you should have plenty of time to make it over. You can even leave the Studios and do anything else while you wait for your boarding group to be called. Eventually, Disney will move away from the boarding group system and over to the regular standby/FastPass+ setup that we see at most attractions. This could happen as early as the first week in January 2020, or much later in in the year. When it does happen, it will still be crucial to arrive two hours before the park opens in order to be among the first inside. You'll then need to rush to Rise of the Resistance first thing. Otherwise, plan on riding last thing at night or do your best to acquire FastPass+ once the changeover happens. **EXPECT TO WAIT** With the virtual queue system, waits of 20 to 30 minutes are common after your boarding group is called. Once standby is available, multiple-hour waits will be the norm all day. **WHERE TO SIT** When applicable, the front row of the eight-person vehicle should provide the best views.

COMMISSARY LANE

Located behind Grauman's Chinese Theatre, Commissary Lane is home to the Red Carpet Dreams Mickey and Minnie meet, in addition to the ABC Commissary quick service and Sci-Fi Dine-In restaurant. ABC Commissary is a decent quick service with plentiful air-conditioned seating, but a limited lunch menu. Beginning at 4pm, a fast casual concept takes over with higher-priced entrées. Guests still order at the register, but food is delivered to the table. Sci-Fi, with its fun drive-in theater theme, is Josh's favorite Studios restaurant, serving reliably good sandwich and burger fare. The more expensive options at Sci-Fi are over-priced given the quality, and best skipped by those paying cash.

Red Carpet Dreams Mickey and Minnie Meet and Greet

Mickey and Minnie greet guests at this glamorous location that opened in spring 2016. Mickey is in his classic sorcerer's robes and hat, while Minnie meets separately in her iconic pink dress. There is just the one line for both characters and waits typically top out at 30 minutes, making this a decent stop in the late afternoon when you'd spend at least that long to do most other attractions. If possible, meet before 10:30am or with two hours to close to minimize waits further.

PIXAR PLACE

Pixar Place closed in July 2018, shortly after Toy Story Land opened. An Incredible Celebration took its place in January 2019. The dance party with Frozone, Mr. Incredible, and Mrs. Incredible has since closed, but guests still have an opportunity to meet Edna Mode to very short waits, in addition to taking advantage of some fun photo ops and potentially picking up a drink or snack from the market kiosk.

TOY STORY LAND

Toy Story Land opened on June 30, 2018, and is the new home to Toy Story Mania, in addition to the new whip-around Alien Swirling Saucers ride and Slinky Dog Dash roller coaster. Jessie and Woody meet inside the land, and Buzz Lightyear welcomes guests closer to the entrance. Bo Peep joined Woody with the release of Toy Story 4. A new, all-outdoor quick service also opened under the Woody's Lunch Box banner, serving breakfast, lunch, and dinner. We like to stop by for sandwiches and a cold drink when temperatures are more moderate as there's no indoor seating. Disney announced another table service restaurant coming to Toy Story Land, called Roundup Rodeo BBQ, in April 2019, with an expected opening date of sometime in 2020. We don't expect it to outshine 50's Prime Time, Hollywood Brown Derby, or Sci-Fi Dine-In.

Alien Swirling Saucers

RANKING Worth experiencing at least once. **EMH** Morning, Evening. **FP+** Yes, a lower priority than Slinky Dog Dash, but a good pickup when it's available. **TYPE** Spinning ride. **REQUIREMENTS** 32" or taller.

WHAT TO EXPECT Anyone familiar with Mater's Junkyard Jamboree will recognize the setup, which seats two to three people in each of the eleven vehicles that circle a set of turntables. While similar to Mad Tea Party at Magic Kingdom, the spinning is milder with more of a whip-around feeling as your alien-helmed rocket spins around and moves from turntable to turntable. A quick YouTube search may help picture the setup better. The queue is all outdoors, but the portion usually in use is covered and the ride doesn't typically close due to adverse weather conditions. **SCARY FACTOR** Low. Those prone to motion sickness may want to think twice, but the vehicles don't spin all the way around and the ride is mercifully short.

WHEN TO GO During the first or last hour of operation or with FastPass+. **EXPECT TO WAIT** Peak waits of 30 to 45 minutes in the afternoon are common. **LENGTH** Under 90 seconds. **WHERE TO SIT** Each rocket seats up to two adults and a child. All rockets provide a similar experience.

Slinky Dog Dash

RANKING Don't miss. **EMH** Morning, Evening. **FP+** Yes. Highest Toy Story Land priority. **TYPE** Roller coaster. **REQUIREMENTS** 38" or taller.

WHAT TO EXPECT Much more than "just a kiddie coaster," Slinky Dog Dash packs a surprising amount of thrills into a low intensity, family-friendly ride similar to Seven Dwarfs Mine Train with beautiful views of Hollywood Studios below. The fact that Slinky travels all across Andy's Backyard as part of his Mega Coaster Play Kit makes the ride all the more charming. Unfortunately, the queue is entirely outdoors and less than half is covered, which can make waiting uncomfortable in the heat or rain. Slinky also closes if lightning is in the area, so don't plan to ride in the middle of a storm. Riding during a recommended time outlined below will mitigate these issues. **SCARY FACTOR** Low as far as roller coasters go. The ride is smooth with no loops, big drops, or fast turns.

WHEN TO GO Immediately after the park opens, in the last 30 minutes of operation, or with FastPass+. **EXPECT TO WAIT** Peak waits of 75 to 90 minutes are common. **LENGTH** About 2 minutes. **WHERE TO SIT** Each Slinky Dog seats up to 18 guests in nine rows of two guests each with individual lap bars. The back row offers the wildest ride, while things are tamer up front. Request your desired position when the cast member is assigning rows at the front of the ride.

Toy Story Mania!

RANKING Don't miss. **EMH** Morning, Evening. **FP+** Yes. Moderate Toy Story Land priority. FastPass+ experiences are easier to acquire than for Alien Swirling Saucers, though using FastPass+ at Toy Story Mania may save more time. **TYPE** Interactive 3D shooting game. **REQUIREMENTS** None.

WHAT TO EXPECT Riders enter slow-moving vehicles and shoot targets to score points with toy guns attached to the front of the ride vehicle. Toy Story Mania is in 3D (with required 3D glasses) and also includes 4D elements. There are five midway style games to play during the ride, none of which are violent. It's a lot more fun to experience than to read about! **SCARY FACTOR** Mild spinning should not upset even the most prone to motion sickness.

WHEN TO GO Within 20 minutes of opening, in the last hour of operation, or with FastPass+. **EXPECT TO WAIT** 45 to 60 minutes in the afternoon. **LENGTH** 5 minutes. **WHERE TO SIT** Pairs of riders sit next to each other and compete with the pair facing the opposite direction in the same vehicle.

MICKEY AVENUE

Mickey Avenue is the corridor behind Grauman's Chinese Theater that connects Animation Courtyard with the walkway into Toy Story Land.

Walt Disney Presents

RANKING Minor attraction. **EMH** Morning, Evening. **FP+** No. **TYPE** Walkthrough exhibit with an optional film and meet-and-greet opportunity. **REQUIREMENTS** None.

WHAT TO EXPECT A sincere, interesting look at the man behind the Walt Disney Company, featuring memorabilia and artifacts from Walt Disney's life and models of Disney park attractions from around the world. When available, the optional 15-minute film at the end is highly recommended, but more often than not, Disney uses the space to promote a preview of one of their new feature films. In the back of the building, Mike and Sulley from "Monsters, Inc." meet guests. **SCARY FACTOR** None.

WHEN TO GO See the exhibit portion when waits are long at other rides, or you simply are nearby. For Mike and Sulley, try to get in line during the last half hour they appear, which may be as early as 6pm. Double check the Times Guide. **EXPECT TO WAIT** No wait to enter the exhibit, but the character meet and greet wait usually peaks around 30 minutes and it may be five to ten minutes until the next film begins. **LENGTH** As long as you like—most guests spend about 30 minutes, including the film.

ANIMATION COURTYARD

Star Wars Launch Bay, located in the back of the courtyard, anchors this area. Inside, you'll find Star Wars character meet and greets, props from the movies, interactive games, and a large store filled with high-end merchandise. Back outside, the area is lined with Disney Junior character meet and greets. Voyage of the Little Mermaid, an enchanting stage show featuring a live Ariel, is arguably the land's best attraction. Disney Junior Dance Party! debuted in December 2018, replacing Disney Junior Live on Stage. The premise of the show, aimed at young children, is similar. There are no dining options here, but two shops are located on the Voyage of the Little Mermaid side, including one that's almost entirely princess merchandise.

Disney Junior Dance Party!

RANKING Don't miss for young kids, skippable for everyone else. **EMH** No. **FP+** Yes, low priority. **TYPE** Musical show and dance party. **REQUIRE-MENTS** None.

WHAT TO EXPECT Join DJ Deejay and host Finn Fiesta for this raucous dance party as Disney Junior favorites like Vampirina, Timon, Mickey Mouse, and Doc McStuffins join in on the fun. With a loose storyline based around whether Mickey will descend from the Hot Dog Hills and arrive at the party on time, this is a fun opportunity for the kids to interact with the characters in a casual environment without the typical lines and short interaction times of most meet and greets. **SCARY FACTOR** Only for single adult Disney bloggers tasked with reviewing the show without kids in tow.

WHEN TO GO Try to see one of the first two or last two shows.. **EXPECT TO WAIT** Arrive at least 15 minutes early. **LENGTH** 20 minutes. **WHERE TO SIT** Rambunctious kids will enjoy the show from the middle of the dance floor, while parents may want to keep some distance.

Star Wars Launch Bay

RANKING Minor attraction. **EMH** Morning, Evening. **FP+** No. **TYPE** Part exhibit, film, and character meet and greets. **REQUIREMENTS** None.

WHAT TO EXPECT The Launch Bay is made up of several pieces. Guests first have the option to wait and watch a short film about how much of an impact *Star Wars* has made on popular culture and what it means to the filmmakers, or skip ahead and enter the exhibit portion of the attraction. Here, guests have an opportunity to look at a variety of props and models from the movies. In the next room, Chewbacca, BB-8, and Darth Vader greet guests in separate lines. Finally, guests exit through a gift shop with a number of high-end goods. **SCARY FACTOR** Darth Vader may be intimidating, but the other characters are happy to see you. **WHEN TO GO** Character waits are shortest before 10am and in the last hour of operation. Otherwise, visit in the afternoon. **EXPECT TO WAIT** 15 to 30 minutes each. **LENGTH** With the film, most guests will spend about 30 minutes. Add more time if the characters are of interest.

Voyage of the Little Mermaid

RANKING Major attraction. **EMH** Evening. **FP+** Yes. Moderate priority. **TYPE** Musical stage show. **REQUIREMENTS** None.

WHAT TO EXPECT A mixture of puppets, Animatronics, and live actors tell the story of the Little Mermaid inside of a comfortable, relatively small theater. **SCARY FACTOR** Medium for young kids. Ursula, the wicked octopus, may frighten young children. She is 12-feet tall, 10-feet wide, and accompanied by loud effects and darkness. You might want to prepare youngsters by reminding them that she can't leave the stage.

WHEN TO GO The first two or last two shows of the day are least crowded. **EXPECT TO WAIT** Up to 30 minutes in the afternoon. **LENGTH** 15 minutes. **WHERE TO SIT** Let half of a row file in first to be in the center. Sit at least half way back for a full view of the stage.

SUNSET BOULEVARD

Here, you'll find two of Hollywood Studios' best rides: Rock 'n' Roller Coaster and Tower of Terror. The entrance to the Hollywood Hills Theater, where *Fantasmic!* takes place, is located on the right before Tower of Terror. Nearby, *Beauty and the Beast* is an excellent stage show that has been running longer than any other WDW show. In March 2019, Lightning McQueen's Racing Academy opened in the old Sunset Showcase building, which is located through a gate to the right of the entrance to Rock 'n' Roller Coaster. With continuous shows, prospective viewers typically need to wait just the ten-or-so minutes for Lightning to appear on-stage for his next performance. Outside the building, Cruz Ramirez from the *Cars* franchise takes pictures with guests.

Sunset Boulevard is primarily lined with retail on the left and right sides of the street before the attractions. On the right, Legends of Hollywood offers one of the largest selections of Pandora jewelry along with dresses, bags, and other couture items. The Once Upon A Time store follows, mixing higher-end watches and purses along with Disney's usual variety of less expensive toys, clothing, and souvenirs. On the left, Beverly Sunset Boutique replaced Sweet Spells on June 30, 2018. The store now offers merchandise with Toy Story tie-ins, including apparel, toys, and of course, treats. Further up is Reel Vogue, which stocks a variety of merchandise based on other Disney properties. At the exit to Rock 'n' Roller Coaster is a store selling a smorgasbord of rock 'n' roll-inspired merchandise. The shop at the exit to Tower of Terror features over a hundred items themed to the attraction, including Hollywood Tower Hotel robes and bells.

Sunset Ranch Market, an outdoor collection of six individual stands, serves all kinds of food—pizza, burgers, sandwiches, salads, ice cream, fruit, snacks, and more. The common seating area is outdoors. Hollywood Hills Theater offers snacks and drinks, in addition to heartier items like hot dogs for about 90 minutes before Fantasmic! starts.

Beauty and the Beast Live on Stage

RANKING Major attraction. **EMH** No. **FP+** Yes. Low priority. **TYPE** Stage show. **REQUIREMENTS** None.

WHAT TO EXPECT This 25-minute Broadway-style musical features characters, music, and scenes from *Beauty and the Beast*. The sets are elaborate, the costumes are first-rate, and the acting is excellent. **SCARY FACTOR** None.

WHEN TO GO The first and last shows are typically least crowded. **EXPECT TO WAIT** Arrive at least 20 minutes early. **LENGTH** 30 minutes. **WHERE TO SIT** At least half way up in the center section.

Lightning McQueen's Racing Academy

RANKING Minor attraction. **EMH** No. **FP+** No. **TYPE** Stage show. **REQUIREMENTS** None.

WHAT TO EXPECT A large Lightning McQueen animatronic appears on stage to show off his racing skills on his state-of-the-art racing simulator. Viewers watch on a massive wrap-around screen as things don't go according to plan. The show is popular with kids, but is more of a diversion for adults. It's easy enough to see that you might fit it into your itinerary around the time you're planning on visiting the Sunset Boulevard attractions anyway. **SCARY FACTOR** Virtually none. Lightning gets himself into a little trouble, but the audience is never in any danger and there are no overtly scary moments.

WHEN TO GO Whenever it's convenient later in the day. Shows are continuous from park open through close. **EXPECT TO WAIT** Up to 15 minutes. **LENGTH** 12 minutes. **WHERE TO SIT** Seating is on bleachers. Find a seat towards the center of a row at least half way back from the stage to take in the whole show with ease.

Rock 'n' Roller Coaster

RANKING Don't miss. **EMH** Morning, Evening. **FP+** Yes, high priority. **TYPE** Roller coaster. **REQUIREMENTS** 48" or taller.

WHAT TO EXPECT An Aerosmith video pre-show explains why you are about to drive really fast. Next you board a limousine-themed roller coaster vehicle that seats 24 people in rows of two. The vehicle will then propel out of the gate with the force of a supersonic jet. **SCARY FACTOR** With max speeds over 60 miles per hour, three inversions, and multiple corkscrews, this is arguably Disney's most intense roller coaster. The dark setting may actually ease fears as the track is never fully visible to riders. **CAN WE HANDLE IT?** The initial launch is the most intense part—the rest of the ride is relatively tame compared to any major coaster at Six Flags or Universal. Anyone that made it through Everest or Space Mountain should be fine.

WHEN TO GO First thing, in the final hour of operation, or with FastPass+. Rock 'n' Roller Coaster offers a single-rider line, but because it's impossible to know how many people are ahead of you in it before you actually get to the indoor pre-show area, it's not recommended. **EXPECT TO WAIT** 50 to 100 minutes in the afternoon. **LENGTH** 90 seconds. **WHERE TO SIT** Request the front row for the best view, the middle if you're apprehensive, or the back to see all the twists and turns.

Twilight Zone Tower of Terror

RANKING Don't miss. **EMH** Morning, Evening. **FP+** Yes, high priority. **TYPE** Elevator drop. **REQUIREMENTS** 40" or taller.

WHAT TO EXPECT A pre-show video in the dilapidated hotel's library explains the circumstances surrounding your unfortunate visit. After a short wait in the boiler room, you board your elevator, which will embark on an eerie journey through the hotel. Anyone going down? **SCARY FACTOR** High. The most obviously frightening ride at Disney World, and one of few that puts an emphasis on fear. There are no particularly scary images or scenes, but Disney does an excellent job of building tension up to the final drop, which begins at 170 feet above ground at a speed faster than gravity would naturally pull. **CAN WE HANDLE IT?** Motion sickness can be an issue, but otherwise walk the nervous past the ride exit and note that almost everyone leaves with a smile on their faces.

WHEN TO GO Immediately after Rock 'n' Roller Coaster, in the final hour of operation, or with FastPass+. **EXPECT TO WAIT** 50–100 minutes in the afternoon. **LENGTH** 5 minutes. **WHERE TO SIT** All seats are good, but the view from the front row is the least obscured.

NIGHTTIME FIREWORKS AND SHOWS

Fantasmic!

RANKING Don't miss. **EMH** No. A show may be scheduled during evening EMH, but anyone is welcome to attend. **FP+** Yes, low priority in most situations. There is dedicated FastPass+ seating near the center, but getting a good seat within the section requires an early arrival. Booking Fantasmic! as one of your three initial selections also means you won't be able to schedule any other FastPass+ experiences after the show, because it's typically scheduled at the very end of the night. If Fantasmic FastPass+ is a priority, look for it as a 4th or subsequent selection in the afternoon or early evening. Thousands of experiences are available with the same return time every night and people are constantly changing or canceling plans. Those canceled FastPass+ experiences will become available for anyone else to book. **TYPE** Fireworks and live action show. **REQUIREMENTS** None.

WHAT TO EXPECT The theater seats about 9,000 people on bleacher seating without backs. Mickey is the star of the show as he appears on stage with over 50 live performers as film sequences featuring many best-loved Disney moments and characters, plus Pocahontas, play on screens made of water, fireworks shoot overhead, and fire and magic potions abound. **SCARY FACTOR** Moderate for the young. Mickey is in a considerable amount of danger with a 40-foot-tall dragon and all the villains. Sit near the back with anxious toddlers for a quick escape.

TYPICAL SCHEDULE: Presented once or twice per evening almost every evening of the year. Show times vary, depending on when it gets dark, and may be as early as 7pm or as late as 10.30 pm. The second show, if scheduled, will be less crowded. **LENGTH** 30 minutes. **WHERE TO SIT:** Arrive at least 45 minutes early for the first show. Arriving 20 minutes early is sufficient for the second show. Sit at least half way up, as close to the center as possible.

Star Wars Galactic Spectacular

RANKING Don't miss for avid Star Wars fans; entertaining for everyone else. **EMH** No. A show may be scheduled during evening EMH, but anyone is welcome to attend. **FP+** No. **TYPE** Projection show and fireworks. **REQUIREMENTS** None.

WHAT TO EXPECT This is now predominantly a projection show on the Grauman's Chinese Theatre façade with the addition of fire, lasers, and fireworks. Many clips from the Star Wars franchise are played along with some of the films' most iconic music. It's a stirring mixture of visuals, sound, and effects. **SCARY FACTOR** Low for anyone but the most susceptible to darkness and loud noises. The audience is never in any danger and the fireworks are typically shot low to the ground.

TYPICAL SCHEDULE: Usually begins at park close. Anyone is welcome to stay and enjoy the show. **LENGTH** 10 minutes. **WHERE TO SEE IT:** About half way in between the Chinese Theatre entrance and the two tall projection towers. If you're seeing Disney Movie Magic, the same spot should be fine for this show.

Disney Movie Magic

RANKING Good filler before nighttime fireworks. **EMH** No. A show may be scheduled during evening EMH, but anyone is welcome to attend. **FP+** No. **TYPE** Projection show. **REQUIREMENTS** Ability to arrive in the Center Stage area in front of Grauman's Chinese Theatre at least ten minutes before show time.

WHAT TO EXPECT Similar to the Disney Movie Magic show that preceded it, The Wonderful World of Animation is a laser light show featuring scenes from 90 years of Disney animated movies projected onto the Chinese Theater facade with a smattering of fireworks intermixed. Every Disney and Pixar film is represented during the 12-minute show, which is accompanied by a unique soundtrack recorded specifically for the production. **SCARY FACTOR** Low. The limited number of fireworks at the end shouldn't startle most. **TYPICAL SCHEDULE:** Usually begins 20–30 minutes before fireworks. **LENGTH** 12 minutes. **WHERE TO SEE IT:** About halfway in between the Chinese Theatre entrance and the two tall projection towers.

The Magic Kingdom

The original Walt Disney World theme park, and the most popular theme park in the world, Magic Kingdom offers more attractions, entertainment, and atmosphere than any of the other theme parks. Its offerings are varied, from elaborate stage shows to classic dark rides to roller coasters. Magic Kingdom is best toured over two or more days, but guests with limited time still have the opportunity to visit the highlights and take in the fabulous nighttime entertainment.

FASTPASS+ PRIORITY

There are far more FastPass+ opportunities at Magic Kingdom than at any of the other theme parks, making the decision on which to pick difficult. Consider picking three high-priority attractions in a Land that you don't plan to visit until the afternoon or evening. For example, if you plan to start your day with The Magic Carpets of Aladdin, Jungle Cruise, Big Thunder Mountain, and Splash Mountain, then you may want to use FastPass+ in the afternoon in Fantasyland at Peter Pan's Flight, Cinderella, and the Mine Train, or in Tomorrowland at Space Mountain, Tomorrowland Speedway, and Buzz Lightyear.

FastPass+ Priority

1. Seven Dwarfs Mine Train
2. Peter Pan's Flight
3. Space Mountain
4. Splash Mountain (when high temperatures are 80+ degrees)
5. Meet Mickey at Town Square Theater
6. Big Thunder Mountain Railroad
7. Meet Cinderella and a Visiting Princess
8. Meet Rapunzel and a Visiting Princess
9. Enchanted Tales with Belle
10. Meet Ariel at Ariel's Grotto
11. Buzz Lightyear's Space Ranger Spin
12. Tomorrowland Speedway
13. Jungle Cruise
14. Haunted Mansion
15. Pirates of the Caribbean
16. Splash Mountain (when high temps are less than 80 degrees)
17. Meet Tinker Bell at Town Square Theater
18. "it's a small world"
19. Barnstormer
20. Dumbo the Flying Elephant
21. The Many Adventures of Winnie the Pooh
22. Magic Carpets of Aladdin

23. Under the Sea ~ Journey of the Little Mermaid
24. Mad Tea Party
25. Monsters Inc. Laugh Floor
26. Mickey's PhilharMagic

ARRIVING AT MAGIC KINGDOM

Magic Kingdom's parking lot is located at the Transportation and Ticket Center (TTC) across Seven Seas Lagoon. Guests arriving via their own automobile or buses from non-Disney-owned resorts (except the Swan and Dolphin) will need to transfer from the TTC to Magic Kingdom via the resort monorail, express monorail, or ferry boat. The express monorail is the fastest because it's a direct route that takes about three minutes. There are also more monorails on the express beam, so a fresh monorail arrives every 3–5 minutes. The resort monorail is often less crowded, but the trip takes about 20 minutes with stops at the Polynesian and Grand Floridian resorts first. The five-minute ferry ride is scenic and less cramped because there's more room to spread out. Our preference is the ferry, though the express monorail is often a few minutes faster. Guests traveling from Epcot will also transfer at the Transportation and Ticket Center. Occasionally, guests will instead take buses if other methods of transportation are unavailable.

Most guests from Disney-owned resorts and the Swan and Dolphin arrive at Magic Kingdom via Disney buses, which pick-up and drop-off just a couple minutes walk from the park's main entrance. Guests from the Contemporary have the option of walking about ten minutes or taking the resort monorail. Guests at the Polynesian and Grand Floridian may take the resort monorail or watercraft. Guests at the Wilderness Lodge and Ft. Wilderness may take a bus or watercraft. Watercraft trips are usually slower, but more scenic.

Guest services is located on the far right outside the entrance and on the left at City Hall inside the entrance. Lines are often shorter inside at City Hall. Wheelchair and ECV rentals are located on the right just inside the entrance. Stroller rental is located underneath the train station.

MAIN STREET, U.S.A.

Main Street, U.S.A. is themed to a small town at the turn of the 20th century. The train station blocks the view of what's inside as guests pass underneath. Once through, the magnificent Cinderella Castle shines in the distance. To the right in Town Square Theater is a Mickey Mouse meet and greet. Tinker Bell meets separately in the same building. Next door is the below-average Tony's Town Square restaurant themed to *Lady and the Tramp*, with Italian food that's generally done better at Olive Garden.

On the left is package pickup and Guest Services. Inside the fire station, guests can sign up to play the interactive Sorcerers of the Magic Kingdom game. Five playing cards per person may be picked up daily. Next to it is Harmony Barber Shop with surprisingly reasonable prices. Stop in for a fun first haircut or some "pixie dust" for a lot less money than the Bibbidi Bobbidi Boutique in Fantasyland. Also on the left, the

Emporium stretches for much of Main Street, offering just about every piece of theme park merchandise from toys and plush to Mickey Crocs.

On the right, The Chapeau offers a wide selection of hats, and Main Street Confectionery is your best spot for handmade treats and cupcakes. Further up on the right is Main Street Bakery, which now hosts the park's Starbucks. Past that is Main Street Cinema, Uptown Jewelers, and Crystal Arts, all offering upscale items like Dooney and Bourke bags and Ray-Ban sunglasses. Uptown Jewelers is also home to the Pandora store that offers theme park-exclusive charms.

At the end of Main Street on the left is Casey's Corner, serving hot dogs with interesting toppings along with corn dog nuggets and, more recently, a vegan, plant-based dog. Farther on the left is Crystal Palace, which hosts a Winnie the Pooh and friends buffet for all three meals. On the right is Plaza Ice Cream Parlor, a great spot for a sundae in the afternoon. To the right of it is The Plaza Restaurant, serving the most inexpensive table service sandwich fare on property.

Mickey Mouse at Town Square Theater

RANKING Don't miss for little kids who need to meet Mickey; skippable for others. **EMH** No. **FP+** Yes. High priority for guests wanting to meet Mickey. **TYPE** Character meet-and-greet. **REQUIREMENTS** None.

WHAT TO EXPECT Magician Mickey greets guests inside Town Square Theater with a fun backstage backdrop. **SCARY FACTOR** None.

WHEN TO GO First or last hour of operation, during a parade, or with FastPass+. **EXPECT TO WAIT** 35–50 minutes in the afternoon. **LENGTH** A minute or two of exchanging pleasantries and taking pictures.

Tinker Bell at Town Square Theater

RANKING The only place (normally) to meet Tink. **EMH** No. **FP+** Yes, low priority. **TYPE** Character meet-and-greet. **REQUIREMENTS** A willingness to be shrunk down to fairy size.

WHAT TO EXPECT Tinker Bell meets alone in a location that doesn't make a lot of thematic sense, but it does feature a nice backdrop and it is air-conditioned. **SCARY FACTOR** None.

WHEN TO GO In the first two or last two hours of operation or with FP+. **EXPECT TO WAIT** 25–40 minutes in the afternoon. **LENGTH** About a minute of one-on-one time.

The Walt Disney World Railroad

RANKING Minor attraction. **EMH** No. **FP+** No. **TYPE** Steam train tour around the outer perimeter of the park, with additional stops in Frontierland near Splash Mountain and Fantasyland near Barnstormer. **REQUIREMENTS** None.

WHAT TO EXPECT The Disney World Railroad is a relaxing way to see parts of the Magic Kingdom that you might miss by walking around in a hurry. Some minor vignettes are only visible from the train (and the steamboat).

You board at any of the three stations and ride for as long as you like around the 1.5 mile track. If you are walking between areas near two of the stops, the train is a nice break. The strollers Disney rents at the park are not allowed on the train. You will need to remove your belongings, name card, and have your receipt handy to pick up a new stroller at your final destination. Note that the railroad will be closed for the foreseeable future, due to Tron construction in Tomorrowland. Skippable for those on shorter visits. **SCARY FACTOR** None.

WHEN TO GO Anytime attraction. See it when waits are long at other rides, or when you want to use it as transport to save walking. The train stops operating prior to Happily Ever After in the evening and does not usually resume service. **EXPECT TO WAIT** Only for the next train—7–10 minutes. **LENGTH** A full circle around the Magic Kingdom takes about 20 minutes. **WHERE TO SIT** Views are best from the side where you board.

ADVENTURELAND

Split into two distinct areas—the Arabian Village and Caribbean Plaza—Adventureland is distinctively adventure-y. In the Arabian section, you'll find most of the attractions—Tiki Room, Jungle Cruise, Magic Carpets of Aladdin, and Swiss Family Treehouse—as well as the cult favorite Citrus Swirl, a blend of frozen orange juice and vanilla ice cream, at Sunshine Tree Terrace. The Jungle Skipper Canteen restaurant, themed to the nearby Jungle Cruise attraction, opened in December 2015 in the old Adventureland Veranda space to the right of Sunshine Tree Terrace. The immersive atmosphere offers plenty of fun little details and the menu is a little out there with appetizers like falafel or shu mai and entrees like whole fried fish, though other dishes like grilled steak and crispy chicken should be more familiar. Because of its large size and the perceived exoticness of the menu, reservations are easy to secure, particularly for lunch. We like it more for the atmosphere and fun overall experience than the food, which typically sounds bolder than it ends up being flavorful.

Agrabah Bazaar is the primary, smallish store offering wares perfect for adventurers. A store sponsored by Sunglass Hut is across from Swiss Family Treehouse, offering sunglasses that mostly cost hundreds of dollars. To the right of the Pirates entrance is the signup building for the fun Pirate's Adventure Treasures of the Seven Seas interactive game. It includes a free, high-quality souvenir map that sends players around Adventureland unlocking secrets and setting off surprises. Visit in the afternoon as a fun diversion when waits peak elsewhere.

Arabian Village opens up to Caribbean Plaza on the Frontierland side, hosting the Pirates of the Caribbean attraction with an expansive store at its exit offering everything pirate. Tortuga Tavern is the land's quick service, currently offering primarily hot dogs and sandwiches. Aloha Isle behind The Magic Carpets of Aladdin, which recently relocated from its spot now occupied by Sunshine Tree Terrace, serves the popular Dole Whip, a frozen pineapple-flavored treat.

Enchanted Tiki Room

RANKING Minor attraction. **EMH** Evening. **FP+** No. **TYPE** Audio-Animatronics show. **REQUIREMENTS** None.

WHAT TO EXPECT A groundbreaking attraction when it originally opened at Disneyland in the early 60s, the Enchanted Tiki Room entertains with singing Animatronic birds. Today it feels quaint—kids don't enjoy it a lot, and while adults are charmed, it's not a priority. Many Disney fans love it because of its history, but it's ultimately skippable for those immune to nostalgia. **SCARY FACTOR** Not much—just a bit of thunder and lightning.

WHEN TO GO Anytime attraction. See it when waits are long at other rides, or you need to get out of the weather. **EXPECT TO WAIT** 10–15 minutes. **LENGTH** 10 minutes. **WHERE TO SIT** Sit in the last row, towards the center.

Jungle Cruise

RANKING Don't miss. **EMH** No. **FP+** Yes. Medium priority. **TYPE** Comedy disguised as a river cruise. **REQUIREMENTS** None.

WHAT TO EXPECT This boat ride takes you through areas themed as several of the world's great rivers, inhabited by Audio-Animatronic people and animals. Your (human) skipper guides the tour, making corny jokes and telling silly puns along the way. The effects are dated, but the skipper can make the ride so much fun that it's not to be missed. **SCARY FACTOR** Low. There is a short section in dark ruins, but that's it.

WHEN TO GO First two or last two hours of operation, or with FastPass+. **EXPECT TO WAIT** 35–70 minutes in the afternoon. **LENGTH** 10 minutes. **WHERE TO SIT** Anywhere along the edge of the boat—avoid the interior seats.

Magic Carpets of Aladdin

RANKING Skippable but fun. **EMH** Evening. **FP+** Yes. Low priority. **TYPE** Spinning ride. **REQUIREMENTS** None.

WHAT TO EXPECT This slow-loading, low capacity ride raises four-person magic-carpet themed vehicles and then spins riders in the air over Adventureland. You can control how high you go. The ride is fun and offers some spectacular views, but most guests won't want to spend more than a few minutes waiting. **SCARY FACTOR** Low. **CAN WE HANDLE IT?** Motion sickness is rarely an issue. A camel may spit water in your general direction.

WHEN TO GO Anytime attraction. See it when waits are long at other rides, or you simply are nearby. **EXPECT TO WAIT** 10–20 minutes in the afternoon. **LENGTH** 2 minutes. **WHERE TO SIT** Cast Members will assign your group a carpet—the experience is the same from all. The front seat controls height, the back seat tilt.

Pirates of the Caribbean

RANKING Don't miss. **EMH** Evening. **FP+** Yes. Low priority. **TYPE** Boat ride through pirate-themed Audio-Animatronics and settings. **REQUIREMENTS** None.

WHAT TO EXPECT One of the most famous rides at the park, Pirates sends riders floating through a Disneyfied version of a town ransacked by pirates. In a reversal of what usually happens, the Jack Sparrow films were based on the ride, and Jack and others from the films are present in many scenes. **SCARY FACTOR** This is a lighthearted, playful ride, yet one with lots of skeletons and implied violence. Skip it if Haunted Mansion was too much. **CAN WE HANDLE IT?** There's a mild drop towards the beginning of a few feet that may result in a bit of water splashing over the first row, but that's it. **WHEN TO GO** In the first two or last two hours of the day is best. **EXPECT TO WAIT** 30–50 minutes in the afternoon. **LENGTH** 10 minutes. **WHERE TO SIT** All seats have a similar experience. The front row has slightly better views, and a better chance of getting a little wet.

Swiss Family Treehouse

RANKING Skippable but fun. **EMH** Evening. **FP+** No. **TYPE** Self-guided walking tour. **REQUIREMENTS** There are a lot of stairs up and down.

WHAT TO EXPECT The Treehouse replicates the living conditions from the popular film that few probably remember. While interesting, the attraction is not particularly compelling and guests visiting over one day usually have higher priorities. **SCARY FACTOR** Low. **CAN WE HANDLE IT?** The top of the tree is high; the stairs all the way up and down can be tough on cranky knees or hips.

WHEN TO GO Anytime attraction. See it when waits are long at other rides, or you simply are nearby. **EXPECT TO WAIT** No wait to 5 minutes in the afternoon. **LENGTH** 10 minutes or so.

FRONTIERLAND

Home to Big Thunder Mountain, Splash Mountain, and one of the park's most popular quick services, most guests will spend a considerable amount of time here. Fortunately, both rides enjoy hefty capacities that make it possible to visit them in the second hour of operation. You'll also find two anytime attractions: the comfortable serenading of bears in Country Bear Jamboree, and Tom Sawyer Island, where adventures await.

Pecos Bill is the principal quick service, now offering a menu featuring fajitas, nachos, salads, and burgers with an expansive toppings bar. Diamond Horseshoe serves a menu featuring serviceable barbecue that works in a pinch, but probably isn't a restaurant that you want to go out of your way to experience. Golden Oak Outpost is located at the Pecos' side exit, serving a variety of fried snacks to normally non-existent lines when it's open. Westward Ho alongside the river serves snacks and drinks. Two to three carts also position themselves along the river across from Diamond Horseshoe, serving hot dogs, churros, and pretzels. Lines are usually shorter at similar stands around the corner in Liberty Square.

Of course, you'll find several merchandise opportunities here, too. Splash Mountain's exit offers some attraction-branded merchandise, in addition to several shops between Pecos Bill and Diamond Horseshoe that offer everything from freshly baked treats to limited-edition pins.

Big Thunder Mountain Railroad

RANKING Don't miss. **EMH** Evening. **FP+** Yes. High priority. **TYPE** Runaway train-themed roller coaster. **REQUIREMENTS** 40" or taller.

WHAT TO EXPECT Prospective miners board trains consisting of five cars, each with three rows that seat two to three people each. With top speeds under 30 miles per hour, Big Thunder is not an intense experience, but the theming is first rate. **SCARY FACTOR** Minimal for a roller coaster—there are two scenes inside caves that are loud and dark, but anyone that made it through any other Disney coaster will be just fine. **CAN WE HANDLE IT?** Some motion sickness issues for the highly susceptible, and jostling.

WHEN TO GO First or last two hours of operation, or with FastPass+. **EXPECT TO WAIT** 40–60 minutes in the afternoon. **LENGTH** 4 minutes. **WHERE TO SIT** The back provides the wildest experience. Sit up front for a tamer ride.

Country Bear Jamboree

RANKING Minor attraction. **EMH** Evening. **FP+** No. **TYPE** Audio-Animatronics show. **REQUIREMENTS** None.

WHAT TO EXPECT A musical review and show with country-and-western songs performed by Animatronic bears. Wildly popular when it opened, it is now attended largely by roots/country music fans, diehard Disney fans, and visitors looking for a bit of a rest and some air conditioning. The characters are fun but the jokes are hokey, and the songs, while fun to those with wide musical tastes, aren't everyone's favorite. Skippable for many on shorter visits. **SCARY FACTOR** None. **CAN WE HANDLE IT?** The music is more bluegrass/western than modern country.

WHEN TO GO Anytime attraction. See it when waits are long at other rides, or you need to get out of the weather. **EXPECT TO WAIT** 10–15 minutes for the next show. **LENGTH** 15 minutes. **WHERE TO SIT** Sit in the middle row, toward the center. Wait for 25 people or so to enter a row first, and follow them.

Splash Mountain

RANKING Don't miss. **EMH** Evening. **FP+** Yes. High priority on hot days, medium on cool days. **TYPE** Mostly a gentle log ride, with fewer thrills than you'd guess from outside. **REQUIREMENTS** 40" or taller.

WHAT TO EXPECT Splash Mountain is the ride that most showcases all of the best of Disney. You float past brilliantly executed scenes based on the Br'er Rabbit character from Disney's (unavailable) *Song of the South*. And here and there—especially towards the end—there's some thrilling drops. **SCARY FACTOR** The very visible final drop, from 52 feet up and at 40 miles per hour at a 45-degree angle, is greatly misleading. Most of this ride is gentle floating through darling settings. But besides the final drop, there are several much shorter drops. **CAN WE HANDLE IT?** You may get wet—especially if you sit in the front, but possibly from any seat. The visible final drop scares many off who would absolutely love this ride. Trust us and give it a chance.

WHEN TO GO First two or last two hours of operation, or with FastPass+. **EXPECT TO WAIT** 15–90+ minutes in the afternoon (the longer waits on crowded hot days, the shorter on cold low-crowd days). **LENGTH** 12 minutes. **WHERE TO SIT** The front seat has the best view, but is most likely to get wet. Those seated on the left side of the log enjoy the best views of the animatronics.

Tom Sawyer Island

RANKING Minor attraction. **EMH** No. **FP+** No. **TYPE** Self-guided walking tour and playground. **REQUIREMENTS** None.

WHAT TO EXPECT Tom Sawyer Island is only accessible via motorized rafts that board near the entrance to Big Thunder Mountain Railroad. Once on the island, visitors can explore numerous areas themed to Tom Sawyer and Huck Finn—caves, a mine, two bridges, a working water wheel, and Fort Langhorn, a play area. Benches are plentiful and the Island is a terrific spot to take a break. Skippable for those without kids, or on a short visit. **SCARY FACTOR** None.

WHEN TO GO Anytime attraction. See it when waits are long at other rides, or you simply are nearby. Afternoons tend to be best, but note that it closes before dusk. **EXPECT TO WAIT** 5–15 minutes to get raft transport in the afternoon. **LENGTH** Allow 30–45 minutes+ including time spent waiting for the rafts, more if your kids really need to run around.

The Walt Disney World Railroad

See the "Main Street" entry on the railroad, which stops in Frontierland near the exit to Splash Mountain.

LIBERTY SQUARE

To the left of Cinderella Castle, Liberty Square offers the fewest attractions and eateries of any land, but what is offered is mostly above average in quality. Hall of Presidents is a perfect way to spend a hot afternoon, while Haunted Mansion is quintessential Disney.

Columbia Harbour House, across from Haunted Mansion, is our favorite quick service, offering a delicious fried shrimp platter, in addition to salads, unique sandwiches, grilled salmon, and excellent soups. Sleepy Hollow Refreshments serves funnel cakes, waffles, and other ice cream treats. We prefer lunch to dinner at Liberty Tree Tavern for guests paying cash, when an assortment of less expensive appetizers and entrees are available. Best is to start with the tavern cheese dip with griddled Boston brown bread followed by any of the entrees, which include turkey, pot roast, lobster rolls, burgers, and more. The all-you-care-to-enjoy platter, featuring turkey, pot roast, pork loin, and all the fixings, is available for lunch and dinner. For dinner, the fixed-price, per-person platter is the only option on the menu. It includes a non-alcoholic beverage and dessert.

Across from Hall of Presidents is Ye Olde Christmas Shoppe, which offers primarily Christmas-related merchandise. Memento Mori near Haunted Mansion's exit offers the full line of Haunted Mansion merchandise, along with kitchen-related items.

Hall of Presidents

RANKING Minor attraction. **EMH** No. **FP+** No. **TYPE** Audio-Animatronics show. **REQUIREMENTS** None.

WHAT TO EXPECT A theater show featuring film clips and animatronics of all of the U.S. Presidents. The show is patriotic and expounds on the hardships and triumphs of the United States through the years. The theater is air-conditioned, comfortable, and seats over 700 people, which makes it a nice and easy attraction to enjoy in the afternoon heat. Enjoyed most by adults and patriotic Americans, dull for most kids. Skippable for those on shorter visits. **SCARY FACTOR** None, other than it's full of politicians.

WHEN TO GO Anytime attraction. See it when waits are long at other rides, or you need to get out of the weather. **EXPECT TO WAIT** Arrive either at 20 or 50 minutes past the hour and your wait should be just ten minutes. **LENGTH** 25 minutes. **WHERE TO SIT** In the middle row, toward the center.

The Haunted Mansion

RANKING Don't miss. **EMH** Evening. **FP+** Yes. Medium priority. **TYPE** Light-hearted, slow-moving ride through a haunted house and its grave-yard. **REQUIREMENTS** None.

WHAT TO EXPECT One of the most famous rides at the park, the Haunted Mansion is one of Disney's best and most enduring attractions. Intended to be a fun and goofy ride, not a frightening experience, you won't see anything truly gruesome or disgusting. This is a must-ride for almost all guests. **SCARY FACTOR** Haunted Mansion is much more spooky than it is scary, but a lot of kids are going to be apprehensive about entering the foreboding building. Rest assured that it's a lot of fun. **CAN WE HANDLE IT?** Yes, those brave enough to enter enjoy the experience.

WHEN TO GO First two or last two hours of operation, or with FastPass+. **EXPECT TO WAIT** 20–50 minutes in the afternoon, longer if the Hall of Presidents and Liberty Square Riverboat have just let out guests, as they do every thirty minutes. **LENGTH** 10 minutes. **WHERE TO SIT** Each Doom Buggy seats two to three. Sit apprehensive youngsters (or dads) in the middle.

The Liberty Square Riverboat

RANKING Minor attraction. **EMH** No. **FP+** No. **TYPE** Steamboat tour around the Rivers of America. **REQUIREMENTS** None.

WHAT TO EXPECT The Liberty Square Riverboat is a stately three-tiered paddle-wheel boat that slowly circles Tom Sawyer Island and offers fantastic views of Splash Mountain, Big Thunder Mountain Railroad, and several other popular attractions. Some minor vignettes otherwise visible only from the Walt Disney World Railroad also appear. The voice of Mark Twain narrates the journey. Skippable for those on short visits. **SCARY FACTOR** None.

WHEN TO GO Anytime attraction. See it when waits are long at other rides, or you need to get out of the weather. **EXPECT TO WAIT** Arrive either at

20 or 50 minutes past the hour and your wait should be just ten minutes. **LENGTH** 17 minutes. **WHERE TO SIT** Bow and stern locations where you can easily see both riverbanks are best. Otherwise sit on the port side. (That's left when facing the bow—the end without the paddlewheel.)

FANTASYLAND

With the longest list of attractions, this is where most guests will spend the majority of their time. Fortunately, most attractions enjoy short durations and healthy capacities, making it relatively easy to bang out the majority of rides in under an hour first thing in the morning or when crowds ease in the late evening. Mickey's PhilharMagic is an outstanding 3D anytime attraction, and Enchanted Tales with Belle is an afternoon FastPass+ priority.

Be Our Guest Restaurant remains one of the most popular places to eat on property, serving quick service breakfast and lunch, in addition to table service dinner. Reservations are usually required for any of these meals and can be made up to 180 days in advance. We like breakfast for those who can secure a reservation close to 8am with a 9am park open. Diners will be able to beat the rush to a priority Fantasyland attraction like Seven Dwarfs Mine Train so long as they exit the restaurant by 8:45am. Later breakfasts are not recommended because they take up precious morning touring time. Lunch is mostly soups, salads, and sandwiches, in addition to braised chicken and a bean cassoulet. Average entrée prices have climbed to around $15, but most guests find value in the enchanting atmosphere and food is delivered to the table for added convenience. For dinner, the restaurant exclusively serves a 3-course prix-fixe menu with each guest choosing appetizer, entrée, and dessert. More information is available in Chapter 7: Where to Eat.

Pinocchio Village Haus is the primary dinnertime quick service, located to the left of the entrance to New Fantasyland. The flatbread pizzas and salads are above average and there's plentiful air-conditioned seating in addition to outdoor patio seating. Gaston's Tavern between Be Our Guest and Journey of the Little Mermaid serves cinnamon rolls, snacks, and an apple-flavored frozen beverage called LeFou's Brew. Indoor seating is minimal, but the theming is exquisite throughout. Friar's Nook, located across from the entrance to Seven Dwarfs Mine Train, serves tater tots with a variety of toppings, in addition to bratwurst and macaroni and cheese. Storybook Treats is Fantasyland's version of the Plaza Ice Cream Parlor, serving decadent sundaes and other ice-cream treats. Cheshire Café serves snacks, drinks, and treats next to Mad Tea Party, while Prince Eric's Village Market serves drinks, lemonades, and snacks across from the Journey of the Little Mermaid ride in New Fantasyland. Finally, Big Top Souvenirs across from Dumbo is yet another spot to find freshly made treats, including caramel corn, candied apples, and fudge, in addition to the frozen Goofy's Glacier drinks.

Castle Couture, to the left of Mickey's PhilharMagic, is now a check-in and staging area for the Bibbidi Bobbidi Boutique. Across the way is Sir Mickey's, primarily offering princess apparel and toys. Two great stores are located back in New Fantasyland: Bonjour Gifts, to the right of Gaston's Tavern, offers unique glassware, goblets, and other upscale items, and Big Top Souvenirs offers toys and apparel.

Ariel's Grotto

RANKING Don't miss for little kids who need to meet Ariel; skippable for others. **EMH** Morning, Evening. **FP+** Yes. High priority for guests wanting to meet Ariel. **TYPE** Character meet and greet. **REQUIREMENTS** None.

WHAT TO EXPECT After winding through a line themed to undersea rockwork, meet Ariel in her picturesque grotto. **SCARY FACTOR** None.

WHEN TO GO First or last hour of operation, or with FastPass+. **EXPECT TO WAIT** 25–45 minutes in the afternoon. **LENGTH** About a minute with everyone's favorite undersea princess.

The Barnstormer

RANKING Minor attraction. **EMH** Morning, Evening. **FP+** Yes. Low priority. **TYPE** Roller coaster. **REQUIREMENTS** 35" or taller.

WHAT TO EXPECT This slow-loading, low-capacity ride with some light theming around Goofy's stunt plane is the tamest coaster at Disney World, and best thought of as a "starter" roller coaster. Fun, swoopy, and brief, its features are fully visible, so there's no surprises. Great fun for little kids, but skippable for others. **SCARY FACTOR** Low. Mild speeds and heights. **CAN WE HANDLE IT?** If your kids decide after it begins that they aren't ready for coasters, it will be over within seconds. Ride vehicles are low to the ground with just enough room for two average-size adults to sit side by side.

WHEN TO GO First two or last two hours of operation, or with FastPass+. **EXPECT TO WAIT** 25–40 minutes in the afternoon. **LENGTH** Less than 1 minute. **WHERE TO SIT** The front seat has the best view, but no seats are bad.

Dumbo the Flying Elephant

RANKING Minor attraction. **EMH** Morning, Evening. **FP+** Yes. Low priority. **TYPE** Spinning ride. **REQUIREMENTS** None.

WHAT TO EXPECT Charming Dumbos with two riders side by side rise from their delightfully decorated base and slowly spin. Riders control how high or low their Dumbo flies. A favorite of little kids, but skippable for adults. Those not using FastPass+ have the option to wait in an air-conditioned play area instead of the typical queue. **SCARY FACTOR** Low. The mild heights may trouble the most severely acrophobic. **CAN WE HANDLE IT?** Spinning is too slow to affect motion sickness. Little kids can't ride alone.

WHEN TO GO First two or last two hours of operation, or with FastPass+. **EXPECT TO WAIT** 30–50 minutes in the afternoon. **LENGTH** Less than 2 minutes. **WHERE TO SIT** All seats are good.

Enchanted Tales with Belle

RANKING Major attraction. **EMH** Morning, Evening. **FP+** Yes. High priority.
TYPE Combined walk-through tour, Audio-Animatronic show, interactive
show, and character photo op. **REQUIREMENTS** None.

WHAT TO EXPECT It starts as a tour of Maurice's cottage, magically shifts
to the Beast's Mansion where audience volunteers are recruited by Madame
Wardrobe for a show, moves to the Beast's Library where under Lumiere's
direction the volunteers act the show out for Belle, and ends with the show
volunteers getting a chance to meet and have pictures with Belle. Only
show volunteers get photos by default, so if your kids aren't picked for a
part, have them volunteer at the last "anybody else?" casting call. Drop
dead cute, it's Disney at its best. **SCARY FACTOR** None.

WHEN TO GO During the afternoon parade, in the final hour of operation,
or with FastPass+. **EXPECT TO WAIT** 20–40 minutes in the afternoon.
LENGTH 25 minutes.

"it's a small world"

RANKING Minor attraction. **EMH** Morning, Evening. **FP+** Yes. Low priority.
TYPE Boat ride. **REQUIREMENTS** None.

WHAT TO EXPECT Boats seating 20 or so float past miniatures of singing
children from around the world, colorfully attired and accompanied by
toys and representations of their cultures. A world-famous tour-de-force
of design, song writing, and artistic unity. **SCARY FACTOR** None.

WHEN TO GO Before 11am, in the final two hours of operation, or
with FastPass+. **EXPECT TO WAIT** 20–35 minutes in the afternoon.
LENGTH 11 minutes. **WHERE TO SIT** Seats at the sides of the boat have
the best view.

Mad Tea Party

RANKING Minor attraction. **EMH** Morning, Evening. **FP+** Yes. Low priority.
TYPE Spinning ride. **REQUIREMENTS** None.

WHAT TO EXPECT Spinning tea cups lightly themed to *Alice in Wonderland*
delight kids, annoy most adults. Skippable for those on shorter visits. **SCARY
FACTOR** None. **CAN WE HANDLE IT?** There's three simultaneous spins:
the whole ride, a group of cups, and individual cups. Don't ride if you are
subject to motion sickness.

WHEN TO GO Anytime attraction. See it when waits are long at other rides,
or you simply are nearby. **EXPECT TO WAIT** 5–15 minutes in the afternoon.
LENGTH 90 seconds. **WHERE TO SIT** In a different cup than your children,
who will wish to spin much more than you do.

The Many Adventures of Winnie the Pooh

RANKING Minor attraction. **EMH** Morning, Evening. **FP+** Yes. Low priority.
TYPE Dark ride. **REQUIREMENTS** None.

WHAT TO EXPECT Four-person "honey pots" make their way through multiple, richly-detailed Winnie the Pooh-themed scenes featuring Pooh, Eeyore, Piglet, Owl, Tigger, and others. **SCARY FACTOR** Low—a briefly blustery day where the ride vehicle tips up and down slightly for a few seconds.

WHEN TO GO First two or last two hours of operation, or with FastPass+. **EXPECT TO WAIT** 30–40 minutes in the afternoon. **LENGTH** 3 minutes. **WHERE TO SIT** All seats are good.

Mickey's PhilharMagic

RANKING Don't miss. **EMH** Morning, Evening. **FP+** Yes. Lowest priority. **TYPE** 4D show. **REQUIREMENTS** None.

WHAT TO EXPECT This 3D film (supplemented by in-theater effects—hence 4D) tells the tale of Donald getting in trouble, with Mickey ultimately to the rescue. Interwoven between are some of the best bits from some of Disney's most popular films: *Peter Pan, Aladdin, Little Mermaid, Lion King*, and more. It's a must-see because of its fun and diabolically creative celebration of some of Disney's best-loved animation. **SCARY FACTOR** Low. 3D effects and typical cartoon mayhem spook some little ones. Take off their 3D glasses if this happens.

WHEN TO GO Anytime attraction. See it when waits are long at other rides, or you simply are nearby. **EXPECT TO WAIT** Up to 15 minutes for the next show. **LENGTH** 12 minutes. **WHERE TO SIT** Sit in a middle row, towards the center. Wait for 25 people or so to enter a row first, and follow them.

Peter Pan's Flight

RANKING Don't miss. **EMH** Morning, Evening. **FP+** Yes. High priority. **TYPE** Dark ride. **REQUIREMENTS** None.

WHAT TO EXPECT Pirate ships seating 2–3 people fly through scenes from *Peter Pan*. Kids love it, but teens and adults are mixed. For some, the flight over London instantly makes it among their favorite rides at Disney World; others find it pedestrian, a little dull—especially the middle section—and overrated. It's a "Don't miss" so that you can discover for yourself where you stand. **SCARY FACTOR** Dark, but not scary.

WHEN TO GO At park open, in the final hour of operation, or with Fast-Pass+. **EXPECT TO WAIT** 50–70+ minutes in the afternoon. **LENGTH** 3 minutes. **WHERE TO SIT** All seats are good.

Pete's Silly Sideshow: Goofy and Donald

RANKING Don't miss for little kids who need to meet Goofy or Donald; skippable for others. **EMH** No. **FP+** No. **TYPE** Character meet and greet. **REQUIREMENTS** None.

WHAT TO EXPECT Goofy and Donald in elaborate circus costumes greet guests in a tent at Pete's Silly Sideshow. Minnie and Daisy greet in the same tent, but their line is separate. **SCARY FACTOR** None.

WHEN TO GO Anytime attraction. See it when waits are long at other rides, or you simply are nearby. Note that the meet typically begins at 10am and closes by 7pm. **EXPECT TO WAIT** 10–20 minutes in the afternoon. **LENGTH** About a minute with each character individually.

Pete's Silly Sideshow: Minnie and Daisy

RANKING Don't-miss for little kids who need to meet Minnie or Daisy; skippable for others. **EMH** No. **FP+** No. **TYPE** Character meet and greet. **REQUIREMENTS** None.

WHAT TO EXPECT Minnie and Daisy in elaborate circus costumes greet guests in a tent at Pete's Silly Sideshow. Goofy and Donald greet in the same tent, but their line is separate. **SCARY FACTOR** None.

WHEN TO GO Anytime attraction. See it when waits are long at other rides, or you simply are nearby. Note that the meet typically begins at 10am and closes by 7pm. **EXPECT TO WAIT** 20–30 minutes in the afternoon. **LENGTH** About a minute with each character individually.

Prince Charming Regal Carrousel

RANKING Minor attraction. **EMH** Morning, Evening. **FP+** No. **TYPE** Slowly spinning carousel. **REQUIREMENTS** None.

WHAT TO EXPECT As stately and lovely a carousel as you will ever see, the essence of this ride is obvious from simply looking at it. Ride it if you have kids that wish to; just watch it otherwise. **SCARY FACTOR** None, other than getting the spelling right (two r's in carrousel). **CAN WE HANDLE IT?** Spins too slowly to bother most.

WHEN TO GO Anytime attraction. See it when waits are long at other rides, or you are nearby. **EXPECT TO WAIT** 5–10 minutes in the afternoon. **LENGTH** 2 minutes. **WHERE TO SIT** Along the outside for the best photo opportunities.

Princess Fairytale Hall: Cinderella and a Visiting Princess

RANKING Don't miss for those who need to meet Cinderella; skippable for others. **EMH** Morning, Evening. **FP+** Yes. High priority for those who want to greet these characters. **TYPE** Character meet and greet. **REQUIRE-MENTS** None.

WHAT TO EXPECT Cinderella and another princess greet guests in Princess Fairytale Hall. Rapunzel greets in the same building, but her line (and FastPass+) is entirely separate. **SCARY FACTOR** None.

WHEN TO GO At park open, in the final hour of operation, or with Fast-Pass+. **EXPECT TO WAIT** 30–60 minutes in the afternoon. **LENGTH** 3–5 minutes of signing, mingling, and picture taking.

Princess Fairytale Hall: Rapunzel and a Visiting Princess

RANKING Don't miss for those who need to meet Rapunzel; skippable for others. **EMH** Morning, Evening. **FP+** Yes. High priority for those who want to greet these characters. **TYPE** Character meet and greet. **REQUIRE-MENTS** None.

WHAT TO EXPECT Rapunzel and another princess greet guests in Princess Fairytale Hall. Cinderella greets in the same building, but her line (and FastPass+) is entirely separate. **SCARY FACTOR** None.

WHEN TO GO At park open, in the final hour of operation, or with Fast-Pass+. **EXPECT TO WAIT** 30–60 minutes in the afternoon. **LENGTH** 3–5 minutes of signing, mingling, and picture taking.

Seven Dwarfs Mine Train

RANKING Don't miss. **EMH** Morning, Evening. **FP+** Yes. High priority. **TYPE** Combined roller coaster and dark ride. **REQUIREMENTS** 38" or taller.

WHAT TO EXPECT This ride combines the swoops and curves of a moderate roller coaster with richly detailed scenes from *Snow White*, focusing especially on the Dwarfs. The vehicles are small and seating may be uncomfortable for guests over six feet tall. **SCARY FACTOR** Low—the roller coaster parts are mild and the dark scenes brief. **CAN WE HANDLE IT?** A new ride system (cars that swing side to side) both increases the impression of speed and makes the ride smoother and more comfortable for those with motion sickness.

WHEN TO GO Immediately at park open, in the final hour of operation, or with FastPass+. **EXPECT TO WAIT** 50–90+ minutes in the afternoon. **LENGTH** 3 minutes. **WHERE TO SIT** The front row provides the best views while the back row offers the wildest ride.

Under the Sea ~ Journey of the Little Mermaid

RANKING Major attraction. **EMH** Morning, Evening. **FP+** Yes. Low priority. **TYPE** Dark ride. **REQUIREMENTS** None.

WHAT TO EXPECT Two-to three person "clamshells" take you under the sea into a fairly literal re-telling of the *Little Mermaid*. There's much color and movement, and the party scene is particularly well-done, but those who are not Little Mermaid fans may find it dull. If just one Little Mermaid attraction is enough for you, see the one at Disney's Hollywood Studios instead. **SCARY FACTOR** Low. It has its moments shrouded in darkness, but it's not in any way scary.

WHEN TO GO First two or last two hours of operation, or with FastPass+. **EXPECT TO WAIT** 30–40 minutes in the afternoon. **LENGTH** 5 minutes. **WHERE TO SIT** All seats are good.

The Walt Disney World Railroad

See the "Main Street" entry on the railroad for more details. The Fantasyland stop is near the entrance to The Barnstormer.

TOMORROWLAND

One of the most popular lands, and the one located just off the Hub to the right, Tomorrowland is home to several of Magic Kingdom's most popular attractions, including the venerable Space Mountain and Buzz Lightyear's Space Ranger Spin. Several anytime attractions are also situated here, including the Carousel of Progress, Tomorrowland PeopleMover, and Monsters Inc. Laugh Floor. Expect to see construction walls over the next couple of years as Disney begins construction on a Tron roller coaster similar to the ride that debuted in Shanghai. It will be situated in between Space Mountain and Tomorrowland Speedway

Tomorrowland has no table service restaurants, but Cosmic Ray's Starlight Café is one of Magic Kingdom's most popular quick services. Unfortunately, the menu options have been cut recently and ribs are no longer available. You will still find hamburgers, chicken nuggets, chicken sandwiches, hot dogs, salads, and rotisserie chicken, among other items. Tomorrowland Terrace is another major quick service, located closer to the Plaza Restaurant on Main Street than the rest of Tomorrowland, but it's only open when Magic Kingdom is crowded. If it is open, the menu consists of a surprisingly decent mixture of interesting takes on the usual Disney standards. Lunching Pad is located underneath Astro Orbiter in the center of Tomorrowland, serving hot dogs, Mickey Pretzels, frozen beverages, and snacks. Also near Astro Orbiter, Cool Ship serves beverages and snacks. Joffrey's Coffee opened Revive, a fun-looking kiosk in front of Space Mountain, in March 2017. It's a nice change of pace for those who have sworn off Starbucks as it offers a variety of coffee and tea beverages, like the specialty Mission to S'mores Latte, in addition to pastries and other snacks. Rounding out the choices is Auntie Gravity's Galactic Goodies, serving smoothies, snacks, and ice cream treats.

Mickey's Star Traders and Merchant of Venus near Stitch's Great Escape are the two primary stores, though most everything sold here is available elsewhere. There are small shops at the exits to Buzz Lightyear and Space Mountain as well.

Astro Orbiter

RANKING Skippable but fun. **EMH** Morning, Evening. **FP+** No. **TYPE** Spinning ride. **REQUIREMENTS** None.

WHAT TO EXPECT This slow-loading, low capacity ride spins riders high over Tomorrowland. Twelve "rocket ships" load from an elevated platform (two to a vehicle), raise up, and spin. You can control how high you go. Views are nice, and being high is bit of a thrill, but not worth long waits. **SCARY FACTOR** Medium. This is the most intense spinner attraction at WDW, with the high altitude and rocket ships that slant inward. **CAN WE HANDLE IT?** Put a parent with each kid to help with any fears about height. Those with severe fear of heights should sit this out. Motion sickness is rarely an issue. Note that the seating situation is different than other spinner rides. Riders sit one in front of the other with their legs spread out to the sides. Two adults may want to split up as parties of one for a more comfortable ride. The brief elevator ride before and after the ride is packed full and cramped.

WHEN TO GO At park open or in the final hour of operation. **EXPECT TO WAIT** 20–40 minutes in the afternoon. **LENGTH** 2 minutes. **WHERE TO SIT** Seat adults in back with the kids up front.

Buzz Lightyear's Space Ranger Spin

RANKING Don't miss. **EMH** Morning, Evening. **FP+** Yes. Medium priority. **TYPE** Dark ride shooting gallery. **REQUIREMENTS** None.

WHAT TO EXPECT In this slow-moving ride, prospective space rangers protect the universe by turning their ride vehicle and shooting an "ion cannon" at targets as they traverse a series of *Toy Story*-themed spaces. Vehicles hold more than two, but have only two cannons. Scores are tallied, so you compete with your ride-mate. The simple concept—being inside a *Toy Story*-themed video game—delights almost everyone. **SCARY FACTOR** None. **CAN WE HANDLE IT?** A joystick controls much of the spinning. Keep youngsters away to enjoy a ride with less motion.

WHEN TO GO First two or last two hours of operation, or with FastPass+. **EXPECT TO WAIT** 25–80 minutes in the afternoon. **LENGTH** 5 minutes. **WHERE TO SIT** All vehicles and seats give the same experience.

Monsters Inc. Laugh Floor

RANKING Minor attraction. **EMH** Evening (usually first hour only). **FP+** Yes. Low priority. **TYPE** Interactive show. **REQUIREMENTS** None.

WHAT TO EXPECT Mike Wazowski, the one-eyed green monster from *Monsters Inc.*, puts on a comedy show to collect laughs from the audience to power Monstropolis. Cool technology allows the monsters to directly interact with the audience. The laughs typically are weak—though often fun for kids. Turtle Talk with Crush at Epcot uses similar technology much, much better. Those on shorter visits may elect to skip. **SCARY FACTOR** None, if your kids have seen the movies. **CAN WE HANDLE IT?** Avoid if you already have had enough Billy Crystal in your life.

WHEN TO GO Anytime attraction. See it when waits are long at other rides, or you need to get out of the weather. **EXPECT TO WAIT** 10–20 minutes in the afternoon. **LENGTH** 10 minutes. **WHERE TO SIT** As in most shows, the center of the theater seating, midway back, give the best views.

Space Mountain

RANKING Don't miss. **EMH** Morning, Evening. **FP+** Yes. High priority. **TYPE** Roller coaster in the dark. **REQUIREMENTS** 44" or taller.

WHAT TO EXPECT In one of the park's most popular rides, small three-person rockets, coupled together in flights of two, blast into the darkness of space and traverse sharp curves and minor dips past planets, stars, moons, and meteors, before returning to the launch facility. **SCARY FACTOR** Moderate. Because the ride is in the dark, speed seems much higher than it is, and everything that happens is unexpected. This scares some. But otherwise it's a very mild coaster. **CAN WE HANDLE IT?** Motion sickness typically is not an issue, but the ride's jerkiness can aggravate back/neck/shoulder pain.

WHEN TO GO At park open, in the final hour of operation, or with Fast-Pass+. **EXPECT TO WAIT** 45–120+ minutes in the afternoon. **LENGTH** 3 minutes. **WHERE TO SIT** The six seats in each coupled-together ride vehicle are single file. Front seats are the most fun. If you are concerned a kid might panic, sit behind them so you can comfort them by touch.

Stitch's Great Escape!

Stitch's Great Escape officially changed its operation over to "seasonal" in January 2018 with the expectation that the attraction would reopen during peak times. Since then, it hasn't reopened, and while Disney has made no official announcement that it won't in the future, all signs seem to point to a permanent closure. In its place, Stitch meets guests.

Tomorrowland Speedway

RANKING For little kids: don't miss. For everyone else: skippable. **EMH** Morning, Evening. **FP+** Yes. High priority only if you have little kids. **TYPE** Slow, go-cart-style ride on a highly constrained track. **REQUIREMENTS** 32" or taller to ride, 54" or taller to drive.

WHAT TO EXPECT An opportunity for kids to drive or ride along a speed-way-themed track in a small two-seater car, at speeds of less than 8 mph along a guide rail that prevents getting out of their lane. Go-cart-style rides can be fun for adults, but this isn't. Young kids tall enough to drive love it, and waits can be long. **SCARY FACTOR** A reminder that Junior is turning 16 far too soon. **CAN WE HANDLE IT?** Both the queue and the ride reek of exhaust and are largely unprotected from the sun. Getting rear-ended by a gleeful 6 year old is common, which can be rough on your back and neck.

WHEN TO GO At park open, in the final hour of operation, or with Fast-Pass+. **EXPECT TO WAIT** 20–40 minutes in the afternoon. **LENGTH** 5 minutes. **WHERE TO SIT** All vehicles give the same experience. If the kids are tall enough (54"+), let them drive.

Tomorrowland Transit Authority PeopleMover

RANKING Minor attraction. **EMH** Morning, Evening. **FP+** No. **TYPE** Tour above and through Tomorrowland. **REQUIREMENTS** None.

WHAT TO EXPECT This slow-moving elevated attraction sends four-person magnetically powered vehicles around Tomorrowland and through parts of several rides, providing a bit of a tour of the land's attractions, and a rest for weary feet. Skippable for those on short visits. **SCARY FACTOR** None.

WHEN TO GO Anytime attraction. See it when waits are long at other rides, or you need to get out of the weather. **EXPECT TO WAIT** 10 to 20 minute waits in the afternoon are now common. **LENGTH** 10 minutes. **WHERE TO SIT** All vehicles and seats give the same experience.

Walt Disney's Carousel of Progress

RANKING Minor attraction. **EMH** Morning. **FP+** No. **TYPE** Audio-Animatronics show. **REQUIREMENTS** None.

WHAT TO EXPECT The theater-style seating area rotates through four charming scenes of American family life, highlighting changes in home technology from the turn of the last century until the mid-90s. Designed for, and an enormous hit at, the New York World's Fair of 64/65, the ride suffers from the lack of a recent update and is dull for many kids. Many diehard Disney fans love it—and it's the only ride in the park that Walt Disney touched. Unlike most theater shows, leaving midway through is not allowed due to the theater's movement. **SCARY FACTOR** None.

WHEN TO GO Anytime attraction. See it when waits are long at other rides, or you need to get out of the weather. **EXPECT TO WAIT** 5–10 minutes in the afternoon. **LENGTH** 20 minutes. **WHERE TO SIT** As in most shows, the center of the theater seating, midway back, give the best views.

PARADES, FIREWORKS, AND SHOWS

Festival of Fantasy Parade: Afternoon Parade

RANKING Don't miss. **EMH** No. **FP+** No. **TYPE** Parade. **REQUIREMENTS** None.

WHAT TO EXPECT Featuring astonishing floats, a great mix of characters, and wonderful walking entertainers, this parade (which debuted in early 2014) is a don't miss. **SCARY FACTOR** None.

TYPICAL SCHEDULE: Begins at 3pm most days. May start at 2pm in the fall. Unusual events, e.g., tapings of shows on Main Street, may result in different times. The busiest days of the year often see two parades. **LENGTH** 15 minutes once it arrives.

WHERE TO SEE IT: The parade begins in Frontierland to the left of Splash Mountain, takes a turn near Hall of Presidents, and continues down Main Street, exiting between the firehouse and the Emporium. People begin staking out spots on Main Street more than an hour before showtime, but most days there are great spots still available in Frontierland 15–30 minutes before the parade. The height of the floats means that even little kids don't need to be right in front, but the great entertainers and walking characters will be hard for them to see from farther back. See it across from Pecos Bill where crowds are lighter and you can leave sooner. Tony's Town Square offers a fixed price, 3-course meal that includes a ticket to see the parade in a reserved viewing section in Town Square. While there is some value if you order the most expensive items on the menu, we don't recommend it as the food is subpar and seeing the parade from another area, including right across from the reserved section, is usually easy enough.

Happily Ever After: Evening Fireworks

RANKING Don't miss. **EMH** No. **FP+** No. Dessert parties are offered and the courtyard viewing makes seeing the show much easier. The more expensive terrace seating provides an off-center view, and is not recommended. **TYPE** Fireworks show. **REQUIREMENTS** None.

WHAT TO EXPECT Happily Ever After debuted on May 12, 2017, and combines more pyrotechnics than the former show, Wishes, with colorful, emotionally evocative projections on Cinderella Castle. **SCARY FACTOR** The show may prove too loud for some kids.

TYPICAL SCHEDULE: Usually one show nightly scheduled between 8pm and 10pm. **LENGTH** 15 minutes.

WHERE TO SEE IT: The best viewing location is in the Casey's Corner area of Main Street, where it's possible to take in the panoramic view of the fireworks and see the projections on the castle clearly. The fireworks bursts are visible from a variety of locations in Adventureland, Fantasyland, Liberty Square, and Tomorrowland.

Mickey's Royal Friendship Faire: Daytime Stage Show

RANKING Major show. **EMH** No. **FP+** No. **TYPE** Stage show.**REQUIRE-MENTS** None.

WHAT TO EXPECT A wide assortment of characters that includes everyone from Mickey Mouse to Princess Tianna to Olaf to Rapunzel join dancers, singers, and performers in this fun show that takes place on the stage in front of Cinderella Castle. It's a great way to see a lot of characters in a short amount of time. **SCARY FACTOR** Just the sun, potentially blazing down overhead.

TYPICAL SCHEDULE: Two parades are usually scheduled with one in the morning before lunch and another between 4:30pm and 6pm.

WHERE TO SEE IT: The easiest viewing location is in the Hub straight back from the stage just in front of the Partners statue, where the area is raised up higher than the street closer to the stage. This allows guests to see above the heads of those in front.

Move It! Shake It! MousekeDance It! Street Party: Parade

RANKING Minor parade. **EMH** No. **FP+** No. **TYPE** Parade and dancy party. **REQUIREMENTS** Just some slick dance moves and the ability to put up with the music.

WHAT TO EXPECT Mickey and Minnie join an assortment of characters that includes Goofy, Clarabelle, Donald, and Daisy in this parade that begins on Main Street in between The Emporium and Firehouse. MousekeDance It! then continues up to the Hub in front of Cinderella Castle, where the floats stop and a dance party takes hold. It's a fun, high-energy spectacle and a great opportunity to interact with characters in a casual setting. **SCARY FACTOR** Only your dance moves being recorded as part of a popular vlog for all to see.

TYPICAL SCHEDULE: Two parades are usually scheduled with one before lunch and the other between 4:30 pm and 6pm. **LENGTH** 30 minutes.

WHERE TO SEE IT: Unlike Festival of Fantasy and other parades, scouting out a viewing location early is entirely unnecessary. If you'd like to see the parade march up Main Street, wait for it to appear around the Flag Pole or Confectionery and follow it to the Hub. Otherwise, wait for it to arrive at the Hub, about five minutes after it steps off.

Once Upon a Time: Evening Castle Projection Show

RANKING Don't miss. **EMH** No. **FP+** No. **TYPE** Projection show. **REQUIRE-MENTS** Decent eyesight.

WHAT TO EXPECT Once Upon A Time, which has nothing to do with the fairytale soap opera of the same name, is a 15-minute animated show that's cleverly projected onto the front of Cinderella Castle. In addition to all of the characters and stories, including scenes from Frozen, Beauty and the Beast, Winnie the Pooh, Alice in Wonderland, Pinocchio, Cinderella, and a whole lot more, special effects and pyrotechnics help complete this nighttime spectacular. **SCARY FACTOR** None.

TYPICAL SCHEDULE: Double check the Times Guide. It's currently sched-uled 45 minutes after Happily Ever After begins. **LENGTH** 15 minutes.

WHERE TO SEE IT: Somewhere between the Casey's Corner area on Main Street and the Partners statue in the hub is best. The projected images are large enough that they can be seen from further back more easily than previous shows.

The Cheat Sheets

The Cheat Sheets are designed to break down all of our touring advice and principles into an easy guide you can bring along to the theme parks. Print out the newest versions in color at yourfirstvisit.net/easy-guide-2020-changes.

Each Cheat Sheet covers one park, and includes:

- Coded maps
- Touring overviews
- General FastPass+ priorities
- Daily touring plans that include specific FastPass+ suggestions

The maps are shaded based on the best time to visit the various attractions:

- The dark gray attractions are your top morning priorities, or best saved for the very end of the day or FastPass+.
- Medium gray attractions are best visited in the first/second hour of operation, or in the last two hours the park is open. They're a lower priority than the dark attractions because waits build slower and peak lower.
- Light gray attractions are designated "anytime", which is another way of saying they're best saved for the afternoon when waits at the higher priority attractions are longer. Most shows are designated "light gray" because you want to save them for the afternoon or evening when waits are longer at the major attractions.

Attractions that offer FastPass+ are followed by a +. FastPass+ kiosks are noted with the FP+ symbol. Also included are bathrooms, quick services, restaurants, and the larger stores.

Several touring plans are included with each Cheat Sheet. You may need to make changes based on the previous reviews (which is why we offer them), particularly with kids too short or too easily scared to experience certain attractions. For example, you may want to avoid roller coasters, character meets (at press time, no rides include both), or motion simulators, etc. Once you've picked your plan, it's easiest to simply cross off attractions the group isn't interested in experiencing. That will only result in shorter waits at the next attraction. Also consider substituting attractions coded the same. For example, you may want to substitute a second ride on Toy Story Mania over Rock 'n' Roller Coaster if coasters are problematic.

Animal Kingdom Cheat Sheet

PARK MAP

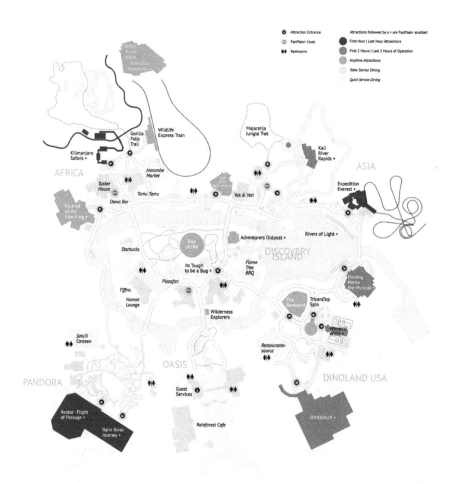

TOURING AT ANIMAL KINGDOM

GENERAL TOURING PHILOSOPHY The 2017 opening of Pandora: World of Avatar complicates touring, but it's possible to experience most of Animal Kingdom's attractions in one day—and all in one hard day. A visit over parts of two days doubles the number of FastPass+ available to you and greatly simplifies seeing everything at Animal Kingdom. How you go about your visit comes down to whether you can acquire FastPass+ for Avatar Flight of Passage, which are typically not available 59 or less days from a given date. That means little or no availability for those staying off-site or planning a trip less than 60 days in the future.

- *If you are able to acquire Flight of Passage FP+:* With one day, the easiest way to do most everything is to arrive at least 30–45 minutes before open and head straight to Pandora to ride Na'vi River Journey in standby. After, head to priority attractions outside of Pandora where waits will be short. If you can't arrive that early but can stay late, get in line for Na'vi River Journey about 5 minutes before park close. If neither is possible, ride Na'vi sometime between 1pm and 5pm when waits are actually shorter than the morning or evening, or search for River Journey FP+ availability throughout the day and book it when it becomes available. Use FastPass+ at Flight of Passage and other priority attractions in the late morning and earlier afternoon. With two days, book FastPass+ for Flight of Passage on one day and Na'vi River Journey on the second, in addition to two other selections each day.

- *If you are unable to acquire Flight of Passage FP+:* With one day, the easiest way to do most everything is by arriving at least 75 minutes before open and heading straight to ride Flight of Passage in standby. After, head to Na'vi River Journey or priority attractions outside of Pandora where waits will be short. If you can't arrive early but can stay late, get in line for Flight of Passage a few minutes before park close. If neither is possible, ride sometime between 1pm and 5pm when waits are shorter than the morning or evening. Use FastPass+ in the late morning and afternoon at Na'vi River Journey and other priority attractions. Visiting over two days will allow more FastPass+ usage and an easier time seeing the nighttime entertainment.

Either way, with an early arrival and plans to stay for the nighttime entertainment, including the Tree of Life Awakenings and Rivers of Light, on days when late sunsets push evening shows until after 9pm, most guests will want to plan a lengthy afternoon break to rest. For those without interest in the nighttime entertainment, a three-quarters day should work. For a single-day visit with a late morning or early afternoon arrival, some compromises will need to be made as it will be difficult to experience both Pandora rides and all of the headliners with short waits, in addition to the evening entertainment. Plan to use FastPass+ upon arrival and then make as many subsequent selections as possible after using the initial three.

CHARACTERS Mickey & Minnie in Adventurers Outpost and the Wilderness Explorers meet to the left of It's Tough To Be A Bug are the only priorities and both usually see actual waits under 20 minutes.

ROPE DROP Animal Kingdom usually begins letting guests inside the park 30-45 minutes prior to the scheduled open and holds guests in four places inside the park. Those headed to Asia or DinoLand wait at the respective bridges leading into those lands. Those waiting for Pandora are held just outside the land along the bridge leading into it. Those heading to Africa are held in the Pizzafari/Starbucks area. Guests are typically walked into Pandora 20-30 minutes before official open with guests headed elsewhere held until closer to official park open.

The main rope drop priority is Avatar Flight of Passage, where it's essential to arrive at least an hour before open (75 minutes before is better) and hurry as fast as possible to the holding area. For Flight of Passage, stay to the right. The walk can be a congested experience. The walk to Na'vi River Journey on the left is much less stressful. Very few people will be heading anywhere other than Pandora first thing.

PRIMEVAL WHIRL Disney has changed Primeval Whirl's status to "seasonal," which means it may not be open during your visit. If it's not open, in the touring plans that follow simply skip the step for it and move on to the next.

ANIMAL KINGDOM AT NIGHT AND RIVERS OF LIGHT Disney began keeping Animal Kingdom routinely open past dark in mid 2016, adding plentiful nighttime entertainment and, in February 2017, a new after-dark show, Rivers of Light, which we consider subtle rather than spectacular but still worth a visit.

Rivers of Light during busy periods is shown twice a night. During less busy periods, once a night is more common.

Rivers of Light has proven unpopular with guests, which has made standby seating much more plentiful. While it is bookable as a FastPass+, the problem with booking FP+ in advance for it is that the show is late at night and because of that, you'll be limited to just two FP+ during the day without the ability to book more. The easiest way to see the show is with the dining package, which guarantees a seat in the reserved section and allows booking FP+ elsewhere. A dessert party that offers similar reserved seats is also available—we think the dining package offers better value. Without the package or party, on a single-day visit afternoon/evening arrivers probably want to book FP+ in advance as doing so won't much limit using FP+ elsewhere. Morning arrivers may want to see the last show in standby when applicable or refresh FP+ availability to try to score additional FP+ that someone else canceled closer to show time.

Those uninterested in the show still ought to take advantage of Animal Kingdom's later hours, when wait times drop substantially at priority attractions. Expedition Everest at night is a whole new experience, as is Pandora, and the Tree of Life Awakenings, which happen sporadically from sundown through about 30 minutes after park close, are not to be missed.

FASTPASS+ AT ANIMAL KINGDOM

FASTPASS+ PRIORITY FastPass+ at Animal Kingdom is divided into two groups. One group includes the two rides that opened with the Pandora: World of Avatar land. From these two you can pick just one. The other group includes all other Animal Kingdom FastPass+ rides, and from these you can pick two more.

Pandora (choose one):

1.   Avatar Flight of Passage
2.   Na'vi River Journey

Everything else (choose two):

1.   Kilimanjaro Safaris
2.   Expedition Everest

3. Animation Experience at Rafiki's Planet Watch (if you wish to participate, due to very few experiences available)

4. Kali River Rapids (when highs are 80+ degrees)

5. DINOSAUR

6. Adventurers Outpost Mickey and Minnie Meet (due to fewer experiences available)

7. Rivers of Light (primarily the first show; last show is easier to see in standby)

8. Kali River Rapids (when highs are less than 80 degrees)

9. Festival of the Lion King

10. Finding Nemo: The Musical

11. UP! A Great Bird Adventure

12. Primeval Whirl

13. It's Tough To Be A Bug

FOURTH FASTPASS+ SELECTION AVAILABILITY Avatar Flight of Passage and Na'vi River Journey will have no day-of availability outside of cancellations. "Everything Else" attractions 1–10 will have limited availability on busier days by noon, but with so much capacity at most attractions, each will become available when refreshing availability. Primeval Whirl and It's Tough To Be A Bug have plenty of availability.

FASTPASS+ KIOSKS Add or change FastPass+ on your device or at the following locations:

- *Island Mercantile.* On the left just after crossing the bridge into Discovery Island

- *Mandala Gifts.* On the right side on the walk toward Kali River Rapids

- *Kilimanjaro Safaris.* To the left of the entrance

Two-Day Touring Plan
with an Early and a Late Arrival

Use FastPass+ at Avatar Flight of Passage or Na'vi River Journey 12:30–1:30pm, Kilimanjaro Safaris 1:30–2:30pm, and Kali River Rapids 3–4pm.

TWO-DAY EARLY AND LATE ARRIVAL PLAN, DAY ONE
(8AM OPEN OR EMH)

1. Ride the Pandora ride for which you were unable to acquire a FastPass+: 7:45–8:25am.

2. Ride Expedition Everest, twice if time allows: 8:40–9:10am.

3. Ride Primeval Whirl: 9:15–9:35am.

4. Ride DINOSAUR: 9:40–10am.

5. Ride TriceraTop Spin: 10:02–10:15am.

6. See It's Tough to Be a Bug and/or meet a character: 10:20–11am.

7. Have lunch (your choice): 11–11:45am

8. See Finding Nemo the Musical: 11:50am–12:45pm.
9. Ride Avatar Flight of Passage or Na'vi River Journey with FP+. Explore Pandora: 1–2pm.
10. Ride Kilimanjaro Safaris with FastPass+: 2–2:40pm.
11. See Festival of the Lion King: 2:40–3:30pm.
12. Ride Kali River Rapids with FastPast+: 3:40–4pm.
13. Visit additional attractions you'd like to experience, then depart.

TWO-DAY EARLY AND LATE ARRIVAL PLAN, DAY ONE (9AM OPEN)

1. Ride the Pandora ride for which you were unable to acquire a FastPass+: 8:45–9:25am.
2. Ride Expedition Everest, twice if time allows: 9:40–10am.
3. Ride DINOSAUR: 10:05–10:30am.
4. Ride TriceraTop Spin: 10:32–10:45am.
5. Have lunch (your choice): 11–11:45am
6. See Finding Nemo the Musical: 11:50am–12:45pm.
7. Ride Avatar Flight of Passage or Na'vi River Journey with FP+. Explore Pandora: 1–2pm.
8. Ride Kilimanjaro Safaris with FastPass+: 2–2:40pm.
9. See Festival of the Lion King: 2:40–3:30pm.
10. Ride Kali River Rapids with FastPast+: 3:40–4pm.
11. Book Primeval Whirl as a 4th FastPass+ and ride as soon as return window opens.
12. Visit additional attractions you'd like to experience, then depart.

TWO-DAY EARLY AND LATE ARRIVAL PLAN, DAY TWO

With variable closing times, the plan below goes by hour after arrival rather than time of day. With a 9:30pm close and 8:45pm Rivers of Light, the plan starts around 5:30pm.

Use FastPass+ at an attraction of your choice, Avator Flight of Passage or Na'vi River Journey, and Rivers of Light.

1. Use FastPass+ at desired attraction and eat dinner: 00:00–01:30.
2. Ride a Pandora ride with FastPass+ and look around: 01:30–02:30.
3. See Rivers of Light with FastPass+: arrive at least 30 minutes before show time.
4. Ride Expedition Everest or Kilimanjaro Safaris or visit Pandora after dark: 03:35–04:15.
5. See Tree of Life Awakenings: 04:20–04:45.

With Animal Kingdom closing anywhere between 7pm and 11pm, and the potential for one, or two, or three Rivers of Light shows per night, how you go about your evening depends on the Rivers of Light schedule and how late the park is open. Modify the loose plan above to work with the actual operating hours and whether or not you'd like to see Rivers of Light. If you don't, it opens your evening up to experience other attractions at night and spend more time in Pandora after dark.

One-Day Ride-Focused Touring Plan with Optional Evening Return

For an 8am open, or if you are attending morning EMH, use FastPass+ at Avatar Flight of Passage or Na'vi River Journey 10–11am, Kali River Rapids 12:30–1:30pm, and Expedition Everest 1:30–2:30pm.

For a 9am open, shift the Avatar FastPass+ to 10:30–11.30am, keeping the other two FastPass+ the same.

MORNING PLAN (8AM OPEN)

1. Ride the Pandora ride for which you were unable to acquire a FastPass+: 7:45–8:25am.
2. Ride Kilimanjaro Safaris: 8:30–9:10am.
3. Ride Expedition Everest: 9:20–9:40am.
4. Ride Primeval Whirl: 9:45–10am.
5. Ride DINOSAUR: 10:02–10:30am.
6. Ride Avatar Flight of Passage or Na'vi River Journey with FP+. Explore Pandora: 10:40–11:40am.
7. Have lunch. Satu'li Canteen is easy: 11:45am–12:45pm.
8. Ride Kali River Rapids with FastPass+: 1–1:20pm.
9. Ride Expedition Everest with FastPass+: 1:30–1:45pm.
10. Experience anything else you'd like, make a fourth FastPass+ reservation for the evening, and return to resort.

MORNING PLAN (9AM OPEN)

1. Ride the Pandora ride for which you were unable to acquire a FastPass+: 8:45–9:25am.
2. Ride Expedition Everest: 9:35–9:50am.
3. Ride Primeval Whirl: 9:55–10:15am.
4. Ride DINOSAUR: 10:17–10:45am.
5. Ride Avatar Flight of Passage or Na'vi River Journey with FP+. Explore Pandora: 11am–12:00pm.
6. Have lunch. Satu'li Canteen is easy: 12–12:55pm.
7. Ride Kilimanjaro Safaris with FastPass+: 1–1:40pm.
8. Ride Kali River Rapids or Expedition Expedition with FastPass+: 1:50–2:10pm.
9. Experience anything else you'd like, make a fourth FastPass+ reservation for the evening, and return to resort.

EVENING PLAN

Time your evening return based on what you'd like to accomplish. Pandora and Expedition Everest are completely different, recommended experiences after dark. To do both, arrive at least three hours before close. Rivers of Light and Tree of Life Awakenings will add at least another hour.

Two-Day, Two Late Arrivals Touring Plan

TWO DAY, TWO LATE ARRIVAL PLAN, DAY ONE

With variable closing times, the plan below goes by hour after arrival rather than time of day. With a 9:30pm close and 8:45pm Rivers of Light, the plan starts around 3pm.

Use FastPass+ at Expedition Everest 00:00–01:00 (the first hour after arrival), Kilimanjaro Safaris: 01:00–02:00, and Avatar Flight of Passage or Na'vi River Journey 03:00–04:00.

1.   Ride Expedition Everest with FastPass+: 00:00–00:15.
2.   Walk Maharajah Jungle Trek or see a show: 00:15–01:00.
3.   See It's Tough to Be a Bug or meet a character: 01:05–01:30.
4.   See Festival of the Lion King: 01:40–02:30.
5.   Ride Kilimanjaro Safaris with FastPass+: 02:40–03:20.
6.   Ride Flight of Passage or Na'vi River Journey with FP+. Explore Pandora: 03:30–04:30.
7.   Have dinner. Satu'li Canteen is convenient: 04:45–05:30.
8.   Ride Pandora ride for which you were unable to acquire FastPass+: 05:35–06:30.
9.   See Tree of Life Awakenings: 06:35–07:00.

TWO-DAY, TWO LATE ARRIVAL PLAN, DAY TWO

With variable closing times, the plan below goes by hour after arrival rather than time of day. With a 9:30pm close and 8:45pm Rivers of Light, the plan starts around 4:30pm.

Use FastPass+ at DINOSAUR 01:00–02:00 (the second hour after arrival), Kali River Rapids or Expedition Everest 02:30–03:30, and Rivers of Light (arrive at least 30 minutes before show time).

1.   See a show, meet a character, or look around: 00:00–01:00.
2.   Ride DINOSAUR with FastPass+: 01:10–01:35.
3.   Ride TriceraTop Spin: 01:37–01:50.
4.   Ride Primeval Whirl: 01:52–02:30.
5.   Have dinner. Restaurantosaurus, Flame Tree, Yak & Yeti are convenient: 02:30–03:30.
6.   Ride Kali River Rapids or Expedition Everest with FastPass+: 03:30–03:50.
7.   See Rivers of Light with FastPass+: arrive 30 minutes before show time.
8.   Ride Expedition Everest or another ride if time allows: 04:50–05:10.
9.   See Tree of Life Awakenings or visit another attraction: 05:10–06:00.

TYPICAL ANIMAL KINGDOM WAIT TIMES IN MINUTES

Low Crowds, 8pm Close

	9:30am	10am	11am	12pm	1pm	2pm	3pm	4pm	5pm	6pm	7pm	8pm
Avatar Flight of Passage	120	90	90	90	90	90	90	90	90	70	70	60
DINOSAUR	10	10	20	20	20	20	20	20	10	10	5	5
Expedition Everest	10	15	20	20	20	20	20	20	15	10	5	5
It's Tough to be a Bug	5	5	5	5	5	5	5	5	5	5	5	5
Kali River Rapids (hot)	10	15	25	40	40	40	40	30	30	20	15	10
Kali River Rapids (cool)	5	10	10	10	10	10	10	10	5	5	5	5
Kilimanjaro Safaris	10	20	30	30	20	20	20	20	15	30	20	10
Na'vi River Journey	50	60	60	60	50	50	50	50	50	60	50	40
Primeval Whirl	10	10	15	20	20	20	20	20	10	10	10	5
TriceraTop Spin	5	5	5	5	5	5	5	5	5	5	5	5

Moderate Crowds, 8pm Close

	9:30am	10am	11am	12pm	1pm	2pm	3pm	4pm	5pm	6pm	7pm	8pm
Avatar Flight of Passage	120	150	120	120	100	100	100	100	120	120	90	70
DINOSAUR	10	20	30	40	40	40	40	30	20	20	10	10
Expedition Everest	15	20	35	40	40	40	30	25	20	20	10	5
It's Tough to be a Bug	5	5	5	5	5	5	5	5	5	5	5	5
Kali River Rapids (hot)	15	20	50	60	60	60	60	50	40	30	20	5
Kali River Rapids (cool)	5	15	15	20	20	15	15	15	10	5	5	5
Kilimanjaro Safaris	20	30	40	50	50	50	40	30	30	40	30	10
Na'vi River Journey	70	80	80	80	70	60	60	60	70	70	60	50
Primeval Whirl	10	10	20	30	30	30	30	30	20	20	10	5
TriceraTop Spin	5	5	5	10	10	10	5	5	5	5	5	5

Moderate Crowds, 11pm Close

	9:30am	10am	11am	12pm	1pm	2pm	3pm	4pm	5pm	6pm	7pm	8pm	9pm	10pm	11pm
Avatar Flight of Passage	120	150	120	120	100	100	100	100	120	120	90	90	90	90	70
DINOSAUR	10	20	30	40	40	40	40	30	30	30	20	20	10	10	5
Expedition Everest	15	20	35	40	40	40	30	30	30	30	20	20	20	15	5
It's Tough to be a Bug	5	5	5	5	5	5	5	5	5	5	5	5	5	5	5
Kali River Rapids (hot)	15	20	50	60	60	60	60	50	40	30	20	15	10	5	5
Kali River Rapids (cool)	5	15	15	20	20	15	15	15	10	10	10	10	5	5	5
Kilimanjaro Safaris	20	30	40	50	50	50	40	30	30	30	30	30	30	30	10
Na'vi River Journey	70	80	80	80	70	70	70	70	70	80	80	80	70	60	40
Primeval Whirl	10	10	20	30	30	30	30	30	20	20	15	10	10	10	5
TriceraTop Spin	5	5	5	10	10	10	5	5	5	5	5	5	5	5	5

Heavy Crowds, 8pm Close

	8:30am	9am	10am	11am	12pm	1pm	2pm	3pm	4pm	5pm	6pm	7pm	8pm
Avatar Flight of Passage	150	180	180	150	120	150	120	120	150	150	150	120	90
DINOSAUR	10	10	20	40	60	70	60	60	50	40	40	20	10
Expedition Everest	15	25	45	60	60	60	60	50	50	50	35	20	10
It's Tough to be a Bug	5	5	10	15	20	20	20	15	15	15	10	10	5
Kali River Rapids (hot)	15	20	35	70	80	90	90	90	80	70	60	30	20
Kali River Rapids (cool)	5	5	15	25	25	25	20	20	20	15	10	5	5
Kilimanjaro Safaris	10	20	60	70	80	90	90	80	70	60	50	40	20
Na'vi River Journey	90	100	100	100	90	80	80	90	90	90	80	80	70
Primeval Whirl	10	20	20	30	40	50	50	40	40	30	30	20	5
TriceraTop Spin	5	5	10	20	20	20	20	20	20	15	10	5	5

Heavy Crowds, 11pm Close

	8:30am	9am	10am	11am	12pm	1pm	2pm	3pm	4pm	5pm	6pm	7pm	8pm	9pm	10pm	11pm
Avatar Flight of Passage	150	180	180	150	120	150	120	120	150	150	150	150	150	150	120	90
DINOSAUR	10	10	20	40	60	70	60	60	50	40	40	20	20	15	10	5
Expedition Everest	15	25	45	60	60	60	60	50	50	50	35	30	25	25	15	5
It's Tough to be a Bug	5	5	10	15	20	20	20	15	15	15	10	10	5	5	5	5
Kali River Rapids (hot)	15	20	35	70	80	90	90	90	80	70	60	40	20	15	10	5
Kali River Rapids (cool)	5	5	15	25	25	25	20	20	20	15	10	10	5	5	5	5
Kilimanjaro Safaris	10	20	60	70	80	90	90	80	70	60	50	40	30	40	30	20
Na'vi River Journey	90	100	100	100	90	90	90	90	90	100	100	100	90	80	70	60
Primeval Whirl	10	20	20	30	40	50	50	40	40	30	30	20	20	15	10	5
TriceraTop Spin	5	5	10	20	20	20	20	20	20	15	10	5	5	5	5	5

Epcot Cheat Sheet

PARK MAP

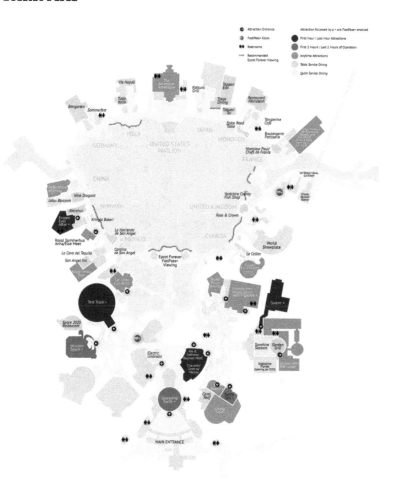

TOURING AT EPCOT

GENERAL TOURING PHILOSOPHY Because of its massive size and the long duration of many of its attractions, Epcot is best experienced over two days. By visiting the attractions in roughly half of the park on two separate days, you cut down on the amount of walking necessary and you won't run into waits longer than a few minutes all day. On one day, start with Test Track and visit Future World East and the World Showcase Pavilions from Mexico through the U.S., riding Frozen with FP+ in the early afternoon. On your other day, start with Soarin' and hit Future World West and the Pavilions from Canada through Japan, using FastPass+ again at Frozen or elsewhere..

With just one day, things are more complicated if you want to try to do each of Soarin', Test Track, Frozen, and Epcot Forever. The best way to accomplish that is to ride Test Track at rope drop, use FastPass+ at Frozen, ride Soarin' around 7pm, and then see Epcot Forever after. If you're willing to forego seeing Epcot Forever, Frozen typically has an actual wait under 20 minutes at the very end of the night, but the ride may not be operational. If you're willing to risk it, ride Test Track or Soarin' first thing, use FastPass+ at the other, and get in line for Frozen about five minutes before park close. Those skipping Frozen can instead enjoy Epcot Forever. Seeing Test Track via its single rider line is a viable option with actual waits typically under 20 minutes all day.

CHARACTERS Joy and Sadness, inside Innoventions West, are the highest priority, and see waits of 30 to 60+ minutes. Visit first thing if possible or late at night. Mickey, Minnie and Goofy at Character Spot in Innoventions West also post 20 to 40 minute waits. None of these characters offer FastPass+. Wreck-It Ralph and Vanellope inside ImageWorks in the Imagination Pavilion typically sport 20 to 30 minute waits. The Princesses in World Showcase, including Belle, Jasmine, Snow White, and Aurora can see substantial waits. Most other characters will have 5 to 20 minute waits. Random characters may also appear in between the Canada and United Kingdom Pavilions and on the pathway on the left in between the United States and Italy Pavilions.

ROPE DROP Epcot has two entrances. Guests arriving via Disney bus, monorail, or their own vehicles will enter via the main entrance at the front of the park. The International Gateway entrance in between the France and UK pavilions in World Showcase is used by those arriving from the BoardWalk, Beach Club, Yacht Club, Swan, and Dolphin resorts, and will also be used by those arriving via Disney's Skyliner from Pop Century, Art of Animation, Riviera, and Caribbean Beach.

If you're headed to a priority ride from the main entrance, arrive at least 45 minutes before open to be among the first to enter the park. From the International Gateway, arrive at least 30 minutes early.

Disney will begin letting guests enter the park from both entrances at 20–40 minutes before open. If your group arrives at the main entrance later than you'd like, check to see if Disney is still letting in guests with breakfast reservations on the far right (sometimes left) side of the entrance. If yes, wait until these lines open to everyone and hurry over for a shorter wait.

Guests at the main entrance are then held at Spaceship Earth typically until 10 to 15 minutes before official open and then allowed to head to the attraction of their choice freely. Guest at the International Gateway are held at the top of the hill in front of Yorkshire Fish in the UK Pavilion until 10 to 15 minutes before official open and then allowed to head to the attraction of their choice freely.

The International Gateway entrance is typically better for Frozen, but will put you at a slight disadvantage at Soarin' or Test Track due to how far away it is. Those with pre-opening breakfast reservations at Akershus in Norway have an advantage if they are able to finish breakfast and be outside by 8:50am.

FASTPASS+ AT EPCOT

FASTPASS+ PRIORITY FastPass+ at Epcot is divided into two tiers. Guests may initially select only one Tier 1 experience. Test Track is the highest priority because waits are longest, they are the hardest FP+ to acquire, and FP+ makes it easier to ride should the attraction go down for technical difficulties. Frozen gets the nod now that capacity at Soarin' has increased and waits are down. Test Track is typically more convenient to ride in standby first thing, so some guests may still elect to use FastPass+ at Frozen instead. Those willing to ride Test Track in single rider may also favor using FP+ elsewhere.

There are seven options for Tier 2 and you may initially select two of them. Most guests will want to initially select two of the top four choices. Note that Mission: SPACE does not require selecting Orange/Mars or Green/Earth in advance, but Orange/Mars waits are routinely longer and those that prefer the more intense Mars version will save more time using FP+ for it.

Tier One (choose one)
1. Test Track
2. Frozen Ever After
3. Soarin'
4. Epcot Forever

Tier Two (choose two)
1. Mission: SPACE
2. Spaceship Earth
3. Living with the Land
4. Journey into Imagination with Figment
5. The Seas with Nemo and Friends
6. Turtle Talk with Crush
7. Disney & Pixar Short Film Festival

FOURTH FASTPASS+ SELECTION AVAILABILITY Tier 1 selections will be limited by noon and only cancellations may be available. Refresh the app as often as possible for the most availability. Lower Tier 2 priorities will have plentiful availability for most of the day and may save a handful of minutes at each, though it's usually easy enough to see the attractions in standby during a recommend time.

FASTPASS+ KIOSKS Add or change FastPass+ at the following locations, or over your phone:

- Future World West breezeway outside Character Spot
- Future World East breezeway outside Mouse Gear and across from Electric Umbrella
- International Gateway in between UK and France pavilions near entrance/exit

Two-Day Early Arrival Touring Plan

TWO-DAY EARLY ARRIVAL PLAN, MORNING, DAY 1

Use FastPass+ at The Seas with Nemo (9:30–10:30am), Turtle Talk with Crush (10:30–11:30am), and Frozen Ever After (1–2pm).

1. Ride Soarin': 9–9:25am.
2. Ride Living with the Land: 9:30–9:45am.
3. Visit characters if desired: 9:50–10:10am.
4. Ride Journey into Imagination with Figment: 10:15–10:30am.
5. Ride The Seas with Nemo and Friends with FastPass+: 10:40–10:55am.
6. See Turtle Talk with Crush with FastPass+ and look around the Seas: 11–11:45am.
7. Have lunch—something in World Showcase makes the most sense: 12–1:15pm
8. Ride Frozen Ever After with FastPass+: 1:30–1:45pm.
9. Book a 4th FastPass+.

TWO-DAY EARLY ARRIVAL PLAN, AFTERNOON AND EVENING, DAY 1

You have a lot of options depending on what you want to do and where you'll have dinner. Consider heading up to World Showcase beginning with the Canada Pavilion. Even though there aren't waits at the attractions in Canada, France, etc., touring the area in low crowds means you'll have an easier time in the shops and fewer people in front of you at the various acts. Consider returning to Future World around 5pm. You'll be exiting World Showcase when crowds peak there and returning to Future World where waits will be short for everything other than Soarin' and Test Track. See Epcot Forever tonight or on your second night.

TWO-DAY EARLY ARRIVAL PLAN, MORNING, DAY 2

Use FastPass+ at Test Track (9:15–10:15am), Spaceship Earth (10:30–11:30am), and a third attraction.

1. Ride Test Track: 8:55–9:20am.
2. Ride Mission: SPACE: 9:25–9:45am.
3. Ride Test Track with FastPass+: 9:50–10:15am.
4. Ride Spaceship Earth with FastPass+: 10:25–10:45am.
5. Experience a third attraction with FastPass+.

TWO-DAY EARLY ARRIVAL PLAN, LATE MORNING AND EVENING, DAY 2

You have some options depending on what you plan to do in World Showcase and whether you're planning to head back to Future World. Consider heading up to World Showcase beginning with the Gran Fiesta Tour in the Mexico Pavilion. You can stay in World Showcase or take the boat in Germany back to Future World around 5pm when crowds thin. Standby waits will be short for anything other than Test Track, which has the single rider line, and Soarin'. See Epcot Forever if you did not see it on Day 1.

One-Day Touring Plan

Use FastPass+ at Spaceship Earth (10–11am), Journey into Imagination (11am–12pm), and Frozen Ever After (whatever is available; ideally earlier in the day).

1. Ride Test Track: 8:55–9:20am.
2. Ride Mission: SPACE Green or Orange: 9:25–9:50am.
3. Visit characters, if desired: 10–10:35am.
4. Ride Spaceship Earth with FastPass+: 10:45–11:10am.
5. Ride Journey into Imagination with Figment with FastPass+: 11:20–11:35am.
6. Tour World Showcase. Start on the Mexico/Norway side if you have an earlier Frozen FastPass+ time. Start with Canada/UK if it's later. Have lunch and check for additional FastPass+ availability after riding Frozen: 11:45am–5:30pm.
7. Ride The Seas with Nemo and Friends: 5:35–5:50pm.
8. See Turtle Talk with Crush or look around The Seas: 5:55–6:30pm.
9. Ride Living with the Land: 6:40–7pm.
10. Ride Soarin' standby unless you have FastPass+: 7–7:45pm.
11. Have dinner at Sunshine Seasons or grab snacks in World Showcase: 7:50–8:30pm.
12. See Epcot Forever: 8:50–9:15pm (The show is sometimes at 9:30pm or 10pm).

Two-Day Late Arrival Touring Plan

Frozen Ever After complicates late arrivals on two days as there are now three high priority attractions that all see long waits and most guests will only be able to initially select two Tier 1 FastPass+ experiences. Try to book Soarin', Test Track, or Frozen as a 4th FastPass+ on both days and you'll have an easier time. Otherwise, ride one at park close to experience short waits.

TWO-DAY LATE ARRIVAL PLAN, DAY 1

Use FastPass+ at Spaceship Earth (10:15–11:15am), Mission: SPACE (11:15am–12:15pm), Frozen Ever After (ideally around 1pm).

1. Arrive between 10:30 and 11am.
2. Ride Spaceship Earth with FastPass+: 11–11:20am.
3. Ride Mission: SPACE with FastPass+: 11:30am–12pm.
4. Ride Gran Fiesta Tour: 12:10–12:25pm.
5. Have lunch. There are lots of options in World Showcase: 12:30–1:15pm.
6. Ride Frozen Ever After with FastPass+: 1:15–1:30pm.
7. Meet Anna and Elsa at Royal Sommerhus if desired: 1:35–2pm.
8. Check FastPass+ availability for a priority attraction with a return time around 8pm.

9. Enjoy World Showcase through the United States or Japan pavilions.

10. Have dinner in World Showcase and walk back to Future World around 8pm.

11. Use the 4th FastPass+ at the attraction of your choice: 8:15–8:425pm.

12. Ride Test Track: 8:55–9:20pm.

TWO-DAY LATE ARRIVAL PLAN, DAY 2

Use FastPass+ at The Seas with Nemo and Friends (10:15–11:15am), Living with the Land (11:45am–12:45pm), and Soarin' (1:15–2:15pm).

1. Arrive between 10:30 and 11am.

2. Ride The Seas with Nemo and Friends with FastPass+: 11–11:15am.

3. See Turtle Talk with Crush and look around The Seas Pavilion: 11:20am–12:20pm.

4. Ride Living with the Land with FastPass+: 12:30–12:50pm.

5. Have lunch at Sunshine Seasons: 12:55–1:40pm.

6. Ride Soarin' with FastPass+: 1:45–2:15pm.

7. Ride Journey into Imagination with Figment and look around the Imagination Pavilion: 2:30–3pm.

8. See Disney Pixar Short Film Festival, if desired: 3:05–3:30pm.

9. Tour World Showcase from Canada to Japan.

10. Enjoy dinner in World Showcase or back in Future World.

11. See Epcot Forever or get in line for Soarin', Test Track, or Frozen at 8:55pm.

EPCOT FOREVER

Epcot Forever is the nightly entertainment at Epcot, scheduled at 9pm most nights. For the best spots, arrive 15–30 minutes before the show starts. The best spots are listed below, but plan a backup spot in case your first choice is booked for a private event or there is little front row space.

BEST SPOTS

1. Base of the World Showcase directly across the lagoon from the United States Pavilion. This "front of house" view is elevated with a direct view of the globe and fireworks. Parts of this area are reserved for FastPass+.

2. The next best spot is the bridge connecting the UK and France. It can't be reserved and those who booked expensive boat cruises for the show will stop below you, enjoying a similar view.

3. The Italy Isola, or raised section across from Italy. Parts can be reserved, but the viewing location behind the seated guests is almost as good.

4. The stretch from Mexico to Norway is good. Areas closer to Norway have fewer people.

5. Other options: There's limited space outside Tokyo Dining on the second level in Japan. Limited viewing is available along Canada into the UK. There are areas to the right of the UK downstairs that are good locations, but they may be reserved for private events.

6. Rose & Crown has patio seating and a reserved platform for those dining inside prior to the show. La Hacienda de San Angel also has indoor viewing, but only some of the tables face the windows. It isn't a great choice if you're looking for a guaranteed view. Consider a meal that begins after 7:45pm.

After Epcot Forever, hang out for 20–45 minutes and let others exit in front of you. With people eating dinner for 90+ minutes after Epcot officially closes, you can enjoy World Showcase's atmosphere and architecture freely during that time.

TYPICAL EPCOT WAIT TIMES IN MINUTES

Low Crowds

	9:30am	10am	11am	12pm	1pm	2pm	3pm	4pm	5pm	6pm	7pm	8pm	9pm
Character Spot	10	20	20	20	20	20	20	20	20	10	10	10	10
Frozen Ever After	15	20	25	35	45	45	45	45	45	45	45	35	30
Gran Fiesta Tour	n/a	n/a	5	5	5	5	5	5	5	5	5	5	5
Journey into Imagination	5	5	5	10	10	5	5	5	5	5	n/a	n/a	n/a
Living with the Land	5	5	5	5	5	5	5	5	5	5	n/a	n/a	n/a
Mission: Space Green	10	10	15	15	15	15	15	15	15	15	20	15	10
Mission: Space Orange	15	15	20	25	20	20	20	20	20	20	25	20	10
Royal Sommerhus Meet	5	10	15	15	10	10	10	10	10	10	10	10	10
Seas with Nemo	5	5	10	10	10	10	10	5	5	5	5	5	10
Soarin'	15	30	40	40	40	40	40	30	30	30	20	20	10
Spaceship Earth	5	10	20	20	15	10	10	10	5	5	5	5	5
Test Track	30	30	50	60	50	40	40	40	40	40	30	20	20

Moderate Crowds

	9:30am	10am	11am	12pm	1pm	2pm	3pm	4pm	5pm	6pm	7pm	8pm	9pm
Character Spot	25	30	35	30	30	30	30	30	20	20	20	15	10
Frozen Ever After	35	45	60	60	60	60	60	60	60	60	60	55	30
Gran Fiesta Tour	n/a	n/a	5	5	5	5	5	5	5	5	5	5	5
Journey into Imagination	5	10	20	30	30	30	30	30	20	10	n/a	n/a	n/a
Living with the Land	5	10	20	30	30	20	20	10	10	10	n/a	n/a	n/a
Mission: Space Green	10	25	35	35	30	30	30	25	25	15	25	25	10
Mission: Space Orange	15	30	40	40	40	35	30	30	25	20	30	30	15
Royal Sommerhus Meet	20	25	20	20	20	20	20	15	15	15	10	10	10
Seas with Nemo	5	10	35	30	20	10	10	10	10	5	5	5	5
Soarin'	30	45	60	60	60	60	60	60	45	45	45	40	20
Spaceship Earth	15	30	30	30	25	25	20	15	10	10	5	5	5
Test Track	45	60	70	80	80	70	60	60	60	60	50	40	30

Heavy Crowds

	9:30am	10am	11am	12pm	1pm	2pm	3pm	4pm	5pm	6pm	7pm	8pm	9pm
Character Spot	25	35	45	45	40	40	40	40	30	30	30	20	10
Frozen Ever After	60	70	80	90	90	90	90	90	90	90	90	75	40
Gran Fiesta Tour	n/a	n/a	10	15	15	15	15	15	15	15	10	10	5
Journey into Imagination	5	10	35	45	45	40	40	35	30	20	n/a	n/a	n/a
Living with the Land	5	15	30	40	40	40	30	30	20	10	n/a	n/a	n/a
Mission: Space Green	10	25	55	65	65	50	50	45	35	35	50	35	15
Mission: Space Orange	15	35	65	80	80	65	65	55	55	45	55	45	20
Royal Sommerhus Meet	20	30	25	25	25	25	25	25	20	15	15	15	10
Seas with Nemo	5	20	45	40	40	25	20	20	15	10	10	5	5
Soarin'	40	60	70	80	80	70	70	70	70	60	50	45	30
Spaceship Earth	15	35	45	45	35	30	25	25	20	15	15	10	5
Test Track	80	90	100	120	120	120	100	100	90	80	70	60	50

Hollywood Studios Cheat Sheet

PARK MAP

TOURING AT DISNEY'S HOLLYWOOD STUDIOS

GENERAL TOURING PHILOSOPHY With Galaxy's Edge now completely operational, Disney has been opening the Studios as early as 6:15am, even with official 8am or 9am opens. Expect the park to open by 6:45am most days moving forward, with the possibility that it will be even earlier on busier days. Disney has moved the official open as early as 6am around Christmas, which means the park will likely open before 5:30am.

Currently, all of the rides that offer a standby line are operating at the actual—not the scheduled—opening. While opening crowds are bigger than we've ever seen, the Studios does a decent job of distributing them around the park upon open, making for short waits at most attractions.

Most guests arriving that early will want to start with Smugglers Run in Galaxy's Edge, then move on to Slinky Dog Dash, Alien Swirling Saucers, and Toy Story Mania in Toy Story Land. After that, it should be about time to experience Rise of the Resistance. Rely on FastPass+ at the Sunset Boulevard thrill rides, by booking Rock 'n' Roller Coaster in advance and Tower of Terror as a fourth FastPass+ option. Use FastPass+ at Star Tours and a show and you've experienced all of the Studios' rides without much trouble. Continue securing additional FastPass+ experiences, while mixing in other attractions, as the day goes on.

STAR WARS: GALAXY'S EDGE Most of Star Wars: Galaxy's Edge opened on August 29, 2019, including the Millennium Falcon: Smugglers Run simulator ride, Oga's Cantina lounge, Docking Bay 7 Food and Cargo quick service, Ronto Roasters meat stall, Milk Stand takeaway bar, Kat Saka's Kettle popcorn stand, Savi's Workshop lightsaber customization experience, Droid Depot assembly experience, and a host of small shops. The second ride, Star Wars: Rise of the Resistance, opened on December 5th, 2019.

Neither Smugglers Run nor Rise of the Resistance currently offers FastPass+, though one or both attractions will likely add the service at some point in the future. Fortunately, Oga's Cantina, Savi's Workshop, and the Droid Depot do offer reservations. This makes touring the new land much easier as it won't be necessary to visit any of these locations early in the day to secure spots. Fewer than 50 people are able to build a lightsaber per hour at Savi's Workshop, and Oga's Cantina has room for fewer than 250 people. Smugglers Run, on the other hand, moves through about 1,500 riders per hour – a much higher capacity. During the first couple months of operation, the average wait for Smugglers Run has been about an hour.

There is currently only one way to experience the Star Wars: Rise of the Resistance attraction, and that is to sign up for a boarding group on the morning of your visit via the My Disney Experience app or with the help of a Guest Experience Team or Guest Services Cast Member. To be eligible to join a boarding group, you must have first scanned your ticket/ MagicBand and entered the park. Only those who have scanned are eligible to join a boarding group, and everyone in a party signing up together must have scanned in to be eligible.

To join a boarding group after you've entered the park, open up the My Disney Experience app and click on the "Join Boarding Group" button on the first screen, which should be illuminated in red. If it's greyed out, it means that boarding groups have either not yet opened for the day, or they have filled to capacity. During the first week of operation, Rise of the Resistance boarding groups filled to capacity before 8am most days, and as early as 7:20am. To guarantee a position, it is imperative that you arrive by 6:30am and immediately join a boarding group. A 5:45am arrival is wise, and even earlier would be better if the official opening is at 6am, as it will be on the busiest days.

Disney will call boarding groups over to experience Rise of the Resistance as space in the queue opens up. The My Disney Experience app keeps track of the current boarding groups that are eligible to ride and screens around the park display the same information.

Typically, around seven boarding groups are called per hour. Once your boarding group has been called, you'll have up to two hours to arrive at the attraction entrance and scan your tickets/MagicBands to redeem your boarding passes. While you wait for your boarding group to be called, you can do whatever else you'd like, including leaving the park to do something else. You won't lose your place in the queue. Once you redeem your boarding passes, the wait to experience Rise of the Resistance is typically 20 to 30 minutes. Budget a full hour to experience the new ride, including pre-shows.

Eventually, both Rise of the Resistance and Smugglers Run will offer FastPass+, and Rise of the Resistance will switch from the virtual queue to the usual standby line. There is no timeline for when that change will occur, but it could be as early as the first week in January, 2020. When that happens, it will likely be just as necessary to arrive at the park two hours early, but instead of signing up for the virtual queue, you'll have to hurry over to ride in standby, or rely on FastPass+.

CHARACTERS The Woody and friends meet in Toy Story Land is the highest priority with a 30+ minute wait that develops almost instantaneously after they appear at park open. Try to visit immediately after riding Slinky Dog Dash in the morning or as late in the evening as possible. Other characters in Toy Story Land see 20 minute waits. Mickey and Minnie meet across from Sci-Fi Dine-In to 25 to 40 minutes waits. Mike and Sulley from Monsters, Inc. inside Walt Disney Presents are the next priority with 30-minute waits almost all day. Visit in the last half hour that they're scheduled to appear, which is usually 6pm. The Star Wars characters in Launch Bay typically see 20- to 30-minute waits. Visit during the heat of the day as it's inside and air-conditioned. Other priorities include the Disney Junior characters like Doc McStuffins and Fancy Nancy outside Disney Junior, and Olaf sees 15 minute waits across from Star Tours.

JEDI TRAINING ACADEMY Kids between the ages of 4 and 12 have the opportunity to participate in this show held next to Star Tours. To sign them up, bring the participating child to the Adventurers Outpost store to the right of 50's Prime Time Café before 10:30am. With Toy Story Land and Galaxy's drawing heavy crowds, few people head to signups first thing, making it easier to head over later in the day. If Jedi Training is an absolute must-do, visit earlier to guarantee spots. There are usually 12 to 15 shows scheduled throughout the day. Ask for a show in the late morning or afternoon so it doesn't interfere with morning touring and double check the weather as rain cancels shows. Kids participating in Jedi Training are required to return to the sign-up location 30 minutes before the show to practice. Those with pre-opening reservations at the Hollywood & Vine character breakfast may be able to sign their kids up before the meal without a wait, which is an added perk.

ROPE DROP Things have changed considerably with Galaxy's Edge now available, and the Studios typically opening between 6:15am and 6:45am, even with a stated 7am or 8am open. While there will be a thousand or more people waiting to enter the park before 6am, once the park begins accepting guests, all of the rides will be operational, and guests are free to head to the attraction of their choice. Arrive by 5:45am to be among the first to enter, or closer to 6:30am if you don't mind a later boarding group. If the Studios is officially opening at 6am, an arrival before 5am will put you in the best possible position to secure a lower-numbered boarding group and take advantage of short waits at the priority attractions.

If you don't care about joining a boarding group for Rise of the Resistance, then an arrival a half hour before the park is scheduled to open should be sufficiently early to enjoy short waits at the attractions without arriving unnecessarily early.

FASTPASS+ AT HOLLYWOOD STUDIOS

FASTPASS+ PRIORITY The opening of Galaxy's Edge was accompanied by substantially changed FastPass+ tiers. Here's the priority:

Tier 1 (choose one)

1. Slinky Dog Dash
2. Rock 'n' Roller Coaster
3. Tower of Terror
4. Toy Story Mania
5. Alien Swirling Saucers

Tier 2 (choose two)

1. Star Tours
2. Frozen Sing-Along
3. Beauty and the Beast Live on Stage
4. Indiana Jones Epic Stunt Spectacular
5. Disney Junior Dance Party
6. Voyage of the Little Mermaid
7. Fantasmic!
8. Muppet*Vision 3D

Guests may initially select only one attraction from Tier 1 in advance. This includes all five of the most popular rides in the park outside of Galaxy's Edge. Compared ot the recent past, the change complicates touring quite a bit, as previously guests were able to book in advance one of the Toy Story Land rides, like Slinky Dog Dash, in addition to both Rock 'n' Roller Coaster and Tower of Terror. Now, only one of these high-priority attractions may be selected.

FOURTH FASTPASS+ SELECTION AVAILABILITY The placement of all the most popular rides except those in Galaxy's Edge in Tier 1 means that day-of FastPass+ availability should be better for priority attractions. For example, at Epcot, the tier system makes it easier to secure Tier 1 attractions as 4th FastPass+ selections because guests may only select one attraction in advance from Tier 1, which includes Frozen Ever After, Soarin', and Test Track. If people were able to select three of these in advance, then there would be far less availability as most people would pick three priority experiences from the available inventory as soon as they're able. With most guests at the Studios selecting one of the first three rides from Tier 1 in advance, there is more availability for Toy Story Mania and Alien Swirling Saucers later in the day.

FASTPASS+ KIOSKS Add or change FastPass+ at the following locations or on your phone:

- Main tip board near the end of Hollywood Boulevard
- To the right of the entrance to Muppet Vision 3D
- Tower of Terror's old FASTPASS machines to the left of the attraction entrance
- Toy Story Land entrance, to the left of the walkway into the land

Touring Plan with 7am or 8am Scheduled Open and an Actual 6:30am Open

Use FastPass+ at Star Tours (8:30–9:30am), Muppet Vision 3D (10–11am), and Rock 'n' Roller Coaster (11am–12pm).

1. Immediately sign up for a Rise of the Resistance Boarding Group after entering the park
2. Ride Millennium Falcon: Smugglers Run: 6:45–7:05am
3. Ride Slinky Dog Dash: 7:15–7:45am
4. Ride Alien Swirling Saucers: 7:50–8:05am
5. Ride Toy Story Mania: 8:10–8:40am
6. Ride Rise of the Resistance with your boarding group: 8:50–9:45am (See "Fitting in Ride of the Resistance," below)
7. Ride Star Tours with FastPass+: 9:50–10:10am
8. See Muppet Vision 3D with FastPass+: 10:15–10:45am
9. Ride Rock 'n' Roller Coaster with FastPass+: 11–11:20am
10. Book Tower of Terror as a fourth FastPass+ via the app, a kiosk, or DisneyWorld.com
11. Have lunch: Sunset Ranch Market is close: 11:30am–12:30pm
12. See Beauty and the Beast Live on Stage or Lightning McQueen's Racing Academy: 12:40–1:30pm
13. Ride Tower of Terror with FastPass+: 1:35–2pm
14. Select a fifth FastPass+ option and blend shows with additional FastPass+ opportunities
15. Explore Galaxy's Edge. Return to Smugglers Run as near to park close as possible, and/or see the evening shows

FITTING IN RISE OF THE RESISTANCE Boarding groups are called when space in the queue is available, with about seven boarding groups called per hour, on average. Groups are called more slowly when the attraction goes down for technical problems. By 9am, about 20 boarding groups are typically called. If your boarding group hasn't yet been called by step 6, simply skip the step and head over to Rise once you're eligible to board later in the day.

You may have the urge to head over to Rise of the Resistance immediately after your boarding group is called, potentially as early as 7am. Because you have two hours to return to the ride after your boarding group is initially called, and with wait times that typically rise as it gets later in the morning, it makes more sense to experience other attractions in standby first, when waits remain short. You can move Rise of the Resistance to earlier in the day, by riding immediately after your boarding group is called, but your waits for the subsequent attractions in Toy Story Land will be longer.

If you don't care about experiencing Rise of the Resistance, eliminate that step and moves the following attractions up an hour in the day.

AFTER RISE OF THE RESISTANCE MOVES TO STANDBY AND ADDS FASTPASS+ We expect most guests to rush to Rise of the Resistance first, and then ride Smugglers Run after. This phenomenon should make it possible to experience both attractions with short waits, provided you arrive early enough and move quickly. We see the same thing happen at Pandora at Animal Kingdom, where it's possible if you arrive early enough to ride Avatar Flight of Passage and Na'vi River Journey back to back with short waits given the fact that everyone rushes to Flight of Passage first. If you are among the first several hundred people at Flight of Passage, Na'vi River Journey will be a walk-on, and we expect something similar to work well with Smugglers Run. After Galaxy's Edge, move on to Toy Story Land.

Late-Arrival Touring with FastPass+

Use FastPass+ at a Toy Story Land attraction and for two of the attractions from Tier 2 that you would like to experience. Most people will want to select Slinky Dog Dash in advance along with Star Tours and a show. Visit the anytime attractions in the afternoon when crowds are heaviest, prioritizing the shows that run on a set schedule. Visit characters in the last 60 to 90 minutes that they're scheduled to appear. End the evening with Fantasmic or the Star Wars Fireworks or visit Smugglers Run, Toy Story Mania, Alien Swirling Saucers, and Slinky Dog Dash (in that order) in the final two hours of park operation when waits are shorter. Disney allows guests to enter the queue of any operating ride, with the exception of Rise of the Resistance, up to a minute before the parks' posted closing time. Slinky Dog may still post a 40+ minute wait at the end of the night, but actual waits are routinely under a half hour. You may also elect to ride Smugglers Run last thing, when actual waits are usually under an hour. It's not currently possible to experience Rise of the Resistance without an early morning arrival to secure a boarding group position.

STAR WARS SHOW

Hollywood Studios is also home to a Star Wars stage show: Star Wars: A Galaxy Far, Far Away (March of the First Order ended its run in summer 2019). A Galaxy Far, Far Away is typically scheduled at 10:30am, 11:30am, 12:30pm, 1:30pm, 3:30pm, 4:30pm, and 5:30pm. The first show may be scheduled at 11:30am, in which case a show will be scheduled at 6:30pm.

The show happens on the stage in front of Grauman's Chinese Theatre. To see it, arrive about 5 minutes before show time and find a spot further back on the far left or right hand sides of the stage. Because of the low height of the stage, it's difficult to see over people's heads from the center. For front row spots, arrive at least 30 minutes early.

EVENING ENTERTAINMENT: FANTASMIC

Hollywood Studios' nighttime spectacular is scheduled at least once almost every night. During extremely busy times, a second show is scheduled 90 minutes after the start of the first. Shows can start as early as 6:30pm or as late as 10pm. If two shows are scheduled, the second will virtually always be less crowded, especially if it begins at 9pm or later, due to the number of families that opt for the earlier show. If you're headed to the first or only Fantasmic!, arrive 60–75 minutes early to secure good seats together or use FP+ and arrive closer to 40 minutes early. For the second show, arrive 20–30 minutes early. Seating is bleacher-style, uncomfortable, and without backs. The best seats are at least half-way up in the middle section. Any closer and you risk getting wet and won't be able to see what's happening on the water. The Fantasmic! Dining Package, a fixed price meal at Hollywood Brown Derby, Hollywood & Vine, or Mama Melrose, guarantees a seat for the show and a three-course meal. A Dessert Package with reserved seating is also available. Reserved seats for both are front and center. Those using either should arrive at least 20 minutes early. FastPass+ has a reserved section next to the Dining Package section. Because the show is so late at night, most guests will want to use their pre-scheduled FastPass+ selections elsewhere and check to see if the show is available as an additional FastPass+ selection later in the day. While Fantasmic FastPass+ may not initially be available, there are thousands of spots available and people consistently cancel. Keep refreshing the app and Fantasmic should show up sooner or later.

EVENING ENTERTAINMENT: STAR WARS FIREWORKS

Star Wars: A Galactic Spectacular, predominantly a projection show on the façade of Grauman's Chinese Theatre with accompanying fireworks, is usually scheduled once per night. Guests wishing to see the fireworks, which are almost exclusively shot off on the right side of the building, will need to arrive at least 35 minutes prior to the start of the show and position themselves in the Center Stage area about half way between the theater and the two tall projection towers near Hollywood Boulevard. There's typically room to fill in this area without much trouble. This is the ideal location for both the fireworks and the Wonderful World of Animation projection show that precedes them.

EVENING ENTERTAINMENT:
WONDERFUL WORLD OF ANIMATION

Similar to the Disney Movie Magic show that preceded it, this 12-minute projection show features scenes from all of Disney and Pixar's animated movies from the last 90 years projected on the Chinese Theater with a few fireworks at the end. The show is typically scheduled 20-30 minutes before the Star Wars fireworks. Those seeing the fireworks should arrive ten minutes before the start of Movie Magic to take in the show and then wait for the fireworks.

EVENING ENTERTAINMENT: JINGLE BELL, JINGLE BAM!

Disney typically offers a holiday-inspired projection show with accompanying fireworks in place of the Star Wars show from the first week in November through the first week in January. In 2019, the show will run from November 8, 2019 to January 5, 2020. The advice on seeing the show is the same as for Star Wars.

SEEING BOTH NIGHTTIME SHOWS ON THE SAME NIGHT

With the way the two nighttime shows are usually scheduled, it will be difficult or impossible to see both if only one Fantasmic is scheduled. Disney typically schedules the Star Wars Fireworks/Jingle Bell show 15 or 30 minutes after the first Fantasmic. If it's 15 minutes, that makes it impossible to see both. If it's 30 minutes, you'll have to quickly exit Fantasmic and try to find spots as close to the recommended viewing area as possible. With two Fantasmic shows, see the other show first followed by the second Fantasmic.

TYPICAL HOLLYWOOD STUDIOS WAIT TIMES IN MINUTES

Wait Times in Minutes															
Low Crowds	6:30am	7am	8am	9am	10am	11am	12pm	1pm	2pm	3pm	4pm	5pm	6pm	7pm	8pm	9pm
Alien Swirling Saucers	5	5	10	20	30	30	30	30	30	30	30	30	30	25	20	10
Muppet Vision 3D	N/A	N/A	N/A	N/A	5	5	5	5	5	5	5	5	5	5	5	5
Rock 'n' Roller Coaster	5	10	15	30	40	50	60	60	60	60	60	60	50	40	20	20
Slinky Dog Dash	5	15	45	60	60	75	75	75	75	75	75	75	75	60	50	40
Smugglers Run	5	10	15	45	60	60	60	50	50	50	50	50	40	40	30	30
Star Tours	5	5	5	5	10	20	20	20	20	20	20	20	10	10	10	5
Tower of Terror	5	10	20	25	30	40	40	40	40	40	40	40	30	30	20	10
Toy Story Mania	5	15	25	30	40	45	45	45	45	45	45	45	45	30	15	10
Voyage of the Mermaid	10	10	10	10	10	10	10	10	10	10	10	10	10	10	10	10

Moderate Crowds	6:30am	7am	8am	9am	10am	11am	12pm	1pm	2pm	3pm	4pm	5pm	6pm	7pm	8pm	9pm
Alien Swirling Saucers	5	5	15	20	35	40	40	40	40	40	40	40	40	35	30	15
Muppet Vision 3D	N/A	N/A	N/A	5	5	5	5	5	5	5	5	5	5	5	5	5
Rock 'n' Roller Coaster	5	10	15	40	50	60	70	70	70	70	70	70	70	70	60	40
Slinky Dog Dash	5	15	60	75	75	85	85	85	85	85	85	85	85	75	60	40
Smugglers Run	5	10	25	60	75	75	75	60	60	50	50	50	50	40	40	30
Star Tours	5	5	5	10	20	30	30	30	40	40	40	30	30	20	20	10
Tower of Terror	5	10	25	50	60	60	60	60	60	60	60	60	50	40	30	20
Toy Story Mania	5	15	30	40	50	50	60	60	60	60	60	60	60	50	40	30
Voyage of the Mermaid	10	10	10	10	10	10	10	10	10	10	10	10	10	10	10	10

Heavy Crowds	6:30am	7am	8am	9am	10am	11am	12pm	1pm	2pm	3pm	4pm	5pm	6pm	7pm	8pm	9pm
Alien Swirling Saucers	5	5	15	25	40	50	50	50	50	50	50	50	45	35	30	20
Muppet Vision 3D	N/A	N/A	N/A	5	5	5	5	5	5	5	5	5	5	5	5	5
Rock 'n' Roller Coaster	5	15	25	70	80	90	100	100	100	100	100	90	90	80	70	50
Slinky Dog Dash	5	20	75	90	100	100	100	100	100	100	85	85	75	75	60	50
Smugglers Run	5	15	30	75	90	90	90	90	90	90	90	75	60	50	45	30
Star Tours	5	5	5	20	40	50	50	50	50	50	50	40	30	30	15	10
Tower of Terror	5	10	35	50	75	90	100	100	100	100	100	90	80	70	60	30
Toy Story Mania	5	15	35	45	60	75	75	75	75	70	60	60	60	60	40	30
Voyage of the Mermaid	10	10	10	10	10	10	10	10	10	10	10	10	10	10	10	10

Magic Kingdom Cheat Sheet

PARK MAP

TOURING AT MAGIC KINGDOM

GENERAL TOURING PHILOSOPHY With 60+ attractions, Magic Kingdom is best toured over two or more days. The best plans compartmentalize the park by visiting two or three lands each day. Visit the character and attraction priorities in one land before moving on to the next. Have lunch and then head back to the same Lands visiting the "anytime attractions". This minimizes both waiting and walking. One-day touring will require more walking. You can still accomplish a lot in a day by touring intelligently, but some attractions will need to be skipped.

CHARACTERS Home to about 40 characters at any given time, the princesses are typically high priorities, whether it means meeting them early in the morning or with FastPass+ to avoid long waits. Check the My

Disney Experience app or disneyworld.disney.go.com/entertainment/
magic-kingdom for character meeting times and locations.

ROPE DROP With a 9am open, Disney lets guests enter the park around
7:45am. Most of Main Street is open, including Guest Relations, stroller/
ECV rental, most stores, and Starbucks. Guests are held in the hub area
in front of Cinderella Castle with ropes blocking access to the other
lands. At 8:55am, a 4-minute opening show featuring Mickey Mouse
welcomes guests and then the ropes are dropped and guests are free to
visit the attraction of their choice. For Seven Dwarfs Mine Train, arrive
no later than 8:15am and position yourself on the walkway to the right
of Cinderella Castle heading toward Mad Tea Party. Get as close to the
rope as possible. For Peter Pan's Flight or Princess Fairytale Hall, position
yourself in front of the castle at the rope leading up through the castle.
For other attractions, there is much less of a rush and you can enjoy the
Welcome Show front and center in the hub. On morning Extra Magic Hour
days, the Welcome Show still starts five minutes before regular park open.

FASTPASS+ AT MAGIC KINGDOM

FASTPASS+ PRIORITY There are far more FastPass+ opportunities at
Magic Kingdom than any of the other theme parks, making the decision
on which to pick difficult. Consider picking three high priority attractions
in a Land that you don't plan to visit until the afternoon or evening. For
example, if you plan to start your day with Jungle Cruise, Pirates of the
Caribbean, Big Thunder Mountain, and Splash Mountain, then you may
want to use FastPass+ in the afternoon in Fantasyland at Peter Pan's Flight,
Enchanted Tales with Belle, and the Mine Train, or in Tomorrowland at
Space Mountain, Tomorrowland Speedway, and Buzz Lightyear.

1. Seven Dwarfs Mine Train
2. Peter Pan's Flight
3. Space Mountain
4. Splash Mountain (when high temperatures are 80+ degrees)
5. Meet Mickey at Town Square Theater
6. Big Thunder Mountain Railroad
7. Meet Cinderella and a Visiting Princess
8. Meet Rapunzel and a Visiting Princess
9. Enchanted Tales with Belle
10. Meet Ariel at Ariel's Grotto
11. Buzz Lightyear's Space Ranger Spin
12. Tomorrowland Speedway
13. Jungle Cruise
14. Haunted Mansion
15. Pirates of the Caribbean
16. Splash Mountain (when high temps are less than 80 degrees)

17. Meet Tinker Bell at Town Square Theater
18. "it's a small world"
19. Barnstormer
20. Dumbo the Flying Elephant
21. The Many Adventures of Winnie the Pooh
22. Magic Carpets of Aladdin
23. Under the Sea ~ Journey of the Little Mermaid
24. Mad Tea Party
25. Monsters Inc. Laugh Floor
26. Mickey's PhilharMagic

FOURTH FASTPASS+ SELECTION AVAILABILITY Unlike the other parks, Magic Kingdom has plenty of FP+ enabled attractions and 10 or more will still have availability even around 2pm. Schedule a high priority attraction with limited availability for after a break or schedule several lower priority experiences back-to-back if you plan to stay in the park. Continue refreshing the app checking for other people's canceled FastPass+ selections as they will become available for anyone else to book.

FASTPASS+ KIOSKS Add or change FastPass+ at the following locations or on your phone:

- *Adventureland*—Jungle Cruise's old FASTPASS machines to the left of the entrance
- *Adventureland*—Breezeway to the right of Diamond Horseshoe across from Swiss Treehouse
- *Fantasyland*—To the right of Mickey's PhilharMagic
- *Tomorrowland*—To the left of Stitch's Great Escape's old entrance

Two-Day Touring Plan

TWO-DAY PLAN, MORNING, DAY 1

Use FastPass+ at Many Adventures of Winnie the Pooh (9:30–10:30am), Seven Dwarfs Mine Train (11:15am–12:15pm), and Enchanted Tales with Belle (12:30–1:30pm).

1. Ride Space Mountain: 9–9:20am.
2. Ride Buzz Lightyear's Space Ranger Spin: 9:25–9:40am.
3. Ride Tomorrowland Speedway (if desired): 9:45–10am.
4. Ride The Many Adventures of Winnie the Pooh with FastPass+: 10:05–10:15am.
5. Ride Barnstormer: 10:20–10:40am.
6. Ride Dumbo: 10:42–11:05am.
7. Ride Journey of the Little Mermaid: 11:10–11:30am.
8. Ride Seven Dwarfs Mine Train with FastPass+: 11:35–11:50am.

9. Have lunch. Be Our Guest and Pinocchio Village Haus are closest: 12–12:45pm.

10. Visit Enchanted Tales with Belle with FastPass+: 12:50–1:30pm.

11. Select a nearby 4th FastPass+ via the phone app or the kiosk near Mickey's PhilharMagic.

12. Visit Mickey's PhilharMagic or Prince Charming's Regal Carrousel, and select a 4th FastPass+: 1:35–2:35pm.

13. Find spots for Festival of Fantasy and watch parade: 2:40–3:15pm.

14. Use additional FastPass+, shop, grab snacks, or look around.

TWO-DAY PLAN, AFTERNOON AND EVENING, DAY 1

Consider an afternoon break or visit the anytime attractions in Fantasyland and Tomorrowland like Mickey's PhilharMagic, Prince Charming's Regal Carrousel, Monsters Inc. Laugh Floor, Tomorrowland PeopleMover, and Carousel of Progress. Blend these with additional FastPass+ selections as they become available. Visit priority attractions in the two hours prior to park close when wait times are shorter than the afternoon, ending with a re-visit to a high priority ride like Seven Dwarfs Mine Train or Peter Pan's Flight right before close. See the evening entertainment tonight or the night of Day 2.

TWO-DAY PLAN, MORNING, DAY 2

Use FastPass+ at Peter Pan's Flight (10–11am), Jungle Cruise (11am–12pm), and Pirates of the Caribbean (12–1pm).

1. Ride Big Thunder Mountain Railroad: 9–9:15am.

2. Ride Splash Mountain: 9:18–9:45am.

3. Ride Haunted Mansion: 9:55–10:20am.

4. Ride "it's a small world": 10:22–10:45am.

5. Ride Peter Pan's Flight with FastPass+: 10:48–11am.

6. Ride Jungle Cruise with FastPass+: 11:10–11:30am.

7. Have lunch. Tortuga Tavern, Pecos Bill, and Skipper Canteen are closest. Columbia Harbour House, Liberty Tree Tavern, and Casey's Corner are relatively close. 11:30am–12:30pm.

8. Ride Pirates of the Caribbean with FastPass+: 12:30–12:50pm.

9. Check app or Jungle Cruise kiosk for more FastPass+ selections.

TWO-DAY PLAN, AFTERNOON AND EVENING DAY 2

Consider an afternoon break or visit the anytime attractions like Tom Sawyer Island, Hall of Presidents, Liberty Square Riverboat, Country Bear Jamboree, Enchanted Tiki Room, and Swiss Family Treehouse. Schedule nearby FastPass+ experiences as they become available. See the evening entertainment if you did not see it on Day 1.

Character-Centric Two Day Touring Plan

TWO-DAY CHARACTER-CENTRIC PLAN, MORNING, DAY 1

Use FastPass+ at Seven Dwarfs Mine Train (11:15am–12:15pm) Enchanted Tales with Belle (1–2pm), and Rapunzel at Fairytale Hall (2–3pm).

1. Ride Peter Pan's Flight: 9–9:15am.
2. Ride The Many Adventures of Winnie the Pooh: 9:20–9:30am.
3. Meet Ariel at Ariel's Grotto: 9:35–9:50am.
4. Meet Gaston outside Gaston's Tavern in New Fantasyland: 9:55–10:10am.
5. Meet Daisy and Minnie at Pete's Silly Sideshow: 10:15–10:30am.
6. Meet Donald and Goofy at Pete's Silly Sideshow: 10:31–10:45am.
7. Ride Barnstormer: 10:47–11am.
8. Ride Dumbo the Flying Elephant: 11:03–11:30am.
9. Ride Journey of the Little Mermaid: 11:35am–12pm.
10. Ride Seven Dwarfs Mine Train with FastPass+: 12:05–12:20pm.
11. Have lunch. Be Our Guest Restaurant and Pinocchio Village Haus are closest. Cosmic Ray's is nearby: 12:30–1:20pm.
12. Visit Enchanted Tales with Belle with FastPass+: 1:25–2pm.
13. Meet Rapunzel at Princess Fairytale Hall with FastPass+: 2:05–2:20pm.
14. Check the app or Mickey's PhilharMagic FastPass+ kiosk for a 4th FastPass+.

TWO-DAY CHARACTER-CENTRIC PLAN, AFTERNOON/EVENING, DAY 1

Consider a lengthy afternoon break in preparation of returning for dinner, some late night rides when waits drop, and the nighttime shows. Alternatively, continue scheduling available FastPass+ experiences and work in anytime attractions while waiting for the return windows to open.

TWO-DAY CHARACTER-CENTRIC PLAN, MORNING, DAY 2

Use FastPass+ for Cinderella at Fairytale Hall (10:30–11:30am), Jungle Cruise (1–2pm), and Pirates of the Caribbean (2–3pm).

1. Meet Mickey Mouse: 9–9:10am.
2. Meet Tinker Bell: 9:12–9:20am.
3. Ride Tomorrowland Speedway: 9:30–9:50am.
4. Ride Buzz Lightyear's Space Ranger Spin: 9:55–10:15am.
5. Meet Stitch: 10:25–10:40am.
6. Meet Cinderella at Princess Fairytale Hall with FastPass+ and grab snacks: 10:50–11:15am.
7. See Move It! Shake It! Parade in front of the castle: 11:20–11:55am.
8. See Mickey's Royal Friendship Faire show in front of the Castle: 12–12:30pm.

9. Have lunch. Be Our Guest, Pinocchio Village Haus, Columbia Harbour House are close: 12:35–1:30pm.

10. Ride Jungle Cruise with FastPass+: 1:40–2pm.

11. Ride Pirates of the Caribbean with FastPass+: 2:05 –2:30pm

12. Book a 4th FastPass+ via the app or the kiosk next to Jungle Cruise. Haunted Mansion or it's a small world would be best

13. See Festival of Fantasy Parade in Frontierland or Liberty Square: 2:40–3:20pm

14. Meet Merida, Aladdin/Jasmine, or other skipped characters.

TWO-DAY CHARACTER-CENTRIC PLAN, AFTERNOON/EVENING, DAY 2

Consider an afternoon break or visit the anytime attractions like Tom Sawyer Island, Hall of Presidents, Liberty Square Riverboat, Country Bear Jamboree, Enchanted Tiki Room, and Swiss Family Treehouse. Visit it's a small world, Haunted Mansion, Big Thunder Mountain, Splash Mountain and any other skipped attractions late in the evening or with FP+. Check your Times Guide or app for missed characters and visit them in the last hour they're scheduled to appear. See the evening entertainment if you did not see it on Day One.

One-Day Touring Plan, 9am Open

ONE-DAY PLAN, 9AM OPEN, MORNING AND AFTERNOON

Use FastPass+ at Seven Dwarfs Mine Train (11am–12pm), Big Thunder Mountain (12:15–1:15pm), and Splash Mountain (1:15–2:15pm).

1. Ride Peter Pan's Flight: 9–9:10am.

2. Ride The Many Adventures of Winnie the Pooh: 9:15–9:25am.

3. Ride Space Mountain: 9:35–10am.

4. Ride Buzz Lightyear's Space Ranger Spin: 10:05–10:25am.

5. Ride The Barnstormer: 10:35–11am.

6. Ride Under the Sea ~ Journey of the Little Mermaid: 11:05–11:30am.

7. Ride Seven Dwarfs Mine Train with FastPass+: 11:35–11:55am.

8. Have lunch. Be Our Guest and Pinocchio Village Haus are close: 12–12:45pm.

9. Ride Big Thunder Mountain with FastPass+: 1–1:20pm.

10. Ride Splash Mountain with FastPass+: 1:22-2pm.

ONE-DAY PLAN, 9AM OPEN, AFTERNOON AND EVENING

Continually check the phone app for FastPass+ availability for the best Jungle Cruise, Haunted Mansion, Pirates of the Caribbean, and "it's a small world" return times throughout the day, in addition to whatever other FastPass+ enabled attractions that you would like to experience. Mix in nearby anytime attractions in between FastPass+ windows, and see the evening entertainment if scheduled for your visit.

One-Day Touring Plan, 8am Open

ONE-DAY PLAN, 8AM OPEN, MORNING AND AFTERNOON

Use FastPass+ at Splash Mountain (10:15–11:15am), Big Thunder (11:15am–12:15pm), Peter Pan's Flight (12:30–1:30pm).

1. Ride Seven Dwarfs Mine Train: 8–8:20am
2. Ride The Many Adventures of Winnie the Pooh: 8:22–8:35am
3. Ride Space Mountain: 8:40–9am
4. Ride Buzz Lightyear's Space Ranger Spin: 9:05–9:20am
5. Ride Astro Orbiter or Tomorrowland Speedway: 9:25–9:45am
6. Ride Jungle Cruise: 9:55–10:15am
7. Ride Pirates of the Caribbean: 10:20–10:50am
8. Ride Splash Mountain with FastPass+: 10:55–11:15am
9. Ride Big Thunder Mountain with FastPass+: 11:17–11:35am
10. Have lunch: Pecos Bill and Columbia Harbour House are close: 11:45–12:45pm
11. Ride Peter Pan's Flight with FastPass+ 12:50–1:05pm.

ONE-DAY PLAN, 8AM OPEN, AFTERNOON AND EVENING

Continually check the phone app for FastPass+ availability for the best Jungle Cruise, Haunted Mansion, Pirates of the Caribbean, and "it's a small world" return times throughout the day, in addition to whatever other FastPass+ enabled attractions that you would like to experience. Mix in nearby anytime attractions in between FastPass+ windows, and see the evening entertainment if scheduled for your visit.

Late Arrival

Crowds only diminish most nights as families with small children leave early. The later it gets, the lower wait times will be, particularly if close is 11pm or later. Use FastPass+ when you arrive when wait times are longest. Visit the anytime attractions colored light gray on the map until two to three hours before close. Then move on to the medium gray attractions like Buzz Lightyear and Big Thunder Mountain and finish the night with the highest priority attractions like Peter Pan's Flight, Seven Dwarfs Mine Train, and Space Mountain.

PARADES, SHOWS, EVENING ENTERTAINMENT, AND EXIT

FESTIVAL OF FANTASY PARADE is usually scheduled at 3pm and runs from Frontierland to the left of Splash Mountain, through Liberty Square, and then through Main Street, exiting in between the firehouse and the Emporium. The best/lowest wait viewing locations are from Frontierland in the Pecos Bill area through Liberty Square in front of Hall of Presidents. For Main Street viewing, see the show in front of the Confectionery or Town Square Theater where crowds are thinner. The parade may be scheduled at

2pm during the fall months. If that happens, modify the touring plans above by finding spots for Festival of Fantasy one hour earlier and move the attractions visited between 2pm and 3pm to between 3pm and 4pm.

MOVE IT, SHAKE IT, MOUSEKEDANCE IT STREET PARTY is usually scheduled two times daily and runs from Main Street in between the firehouse and Emporium up to Cinderella Castle, where it stops for about 20 minutes, before returning the same way that it came. Arriving more than five minutes before it steps off is not necessary. Meet the parade on Main Street and follow it to Cinderella Castle or wait at the castle for it to arrive.

MICKEY'S ROYAL FRIENDSHIP FARE is usually scheduled five times per day at the stage in front of Cinderella Castle. Try to arrive ten to fifteen minutes before one of the shows. Earlier shows are typically less crowded. Consider watching from the very back of the area near the statue of Walt and Mickey as it's elevated and thus it is easier to see over the heads of people standing closer to the stage.

HAPPILY EVER AFTER This fireworks and projection show replaced Wishes in May 2017. Fortunately, it actually increases the amount of pyro, in addition to adding impactful projections on Cinderella Castle. The best place to see it is between Casey's Corner on Main Street and the Partners statue in the center of the Hub. Arrive 30-45 minutes before the show begins.

ONCE UPON A TIME A projection show visible on the front of Cinderella Castle, Once Upon a Time usually begins 45 minutes after the fireworks. See it either from the same spot as the fireworks or a little closer to the castle for the best views.

LAST-MINUTE RIDES AND EXIT Consider getting in line for Seven Dwarfs Mine Train, Peter Pan's Flight, or another attraction with a few minutes until close. Disney will let you ride any operating attraction as long as you get in line at least a minute before close, even if the posted wait is long. Main Street stores will remain open for about an hour after park close. Linger a bit while others exit in front of you. The express monorail is the fastest way to the Transportation and Ticket Center (parking lot) unless the line is significantly backed up. The ferry is often a more comfortable ride with more room to spread out, particularly up the stairs on the second level.

TYPICAL MAGIC KINGDOM WAIT TIMES IN MINUTES

Low Crowds, 8pm Close

	9:30am	10am	11am	12pm	1pm	2pm	3pm	4pm	5pm	6pm	7pm	8pm
Ariel's Grotto	10	15	30	30	30	30	30	30	30	20	15	10
Astro Orbiter	10	15	20	30	30	30	30	20	20	20	15	10
Barnstormer	5	5	10	20	20	20	15	15	15	10	10	5
Big Thunder Mountain	10	20	30	35	45	40	40	40	30	20	20	10
Buzz Lightyear Spin	5	15	30	30	40	40	30	30	25	20	15	10
Dumbo	10	15	15	20	20	20	20	20	20	15	10	5
Enchanted Tales w/ Belle	15	20	30	40	30	30	30	30	30	20	20	10
Haunted Mansion	10	20	30	35	40	30	30	30	25	20	10	5
it's a small world	5	10	15	20	25	25	20	20	20	15	10	5
Jungle Cruise	10	30	40	40	50	40	40	30	30	30	20	10
Mad Tea Party	5	5	5	10	10	10	10	10	5	5	5	5
Magic Carpets of Aladdin	5	10	15	20	20	20	20	20	15	15	10	5
Many Adventures of Pooh	10	20	30	40	40	30	30	30	20	20	10	5
Monster's Inc Laugh Floor	10	10	10	10	10	10	10	10	10	10	10	10
Peter Pan's Flight	60	60	70	70	70	70	60	60	60	45	30	20
Pirates of the Caribbean	5	10	20	30	35	30	30	30	20	15	10	5
Prince Regal Carrousel	5	5	5	5	5	5	5	5	5	5	5	5
Princess Fairytale Cinderella	20	30	40	50	50	40	30	30	30	30	20	10
Princess Fairytale Rapunzel	20	30	40	50	50	40	30	30	30	30	20	10
Seven Dwarfs Mine Train	60	60	70	80	80	80	70	60	60	50	50	40
Space Mountain	10	20	30	40	50	50	40	40	35	25	15	10
Splash Mountain (Hot)	10	30	40	50	50	40	35	30	30	25	20	10
Splash Mountain (Cold)	5	5	10	15	20	20	20	15	10	10	5	5
Stitch's Great Escape	5	5	5	5	5	5	5	5	5	5	5	5
Swiss Family Treehouse	0	0	0	0	0	0	0	0	0	0	0	0
Tomorrowland Speedway	10	20	20	30	30	30	20	20	20	20	10	10
Tomorrowland PeopleMover	0	0	0	0	0	0	0	0	0	0	0	0
Town Square Mickey	20	30	50	40	30	30	15	30	30	20	10	10
Under the Sea ~ Little Mermaid	10	15	20	20	20	20	15	10	10	10	10	10

Moderate Crowds, 11pm Close

	9:30am	10am	11am	12pm	1pm	2pm	3pm	4pm	5pm	6pm	7pm	8pm	9pm	10pm	11pm
Ariel's Grotto	15	20	35	50	45	45	40	40	40	40	30	20	20	15	10
Astro Orbiter	10	20	20	30	40	30	30	30	30	20	20	20	20	15	10
Barnstormer	5	10	20	20	30	20	20	20	20	20	15	15	15	10	5
Big Thunder Mountain	10	20	40	50	60	60	40	40	40	40	35	30	20	15	10
Buzz Lightyear Spin	5	25	40	45	50	50	40	40	40	30	30	20	20	15	10
Dumbo	10	15	25	30	40	30	30	30	25	20	15	15	15	10	5
Enchanted Tales w/ Belle	20	30	40	40	40	40	40	40	40	30	30	30	20	20	10
Haunted Mansion	10	20	30	40	50	45	40	40	40	30	25	20	15	10	10
it's a small world	10	15	20	30	30	35	30	30	30	20	15	10	10	10	10
Jungle Cruise	10	20	35	45	50	50	40	40	40	40	35	30	25	20	10
Mad Tea Party	5	5	10	15	15	15	15	15	10	10	10	10	5	5	5
Magic Carpets of Aladdin	5	10	20	30	30	30	20	20	20	15	20	10	10	5	5
Many Adventures of Pooh	20	35	45	50	50	40	40	40	30	30	20	20	15	10	5
Monster's Inc Laugh Floor	10	10	10	20	20	20	20	10	10	10	10	10	10	10	10
Peter Pan's Flight	60	60	70	80	90	90	80	70	70	70	60	60	50	40	20
Pirates of the Caribbean	5	15	30	40	45	40	40	30	30	30	20	20	15	5	5
Prince Regal Carrousel	5	5	5	5	5	5	5	5	5	5	5	5	5	5	5
Princess Fairytale Cinderella	20	30	40	50	50	50	30	40	40	40	30	30	20	20	10
Princess Fairytale Rapunzel	20	30	40	50	50	50	30	40	40	40	30	30	20	20	10
Seven Dwarfs Mine Train	60	70	80	90	80	80	80	70	70	60	60	60	50	50	30
Space Mountain	10	35	50	60	70	80	60	60	60	50	45	40	30	20	10
Splash Mountain (Hot)	15	30	60	70	70	60	60	60	60	60	50	40	30	15	10
Splash Mountain (Cold)	5	10	20	25	25	20	20	20	20	20	15	15	10	5	5
Stitch's Great Escape	5	5	5	5	5	5	5	5	5	5	5	5	5	5	5
Swiss Family Treehouse	0	0	0	0	0	0	0	0	0	0	0	0	0	0	0
Tomorrowland Speedway	10	20	25	40	40	30	30	30	30	30	20	20	15	10	10
Tomorrowland PeopleMover	0	0	0	5	5	5	5	5	5	5	5	0	0	0	0
Town Square Mickey	20	40	50	60	50	50	25	40	40	30	20	20	20	15	10
Under the Sea ~ Little Mermaid	10	15	20	30	30	30	30	20	20	20	20	10	10	10	5

TYPICAL MAGIC KINGDOM WAIT TIMES IN MINUTES

Heavy Crowds, Midnight Close

	9:30am	10am	11am	12pm	1pm	2pm	3pm	4pm	5pm	6pm	7pm	8pm	9pm	10pm	11pm	12am
Ariel's Grotto	15	20	50	60	60	60	50	50	50	40	35	25	20	15	10	5
Astro Orbiter	15	20	40	50	50	50	40	30	30	30	30	25	20	15	10	10
Barnstormer	5	10	25	30	40	35	35	30	30	30	20	20	10	5	5	5
Big Thunder Mountain	25	35	50	60	70	70	70	70	60	60	50	40	30	25	20	10
Buzz Lightyear Spin	10	15	50	60	60	60	60	60	50	50	40	30	25	15	10	10
Dumbo	15	20	30	40	50	60	50	50	50	45	30	25	15	10	5	5
Enchanted Tales w/ Belle	25	30	40	50	40	40	40	40	40	30	30	30	15	15	10	5
Haunted Mansion	15	25	50	60	60	60	50	50	45	40	30	20	10	10	5	5
it's a small world	15	20	30	40	40	40	40	30	30	30	30	25	20	15	10	5
Jungle Cruise	25	40	60	75	75	75	60	60	60	60	45	40	30	20	15	10
Mad Tea Party	5	5	10	30	30	30	20	20	20	20	15	10	10	5	5	5
Magic Carpets of Aladdin	10	15	20	30	30	30	25	25	25	25	20	20	15	10	5	5
Many Adventures of Pooh	45	60	60	60	60	50	45	40	40	40	40	40	25	20	15	10
Monster's Inc Laugh Floor	10	10	20	30	30	20	20	20	20	20	20	10	10	10	10	10
Peter Pan's Flight	65	75	80	90	100	100	90	90	80	80	80	70	60	50	35	25
Pirates of the Caribbean	10	15	45	60	70	60	60	50	50	40	40	30	20	15	15	10
Prince Regal Carrousel	5	5	10	10	10	10	10	10	10	10	10	5	5	5	5	5
Princess Fairytale Cinderella	30	40	60	60	70	60	40	60	60	50	40	30	20	20	20	10
Princess Fairytale Rapunzel	30	40	60	60	70	60	40	60	60	50	40	30	20	20	20	10
Seven Dwarfs Mine Train	80	90	100	120	120	120	120	120	120	100	90	90	70	70	60	40
Space Mountain	50	60	90	120	120	120	90	90	90	80	80	70	70	60	40	20
Splash Mountain (Hot)	45	60	80	100	100	100	90	90	80	80	70	60	40	30	20	15
Splash Mountain (Cold)	10	15	25	30	30	30	30	30	30	30	25	10	10	5	5	5
Stitch's Great Escape	5	10	10	20	20	20	20	20	20	20	10	10	10	5	5	5
Swiss Family Treehouse	0	0	0	5	5	5	5	5	0	0	0	0	0	0	0	0
Tomorrowland Speedway	25	30	30	40	50	40	40	30	30	30	30	25	20	15	10	5
Tomorrowland PeopleMover	0	0	5	5	5	5	5	5	5	5	5	5	5	0	0	0
Town Square Mickey	25	30	30	40	50	50	30	45	40	30	30	25	20	20	20	10
Under the Sea ~ Little Mermaid	20	20	30	30	40	40	40	40	30	30	30	20	20	10	10	10

Party Night, 7pm Close

	9:30am	10am	11am	12pm	1pm	2pm	3pm	4pm	5pm	6pm	7pm
Ariel's Grotto	10	15	30	30	30	30	30	30	30	20	10
Astro Orbiter	10	15	20	30	30	30	30	20	20	20	15
Barnstormer	5	5	10	20	20	20	15	15	15	10	10
Big Thunder Mountain	10	20	30	35	45	40	40	40	30	20	15
Buzz Lightyear Spin	5	15	30	30	40	40	30	30	25	20	10
Dumbo	10	15	15	20	20	20	20	20	20	15	10
Enchanted Tales w/ Belle	15	20	30	40	30	30	30	30	30	20	10
Haunted Mansion	10	20	30	35	40	30	30	30	25	20	10
it's a small world	5	10	15	20	25	25	20	20	20	15	10
Jungle Cruise	10	30	40	40	50	40	40	30	30	30	20
Mad Tea Party	5	5	5	10	10	10	10	10	5	5	5
Magic Carpets of Aladdin	5	10	15	20	20	20	20	20	15	15	10
Many Adventures of Pooh	10	20	30	40	40	30	30	30	20	20	10
Monster's Inc Laugh Floor	10	10	10	10	10	10	10	10	10	10	10
Peter Pan's Flight	60	60	70	70	70	70	60	60	60	45	30
Pirates of the Caribbean	5	10	20	30	35	30	30	30	20	15	10
Prince Regal Carrousel	5	5	5	5	5	5	5	5	5	5	5
Princess Fairytale Cinderella	20	30	40	50	50	40	30	30	30	20	20
Princess Fairytale Rapunzel	20	30	40	50	50	40	30	30	30	20	20
Seven Dwarfs Mine Train	60	60	70	80	80	80	70	60	60	50	50
Space Mountain	10	20	30	40	50	50	40	40	35	25	10
Splash Mountain (Hot)	10	30	40	50	50	40	35	30	30	25	10
Splash Mountain (Cold)	5	5	10	15	20	20	20	15	10	10	5
Stitch's Great Escape	5	5	5	5	5	5	5	5	5	5	5
Swiss Family Treehouse	0	0	0	0	0	0	0	0	0	0	0
Tomorrowland Speedway	10	20	20	30	30	30	20	20	20	20	10
Tomorrowland PeopleMover	0	0	0	0	0	0	0	0	0	0	0
Town Square Mickey	20	30	50	40	30	30	15	30	30	20	10
Under the Sea ~ Little Mermaid	10	15	20	20	20	20	15	10	10	10	10

CHAPTER SEVEN

Where to Eat

There are three keys to successfully navigating Walt Disney World dining:

- Several dining venues are among the most memorable and delightful experiences Walt Disney Word has to offer. Options range from dining in the banquet hall inside Cinderella Castle with the Disney Princesses to sharing sushi and filet mignon on the 15th floor of the Contemporary to joining Mickey and the Gang for lunch in an exotic African marketplace.

- Table service reservations open 180 days in advance, and availability at the most sought-after restaurants is gobbled up almost immediately. A list of the hardest restaurants to reserve follows later.

- Disney World dining is expensive. Expect to pay 25–40% more on-property than you would for comparable meals off-property, whether we're talking about a fast food hamburger at Cosmic Ray's or a 28-ounce Porterhouse at Yachtsman Steakhouse. In effect, most of the upcharge is a convenience fee, but the Disney restaurants offer a reliably consistent experience, many times in unique settings.

The rest of this chapter:

- Offers suggestions on where to eat
- Explains how to reserve meals at Disney World—and why starting to do so 180 days before your visit is crucial
- Introduces and compares the various Disney Dining Plans
- Shares some thoughts on saving money

The chapter ends with overviews of dining at the parks and brief reviews of all the Disney World table service dining options.

Where to Eat at Walt Disney World

Service, food quality, and atmosphere vary immensely among the Disney World restaurants, even those inside the same park with similar price points. The information and reviews that follow will help identify restaurants that are the perfect fit for your group's budget and preferences. Disney World dining locations come in several shapes and sizes:

QUICK OR COUNTER SERVICE Basically a fancy name for fast food, quick service locations don't typically accept reservations and food is usually ordered at a register and then available for pickup several minutes later. Be Our Guest is one exception. It accepts and usually requires a reservation for quick service breakfast and lunch. ABC Commissary at Disney's Hollywood Studios also takes reservations for a fast-casual dinner that begins at 4pm. Pizzafari, typically a fast food pizza joint at Disney's Animal Kingdom, offers reservations for a family-style meal for dinner. Restaurantosaurus also takes reservations in the evening for a fixed price burger and sundae dinner. An increasing number of outlets are also introducing mobile order as an option. At participating locations, guests have the opportunity to use the My Disney Experience app to create their order and then pay for it using an attached credit card, or when applicable, the Disney Dining Plan. When it's time to eat, simply click the "I'm here" button and the order will be prepared fresh for retrieval. That gives users the ability to discuss orders and look over menus well ahead of meal time rather than having to rush to judgment in a crowded ordering area while looking at a distant menu board. A separate counter is used for mobile order pickup, so no waiting in line is usually necessary. It's incredibly useful during peak meal times when waits are long. Quick service is usually cheaper and faster than table service. Menus, food quality, and atmosphere vary wildly among the various options, making your choices more important than you might expect.

TABLE SERVICE These venues are typical restaurant experiences, where a host will seat your party and a server will take your order and deliver the food to the table. Most require reservations, particularly for dinner. Prices range from $15 sandwiches at The Plaza Restaurant in Magic Kingdom to $185+ for a seven-course meal at Victoria & Albert's. Buffets are generally lumped into this category, even when guests typically serve themselves.

DINNER SHOWS Spirit of Aloha at the Polynesian and Hoop-Dee-Doo Revue at Fort Wilderness offer all-you-care-to-enjoy family-style dining accompanied by two-hour shows.

FAVORITE FAMILY DINING

In addition to the food, the most fun and best-loved family dining contains some or all of the following:

- A fun setting
- Some kind of show and/or interactive play-along elements
- Visits by Disney characters like Mickey, Tigger, or the Disney Princesses

On almost every family's list of the best among these are:

- The Hoop-Dee-Doo Musical Revue, a silly, energetic dinner show with interactive elements and plenty of audience participation at Disney's Fort Wilderness Resort
- The Princess meals: Cinderella's Royal Table in the Magic Kingdom and Akershus Royal Banquet Hall in Epcot. The first has the better setting, the second is much less expensive
- Dining with Tigger, Pooh, and friends at the Crystal Palace in the Magic Kingdom

- Joining Snow White, Dopey, Grumpy, and Evil Queen at Artist Point at Disney's Wilderness Lodge
- Dining with Mickey and friends at Chef Mickey's at Disney's Contemporary Resort and 'Ohana breakfast at Disney's Polynesian Resort
- Dining in the Beast's Castle at Be Our Guest in the Magic Kingdom
- Various degrees of wait-staff induced silliness at 50's Prime Time Café in Disney's Hollywood Studios and Whispering Canyon Café at Disney's Wilderness Lodge
- Exotic settings in the local versions of national chain restaurants like the Rainforest Café, in both Disney's Animal Kingdom and Disney Springs, and T-REX in Disney Springs

SELECTING CHARACTER MEALS

Character meals are table service meals or dinner shows where the group has the opportunity to interact and take pictures with the characters during the dining experience. There are several benefits to these meals. First, they replace the lengthy waits to meet the characters inside the theme parks. At Magic Kingdom, meeting Mickey, Minnie, Goofy, Donald, and Pluto might take 90 or more minutes standing in line, often outdoors and unprotected from the heat and rain. At Chef Mickey's, you can enjoy your ice cream sundae while they all come to you. In addition, several characters don't ordinarily meet outside of character meals, including Piglet, Beast, and Prince Charming.

When deciding on a character meal, first identify which characters you'd like to meet. Then narrow down the potential choices by cost, setting, and convenience via the reviews that follow.

Character meal options include:

ANIMAL KINGDOM:

- Tusker House: Mickey, Donald, Daisy, Goofy in safari gear.

EPCOT:

- Garden Grill: Mickey, Pluto, Chip, Dale in farming apparel
- Akershus Royal Banquet Hall: Belle, in her yellow gown, joins diners for a picture before they're seated. Ariel, Aurora, Jasmine, and Snow White usually greet tableside

HOLLYWOOD STUDIOS:

- Hollywood & Vine (breakfast only): Sofia, Doc McStuffins, Vampirina, Goofy
- Hollywood & Vine (lunch and dinner): Minnie, Mickey, Donald, Daisy, and Goofy in seasonal costumes

MAGIC KINGDOM:

- Be Our Guest Restaurant (dinner only): While not a "character meal" per se, guests have the opportunity to meet and take pictures with Beast after the meal

- Cinderella's Royal Table: Pictures with Cinderella before the meal, with Ariel, Aurora, Jasmine, and Snow White usually meeting tableside.
- Crystal Palace: Pooh, Tigger, Eeyore, and Piglet

RESORTS:

- 1900 Park Fare Breakfast at Grand Floridian: Mary Poppins, Alice, the Mad Hatter, Tigger, and Winnie the Pooh
- 1900 Park Fare Dinner at Grand Floridian: Cinderella and Prince Charming, Lady Tremaine, Anastasia, Drizella, Fairy Godmother
- Artist Point at Wilderness Lodge: Snow White, Evil Queen, Dopey, and Grumpy
- Cape May Café at Beach Club Resort (breakfast only): Goofy, Minnie, Daisy, and Donald in ridiculous beach outfits
- Chef Mickey's at the Contemporary Resort: Mickey, Minnie, Daisy, Donald, Pluto, and Goofy in culinary outfits
- 'Ohana at the Polynesian (breakfast only): Mickey, Pluto, Lilo, and Stitch in Hawaiian outfits
- Trattoria al Forno (breakfast only) on the BoardWalk: Rapunzel, Flynn, Ariel, Eric
- Topolino's Terrace—Flavors of the Riviera at the Riviera Resort (breakfast only): Mickey, Minnie, Donald, and Daisy

For the princesses, we prefer Cinderella's Royal Table, which is also the only opportunity to see inside the beautiful castle. Absurdly expensive? Yes, but it's a special experience that can't be duplicated elsewhere.

For Mickey, we like Garden Grill breakfast at Epcot and Tusker House lunch or dinner at Animal Kingdom. Both are conveniently located inside the theme parks, making them easy to access while you're visiting those parks. For Mickey at the resorts, Chef Mickey's is a family favorite, as is breakfast at 'Ohana.

DINING FOR COUPLES

For couples looking for the most romantic atmosphere and the best food, we suggest:

- *California Grill.* Located on the 15th floor of the Contemporary, California Grill offers breathtaking views of Magic Kingdom during the evening fireworks, in addition to a great menu focused on fresh ingredients, sushi, and contemporary cocktails.
- *Flying Fish.* Located amidst the playful fun of the BoardWalk, Flying Fish offers a romantic retreat into luxury. Start the meal with inventive appetizers and then enjoy some of the freshest fish on property at one of Disney's best signature restaurants.
- *Victoria & Albert's.* For a truly special occasion; astonishing dining.

Guide to Disney World Dining

Bold=Character Meal; <u>Underline</u>=Requires 2 Dining Plan Credits; (paren)=which meal, if ratings differ; *Italic*=Resort Casual Dress Code; CAPS=Location (see key below)

			LOW	MEDIUM	HIGH
K I D A P P E A L	High	Chef **Mickey's** C, 50's Prime Time Café HS	**Akershus** E, *Artist Point* WI, Beaches & Cream BC, Biergarten E, <u>**Cinderella's Royal Table**</u> MK, **Crystal Palace** MK, Hollywood & Vine H<u>S (l,d), Hoop-dee-Doo</u> Revue FW, <u>**Mickey's Backyard Barbecue**</u> FW, **'Ohana** P (b), Rainforest Café AK DS, San Angel Inn E, Sci-Fi Dine-in Theater HS, Trattoria al Forno BW (b), **Tusker House** AK, Whispering Canyon Café WL	
	Medium	**Hollywood and Vine*** HS (b)	**Cape May Café** BC (b), Cape May Café BC (d), Coral Reef E, ESPN Club BW, **Garden Grill** E, La Hacienda de San Angel E, Liberty Tree Tavern MK, Mama Melrose's HS, Nine Dragons E, **1900 Park Fare** GF (b,d), 'Ohana P (d), Olivia's OKW, Plaza MK, Restaurant Marrakesh E, Rose & Crown E, Jungle Skipper Canteen MK, Tony's Town Square MK, Turf Club SS, Tutto Italia E, Via Napoli E, Yak & Yeti AK	Be Our Guest MK (d), *California Grill* C, Boma AKL, Hollywood Brown <u>Derby</u> HS, <u>Le Cellier</u> E, Sanaa KAKL (l,d),Teppan Edo E
	Low	<u>Spirit of Aloha</u> Polynesian *Luau* P	Big River Grille BW, Ale & Compass YC, Grand Floridian Café GF, Kona Café P, Les Chefs de France E, Spice Road Table E, Trattoria al Forno BW (l,d)	Monsieur Paul's E, *Citricos* GF, *Flying Fish Café* BW, *Jiko* AKL, *Narcoossee's* GF, Queen Victoria's Room** GF, *Tiffins* AK, Tokyo Dining E, Victoria & Albert** GF, The Wave C, *Yachtsman Steakhouse* YC
			Low	Medium	High
				ADULT APPEAL	

Locations: AK=Animal Kingdom, AKL=Animal Kingdom Lodge, BC=Beach Club, BW=BoardWalk, C=Contemporary, DS=Disney Springs, E=Epcot, FW=Fort Wilderness, GF=Grand Floridian, HS=Hollywood Studios, KAKL=Kidani Village at AKL, MK=Magic Kingdom, OKW=Old Key West, SS=Saratoga Springs, WL=Wilderness Lodge, YC=Yacht Club

* Though a character meal, low kid appeal except for fans of Playhouse Disney
** Not on Dining Plan; jacket required; no kids under 10

WHAT ABOUT EARLY BREAKFAST AT THE PARKS?

Tusker House at Animal Kingdom, Akershus Royal Banquet Hall and Garden Grill at Epcot, Hollywood & Vine at Hollywood Studios, and Cinderella's Royal Table, Crystal Palace, and Be Our Guest Restaurant at Magic Kingdom all routinely open at 8am for breakfast, which is often a full hour before the rest of the park. Many people recommend these 8am breakfasts because they afford an opportunity to get pictures in the park "when nobody else is around". Unfortunately, and particularly at Magic Kingdom and Hollywood Studios, this is not usually the case because hundreds of other people have the same idea. 8am reservations are also awfully early and awfully expensive. Transportation from the resorts is also dodgier and less consistent so early. With the parks routinely opening as much as an hour prior to the officially stated time, an 8am reservation either means rushing through the meal and hoping the characters arrive in time for a hasty exit, or wasting precious morning touring time eating. Instead, we recommend a late breakfast or early lunch, which allows you to sleep in an extra hour and hit the priority attractions when crowds are lowest before taking a restful, air-conditioned break with the characters.

There are two possible exceptions, the first of which is Be Our Guest, which currently serves quick service breakfast without characters for $29 for adults and $16 for kids. It includes choice of entrée, beverage, and a pastry platter for the table to share. With a 9am open, everyone with a reservation before then will be allowed to enter Magic Kingdom around 7:45am, even if your reservation is for 8:30am or 8:45am. With a pre-opening reservation, do your best to arrive by 7:30am and be done with breakfast and back outside the restaurant no later than 8:45am. This offers a great advantage for those planning to visit Seven Dwarfs Mine Train or Princess Fairytale Hall first thing because diners have the ability to arrive before anyone entering from the main entrance.

The second exception is Akershus Royal Banquet Hall in Norway at Epcot, where a reservation before 9am offers a substantial advantage in getting to the Frozen Ever After ride. Guests with pre-opening reservations will be allowed to enter the park just before 8am regardless of whether their reservation is for 8:15am or 8:45am. Hurry to the restaurant, eat quickly, and be out in front of the attraction entrance by 8:45am in order to basically walk on Epcot's most popular new ride.

Note that this advantage is moot on days with morning extra magic hours or with regular 8am opens and those with reservations will likely want to cancel them or schedule a reservation for later on these days.

RECOMMENDED DINING

Families using the 9-day itineraries introduced in Chapter 6 will find recommended dining at the top of each day in the graphic of the itinerary. The associated To-Do Lists for these itineraries have instructions on when and how to book the reservable table service meals, in addition to walking you through each step of the planning process. Each of the park "Cheat Sheets" in the previous chapter has recommended counter-service options.

Our recommendations are not set in stone. Families with much younger kids may wish to cut some of the non-character meals and replace them with character meals. Families with teens might want to do the opposite. Substitutions can be based on the "Guide to Disney Dining" graphic—which ranks the Disney World theme park and resort table service options based on kid and adult appeal—or on the capsule reviews that follow at the end of this chapter.

In the graphic, high adult appeal is based on "date night" criteria: a restaurant offering elevated cuisine, fine service, and a lovely setting. High kid appeal means that a restaurant has the elements that make the rest of Disney World a joy for kids—playful action, characters, and a fun setting—and also has a menu suited to picky eaters. By these criteria, it's hard for a restaurant to appeal to both. Be Our Guest in the Magic Kingdom comes closest, and if it had a better kids menu for picky eaters, would be ranked with high appeal for both groups.

Because kids and adults vary, it's best to use the chart and the reviews at the end of this chapter together.

Advance Dining Reservations

Make Advance Dining Reservations (ADRs) beginning 180 days before your arrival date.

The best Disney World dining options have limited capacity and are wildly popular. Because of this, these restaurants can be filled almost as soon as reservations open for them.

One topic that surprises first-time visitors is the importance and fun of dining experiences. Because quality and price vary so much between restaurants in the same vicinity, researching your options and booking the best restaurants far in advance puts you in the best possible position to have a fun, stress-free vacation. Identify your table service dining favorites as soon as possible and then make your ADRs as soon as reservations open.

Note that ADRs are not "reservations" in the traditional sense. With the exception of Victoria & Albert's and the dinner shows, the restaurant does not actually reserve a table. Instead, your party will receive the next available table that opens up. This can lead to the occasional long wait, particularly at the popular buffets that are often overbooked. To help mitigate this, book a meal right after the restaurant starts service or near the end of service when empty tables are more common.

MAKING YOUR RESERVATIONS

Reservations currently open 180 days before the date of dining—online at 6 a.m. and over the phone at 7 a.m. Moreover, if you are staying at a Disney World hotel, once 180 days from your hotel arrival date rolls around, you can make ADRs for not just that day, but also for the first ten days of your visit. You'll sometimes see this referred to as 180+10. Input your arrival date into pscalculator.net/pscalc.php to identify the first day you can make reservations. As an example, let's say you're visiting from December 1–8 and staying on property at Art of Animation. According to the calculator, the first day you can make reservations is June 4. Not only could you make reservations for December 1, the first day of our hypothetical vacation, but you can also make reservations for up to ten additional days because you're staying at a Disney-owned resort. Off-site guests visiting on the same dates would also be able to make their reservations for December 1 on June 4, but they would need to call or go online again on June 5 to book December 2, June 6 to book December 3, and so forth.

Most table service reservations require prospective diners to put a credit card on file. A $10 per person fee will be assessed if the group does not show up within 15 minutes of the reservation time. To avoid this fee, cancel the reservation no later than the day before. Same-day cancellations will be charged the no-show fee. Note that only one person needs to show up regardless of how many people are on the reservation. So if you have a reservation for six and only three show up, your party will not be assessed any fees. If weather, transportation delays, or something else causes you to miss your reservation, visit Guest Services and explain your case. Disney will likely waive the charge for worthy stories.

The hardest reservations to get, and which you should book as soon as you can, are:

- Be Our Guest Restaurant [Magic Kingdom]
- California Grill brunch
- Artist Point dinner [Wilderness Lodge]
- Trattoria al Forno breakfast [Boardwalk]
- Cinderella's Royal Table [Magic Kingdom]
- Chef Mickey's [Contemporary Resort]
- 'Ohana [Polynesian Resort]
- Akershus Royal Banquet Hall [Epcot]
- 1900 Park Fare Dinner [Grand Floridian Resort]
- California Grill dinner [Contemporary Resort]

Typically, over 40 restaurants will have same-day reservations available at some point during the day. It's always best to secure reservations via 407-WDW-Dine, DISNEYWORLD.COM, the My Disney Experience mobile app, or in person at Guest Services or the restaurant itself. It's not uncommon for a restaurant to entirely turn guests away without reservations, particularly at peak dinner times. Make reservations as soon as you know where you want to eat.

If there is a reservation that you would like but were unable to initially secure, refresh availability on the day before as many people cancel their reservations, which are subsequently offered to other guests.

The Disney Dining Plan

Disney World dining is expensive. For some guests, it may even be the priciest component of the vacation, eclipsing the cost of lodging and theme park tickets. The three versions of the Disney Dining Plan (Quick Service, Regular, and Deluxe) are a way to prepay some of these dining expenses.

Years ago, when the Regular Dining Plan included appetizer and tip at sit-down restaurants, you could save some money by using these plans. These days it's hard for us to recommend them, although the inclusion of a single alcoholic drink per meal will improve the value payoff of these plans for some, and for others make the cost of the plans easier to forget.

Ignoring alcohol:

- The Quick Service Dining Plan is priced so high that it's only possible to break even or come out ahead if you use the credits solely for lunch and dinner. From there, you'll need to order only the most expensive items to eke out a potential savings of a dollar or two per day.
- At a cost just over $78 per adult per night, the Regular Dining Plan is expensive and saving money with it requires planning only the most expensive meals.
- The Deluxe Dining Plan comes with three quick or table service meals per day at a cost of about $119 per night per adult. Users either spend three or more hours per day eating table service meals or use their credits on faster quick service meals, in turn reducing the value of each credit.

The addition of one alcoholic drink for each quick and table service credit will change the value equation of these plans for some. The Dining Plan includes most beers, wines, cocktails, and other drinks up to around $17. Certain pricier pours, particularly at Disney signature restaurants, are excluded. But those who would otherwise have paid cash for at least one less-expensive alcoholic drink at most of their meals anyway will see an additional value of around $15–30 per night for the Quick Service and Regular Plans, and even more for the Deluxe Plan. This additional value may well turn the plans into more reasonable economic choices for those who imbibe in the ways that they reward.

In place of an alcoholic drink, all guests may instead select a single non-alcoholic specialty drink at each meal. These include milkshakes, smoothies, mocktails, and the like. These drinks are typically more expensive than fountain beverages and those ordering them will see additional value to the change.

We suggest skipping the dining plans, with these exceptions:

- If you take comfort in pre-paying some of your dining expenses as a budgeting tool (even if this means you spend more money), the Quick Service or Regular plans may make sense for you—the cash loss may be worth the budget comfort. It's nice knowing that food is pre-paid and users are free to order whatever entrees and desserts that they like, even if those prices are higher than they're accustomed to paying. As an alternative, consider loading a Disney gift card with the amount of money you plan to pay for meals, and use that instead.

- Pricing on the Regular Plan is advantageous for groups with kids under the age of ten that plan multiple buffets and character meals. The cost of a child buffet at many character meals exceeds their cost of the Regular Dining Plan for that day.

- Those 21 and over who would have had an eligible alcoholic drink at most of their quick and table service meals anyway may come out ahead, especially on the Quick Service Plan, which gives you just as many free drinks per night as the Regular Plan but costs about $23 per night less.

With or without a dining plan, the typical family eating their meals on property should budget $40–$75+ per adult per day, and between $20 and $40/day for the kids—depending on their ages and appetites.

DINING PLAN CREDITS AND WHAT THEY COVER

The Dining Plans are only available to guests staying at Disney owned and operated resorts. All guests on a single reservation (except children under three—not covered on any plan) must opt for the same Dining Plan if you elect to purchase it. There's no such thing as having four people on a room reservation and only three people on the Deluxe Plan. And it isn't possible for one person to purchase Deluxe, while the other chooses Regular. The plan must be purchased for each night of the booked stay. Everyone over the age of nine must pay the adult rate, regardless of how much they plan to eat. And kids 3–9 might be required to order from the Kids' Menu if the dining location has one.

Those on the Dining Plan receive credits based on the number of nights they're staying. The Dining Plan and credits are not connected to theme park tickets—just the number of nights on the reservation. Credits are usable from check-in day through midnight on checkout day, and can be used in any order on any of these days. On a three-night stay, a guest could use all their credits on the first day, the last day, or space them out.

Quick service meals generally consist of one entrée or combo meal, and one beverage—for 2020 plans, as noted above, this beverage can be a "regular" beverage (think milk or Coke), "specialty" non-alcoholic beverage (think milkshake or smoothie), or for those over 21, an alcoholic beverage. In 2017, Disney eliminated the former dessert entitlement and added in its place an additional snack credit per day, which can be used either on dessert or on something else at any time, making these plans much more flexible. Virtually every quick service on property participates in the Dining Plan, although not all of them—especially at Magic Kingdom—offer alcohol or specialty drinks. All quick service meals cost one credit.

In 2020, table service meals include one entrée, one dessert, and one regular, specialty, or alcoholic beverage, and cost one or two credits. The Deluxe Dining Plan credits also include an appetizer, in addition to the entrée, dessert, and the three beverage options. Snack credits can be used on small food or drink items like candy apples, ice cream bars, pastries, and bottles of water and soda. Look for the Dining Plan symbol on any menu to see what qualifies as a snack credit.

The credits don't always cover everything you might want at a meal and most don't cover tips. Most guests have some additional dining expenses, in addition to the cost of the Dining Plan.

THE QUICK SERVICE DINING PLAN

The 2020 Quick Service Dining Plan includes per person, per night:

- Two quick service meals (entrée/beverage)
- Two snacks

In addition, each guest receives a refillable mug for use at their resort's quick service, and, if available, pools.

So a family of four staying for five nights would receive ten quick service meals, ten snacks, and a refillable mug each. For 2020, after-tax pricing is:

- $55.00 per night for those ten and older
- $26.00 per night for kids ages three to nine

Ignoring alcohol, adult quick service entrees are typically $11–$15 in the theme parks. Add a $4 fountain beverage and your average meal comes to around $17. Eat two of those, in addition to a $6 Churro and $6 Mickey Ice Cream Bar, and add about $3 for a day's worth of the refillable mug, and you're close to breaking even, after adding tax. Substitute an $8 beer or $10 mixed drink for the soda and you've eked out a savings of about four dollars assuming you've eaten and enjoyed everything. Kids' Picks generally come in around $7 each. Eat two and add a $5 Popcorn and $7 Mickey Pretzel and the use of the refillable mug, and you've covered the day's cost.

While it's more possible now than it has been for the past several years to save a few dollars per day on the Quick Service Dining Plan, those savings evaporate whenever you eat breakfast, when prices are usually lower, or whenever someone feels forced to order and eat something that they ordinarily wouldn't. It also makes it difficult to schedule a table service meal or character buffet since those meals aren't included on the Plan. You can pay cash for such meals, but if doing so pushes you to using a credit for breakfast—or worse, ending your vacation with unused credits—the Quick Service plan will cost you money. On the other hand, as noted, the value of an alcoholic drink at each meal may well put those 21 and older ahead of the cost of this plan.

THE "REGULAR" DINING PLAN

The 2020 "Regular" Dining Plan—often known simply as the Disney Dining Plan—includes per person, per night:

- One quick service meal (entrée/beverage)
- One table service meal (entrée/dessert or select side/beverage)
- Two snacks

In addition, each guest receives a refillable mug for the duration of the stay. For 2020, after-tax pricing is:

- $78.01 per night for those ten and older
- $30.50 per night for kids ages three to nine

Child pricing is advantageous with a cost just about $4 more than the Quick Service Plan. With several character buffets priced over $20, it's easy for kids to come out ten dollars or more ahead each day they dine at such a venue. For those older than 9, the price of $23/per day more than the Quick Service is harder to justify. There are meals where you do well—Akershus for lunch or dinner, after tax, costs $66 per adult, and standard character meals now cost about $58 per adult, after tax. Over the course of a day, an adult ordering a typical quick service lunch alongside a beer, a snack, and dinner at Akershus will pay less under the Dining Plan than with cash.

Outside of buffets and ignoring alcohol, it's difficult to find restaurants with average entrée and dessert prices high enough to cover the cost of the plan. Let's assume you're spending the day at Hollywood Studios and select 50's Prime Time Café for dinner. You select the third most expensive entrée, the $24 Golden Fried Chicken, and the most expensive dessert, the $10 Peanut Butter Layered Cake, along with an $8 Root Beer Float as your beverage. With tax, the meal comes out to $44, which is $34 away from covering the cost of the Dining Plan with just a quick service meal and two snacks to go. At the costliest quick service, Docking Bay 7 Food and Cargo, the most expensive quick service lunch you could put together with a non-alcoholic beverage is $26 with tax. That's about $6 higher than average. Even so, add a $6 Mickey Ice Cream Bar and $7 Mickey Pretzel as snacks and you've only "saved" about $5 on the Dining Plan after going out of your way to order some of the most expensive items at the park. If you had simply ordered the meatloaf instead of the fried chicken at 50's Prime Time, and the chicken instead of the pot roast at Docking Bay 7, then you would come out behind the cost of one day on the Dining Plan.

The economics of two-credit meals are even worse. Signature restaurant entree prices are about 1.5x the cash cost of regular restaurants, but cost twice the number of credits, resulting in a lower per-credit value. For example, the most expensive meal you could put together on the Dining Plan at California Grill is a $65 lobster and scallops, $16 chocolate cake, and $14 cocktail. That's $95 after tax, or just $42.50 per credit for the most expensive meal at one of the most expensive restaurants on property. To compare, the most expensive dinner you could put together at Trattoria al Forno, a single credit restaurant, is a $42 Whole-roasted fish, $8 tiramisu, and $13 cocktail. The value of that single credit with tax is $67.10, or 58% more value than you'd find at California Grill.

THE DELUXE DINING PLAN

The 2020 Deluxe Dining Plan includes per person, per night:

- Three meals per day—either quick service or table service. Table service meals include an appetizer where applicable, and all meals include the specialty and alcoholic beverage credit
- Two snacks

In addition, each guest receives a refillable mug for the duration of the stay. For 2020, after-tax pricing is:

- $119.00 per night for adults
- $47.50 per night for kids ages three to nine

On paper, there is a lot of value potential here, particularly for kids under the age of ten and those over 21 who drink at every meal. To maximize that value, however, you could be spending more than three hours a day dining—even more if you avoid two-credit meals—and building an itinerary largely around being at specific restaurants at specific times. And let's not forget the actual cost. A family of two adults, a 15-year old, and a 7-year old would cost a whopping $404.50 per night. For that, Josh and Dave will cook and serve your family of four both lunch and dinner, and offer all the Bud Light you can handle, while intermittently breaking out into song and dance. (A word to the wise though: Josh's specialty is Hot Pockets and Dave's favorite ingredient is Sriracha.)

Saving Money on Dining

Purchasing ingredients and preparing meals where you're staying is the easiest way to slash a food budget. This works best for quick breakfasts in the room. Pack or purchase a dozen bagels or donuts, fruit, cereal and milk, and some protein bars and you can easily eliminate busy breakfasts at the resort food court, in addition to cutting meal time down to a few minutes from 30+.

Unfortunately, Disney doesn't make purchasing these items economical at its resort gift shops, for reasons you might be able to guess. Other than Fort Wilderness and the Disney Vacation Club properties, pickings can be slim and prices are high. On top of that, only Ft. Wilderness cabins and the villas in the DVC resorts have kitchens, making even simple prep work difficult in most situations. If you have a car and the time to shop, we recommend the Speedway stores on property for convenience. One is located across the street from the BoardWalk Inn near Epcot, another after the exit to Magic Kingdom parking, and the third is across the street from the Marketplace section of Disney Springs. For a better selection, visit the Winn-Dixie (and nearby liquor store) at 1957 S Apopka Vineland Rd, in Orlando, or the Publix (and nearby liquor store) at 29 Blake Boulevard, in Kissimmee. The nearest to your hotel will be about a 10–15 minute drive.

Without transportation or the ability to venture out to a supermarket on vacation, consider a grocery delivery service. Amazon Prime users will want to consider Prime Now, which will deliver directly to you at the resort lobby or to the resort concierge for pickup later. Delivery is free on orders over $35 and a specific two-hour window can be selected. Prices are typically in-line with area grocery stores and thousands of products from Whole Foods are available for the same cost as the store. GardenGrocer. com and WeGoShop.com are two legacy recommendations that also work, but may be more expensive and less streamlined. All three deliver beer and wine, but someone over the age of 21 will need to be present to accept the order if alcohol is purchased.

Dining Reviews

Brief reviews of the table service restaurants in the parks, Disney Springs, and the Disney resorts follow.

First, you'll find reviews of the restaurants inside each theme park, in alphabetical order. Next, you'll find an alphabetized list of the resorts, with reviews of all restaurants located at that resort.

We start with the venue name and location within its area, indicating also whether a meal is a character meal or a dinner show. We then note cuisine, operating hours, and whether or not it is on the Disney Dining Plan (abbreviated as DDP)—note that some DDP meals require two credits and are so indicated. Next, we note current price ranges for adult appetizers and entrees, in addition to kids' meals. Buffet prices with tax included are also noted where applicable. We then get into the food and ambiance of the restaurants themselves. This material is necessarily brief—for more, see Josh's EASYWDW.COM. Prices, menus, hours, required credits, discounts etc., are all subject to change.

We also throw some Disney jargon around:

- Signature Restaurant: two credit venues usually aimed at adults— that is, thin on kid appeal, but with finer and more elegant dining. Most have a mild dress code, e.g., on men, pants are preferred, nice shorts are OK, but no tank tops.
- Family Style: food for the entire table is served on platters and shared amongst the table.
- Walk-up: trying to get a seating without having a reservation.

Note also that some venues will require full pre-payment—at press time, Hoop-Dee-Doo, Spirit of Aloha, and Cinderella's Royal Table—and most others will require a credit card so that a no-show fee can be charged. To avoid no-show fees, cancel no later than 11:59pm on the day before the reservation.

Dining Reviews: The Theme Parks

DINING AT DISNEY'S ANIMAL KINGDOM

Disney's Animal Kingdom offers a nice variety of consistently high-quality restaurants and quick services, and we like each for different reasons. The Rainforest Café at the front of the park is much less crowded than the Disney Springs iteration, and offers the same fun atmosphere fueled by Animatronics and a vast menu. Theme park admission is not required to dine there. Tusker House in Africa is a low-key character meal featuring Donald and Mickey for all three meals. The expansive buffet area makes sampling the 30+ items easy, and the characters have more time to spend with guests than at the more crowded resort character meals. Yak & Yeti serves up fantastic Pan-Asian food in a restaurant full of authentic artifacts from India, China, and elsewhere. Tiffins is a new signature restaurant featuring African, Asian, and South American flavors that's quickly become one of Disney's best overall dining experiences. Food might seem adventurous at first blush, but flavors should be more accessible than you might expect. Diners also have the opportunity to visit Nomad Lounge with a menu featuring carefully crafted cocktails along with wines and beers from around the world.

Like the other theme parks, Animal Kingdom quick service is largely hit or miss. Pizzafari serves up standard Disney reheated pizzas that are edible, but unlikely to wow. Beginning at 5pm daily, a family-style pizza dinner is offered for $25/adult and $14/child ages 3-9. Start with Caesar and caprese salads before cheese or pepperoni pizza, baked ziti, and fettuccine alfredo with chicken are delivered for the main course. Miniature cannoli follow for dessert. A non-alcoholic beverage is included in the price. If you're planning on dining at Pizzafari after 5pm anyway, then the meal may be a good value versus paying a la carte. The fact that the pizzas are made fresh is also a benefit versus the reheated frozen pies that the quick service serves to those ordering a la carte.

Restaurantosaurus in DinoLand USA is your burger and nugget option. You'll find plenty of air-conditioned seating, in addition to outdoor patio tables. On select nights for dinner, the quick service also offers a burger, side, sundae, and non-alcoholic drink combo for $25 for adults and $16 for kids. Better is Yak & Yeti Local Food Cafes, which serves up Asian specialties like Teriyaki Beef and Honey Chicken. Unfortunately, all seating is outdoors, and it can be uncomfortably hot and wet in the summer. Harambe Market opened in May 2015 in the Africa section behind the Mombasa Marketplace store and to the right of the entrance to Kilimanjaro Safaris. It adds another open-air quick service option with outdoor seating and a unique menu. It's an excellent choice if the weather cooperates, but with all seating outdoors, it can be unpleasant in the rain or heat. Better is Flame Tree Barbecue, where you'll find Disney's best quick service ribs, pork sandwiches, and half chickens. While seating is outdoors, it's better covered with fans overhead. Walk all the way down to the water for expansive views of Asia and Expedition Everest. Satu'li Canteen in Pandora is the new kid on the block, offering some surprisingly unique flavors in their various bowl entrees that feature grilled beef, chicken, shrimp, or tofu on top of bases that include salad or rice. Air-conditioned seating is available, in addition to patio seating outside. We recommend Flame Tree and Satu'li the most based on food quality, value, and atmosphere.

Rainforest Café

Front of park; theme park admission not required to dine

CUISINE American. **HOURS** 8:30am–late. **DDP** Yes.

PRICES *Breakfast*: $12–$15. *Lunch/Dinner Appetizers*: $9–$21. *Entrées*: $15–$37. Kids: $10.

OVERVIEW Part of a chain of 25+ restaurants around the world, Rainforest Cafe blends an immersive environment with a laundry list menu. Dine on steaks, pastas, salads, burgers, or one of 50+ other items, while Animatronic gorillas pound their chests, birds sing, and thunder booms from the starry night sky. The food may not always impress, but it's all serviceable and portions are huge. The restaurant is extremely loud and the atmosphere may startle young children apprehensive about rides like DINOSAUR and Haunted Mansion, although older children love the atmosphere. Because it's located at the front of the park, plan to eat when you're near the entrance/exit.

Tiffins

Attached to the back of Pizzafari, on Discovery Island

CUISINE Global, but mostly Asian, African, and South American. **HOURS** 11:30am–late. **DDP** 2 credits.

PRICES Lunch/Dinner Appetizers: $10–$18. Entrées: $30–$65. Kids: $10–$15.

OVERVIEW Tiffins extends Animal Kingdom's keen eye for detail at a restaurant that celebrates the bold globetrotting spirit of Disney's Imagineers as they explored the world to create Disney's Animal Kingdom. Of the three elegant dining rooms, we recommend requesting the Grand Gallery, where concept art for Rivers of Light lines the walls, or the Safari Gallery, where guests dine amidst authentic artifacts and actual field notes from the Imagineers' adventures in Africa. The menu skews toward the foreign for most people, but flavors should be more accessible than you might expect with the usual beef, chicken, lamb, and vegetables making up the majority of most dishes. The steak is a crowd favorite as is the Chocolate Ganache dessert. The atmosphere is casual and inviting with service that should exceed expectations. It's our favorite new restaurant.

Nomad Lounge is located to the left of the main lobby area and enjoys its own menu of small plates and an expanded drink menu. We love stopping by for a cocktail or draft beer, the Kungaloosh Excursion Spiced Ale being our favorite, but food portions are small for the money. Consider noshing on a couple of appetizers, but most people will need to spend $40 or $50 in the lounge to truly fill up. Tiffins presents more value for a full meal.

Tusker House

Character meal, in Africa

CUISINE African-inspired. **DDP** Yes.

HOURS AND PRICES *Breakfast* (8–10:55am): $44 adults, $26 kids. *Lunch* (11am–3:30pm; may extend later): $58 adults, $34 kids. *Dinner* (4:30pm–late): $55 adults, $34 kids. Pricing may vary depending on the season.

OVERVIEW Donald, Daisy, Mickey, and Goofy greet guests tableside inside this vibrant African marketplace. Some of the 30+ items at each meal retain touches of African flair and spice, but Disney is careful to cater to the typical American palate. Character interaction is among the best, with the characters leading parades around the restaurant and playing games with guests.

Yak & Yeti

Asia, between UP! A Great Bird Adventure and Kali River Rapids

CUISINE Asian. **HOURS** 11am–late. **DDP** Yes.

PRICES Lunch/Dinner Appetizers: $6–$17. Entrées: $17–$35. Kids: $10.

OVERVIEW Located in Asia, this air-conditioned respite is appropriately themed to a rural countryside sanctuary set in the heart of the Himalayan Mountains. The menu is reminiscent of P.F. Chang's and features such favorites as Lettuce Cups, Crispy Honey Chicken, and Sweet-and-Sour Pork, in addition to a Kobe Beef Burger or Steak. Portions are large and service is friendly as guests dine amongst hundreds of authentic artifacts from all over Asia. Request a window table upstairs for a great view.

DINING AT EPCOT

Epcot offers an overwhelming number of dining options, mostly in World Showcase with national cuisines tied into the respective pavilions. You could visit Epcot every day for a month and dine in a different venue each day. We present reviews of all the table service options below, but our recommended restaurants are Biergarten in Germany, Via Napoli in Italy, Akershus Banquet Hall in Norway, and San Angel Inn in Mexico.

Biergarten is a richly themed buffet restaurant with authentic German items like beer cheese soup, sauerbraten, spaetzle, veal sausage, mini frankfurters, and a whole lot more. A live oompah band plays intermittently, with guests invited up to the dance floor to sing and dance along.

Via Napoli, an authentic Neapolitan pizzeria, serves some of the best pizza on property. A large mezzo-metro pizza is plenty to feed a family of four for about $11 per person, making it a great value. Stay conservative with a signature pepperoni pie or try something like the Prosciutto e Melone Signature Pie (fontina, mozzarella, prosciutto, and cantaloupe).

Akershus is the part-buffet, part-table service character meal in Norway. While pricey, it's significantly less expensive than Cinderella's Royal Table at the Magic Kingdom, and the price includes a digital picture with Belle in her yellow gown, along with four other princesses meeting tableside. The cold buffet guarantees everyone will have plenty to eat, and the entrees are varied and above average as well.

At San Angel Inn, guests dine underneath perpetual twilight as the boats from the Gran Fiesta Tour next door glide by. Food quality is a bit lower than at our other three picks, but the unique atmosphere can't be replicated elsewhere.

Quick service options at Epcot are even more abundant.

Of the Future World options, Sunshine Seasons near Soarin' in the Land Pavilion receives nearly universal acclaim. Serving freshly grilled pork chops, rotisserie chicken, salmon, salads, sandwiches, Asian entrees, and more, with plentiful air-conditioned seating, it's a great choice for a convenient Future World lunch. Electric Umbrella is your Future World spot for the usual Disney hamburgers and chicken nuggets, but it's expected to close in late 2019 or early 2020 for a lengthy remodel.

In World Showcase, you may pick a quick service based on the mood—or location—of the group at the time. We both highly recommend Tangierine Café in Morocco. While the menu of shawarma, falafel, kefta, and tabouleh might initially seem exotic, the typical Mediterranean flavors are more familiar than you might expect. Food is also higher quality and portions are larger than at just about any other quick service. Josh likes the U.K.'s Fish and Chips, particularly when a table overlooking the lagoon is available. Liberty Inn in the U.S. closed in the middle of 2019 to make way for Regal Eagle Smokehouse, a new quick service that will offer barbecue and craft beers, likely opening in the middle of 2020. Sommerfest in Germany is quite good, but the seating section consists of only a handful of tables, and there's rarely anywhere comfortable to sit.

La Cantina de San Angel in Mexico and Lotus Blossom Café in China both offer menus that should be familiar to most guests and for that reason, we don't necessarily recommend stopping over more interesting options. But the nachos in Mexico are a very shareable snack and the chicken and beef entrees in China should satisfy most appetites for less money than other options. Katsura Grill in Japan doesn't live up to its potential, but the udon and chicken cutlet curry are good and the outdoor garden seating area is among the most peaceful you'll find. The sushi largely disappoints. Boulangerie Patisserie in France offers some unique quiche, sandwich, and salad fare, but the ordering process is confusing and the seating section is small, loud, and chaotic.

Overall, visiting Tangierine Café or Sunshine Seasons for lunch and one of our recommended table service restaurants for dinner is your best bet. But most guests are satisfied no matter where they choose to dine.

Akershus Royal Banquet Hall

Princess character meal, in Norway Pavilion

CUISINE Norwegian/American. **DDP** Yes.

HOURS AND PRICES *Breakfast* (8–11:10am): $55 adults, $33 kids. *Lunch* (11:55am–3:30pm): $65 adults, $39 kids. *Dinner* (4:55pm–park close): $66 adults, $40 kids.

OVERVIEW Themed to a 14th century Scandinavian castle, Akershus is Epcot's much less expensive version of Cinderella's Royal Table. A picture with Belle begins the adventure and will be available on PhotoPass, and four other princesses meet tableside—usually Ariel, Aurora, Cinderella, and Snow White. For breakfast, guests are brought platters of hot breakfast foods like scrambled eggs, potato casserole, sausage, and bacon. Lunch and dinner feature a set menu of Norwegian and American favorites like Norwegian Meatballs with Lingonberry Sauce, Salmon, and Chicken Breast. All meals include unlimited access to the cold bar, which includes bread, salads, sliced meats, cheeses, fish, and a variety of other chilled foods, including traditional Scandinavian items. Kids' meals include pizza, salmon, pasta, and meatballs. Breakfast is the most consistent and least expensive meal.

Biergarten

Germany Pavilion

CUISINE German. **DDP** Yes.

HOURS AND PRICES *Lunch* (12–3:55pm): $49 adults, $27 kids. *Dinner* (4pm–park close): $49 adults, $27 kids.

OVERVIEW Be transported to a quaint Bavarian village in the heart of Oktoberfest at this German buffet that features live oompah music throughout the day. Selections include bratwurst, rotisserie chicken, pork schnitzel, and a variety of seasonal salads. Dessert includes Apple Strudel and Black Forest Cake. The selection and food quality are both outstanding. Service is genuinely friendly and the music is a lot of fun. Tables seat eight and smaller parties will be seated with others. There is no dedicated buffet section for kids, though most will be happy loading up on macaroni and cheese, chicken, pretzel rolls, and dessert. The liters of beer are a lot of fun and a good value. Note that while lunch used to carry a big discount compared to dinner that both meals now cost the same and offer identical menus.

Chefs de France

France Pavilion, ground level

CUISINE French. **HOURS** 12pm–park close. **DDP** Yes.

PRICES (One all-day menu) Appetizers: $9–$17. Entrées: $20–$36. Kids: $8–$10.

OVERVIEW This family-friendly Parisian café provides a casual atmosphere for guests to sample French cuisine like casserole of Burgundian escargots,

French onion soup, and duck breast and leg confit. Steaks, roasted chicken, and broiled salmon are also available. The charming French service is perhaps a bit too authentic at times, but meals at this busy brasserie are a lot of fun. The kids' menu may be limiting, with just chicken strips, ground beef steak on a brioche bun, pasta, and grilled fish typically available.

Coral Reef

To the right of The Seas with Nemo and Friends

CUISINE American. **HOURS** 11:30am–park close. **DDP** Yes.

PRICES Lunch/Dinner Appetizers: $9–$15. Entrées: $24–$40. Kids: $10–$13.

OVERVIEW More than 4,000 creatures, including sharks, rays, and turtles, join diners seated in front of the 5.7 million gallon aquarium glass. Food is average table service quality and the menu skews towards fish and beef with the shrimp & grits standing out as excellent. Kids love the aquarium view and their menu features steak, cheesy shells, and fish. Request a lower-level aquarium view at check-in.

Garden Grill

Character meal, upper floor of the Land Pavilion

CUISINE American. **DDP** Yes.

HOURS AND PRICES *Breakfast* (8–10:30am): $44 adults, $26 kids. *Lunch* (11:30am–3pm): $58 adults, $34 kids. *Dinner* (4–8:30pm): $58 adults, $34 kids.

OVERVIEW Join Chip, Dale, Mickey, and Pluto at this fun restaurant featuring views of the Living with the Land ride below. All three meals are served family-style with the usual assortment of eggs, bacon, and other favorites at breakfast, though the accompanying warm chocolate-hazelnut sauce helps elevate the Mickey waffles and the cinnamon roll is quite good. For lunch and dinner, garden salad, turkey breast, grilled beef, vegetables, stuffing, mashed potatoes, and non-alcoholic beverages are included. Kids receive chicken drumsticks, macaroni-and-cheese, broccoli, and fries. For dessert, expect cupcakes for the kids and short cake for the adults. Food is quite good, and this is one of the more laid-back character meals, with excellent character interaction.

La Hacienda de San Angel

Mexico Pavilion, outside on the water

CUISINE Mexican. **HOURS** 4pm–park close. **DDP** Yes.

PRICES Dinner Appetizers: $9–$14. Entrées: $18–$34. Two-person platters: $62. Kids: $10–$11.

OVERVIEW This restaurant on the Lagoon features floor-to-ceiling windows with the potential for grand views of World Showcase Lagoon. The menu skews away from typical Tex-Mex and towards grilled and marinated meats and seafood. Parties of two or more should stick to one of the two combination skillets for $62 each; plenty of food for up to three to share. Kids' meals include cheese quesadillas and chicken tacos. Food quality and service range from below average to average. The nearby San Angel Inn is more charming.

Le Cellier Steakhouse

Canada Pavilion (look for the walkway down to the Canada: Far and Wide show)

CUISINE Steak and fish, mostly. **HOURS** Opening varies between 11am and 12:30pm to park close. **DDP** 2 credits.

PRICES Lunch/Dinner Appetizers: $12–$21. Entrées: $33–$59. Kids: $10–$18.

OVERVIEW This dark, wine-cellar-themed restaurant that focuses on Canadian beef is an expensive proposition. No steak currently comes in under $50. While cozy, tables are virtually on top of each other, creating a less-than-intimate atmosphere. Food quality is high and service is typically above average, but it's hard to justify these prices. On the plus side, the $12 cheese soup is excellent, the complimentary pretzel bread is out of this world, and the Unibroue beer is world-class. Kids, who are unlikely to be enthralled by the restaurant, can get in on the action with a grilled steak, seared salmon, and a kids' portion of the cheese soup.

Monsieur Paul

France Pavilion, above Les Chefs de France

CUISINE French. **HOURS** 5:30pm–park close. **DDP** 2 credits.

PRICES Dinner Appetizers: $15-$29. Entrées: $37–$44. Kids: $13–$19.

OVERVIEW This upscale gourmet French restaurant replaced Bistro de Paris above Chefs de France in December 2012. Couples looking for the most intimate experience inside Epcot should look no further, but the formal atmosphere is not particularly kid friendly. Luckily, the restaurant introduced a kids' menu that includes seared chicken, roasted salmon, or beef tenderloin with choice of side to cater better to younger clientele. The very French staff may struggle to communicate in English, but they are among the most attentive property wide. Food impresses in quality and presentation and is not much more expensive than the pricier entrees downstairs.

Nine Dragons

China Pavilion

CUISINE Chinese. **HOURS** 12pm–park close. **DDP** Yes.

PRICES Lunch/Dinner Appetizers: $5–$13. Lunch Entrées: $16–$25. Dinner Entrées: $16–$34. Kids: $8–$11.

OVERVIEW Featuring a beautiful glass mural of two dragons chasing a glowing pearl, rosewood wall panels, and Chinese lantern lighting, Nine Dragons is not your typical neighborhood dive. The menu offers familiar favorites like Kung Pao Chicken and Honey-Sesame Chicken along with traditional dishes like the Fragrant Five-Spiced Fish, all for $25 or less. Kids can get in on the action with interesting items like Pot Stickers,

Sweet-and-Sour Chicken, and Ginger Ice Cream. Portions are huge and the kitchen consistently executes food that is less expensive than other restaurants. Service is friendly but tends to be abrupt. While Nine Dragons suffers from a poor reputation, we think it's improved handily in recent memory and don't have any qualms about recommending it, particularly as a last-minute walk-up.

Restaurant Marrakesh

Morocco Pavilion, in the very back

CUISINE Moroccan/Mediterranean. **HOURS** 11:30am–park close. **DDP** Yes.

PRICES Lunch/Dinner Appetizers: $7–$15. Entrées $22–$36. Kids: $9–$12.

OVERVIEW This hard-to-find restaurant in the back of the Morocco Pavilion is themed to an ornate Moroccan palace as stained glass chandeliers provide the only light for the visiting band and belly dancer who perform throughout the day. Marrakesh updated its menu in the middle of 2018, raising prices during lunch, in addition to adding new, more expensive entrees. It's a curious move considering the restaurant is easily Epcot's least popular. We recommend skipping it at the elevated price points as the quality of food isn't high enough to justify the money.

Rose & Crown Dining Room

United Kingdom Pavilion

CUISINE British. **HOURS** 12pm–park close. **DDP** Yes.

PRICES Lunch/Dinner Appetizers: $9–$14. Entrées: $21–$27. Kids: $9–$12.

OVERVIEW Situated along World Showcase Lagoon, Rose & Crown provides the only guaranteed fireworks viewing from a restaurant. Views are best outside on the patio, but guests seated inside the family-friendly pub, heavy on wooden furniture, will be invited outside shortly before the show. Food quality has fallen in recent years as chefs seem to push out a new menu every couple months. Stick with long-standing favorites like bangers & mash, fish & chips, and shepherd's pie. Kids choose from a menu that includes butter chicken, bangers & mash, and fish & chips.

Rose & Crown Pub

United Kingdom Pavilion

CUISINE Mostly beer. **HOURS** 11:30am–park close. **DDP** No.

PRICES Limited food menu with prices ranging from $10–$12.

OVERVIEW Frosted windows protect the privacy of those imbibing inside this cozy pub, which is virtually always hopping. The entrance is separate from the restaurant and reservations are not accepted here. Draft beer includes Bass, Boddington's, Guinness, Stella, and Harp. Scotch flights, mixed drinks like the Pimm's Cup, and wine are other options.

San Angel Inn

Mexico Pavilion, inside the pyramid
CUISINE Mexican. **HOURS** 11:30am–park close. **DDP** Yes.
PRICES Lunch/Dinner Appetizers: $9–$15. Entrées $19–$36. Kids: $10–$11.

OVERVIEW San Angel Inn sits inside the Mesoamerican pyramid, and is themed as a Mexican village square at twilight. The evening theming makes the restaurant dark, to the point where reading the menu is nearly impossible without the help of tabletop candles. Like La Hacienda outside, the limited menu focuses on grilled meats rather than burritos and enchiladas. Unfortunately, tables are so close together that diners a table over might as well be on your reservation, eliminating any sense of intimacy. A good family choice as parents will find the setting romantic, and kids will find it fun. Request a table on the water for a delightful view of the Gran Fiesta Tour boats gliding by below. Kids' menu items have become more mundane in recent memory, now including grilled chicken, chicken tenders, cheese quesadilla, or pasta.

Spice Road Table

Morocco Pavilion, along the Lagoon
CUISINE Moroccan/Mediterranean. **HOURS** 11am–park close. **DDP** Yes.
PRICES Small Plates: $9–$13. Entrees: $23–35. Kids: $10.

OVERVIEW This water-side eatery offers small-plate Mediterranean specialties like lamb sausage, fried calamari, and harissa chicken rolls. Additional emphasis is placed on mixed drinks, Moroccan wine, and Mediterranean beer. Spice Road accepts reservations, but walk-ups are nearly always available without a wait. Since opening, menu variety and portion size have improved, and we like making a stop here in the middle of the afternoon to cool off, pass around shared appetizers, and try a couple of fruity drinks. More expensive entrees are probably done better elsewhere, as the menu unsuccessfully tries to marry mainstream-sounding dishes with more-interesting spices. Kids can pick from a Beef Slider or Chicken Kebab for about $10 each. The view of the nighttime fireworks is largely blocked by islands and trees, but it's a suitable spot for casual viewing and to enjoy the lovely music.

Takumi-Tei

Japan Pavilion, ground floor, to the right of Mitsukoshi Department Store
CUISINE Japanese. **HOURS** 4pm–park close. **DDP** No.
PRICES Dinner Appetizers: $10-$27. Entrées: $37–$93. Kids: $18–$27.

OVERVIEW The newest kid on the block is also the most expensive, with Takumi-Tei opening during July 2019 with a $93 A-5 Wagyu Tenderloin on the menu and a $58 average entree price. Japanese for "house of the artisan," your money buys you an appreciable amount of serenity with each of the five small dining rooms themed to natural elements with water, wood, earth, stone, and paper represented. Meals here feel incredibly special with dedicated, friendly staff providing an authentic kaiseki, or traditional multi-course, meal. We recommend the Omakase experience, a six-course extravaganza featuring all of the season's freshest flavors accompanied by tableside tea service. The half-dozen nigiri selections are fresh and we also recommend the marinated duck and maki sushi. Our dinner for two took about two and a half hours and cost more than $400 after drinks and tip, but we left more than satisfied. You can save some money by opting for just one omakase meal supplemented by a second entree or sushi selection. Consider Takumi-Tei for that special date night meal, particularly if you don't want to leave the theme park. There isn't a finer experience on property outside of Victoria & Albert's and Takumi-Tei is much more tranquil and welcoming.

Teppan Edo

Japan Pavilion, above Mitsukoshi Department Store

CUISINE Japanese steakhouse. **HOURS** 12pm–park close. **DDP** Yes.

PRICES Lunch/Dinner Appetizers: $4–$14. Sushi: $13–$18. Entrées: $24–$37. Kids: $15–$16.

OVERVIEW This Japanese steakhouse seats eight guests around each of the many hibachi grills in one of six contemporary, windowless dining rooms. Parties with fewer than eight will most likely be seated with other parties. Food is prepared at each grill by Japanese chefs who interact with guests and put on a small show while cooking. Steak, chicken, shrimp, swordfish, vegetables, and other entrees are consistently under-seasoned, but the accompanying dips aid flavor. All meals arrive alongside rice and yakisoba. Kids are usually enamored by the friendly chefs as meals are created before their eyes. Service is sweet and attentive.

Tokyo Dining

Japan Pavilion, above Mitsukoshi Department Store

CUISINE Japanese, mostly tempura and sushi. **HOURS** 12pm–park close. **DDP** Yes.

PRICES Lunch/Dinner Appetizers: $5–$10. Sushi: $6–$18. Entrées: $21–$36. Kids: $14.

OVERVIEW Tokyo Dining is a sleek, traditional Japanese restaurant with floor-to-ceiling windows looking out at World Showcase Lagoon on one side. It is much quieter and calmer than sister restaurant Teppan Edo, and, without the hibachi grills, is a more traditional dining experience. The menu focuses on sushi, steak, and tempura, with over two dozen selections. Kids' options include a California roll, ramen, chicken tempura nuggets, and a teriyaki burger.

Tutto Italia

Italy Pavilion, on the left

CUISINE Italian. **HOURS** 11:30am–park close. **DDP** Yes.

PRICES Lunch/Dinner Appetizers: $9–$20. Lunch Entrées: $19–$35. Dinner Entrées: $22–$36. Kids: $10+.

OVERVIEW Featuring murals of ancient Rome amid shimmering chandeliers, Tutto Italia evokes Old World charm inside this traditional, formal Italian restaurant. Your omnipresent server will cater to your every need as you peruse a menu heavy on pasta, prosciutto, and lean protein. Lunch is less expensive than dinner, with several sandwiches and entrees around $20. Kids choose between pizza, spaghetti, mozzarella sticks, and chicken tenders. The venue is beautiful and service is typically splendid with high-quality food and a keen eye for detail.

Via Napoli

Italy Pavilion, in the back

CUISINE Pizza (predominantly). **HOURS** 11:30am–park close. **DDP** Yes. **PRICES** Lunch/Dinner Appetizers: $9–$19. Entrées: $18–$35. Pizzas: $18–$48+. Kids: $10.

OVERVIEW Themed to a rustic Neapolitan pizzeria, Via Napoli takes its pizza, which is cooked at 900 degrees in one of three wood-fired ovens, very seriously. So seriously that they import their flour and tomatoes from Italy and source water from a secret spring in Pennsylvania that has the same unique properties as water from the homeland. Prices may seem high at first glance, but a $45 specialty mezzo metro pizza is plenty to feed four to five hungry adults, bringing per-person costs lower than most other Disney restaurants. Napoli is loud and service is frequently impersonal, but stick to the big pizzas and you'll leave satisfied for not much more money than quick service.

DINING AT DISNEY'S HOLLYWOOD STUDIOS

Disney's Hollywood Studios runs the food quality gamut more than any of the other theme parks. Our table service recommendations are Sci-Fi Dine-In Theater and 50's Prime Time Café, both of which offer richly themed atmospheres and relatively inexpensive fare. Dave prefers the comfort food favorites at 50's Prime Time, while Josh gives the nod to Sci-Fi, with its fun mockup of a drive-in theater and a menu that focuses on inexpensive sandwiches and hamburgers, in addition to steak and ribs. Much more expensive—and with much finer food—is Hollywood Brown Derby, a signature restaurant (two credits on the Dining Plan) where the servers wear tuxedos and the fancy dinner entrées average $39. Lunch offers good value with several sandwiches and entrees under $25. If you're paying cash, consider an afternoon reservation before 3pm to take advantage of less expensive options. Mama Melrose serves inexpensive basic Italian favorites alongside flatbread pizzas that are higher quality than the nearby quick service pizzeria for only a couple dollars more. Hollywood & Vine is a fun character buffet hosted by singing and dancing Disney Jr. characters for breakfast, followed by a seasonally themed lunch and dinner hosted by Minnie and friends. In April 2019, Disney announced Roundup Rodeo BBQ, a new barbecue restaurant that will situate itself near the entrance to Toy Story Land. We expect it to open in late 2020.

Studios' quick service choices have expanded in recent memory, with newer, more interesting dishes added to legacy outlets and new offerings in Galaxy's Edge. For the most choices, visit Sunset Ranch Market on Sunset Boulevard in front of Tower of Terror, where you'll find everything from burgers to pizza to barbecue to salads to hot dogs to ice cream sundaes. On the downside, the Market is made up of five or six individual kiosks that all offer different menu items and seating is all outside. Woody's Lunch Box opened with Toy Story Land on June 30, 2018, offering breakfast, lunch, and dinner. We like the sandwiches offered during all three meals, but mobile order is a must as there are only two registers for ordering and lines are typically long from 11am onward. Seating is also all outdoors and incredibly limited. The BBQ brisket melt with macaroni salad is our favorite.

We're less enthusiastic about most of the other long-standing options. First, PizzeRizzo, the quick service pizza outlet that replaced Pizza Planet, serves mediocre reheated pizzas. On the plus side, seating is plentiful indoors and out and the atmosphere is fun with all of the Muppets gags. Backlot Express is your spot for typical Disney burgers and chicken nuggets, in addition to some tastier options like the Cuban sandwich and Southwest salad. It's richly themed with a lot of covered outdoor seating and refillable sodas, making for a pleasant experience. Dockside Diner is located on Echo Lake and offers a revolving menu of entrees that currently includes hot dogs, sliders, and snacks. Finally, ABC Commissary offers the most air-conditioning with a lunch menu focusing on burgers, salads, sandwiches, and fried food. After 4pm, a fast casual concept takes over where diners order at the register and food is delivered to the table. Entrees are more expensive with an $18+ Rib Platter leading the way along with a $16 Pot Roast dish and $15 Shrimp Teriyaki Bowl. Outside of Galaxy's Edge, we recommend Sunset Ranch Market first. Backlot Express and ABC Commissary are sound air-conditioned backups.

Luckily, Star Wars: Galaxy's Edge brings a variety of new quick service and bar options, though the table service restaurant originally teased was canceled. All of the new additions impress on quality, though prices are also higher than similar offerings outside of the land.

Batuu is home to five main food and drink outlets. Oga's Cantina offers a wide assortment of concoctions, both alcoholic and non-alcoholic, and all served in unique vessels. The Milk Stand serves the Blue and Green Milk that Luke Skywalker made famous. Both beverages are plant-based, non-dairy drinks, with the option to add alcohol or a souvenir cup resembling a jug. Docking Bay 7 Food and Cargo is the main quick service, offering a bounty of upscale fast food selections that include ribs served with a blueberry corn muffin and a plant-based kefta "meatball" dish with herb hummus and tomato-cucumber relish with pita bread, and much more. Ronto Roasters utilizes an old podracer engine to roast meats that are used in a variety of wraps, including our favorite, the Ronto Wrap with pork sausage. Rounding out the major options, Kat Saka's Kettle is famous for their Outpost Mix, which is a popcorn snack combining savory, spicy, and sweet flavors.

50's Prime Time Café

Echo Lake, near Hollywood & Vine

CUISINE American comfort food. **HOURS** 11am–park close. **DDP** Yes.
PRICES Lunch/Dinner Appetizers: $9–$13. Entrees: $17–$28. Kids: $10–$13.
OVERVIEW This nostalgic throwback to a simpler time features a number of period piece knick-knacks as well as televisions that show clips from 1950s-era shows. Themed to Mom's kitchen, your servers will take responsibility for raising you right and dole out punishment as required. The kids are sure to get a kick out of your server chastising Dad for wearing his Mickey Ears to the table. A good sense of humor is needed to enjoy the fried chicken, pot roast, meatloaf, and Mom's other comfort foods. Fried chicken, the fresh fish, and the chicken pot pie are your best bets. Request a table with a TV.

BaseLine Tap House

To the left of Sci-Fi Dine-In

OVERVIEW While not a restaurant, this bar is worth its own entry, featuring around nine Californian beers on draft and a fantastic charcuterie platter and other snacks. There's plentiful seating indoors and out and to-go cups are offered in 16- and 22-ounce sizes, in addition to a flight of four 5-ounce beers. Stop by to take a load off at your leisure.

Hollywood Brown Derby

End of Hollywood Boulevard, on the right

CUISINE Contemporary American fine dining. **HOURS** 12pm–park close. **DDP** 2 credits.
PRICES Lunch/Dinner Appetizers: $12–$17. Lunch Entrees: $18–$49. Dinner Entrees: $29–$49. Kids: $8–$16.
OVERVIEW Serving up the best food at Hollywood Studios, this signature restaurant focuses on filet of beef and crab rather than burgers and chicken nuggets. A replica of the original Brown Derby, it retains much of the glamour of the 1930s original, with white linen tablecloths, tuxedo-clad servers, and an exquisite eye for detail—if it weren't for all the guests wearing cargo shorts, WDW t-shirts, and Goofy hats. Kids are unlikely to connect here, but they are welcome, with a kids' menu that includes hot dogs and grilled beef, chicken, or fish. We prefer lunch when a couple of sandwiches in the $18-$25 range are typically offered through 3pm.

When the weather is nice, the outdoor patio area works as a walk-up lounge that offers a menu of tapas and drinks, in addition to the full Brown Derby menu. If there's space, it's a great way to indulge on a margarita flight or glass of wine alongside a famous Cobb Salad or innovative sliders.

Hollywood & Vine

Character meal (Disney Junior favorites at breakfast; Minnie, Mickey, Goofy, Donald, and Daisy at lunch and dinner), at Echo Lake near 50's Prime Time Café

CUISINE American. **DDP** Yes.

HOURS AND PRICES *Breakfast* (8–10:20am): $44 adults, $26 kids. *Lunch* (11:20am–3pm): $58 adults, $34 kids. *Dinner* (3:30pm–late): $58 adults, $34 kids. Pricing may vary by season.

OVERVIEW Featuring Disney Junior favorites for Play 'n Dine breakfast, the early morning meal is squarely aimed at kids who are invited to join the characters for singing, dancing, and parading throughout the meal. Minnie takes over for the Disney Junior characters during lunch and dinner alongside Mickey, Goofy, Donald, and Daisy in seasonal attire. The menu features seasonal specialties that have improved in quality in recent years. We prefer late dinners when tables empty and the characters have more time to spend with each table.

Mama Melrose's Ristorante Italiano

Streets of America, across from the exit to Muppet Vision 3D

CUISINE Americanized Italian. **HOURS** 11:30am–park close. **DDP** Yes.

PRICES Lunch/Dinner Appetizers: $8–$18. Entrees: $19–$33; Kids: $10–$12.

OVERVIEW Mama Melrose herself (not really) serves up Americanized Italian food in this backlot warehouse re-purposed (not really) into an eclectic neighborhood eatery. Mama does pizzas ($18 or less), spaghetti ($22), and Chicken alla Parmigiana ($25) better than the more expensive steaks ($33) and Pork Tenderloin ($28). With one menu served all day, Mama is best at dinner. While not as richly themed as Sci-Fi or 50's, Mama's checked curtains, overhead Christmas lights, and old-time photographs of Disney characters create a fun, casual atmosphere. Kids' menu includes cheese pizzas, chicken parmesan, spaghetti, and grilled chicken.

Oga's Cantina

Star Wars: Galaxy's Edge near the Millennium Falcon

OVERVIEW Oga's Cantina is the only eatery in Galaxy's Edge that accepts, and often requires, reservations, but its food menu is limited to just a couple of items, typically including a charcuterie board of sorts that you may need to order off-menu, and a bowl of crispy chips and vegetables served with a spicy chermoula dip. Most guests come to the lounge to order a beer, wine, or cocktail, and then enjoy the original music spun by DJ-R3X, a droid and pilot who you might recognize from the original Star Tours. The dark, seedy atmosphere is a lot of fun, but be aware that cocktails start at $15 and a draft beer will set you back about the same. Unique non-alcoholic drinks are also available for around $8. Because of its small size and incredible popularity, a strict 45-minute maximum stay is usually enforced, and the space is typically cramped. It's not the sort of place where you can leisurely sit for a couple of hours while sipping some innovative cocktails, but even casual Star Wars fans should consider a stop for a drink. Reservations are limited, so book as soon as possible.

Sci-Fi Dine-In Theater

Streets of America, near ABC Commissary

CUISINE American. **HOURS** 11am–park close. **DDP** Yes.

PRICES Lunch/Dinner: Appetizers: $8–$20. Entrees: $16–$33. Kids: $10–$12.

OVERVIEW Diners sit inside classic car-shaped booths at this indoor "drive-in theater," while old black-and-white movie clips, trailers, and commercials play on a large movie screen ahead. Above, the ceiling is lit up like the night sky, complete with twinkling stars. The menu offers several sandwiches and burgers around $20 all day, making this a great value out-of-pocket at dinner. The more expensive steak ($33) and chicken pasta ($24) don't offer as much value. The restaurant is dark, but kids usually love the carhop shtick and campy clips on screen. Kids' meal choices include cheeseburgers, chicken tenders, pasta, and a beef skewer.

DINING AT MAGIC KINGDOM

Three of the most popular restaurants in all of Walt Disney World are in Magic Kingdom. The most popular, Be Our Guest, not only serves upscale, French-inspired fare, but it was also the first place in the Magic Kingdom to offer wine or beer with dinner. It operates as a quick service for breakfast from 8–10:30am and then serves lunch from 11am to 2:30pm daily. It's currently the only quick service that not only accepts reservations for breakfast and lunch up to 180 days in advance, but largely requires them if you'd like to dine. They do accept a limited number of walkups if you're unable to secure a reservation, particularly after 2pm. If you're interested in reserving breakfast or lunch, do so as early as possible. As of July 27, 2018, the restaurant exclusively serves a 3-course prix fixe meal during dinner that includes choice of appetizer and entrée along with a dessert platter. Dinner costs two table service credits on the Dining Plan, while breakfast and lunch run one quick service credit.

Magic Kingdom is also home to two of the most popular character meals: Crystal Palace and Cinderella's Royal Table. The Crystal Palace buffet features Winnie the Pooh, Tigger, Piglet, and Eeyore in a Victorian solarium setting. Royal Table is located inside Cinderella Castle and includes a picture with Cinderella, in addition to four princesses meeting diners tableside. Both are excellent overall experiences for the target audience, but neither is likely to impress on food quality alone.

Liberty Tree Tavern specializes in an all-you-care-to-enjoy platter featuring turkey, pot roast, sliced pork loin, and all the accompaniments for both lunch and dinner. Several a la carte entrees are available for lunch, including fish and chips, pot roast, turkey, hamburgers, and a lobster roll. Tony's Town Square and Plaza Restaurant are two other options. We prefer Plaza, where most sandwiches come in under $20 and the quaint Victorian theming charms. We're less enthusiastic about Tony's Town Square after it went to just one menu served all day in June 2015. Many of the less expensive options were eliminated and what's left is generally overpriced and lower quality than most other restaurants.

Jungle Skipper Canteen is the new kid on the block, having opened in December 2015 in the old Adventureland Veranda space across from Swiss Family Treehouse. The theming and details in each of the three main dining rooms are a lot of fun, and while the food might initially seem exotic, the flavors are more familiar than you might be expecting.

The character meals are excellent if you can swing the cost and have members of the group who want to meet the characters. Otherwise, for table service lunch with cash, we like Skipper Canteen, Liberty Tree Tavern, and Plaza Restaurant. Dinner is best at Be Our Guest and Plaza Restaurant.

Magic Kingdom quick service is mostly burgers, hot dogs, and chicken nuggets, but variety has improved in recent memory. Josh's recommendation is Columbia Harbour House, where you'll find grilled salmon, lobster rolls, fried shrimp platters, a tuna fish sandwich, and great soups and fresh salads. The second floor seating area is usually quiet because there's no elevator access for strollers and the view of the Rapunzel area is more scenic than most. We also like Pecos Bill in Frontierland, where you'll find a variety of southwestern hits like rice bowls and tacos, in addition to burgers and nachos. The extensive toppings bar allows diners to load up their food with as much sour cream, cheese, salsa, and more as they like.

Cosmic Ray's in Tomorrowland usually consolidates its menu into about ten different entrees that are now available at all three bays, which is a departure from how it used to operate with different offerings at each set of registers. Air-conditioning is plentiful, but this is decidedly average Disney fast food with few exceptions, though the Greek salad with or without chicken is quite good. Pinocchio Village Haus in Fantasyland serves interesting flatbread pizzas, salads, and a chicken parmesan in a sandwich or with pasta. Casey's Corner, serving up a few variations of the usual hot dog, is the last major quick service. About $12 buys you a foot-long all-beef hot dog with your choice of chili/cheese or macaroni & cheese/bacon with fries or apple slices. A plain hot dog and corn dog nuggets are also available.

Several quick service outlets are seasonal, based on expected crowds, or operate with limited hours or menus. Tortuga Tavern, across from Pirates of the Caribbean, serves hot dogs and Caribbean favorites. Sleepy Hollow Refreshments serves a fantastic Fruit and Nutella Waffle Sandwich, in addition to a Spicy Chicken Sandwich, waffles, funnel cakes, and more. Gaston's Tavern no longer serves the popular pork shank, instead opting for less-than-stellar temporary fillers. Friar's Nook serves tater tots with a variety of different flavor combinations and bratwurst. When it's open, Tomorrowland Terrace provides a pretty setting and an ever-changing menu that's often inconsistent. But if it is operating, it's a quick, no-nonsense experience. Other kiosks serve a variety of turkey legs and other snacks.

Overall, we suggest Columbia Harbour House, Pecos Bill, and Be Our Guest for quick service lunch, and the first two for a quick service dinner.

Be Our Guest Restaurant

Fantasyland, near Belle's Village

CUISINE French/American. **HOURS** 4pm–late. **DDP** Yes (2 credits).

PRICES Prix-fixe dinner: $64 adults, $38 kids (includes tax). Breakfast and lunch are available as quick-service meals. Make a reservation as early as you can because they're severely limited.

OVERVIEW Set inside Beast's enchanted castle, Be Our Guest is one of Disney's most lavishly themed restaurants. With three elaborately decorated rooms, you may find yourself in the dark and mysterious West Wing, the expansive two-story Grand Ballroom, or the bright Rose Gallery complete with a spinning Belle and Beast music box. During dinner, a 3-course fixed-price menu offering upscale cuisine with a French twist is served. Appetizer choices include Escargots or French Onion Soup, with entrée selections including Center Cut Filet Mignon, Poulet Rouge Chicken, Roasted Lamb Chops, and Pork Tenderloin. Kids' appetizer choices include salad or fruit and cheese along with a choice of chicken, steak, shrimp, or macaroni and cheese for the main course. Dinner reservations remain incredibly difficult to secure, so book as soon as possible, and continue to check for availability as your desired dining date approaches as cancellations are common. Beast meets with guests in a separate room after dinner.

Cinderella's Royal Table

Princess character meal, in Cinderella Castle with check-in at rear of castle
CUISINE American. **DDP** Yes (2 credits).

HOURS AND PRICES *Breakfast* (8–10:15am): $76 adults, $45 kids. *Lunch* (11:40am–2:50pm): $92 adults, $55 kids. *Dinner* (4pm–late): $92 adults, $55 kids.

OVERVIEW By far the most popular character meal, dining here is ordinarily the only way for guests to see the inside of Cinderella Castle. The pricey affair begins in the Grand Hall waiting area and continues through a personal meet and greet with Cinderella on the ground floor. Continue up the red-carpeted spiraling staircase and enter the banquet hall fit for kings and queens. Four princesses greet tableside–usually Ariel, Aurora, Jasmine, and Snow White, and a picture package with Cinderella is available on PhotoPass. Diners select items from a set menu featuring upscale fare. Breakfast choices include the standard plate of bacon, eggs, and sausage, or the more lavish shrimp and grits or grilled beef tenderloin. Lunch and dinner typically begin with choice of soup, salad, or another upscale item like a seared scallop or charcuterie, with entrée selections including beef tenderloin, pork chop, or grilled fish, along with seasonal vegetarian options. Food quality and service are decent, but you're paying for the magical atmosphere, princess interaction, and photos. For cash, breakfast is the best and cheapest meal; on the DDP, all meals are two credits. Lunch is the easiest reservation to secure.

Crystal Palace

Character meal, at end of Main Street on the left, past Casey's Corner
CUISINE American. **DDP** Yes.

HOURS AND PRICES *Breakfast* (8–10:45am): $44 adults, $28 kids. *Lunch* (11:30am–2:45pm): $58 adults, $34 kids. *Dinner* (3pm–late): $58 adults, $34 kids.

OVERVIEW Join Winnie the Pooh, Tigger, Eeyore, and Piglet at this all-you-care-to-enjoy buffet. The bright, airy restaurant is inspired by Victorian greenhouses of the late 1800s, complete with high ceilings, character topiaries, and plenty of natural sunlight. Character interaction is above average, as is the food, which includes Spit-roasted Carved meats, Spice Boiled Shrimp, 20+ salads, and over a dozen desserts. Crystal Palace is often the most over-booked restaurant on property. Even with a reservation, plan to wait 15–30 minutes for your table. For guests paying cash, a late breakfast is the best choice—cheaper than lunch or dinner, shorter waits, and no rush to get through the meal.

Jungle Navigation Co., Ltd. Skipper Canteen

Adventureland near Sunshine Tree Terrace and Swiss Family Robinson Treehouse
CUISINE Primarily Asia, South America, and Africa. **HOURS** 11:30am–late.
DDP Yes.

PRICES Lunch/Dinner Appetizers: $9–13. Entrees: $19–36. Kids: $10–13.

OVERVIEW Skipper Canteen marries innovative design details with a menu of authentic flavors born from the adventures of the punny Jungle Cruise skippers just down the road. With several unique dining rooms, from the bright and airy colonial-era mess hall, to the mysterious secret meeting room used by the famous Society of Explorers and Adventurers, the Canteen may just be Disney's most immersive restaurant yet. Food choices breathe a bit of fresh air into Magic Kingdom's culinary landscape, but the menu may not initially appeal to those uninterested in trying something a little different. But never fear, the flavors are more familiar than you might expect, with the usual chicken, steak, pork, and lamb gussied up with some unique spices and sauces. Kids' choices include steak, chicken, grilled shrimp, chicken noodle soup, and macaroni and cheese. Overall, Skipper Canteen is a unique opportunity to try something completely unlike anything else at Magic Kingdom. We recommend giving it a try.

Liberty Tree Tavern

Liberty Square, near Diamond Horseshoe
CUISINE American. **DDP** Yes.

HOURS AND PRICES *Table-service Lunch* (11am–3pm): Appetizers: $9–$14. Entrees: $18–$26. Kids: $10–$12. *Family-style Lunch and Dinner* (11am–close): $42 adults, $22 kids.

OVERVIEW Liberty Tree is a Colonial-themed tavern featuring candelabra chandeliers, brick fireplaces, and rooms filled with artifacts from some of America's most famous patriots. The Patriot's Platter is the featured item for both lunch and dinner and includes turkey, pot roast, and pork loin, with sides of macaroni & cheese, mashed potatoes, and stuffing. The meal begins with salad and ends with a warm dessert. While the Patriot's Platter is the only dinner item, lunch offers a few a la carte entrée options, like pot roast, fish & chips, and a hamburger. These less expensive options are plenty to fill most appetites and may be preferable over the fixed price dinner for those paying cash. Platter food quality varies between average and above average, making other options more appealing in most situations.

The Plaza Restaurant

End of Main Street, on the right
CUISINE American. **HOURS** Breakfast: 7:45am-10:30am.
Lunch: 11am-2:55pm. Dinner: 3pm-late. **DDP** Yes.

PRICES Breakfast Entrees: $14-$18. Kids: $6-$8. Lunch/Dinner Appetizers: $8–$13. Lunch Entrees: $17–$22. Dinner Entrees: $18-$32. Kids: $9–$11.

OVERVIEW The Plaza features Art Nouveau touches inside a turn-of-the-century ice cream parlor right at the end of Main Street. Now serving all day, breakfast is one of the best meals anywhere with a menu that features a 10-ounce steak or lobster eggs benedict, both under $20. Mickey waffles are on the menu for kids and adults. The lunch menu largely features the same salads, sandwiches, and burgers that have kept The Plaza as the least expensive table service restaurant on property for many years. A couple of more expensive entrees join the mix during lunch service before dinner begins, in turn adding a pricey steak, pork chop, and lobster salad. During dinner, many of the less expensive sandwiches are no longer available. Kids' choices are the same for both lunch and dinner with turkey, grilled cheese, or peanut butter and jelly sandwiches joining chicken tenders or a cheeseburger. We recommend a late breakfast or lunch as the quality of the food doesn't justify the higher prices during dinner. Consider sharing a sandwich and one of their delicious milkshakes or sundaes to help reduce costs further. Portions are large.

Tony's Town Square Restaurant

Entry Plaza, on the right

CUISINE Americanized Italian. **HOURS** 11:30am–late. **DDP** Yes.

PRICES Lunch/Dinner Appetizers: $9–$16. Entrees: $19–$36. Kids: $10–12.

OVERVIEW Modeled after Tony's from *Lady and the Tramp*, guests have an opportunity to relive the romance at this casual family trattoria that serves Olive-Garden-quality Italian food in a relaxing atmosphere. Since moving to one menu all day, Tony's has eliminated many of the less expensive lunch entrées that presented a good value to diners. Quality on the higher-end items doesn't justify the prices, and we usually recommend that people head elsewhere. Kids' choices include spaghetti, pizzas, and pasta. Service is conspicuously fast, with most meals complete within an hour.

Dining Reviews: Disney Springs

Formerly known as Downtown Disney, the Disney Springs ("DS" or occasionally "Springs") shopping and entertainment complex includes more than three dozen table service restaurants and quick services, most on the Dining Plan and reservable on My Disney Experience. Some, like The BOATHOUSE, Paradiso 37, Morimoto Asia, House of Blues, STK, Frontera Cocina, Wolfgang Puck Bar & Grill, and Raglan Road, have additional capacity that can be reserved directly with the restaurant over the phone or via OpenTable.com. In addition to restaurants, you'll find many stores, some Disney and others of the variety you'd find at the local mall. There's also the AMC movie theater, Splitsville upscale bowling alley, and House of Blues concert venue. Note that DisneyQuest permanently closed in July 2017 to make way for a new NBA concept and Cirque du Soleil's final performance of La Nouba was December 31, 2017.

Disney Springs features four distinct neighborhoods: The Landing, Marketplace, West Side, and Town Center. The bulk of the new venues are in The Landing and Town Center, while The West Side and Marketplace remain relatively untouched from their former Downtown Disney days.

THE WEST SIDE West Side quick service options are more diverse than ever. House of Blues opened a decent barbecue joint in late 2013 —seating is also outside, but live music permeates the area beginning daily around 4pm and happy hour offers some drink specials throughout the day. Pepe, attached to Jaleo, is serviceable, but prices are high given the small portions and the atmosphere is incredibly bland, making it an easy skip. The larger of the two Starbucks locations is here, reliably offering the company's usual beverage and food lineup for about the same cost as your local shop. Finally, Disney has gotten into the food truck game with an area dedicated to them located across from the AMC Theater. The trucks serve an ever-changing selection of items, some of which are inspired by classic theme park offerings and others designed exclusively for Disney Springs. Closer to Planet Hollywood, you'll find a collection of quick service kiosks that include Haagen-Dazs, Wetzel's Pretzels, Italian Ice, and a kiosk that serves build your own wraps/rice bowls/noodle bowls, beer, and drinks called YeSake. Each offers quick, no-nonsense snacks mostly between three and ten dollars. Beatrix at Disney Springs may open sometime in late 2020 in the old Bongos spot, and is expected to offer grab-and-go sandwiches, salads, juices, and more.

On the table service front, Splitsville often has last-minute availability and is an easy walk-up when other restaurants are quoting 45+ minute waits without a reservation, as they often are after 6pm. Its pizza, burgers, and sushi are surprisingly good. House of Blues is economically-priced and extremely casual for a nice, no-fuss lunch or dinner. It may be busier if a popular act is scheduled to perform in the club next door. Jaleo, brought by Chef José Andrés, features an incredibly-long menu of Spanish tapas, in addition to several larger, more expensive dishes. With most portions just a few bites and many plates running $12-$15, you can spend a lot of money very quickly, but the food is quite good. The massive NBA Experience now sits in the old DisneyQuest space, bringing with it a slew of interactive experiences tying back to the National Basketball Association. City Works Eatery and Pour House will open next door, offering more than 80 beers on tap along with a food menu featuring bar bites, burgers, and shareables later in 2019. Beatrix may or may not open in 2020, but the restaurant that hails from Chicago's Lettuce Entertain You Enterprises, and is expected to offer "healthful comfort food" focusing on vegan and gluten-free options, will open in place of Bongos Cuban Café.

A new Cirque du Soleil show will debut in the same theater as La Nouba, across from the House of Blues, on March 20, 2020. The show, titled "Drawn to Life," is expected to blend Cirque's unparalleled acrobatics with the magic of Disney animation. We expect a spellbinding show that should put a punctuation mark at the end of visiting Disney Springs. Performances are currently scheduled on Tuesdays through Saturdays with tickets starting at $99 and going up quickly from there.

THE LANDING Once home to Pleasure Island, The Landing shifts focus away from the clubs and dance halls that used to permeate the area and replaces them with restaurants, bars, and outdoor music in the evenings. There are just two holdovers from the previous era: Paradiso 37 and Raglan Road. Portobello survived for a while, but reopened with a new look in the middle of 2018 as Terralina Crafted Italian. Raglan Road Irish Pub is best at dinner. While prices are a couple dollars higher here and there, the live music and dancing are worth the extra cost. Paradiso is great for appetizers and margaritas, but the south-of-the-border entrees are overpriced and the atmosphere is lackluster considering the other options. Fulton's Crab House reopened as Paddlefish in February 2017 with a similar focus on steak and seafood. Our favorite meal is the weekend brunch, when items like the Crab Benedict and Monte Cristo are added to the reasonably priced lunch menu.

The BOATHOUSE (the capitalization is part of the name), offering upscale seafood and steaks, in addition to less expensive salads and sandwiches, opened in May 2015 as the first of the major new restaurants. Operated by Gibsons out of Chicago, we like that the menu offers a wide range of prices in a casual atmosphere. Morimoto Asia, brought to you by Chef Masaharu Morimoto of *Iron Chef* fame, opened in September 2015, serving high-end seafood, sushi, and Asian cuisine in an upscale atmosphere. Jock Lindsey's Hangar Bar might be the best themed dining venue on property, which is saying something when it's going up against the likes of T-Rex and Trader Sam's Grog Grotto. Visit for a fun cocktail served in one of their souvenir glasses or a casual bite to eat. All three offer expansive, walk-up bar areas. STK Orlando joined the field in late May 2016, blending expensive a la carte steaks and seafood in a kind of strange, club atmosphere that seems too loud and contemporary to fit in with most of what Disney Springs offers. It may yet find its intended audience. Helmed by celebrity chef Art Smith, Homecomin' Florida followed in mid-July with a menu emphasizing Southern cooking with specialties like fried chicken & doughnuts, cheddar cheese drop biscuits, and fried catfish. Drinks are particularly inspired.

Patina Group, the same parent company that operates the Italian eateries in Epcot and Morimoto Asia in Disney Springs, opened a trifecta of restaurants in late 2017. The Edison is an interesting venue with an industrial Gothic-style theme designed to look like a 1920s electric company. Before 9:30pm, it operates like most restaurants offering table service lunch and dinner with plenty of bar and lounge areas spread out on two large floors. After 9:30pm, a night-club atmosphere takes over with live music and entertainment that includes contortionists, jugglers, aerialists, and more. We typically recommend dining elsewhere with those interested in a drink and a show arriving later in the evening.

Two Italian restaurants also join the scene. Better is Maria & Enzo's Ristorante, themed to an elegant eatery inside of an old airline terminal from the 1930s. The cocktail menu is diverse and the lunch menu in particular offers large portions of inspired food at reasonable prices. The atmosphere is a lot of fun. Enzo's Hideaway Bar is less impressive with the speakeasy theme falling flat along with an overpriced menu with food that doesn't match the restaurant next door. We don't recommend much more than a stop for a drink and perhaps a shareable appetizer.

Quick service options at The Landing are slimmer with three main options, each operated by its attached restaurant. Cookes of Dublin is operated by Raglan Road—we like their fish & chips, sandwiches, and other Irish fare a lot for lunch and early dinners, but it gets backed up in the evenings and there's rarely anywhere to sit. Morimoto Asia Street Food, which shares part of its kitchen with Morimoto Asia, serves several of the restaurant's specialties. Seating for both is all outdoors. Pizza Ponte resides next to Maria & Enzo's and serves pizza similar to Via Napoli for around $7 per slice, in addition to sandwiches and desserts. It's a good choice for a quick bite when lines are short, but Blaze Pizza offers more customizability and larger portions. You'll also find a great stop for a cold treat in Vivoli il Gelato and at Tea Traders Café by Joffrey's, which offers a variety of inexpensive snacks and a full menu of teas and other drinks. There's also Erin McKenna's Bakery, specializing in vegan/allergy-friendly sweets, and The Ganachery, serving high-end ganache and chocolate.

Retail in The Landing is largely an after-thought, but some guests may enjoy perusing the footwear at Havaianas or Sanuk, the headwear at Chapel Hats, or the jewelry at Erwin Pearl, among a couple of other largely forgettable outlets.

THE MARKETPLACE The Marketplace section is predominantly retail with a few restaurants and quick services mixed in. Shoppers looking for Disney items should pay special attention to World of Disney, Tren-D, Once Upon A Toy, The Art of Disney, and the Marketplace Co-Op. You'll find just about every imaginable theme park item in one of these stores. The LEGO Store is one of the most popular shops in all of WDW, with a huge variety of sets available for purchase, in addition to some interactive opportunities for kids to put together their own LEGO creations. The Bibbidi Bobbidi Boutique, a salon that specializes in magical makeovers for kids between the ages of 3 and 12, is attached to Once Upon A Toy. Consider booking a reservation if you can't find availability at its sister location inside Cinderella Castle.

The Marketplace is home to two of our favorite Springs' quick services from the Downtown Disney days: Earl of Sandwich and Wolfgang Puck Express. Earl of Sandwich serves excellent hot sandwiches for around eight dollars each, in addition to great tasting sides and desserts. Lines can appear long, but service is surprisingly fast. Wolfgang Puck Express is more expensive than most quick services, but its food is table service quality and a server will deliver your meal and take care of drink refills and other needs. Ghirardelli Ice Cream and Chocolate Shop is one of the best places on property to indulge. Decadent sundaes are $9–$10 and, for those looking to be able to walk out after without assistance, best shared. A walk-up Starbucks is located in front of World of Disney and serves the full drink menu to-go, in addition to select food items. Two quick service kiosks are located on the bridge that connects the LEGO Store area with the Rainforest Café area. B.B. Wolf's Sausage Co. specializes in what you might expect, offering a variety of sausage entrees to-go. Aristocrepes, offering sweet and savory crepes, is another option. But with few tables nearby, none of which are air-conditioned, most guests will likely want to seek out more of a destination eatery.

Two kid favorites operated by the same parent company are located in the Marketplace: Rainforest Café and T-REX. Rainforest is best known for providing dining in a tropical setting complete with Animatronic animals that rival some of Disney's best. T-REX is similar, but with a dinosaur theme. We give the nod to T-REX, partly because it's more likely to be new to a visitor (there are only two locations worldwide) but also because the food and drinks are slightly more inspired. Rainforest, however, is fun and less intimidating for some youngsters than T-REX.

TOWN CENTER The majority of Town Center is new construction built on top of what used to be a parking lot. Its addition more than doubles the amount of retail space available to guests visiting the Springs. The new stores are virtually all mall brands from the likes of UGG, Vera Bradley, Under Armour, Sephora, Pandora, Anthropologie, UNIQLO, Zara, and about 35 more. Many are quick to point out that the aesthetic doesn't do much to differentiate itself from the outlet mall up the street, but that isn't necessarily a bad thing as walkways are wide and vibrant and the overall look is quaint and charming. A full listing of stores is available at DisneySprings.com.

Town Center is also home to Planet Hollywood, which reopened in February 2017 with a new planetary theme and Guy Fieri helming the burger menu. Relatively speaking, pricing is reasonable and many of the sandwiches and burgers are quite good. Still, the interior offers a hodgepodge of thematic elements and less memorabilia. It's a safe bet for anyone with limited tastes. Chicken Guy, a quick-service extension attached to Planet Hollywood, opened in August 2018, and serves fast-food chicken dishes served with a wide assortment of sauces.

It also adds Frontera Cocina, a modern Mexican restaurant brought by celebrity chef Rick Bayless and operated by the same company that takes care of dining in the Mexico Pavilion at Epcot and at Coronado Springs. We like to visit the bar area for margaritas and appetizers, but anyone looking for enchiladas, tacos, or other Mexican specialties for lunch or dinner should give it strong consideration.

Wolfgang Puck brings his Bar & Grill concept across from Planet Hollywood. Inspired by a farmhouse for one reason or another, and mixing in a laidback California vibe, the food is among the freshest and most flavorful at Disney Springs, but the atmosphere is too sterile for us to offer a strong positive recommendation. Consider requesting a window table for one of the best people-watching opportunities on property.

As far as quick service options are concerned, Blaze Fast-Fire'd Pizza serves up their own creations, or with any toppings you like, for about $10. The "fast" in the name comes from the fact that it takes less than three minutes to cook your selection. D-Luxe Burger serves up the best quick service hamburgers on property, but a single burger and fry will run you anywhere from $15 to $18, though most people will find an $8 large fry is enough to share between three or more people. With two or more people, consider the popular Duo Combos that pair two burgers, two drinks, and a fry to share for less money than ordering a la carte. The Polite Pig, brought by popular local chefs James and Julie Petrakis, doesn't quite deliver on its potential. We prefer Homecomin', which offers similarly priced food that's more consistent in a more relaxing atmosphere. Amorette's Patisserie, next to the Levi's store, serves exquisite, handmade desserts and is a must-visit for anyone looking for something sweet that isn't served on a stick. Finally, The Daily Poutine is located near World of Disney and offers a menu of french fries topped with things like gravy & cheese curds or fried yucca, black beans, pulled pork, & queso fresco. Each bowl makes for a very share-able snack, but we're not sure we'd make one into a full meal for one.

Finally, the Coca-Cola Store is mostly retail inside of a large building, but does add a rooftop bar offering a variety of cocktails, in addition to fun trays full of Coca Cola soda samples from around the world. For around $15, you can sample sixteen different sodas and eight different ice cream floats with great views of the rest of Disney Springs. Visit for a taste of something different. Literally.

VISITING DISNEY SPRINGS A visit to Disney Springs is not necessar-ily an essential part of a vacation, particularly if it's your first visit. But now that construction has largely concluded and so much is new, many potential guests will want to eye at least one visit, particularly if you're looking to enjoy some of Disney's best restaurants. Our preference is to visit in the late morning through the afternoon when crowds are much lower than the evening, making it easy to visit just about any restaurant without a reservation and enjoy the various shops with few other people around. Take a break at your resort and then consider heading out to enjoy the nighttime entertainment at the theme parks and enjoy crowds as they thin the later it gets.

Disney Springs is served by buses to and from the Disney resort hotels, in addition to slow, low-capacity boats from the Port Orleans resorts, Old Key West, and Saratoga Springs. Walking paths from Saratoga Springs and Old Key West are also available. After 4pm, Disney offers bus service from the theme parks to Disney Springs. These buses can be incredibly popular around park close, but should prove more convenient than trying to take a bus to a resort and then getting on a Disney Springs bus there. Bus service from Disney Springs to the theme parks is not offered at any time.

Getting to Disney Springs is much easier with Buena Vista Drive expanded to ten lanes and the addition of three parking garages, each of which is relatively easy to access from I-4 or on-property locations. Parking remains complimentary. Still, most Friday and Saturday nights see an influx of visitors beginning around 7pm and continuing for a couple of hours. Avoid these times if possible. Bus transportation has improved with the addition of dedicated lanes and less congestion on the roadways immediately surrounding the Springs, but routes remain convoluted and may still include a lengthy trip over to pick up/drop off at Typhoon Lagoon across the street. For those with watercraft access, we recommend taking advantage of it. Those deciding between their own vehicles or Disney buses will strongly want to consider driving them-selves for the quickest trip. But those grabbing cocktails or otherwise not in much of a hurry may still prefer Disney buses. Note that there is only one bus stop now behind the Coca-Cola Store and Planet Hollywood in the Town Center section.

The BOATHOUSE

In between Paradiso 37 and Raglan Road

CUISINE Seafood and steaks. **HOURS** 11am–11pm. **DDP** Yes (2 credits). **PRICES** Lunch/Dinner Appetizers: $8–$19. Entrées: $16–$65+. Kids: $10.

OVERVIEW Offering picturesque waterfront dining, multiple bars inside and out, and a number of diversely themed dining areas, The BOATHOUSE brings upscale cuisine wrapped up in a casual atmosphere to Disney Springs. Entrees vary wildly in price, from the $20 hamburger and $30 lobster roll all the way up to $65 for a 12-ounce filet mignon or well over $100 for the dry-aged tomahawk steak and lobster for two, neither of which include a side. Fortunately, the kitchen reliably executes the pricier steak and seafood options perfectly, and the quality is a step above just about any Disney-operated restaurant. Those who want to spend considerably less can stick with sandwiches, salads, hamburgers, fried shrimp, fish & chips, and more, most of which are under $20. Despite the high price point on some entrées, the atmosphere is decidedly casual and service is largely unrefined. If you're looking for a quiet, intimate steak dinner, this isn't it, but some people may prefer the lack of pretension.

The Edison

The Landing, across from STK Orlando

CUISINE American. **HOURS** 11:30am–1am or 2am. **DDP** Yes. **PRICES** Lunch/Dinner Appetizers: $12–$17. Lunch Entrées: $17–$24. Dinner Entrées: $20–$39. Kids: $15.

OVERVIEW Themed to a 1920s electric company with an aesthetic somewhere between steampunk and industrial-Gothic, The Edison serves up American comfort food favorites like meatloaf, steak, burgers, and fried chicken in an imaginative atmosphere. We think couples and adults 21+ will prefer the late night vibe when live music and unique acts like cabaret dancers and contortionists entertain those nibbling on appetizers and enjoying cocktails from the extensive menu. Dinner food is overpriced if you're not visiting in the evening when the entertainment takes hold, but the lunch menu features several salads and sandwiches under $20 if you'd like to check the space out but aren't as comfortable with the nighttime energy. We were initially hesitant about the after-10pm crowd ourselves, but found a fun, welcoming atmosphere just like everywhere else in Disney Springs not-named-STK. Consider stopping for a bite and a drink, but it may not be the best place to plunk down $35+ on a steak.

Enzo's Hideaway

The Landing, across from Planet Hollywood and underneath Maria & Enzo's

CUISINE Italian. **HOURS** 11:30am–12am or 1am. **DDP** Yes.

PRICES Lunch/Dinner Appetizers: $11–$18. Lunch Entrées: $17–$39. Dinner Entrées: $24–$43. Kids: $12.

OVERVIEW Enzo's Hideaway is supposed to be themed to Prohibition-era rum-running tunnels, but the space ends up being much more cavernous and much less interesting than one might hope to see. Instead of going all-in on the speakeasy vibe, the restaurant is large, open, and boring, and the food is overpriced and unimaginative. We could see stopping for a drink when other venues are crowded, but food is better elsewhere and the atmosphere is forgettable.

Frontera Cocina

Town Center, across the water from Morimoto Asia and across from Sprinkles

CUISINE Mexican. **HOURS** 11am–11pm. **DDP** Yes.

PRICES Lunch/Dinner Appetizers: $5–$14. Entrées: $19–$38. Kids: $9.

OVERVIEW Celebrity Chef Rick Bayless, who operates around ten Mexican restaurants mostly in the Chicago area, brings what is easily Disney's best Mexican restaurant to Disney Springs. The menu is relatively diverse, offering three different guacamoles, in addition to sopes and tostadas to start. Taco, Enchilada, and Carnitas entrees impress for around $25 each with a unique, seasonal menu expanding options further. The food is much more vibrant than the restaurant, but you might care about that less after a couple margaritas, which are priced on the high side at $15–$19. Consider drinks and appetizers or split an entrée at the bar for the best value.

Homecomin'—Florida Kitchen and Shine Bar

The Landing, across from Morimoto Asia

CUISINE Southern American. **HOURS** 11am–11pm or 12am. **DDP** Yes.

PRICES Lunch/Dinner Appetizers: $10–$18. Entrées: $18–$30. Kids: $10.

OVERVIEW Chef Art Smith is perhaps best known as the personal chef of Oprah Winfrey, but those who appreciate his history with Disney will remind you that he completed an internship with their College Program as well. Homecomin' Florida showcases the state's fresh flavors with appetizers like house-made pimento cheese hushpuppies served with red jalapeño jelly. The deviled eggs, which arrive in a precious carton of six, taste as good as they are cute. But many will want to go straight for the signature fried chicken served in a sandwich for $18, with doughnuts for $27, or creamy mashed potatoes and a cheddar drop biscuit for $29. Draft beer offers a nice variety of local choices and the cocktail list is inspired and reasonably priced. While the restaurant is homely and rustic, service is impeccable with a keen eye for detail and a friendly smile. It's one of our favorite new restaurants.

House of Blues

West Side, across from the NBA Experience

CUISINE Southern American. **HOURS** 11:30am–11pm on weekdays, 1am on weekends. **DDP** Yes.

PRICES Lunch/Dinner Appetizers: $8–$16. Entrées: $15–$32. Kids: $9. Bayou Brunch: $35 adults, $16 kids.

OVERVIEW Celebrity Chef Aaron Sanchez took over the menu in July 2011, "incorporating flavors from around the world" in the process. The menu still favors southern favorites like jambalaya, voodoo shrimp, and buttermilk fried chicken, but you'll find inexpensive flatbread pizzas, sandwiches, and pastas, too. Heavy on edgy religious artwork that may appeal to some more than others, Blues is supposed to be themed to a shack on the side of a road down in the New Orleans bayou. Enjoy free live music inside the restaurant on weekends after 10pm; it's calmer and more kid-friendly until then. On Saturdays and Sundays, from 10am until 1pm, the restaurant offers a Bayou Brunch Buffet featuring an assortment of classic and southern breakfast and lunch favorites accompanied by live music.

Jaleo by José Andrés

The West Side across from the AMC theater

CUISINE Spanish tapas. **HOURS** 11:30am–11pm. **DDP** Yes, two credits.

PRICES Lunch/Dinner Appetizers: $4–$40. Large Plates: $25-$69. Kids' Appetizers: $6-$12. Kids' Entrees: $8-$15.

OVERVIEW The brainchild of one of Time Magazine's "100 Most Influential People of 2018," the menu at Jaleo by José Andrés focuses on a diverse array of traditional and contemporary tapas, or small plates, in addition to paellas and other regional Spanish specialties. The interior is layered with dark reds and deep yellows that evoke the Spanish flag in a relaxed atmosphere that's just as heavy on dark woods as it is on playful elements like guests being able to dine at re-purposed foosball tables. With more than 65 selections just on the main food menu, the experience can be a bit overwhelming, but portions are so small that you may find yourself ordering about that many plates anyway. Best are the Spanish cheeses, ibérico hams, patatas bravas, head-on shrimp, bacon-wrapped dates, and any of the paellas, of which two are typically featured each night. We think Jaleo works best with two or three adults splitting a variety of tapas over the course of 90 or more relaxed minutes. With four or more people, you'll find yourself needing to double up on individual plates for everyone to have an opportunity to try everything and costs will quickly rise with stomachs left mostly empty. Those looking for a traditional dining experience should look elsewhere, but those interested in a meandering meal with excellent food and cocktails should take a closer look at the menu. Just be prepared to pay at least $75 per person after tax and tip with a drink.

Jock Lindsey's Hangar Bar

The Landing in between The BOATHOUSE and Paradiso 37

CUISINE Small plate bar food. **HOURS** 12pm–1am. **DDP** No.

PRICES Lunch/Dinner Appetizers: $9–$17.

OVERVIEW As you may or may not be aware, Jock Lindsey is Indiana Jones' longtime pilot, and the bar is ornately themed to his hangar, which was recently converted into a bar for the enjoyment of his fellow members of the Society of Explorers and Adventurers. The atmosphere inside is rich and worth a stop for those with even a passing interest in Indiana Jones, though we think the food and drink options are better at nearby Morimoto Asia and The BOATHOUSE. Still, for about $12 each, you can order a round of easily-shareable appetizers like queso fundido, sliders, a giant soft pretzel, and a whole lot more. The diverse specialty drinks are a little less expensive than other locations, but they rarely pack a punch. Consider a draft beer.

Maria & Enzo's Ristorante

The Landing, across from STK and next to The Edison

CUISINE Italian. **HOURS** 11:30am–10pm or 11pm. **DDP** Yes.

PRICES Lunch/Dinner Appetizers: $8–$18. Lunch Entrées: $12–$39. Dinner Entrées: $24–$46. Kids: $12.

OVERVIEW As the story goes, Maria & Enzo opened their trattoria inside of this 1930s airline terminal, retrofitting it with floor-to-ceiling windows and a grand staircase for good measure. The atmosphere is slightly upscale, but still perfectly welcoming and it's fun to look around the restaurant and take in the bright posters and elegant details. The menu is executed well with a focus on pasta and parmigiana, in addition to steak, fish, and seafood. Start with the calamari or arancini and you're in for a treat. There are a lot of opportunities to eat Italian at Walt Disney World, but this is a safe bet if you're in the mood for good, familiar food and large portions in a pleasant atmosphere.

Morimoto Asia

The Landing across from Raglan Road and The BOATHOUSE

CUISINE Pan-Asian. **HOURS** 11:30am–1am. **DDP** Yes, two credits.

PRICES Lunch/Dinner Appetizers: $7–$21. Lunch Entrées: $16–$36. Dinner Entrées: $16–$52. Sushi: $8–$14. Kids: $12.

OVERVIEW Officially helmed by Iron Chef Masaharu Morimoto and operated by Patina Group, the same company behind the restaurants in the Italy Pavilion at Epcot, Morimoto Asia opened in October 2015 to great fanfare. The restaurant is sleek and stylish, with impressive chandeliers said to resemble jellyfish. We prefer the restaurant's less expensive noodle and rice options with the Singapore laksa noodles and chatsu pork ramen leading the way. Sushi is on point, but the eight choices available in the main dining room all play it safe. Beer and cocktails are above average in price and quality. Consider a more casual meal in one of the two expansive bar areas.

Paddlefish

The Landing, between Terralina and T-Rex

CUISINE Steak and seafood. **HOURS** 11:30am–11pm or 12am. **DDP** Yes, two credits.

PRICES Lunch/Dinner Appetizers: $3–$20. Lunch Entrées: $12–$49. Dinner Entrées: $17–$49. Weekend Brunch Entrees: $16–$23. Kids: $9–$15.

OVERVIEW Paddlefish opened in February 2017 in place of Fulton's Crab House in a refurbished steamboat on the water. Still operated by Levy Restaurants, the problems with uneven service and questionable menu execution that plagued Fulton's seem to linger. On the plus side, the seafood is among the freshest on property and should impress. We like to visit the outdoor lounge on the third floor after it opens at 5pm for the most panoramic views and to share a couple of appetizers and drinks. Best are the lobster corn dogs, crab fries (hand-cut potatoes, lump blue crab, Louie dressing), and beef skewers. Also a great weekend brunch stop, the Bloody Mary is out of this world and the Monte Cristo impresses on size and quality. Unfortunately, inconsistent food quality and service make it difficult to recommend given the high price point for that one "date night" style meal.

Paradiso 37

Old Pleasure Island, between Portobello and West Side

CUISINE North/South American. **HOURS** 11am–2am. **DDP** Yes.

PRICES Lunch/Dinner Appetizers: $6–$19. Entrées: $16–$43. Kids: $8.

OVERVIEW The appetizers and margaritas are better than the entrées at this waterfront restaurant that focuses on cuisine of the Americas. Much busier after 6pm when the live music starts outside, Paradiso is best experienced without kids, who are unlikely to be impressed by the Latin flair or tequila tower stacked with 37 varieties. Walk-up tables are usually available, as are seats at one of the three bars.

Planet Hollywood Observatory

West Side, across from entrance to AMC Fork-and-Screen Theater

CUISINE American; lots of burgers and sandwiches. **HOURS** 11am–1am. **DDP** Yes.

PRICES Lunch/Dinner Appetizers: $12–$18. Entrées: $17–$50. Kids: $10.

OVERVIEW Planet Hollywood reopened with more of a planetarium theme in February 2017 after a lengthy refurbishment that brought many changes, including a burger menu helmed by celebrity chef Guy Fieri and the addition of an expansive outdoor bar. Around $20 each, the burgers and sandwiches should satisfy any appetite. We like the gigantic Pimento Grilled Cheese best, followed by the Bird is the Word fried chicken sandwich. While miles away from high class dining, Planet Hollywood delivers on what it sets out to accomplish and those looking for a wide variety of comfort food favorites may prefer its atmosphere as one of the most casual restaurants on property. Inside, it's quite loud with top 40 hits playing nonstop and music videos projected onto the walls. Consider requesting an outdoor table offering scenic views of Disney Springs, and look at the memorabilia on the way out.

Raglan Road

The Landing, near Fulton's and Portobello

CUISINE Irish. **HOURS** 11am–1am. **DDP** Yes.

PRICES Lunch Appetizers: $6–$17. Lunch Entrées: $11–$22. Dinner Appetizers: $7–$28. Dinner Entrées: $18–$29. Kids: $8–$12.

OVERVIEW The restaurant features a live band playing Irish songs, popular ballads, and pub classics alongside traditional Irish jigs beginning at 6pm nightly (except for Sunday, when the live band plays only during brunch). Each of the four bars, some over 130 years old, were imported directly from Ireland. Celebrity Chef Kevin Dundon is no longer attached to the restaurant, but the menu still includes many of his feature dishes, including Shepherd's Pie, Bangers and Mash, and Fish & Chips, all under $25 each for lunch or dinner. Add Guinness, Smithwick's, and a dozen more beers on draft, and you have yourself an authentically Irish good time. Kids' entrees at this family-friendly, highly-recommended restaurant include shepherd's pie, a burger, and macaroni and cheese. Nearly everything, from the food to the service to the beer, is excellent. A cult favorite among Disney World guidebook authors.

Rainforest Café

Marketplace, near Earl of Sandwich

CUISINE American. **HOURS** 11am–11pm or 12am. **DDP** Yes.

PRICES Lunch/Dinner Appetizers: $12–$21. Entrées: $17–$37. Kids: $9.

OVERVIEW See the Animal Kingdom table service reviews for background info on this raucous chain restaurant. The Disney Springs location is extremely popular with kids and online reservations are hard to come by because only part of the inventory is released to Disney. Call the restaurant directly at 407-827-8500 to book, or visit before 4pm when walk-ups don't require 60+ minute waits. The Lava Lounge next door offers the same menu without any of the restaurant's antics. The water view at the lounge is pleasant for couples, but most families will want to eat inside where the action is.

Splitsville Luxury Lanes

West Side, in between the AMC Theater and the NBA Experience

CUISINE American, Sushi, Pizza. **HOURS** 11:30am–11pm or later. **DDP** Yes.

PRICES Lunch/Dinner Appetizers: $8–$16. Sushi: $12–$20. Entrées: $17–$26. Kids: $8.

OVERVIEW The food at Splitsville is not quite as luxurious as the bowling setup (you've never read a sentence like that before, we bet), but it does offer a bevy of options, including a dozen freshly made sushi rolls, a half-dozen pizzas, a dozen sandwiches and salads, rice bowls, and more. The pricier entrées are best skipped in favor of sushi and pizza, which are executed quite well. The nicest part of dining in this 50,000 square foot complex loosely themed to 1960s kitsch is the lack of a wait for a table when Disney Springs is crawling with people. Eat outside to get away from the bowling noise and stick to beer—the cocktails are overpriced and watered down.

STK Orlando

The Landing, across from Paradiso 37

CUISINE Steak and seafood. **HOURS** 11:30am–11:55pm. **DDP** 2 credits.

PRICES Lunch/Dinner Appetizers: $11–$19. Lunch Entrées: $10–$71. Dinner Entrées: $31–$135+. Kids: $10–$17.

OVERVIEW STK is a significant departure away from anything else at Walt Disney World, blending an ultra-modern aesthetic with an atmosphere that resembles more of a Las Vegas club than a traditional steakhouse. With a live DJ appearing at 8pm nightly in the main dining room, meals are often loud and bustling as partiers mingle about at the same time families with young kids are trying to enjoy a meal. But STK does steak very well, offering a wide variety of cuts cooked to your specifications, in addition to some seafood entrees. Unlike most other steakhouses, side dish portions are incredibly small for around $13 each. We prefer The BOATHOUSE for higher quality beef at a restaurant where we can hear ourselves think, but STK in the company of friends is a unique venue that some people much cooler than these Disney World book authors may prefer. Just be aware of what you're getting into at these prices.

Terralina Crafted Italian

The Landing, to the left of Paddlefish

CUISINE Italian. **HOURS** 11am–11pm. **DDP** Yes.

PRICES Lunch/Dinner Appetizers: $7–$16. Lunch Entrées: $13–$44. Dinner Entrées: $15–$44. Kids: $7–12.

OVERVIEW Previously known as Portobello, Terralina Crafted Italian opened in the middle of 2018, still helmed by James Beard Award-winning chef Tony Mantuano and still operated by Levy. And it's still probably not a restaurant that you want to pick as your single meal at Disney Springs, particularly with other, better Italian restaurants now open. On the plus side, the atmosphere is warm and homely and the staff seems to try their best, even if they're inadequately trained. The outdoor bar area is pleasant and adding a pizza to a drink order only adds about $15. But Terralina doesn't do a single thing better than other nearby restaurants and should only be considered when it's the last eatery with availability.

T-REX Café

Marketplace, near the Lego Store

CUISINE American. **HOURS** 11am–11pm or 12am. **DDP** Yes.

PRICES Lunch/Dinner Appetizers: $9–$15. Entrées: $17–$37. Kids: $10.

OVERVIEW Operated by the same parent company as Rainforest Café, T-REX replaces Rainforest's drizzle with thundering meteor showers and singing birds with a massive undulating octopus and life-sized Animatronic dinosaurs. The T-REX menu offers a staggering number of items, mostly of decent quality and universally in large amounts. Stick with the lower-priced fare or chance a regrettable $35 steak. Younger kids may be scared of the dinosaurs, noise, fire, and occasional darkness, but most kids between the ages of six and twelve love the atmosphere. With apprehensive kids, consider a walk through the restaurant before committing to a meal, or request a table near the entrance. Call the restaurant directly at 407-828-8739 to book because few slots are offered to Disney Reservations.

Wine Bar George

Across from Jock Lindsay's Hangar Bar and next to Raglan Road

CUISINE Mostly Mediterranean. **HOURS** 11am–12am or 2am. **DDP** Yes.

PRICES Lunch/Dinner Small Plates: $9–$28. Lunch Entrées: $12–$19. Dinner Entrées: $265–$39. Kids: $10.

OVERVIEW Master Sommelier George Miliotes, who helped open California Grill back in 1995, oversees this two-story, estate-style wine bar. It offers one of the best wine lists at Walt Disney World at prices that are refreshingly accessible. Pay special attention to the "George's Finds" section of the menu, which offers a number of interesting, high-quality wines at prices that are significantly lower than what you'd pay for better-known labels. The tasty, shareable appetizers and small plates, all of which arrive with suggested wine pairings, enhance the experience further. This is an ideal stop for couples looking to enjoy some time together, but there are more comfortable restaurants for a full meal.

Wolfgang Puck Bar & Grill

The Landing, across from Chicken Guy and Planet Hollywood

CUISINE Californian with a Mediterranean Twist. **HOURS** 11am–11pm. **DDP** Yes.

PRICES Lunch/Dinner Appetizers: $5–$16. Lunch Entrees: $15-$38. Dinner Entrees: $18-$59. Kids: $8-$11.

OVERVIEW Considering the high quality of the freshly-made food, it may be unfortunate that Wolfgang Puck Bar & Grill is located inside such a bland, sterile space. Yes, there is a bit of a farmhouse feel with a laid-back, open floor plan, but you have to ask yourself if you want to enjoy your one meal at Disney Springs inside of said farmhouse. On the other hand, those looking for a standard dining experience with upscale food in a moderately-trendy restaurant will find just what they're looking for. Best are the pizzas, easily shareable as appetizers or individually as less-expensive entrees, in addition to the handmade pastas and fish.

Dining Reviews: The Disney Resorts

Disney's resorts offer the majority of the best Disney-owned restaurants on property, whether we're discussing five-star dining at Victoria & Albert's at the Grand Floridian or the rootin' tootin' good time that is hollering along to Hoop-Dee-Doo Revue at Fort Wilderness. We provide reviews of all these meals in the material that follows.

Unfortunately, complimentary resort-to-resort travel is often inconvenient because Disney does not offer resort-to-resort buses. Guests relying on Disney transportation from the values and moderates in particular will need to wait for a bus to a theme park or Disney Springs, then wait for a bus for the resort they're headed to, and then take the time to ride the bus over to the resort and find the restaurant. Disney recommends allowing 90 minutes each way for such travel. And they're not wrong. Travel is particularly taxing for early morning breakfasts when buses run less frequently (check with your concierge for the schedule) and for late night dinners when the theme parks may already be closed, limiting transfer options.

There are alternatives. Taxis are stationed outside the resorts or bell services will be glad to call, but they add $15-$40 roundtrip to the cost of the meal. We prefer Uber and Lyft, both of which offer on-demand transportation at lower costs. A ride that would cost $30 in a Mears taxi would cost around $11 with Uber. Disney's Minnie Van service, which offers on-demand pickup service from the resorts and theme parks through the regular Lyft mobile app, is another option. For a flat fee, plus an additional cost per mile, service is available to and from anywhere that Disney buses operate on-property, in addition to a number of locations that they can't. There are two main benefits to choosing a Minnie Van. First, the drivers are Disney Cast Members and the vehicles are owned by Disney. Second, each Minnie Van is equipped with two children's car seats and can accommodate up to six people. Unfortunately, the cost is about three times that of a regular Uber or Lyft ride, making the trips less economical and potentially less attractive for repeat use. Guests renting cars have it easiest and can drive directly to the resort hotels with the help of signs and GPS.

Some tips on reducing the hassle using Disney transportation.

- The monorail resorts—Contemporary, Polynesian, and Grand Floridian—are connected by the resort monorail and visiting any of them from any other will only take about 15 minutes each way.

- The Contemporary, Wilderness Lodge, and Fort Wilderness are connected by boat and visiting any of them from any other will only take about 15-30 minutes each way.

- The Epcot resorts—Beach Club, Yacht Club, BoardWalk Inn, Swan, and Dolphin—are all within a 15-minute walk from each other and watercraft transportation is also available between them.

- The Skyliner resorts – Pop Century/Art of Animation, Caribbean Beach Resort, and Riviera Resort are all located on the gondola system, making transportation between them relatively convenient. These resorts are also connected via the Skyliner from Epcot or Hollywood Studios.

- At Magic Kingdom, take the monorail to any of the monorail resorts, or watercraft to Fort Wilderness or Wilderness Lodge.
- At Epcot, exit the park via the International Gateway between the United Kingdom and France Pavilions and either walk or take the boat to any Epcot resorts. The Disney Skyliner is also at this exit.

Particularly for first-time visitors relying on Disney transportation away from the monorail or Epcot area, our strong advice is eat where you otherwise plan to be in order to reduce the time commitment of transferring from one place to another. If you simply can't resist a breakfast with Mickey at the Contemporary or a romantic dinner at the Grand Floridian, that's fine, too. But take a Minnie Van or Uber/Lyft and consider it the low cost of doing business versus the high cost of your time.

DINING AT DISNEY'S ANIMAL KINGDOM LODGE

Boma - Flavors of Africa

Take the elevator to the first floor

CUISINE African-inspired. DDP Yes.

HOURS AND PRICES *Breakfast* (7:30–11:00am): $31 adults, $17 kids. *Dinner* (5-9:30pm): $52 adults, $29 kids.

OVERVIEW Featuring a robust dinner menu of over 50 African-inspired specialties, Boma is a favorite of many for its wide selection and high quality, unique options. Best are the soups and roasted meats, but just about everything from the seasonal salads to the zebra dome desserts are excellent. Kids enjoy the full buffet in addition to items like macaroni-and-cheese, mashed potatoes, pasta, and baked chicken legs. Breakfast is more pedestrian with the usual selection of French toast, Mickey waffles, bacon, sausage, and the like, with the occasional twist. The only downside is that few tables in the African-marketplace-themed dining room have views of the savannas outside.

Jiko - The Cooking Place

Take the elevator to the first floor

CUISINE African. HOURS 5:30–10pm. DDP 2 credits.

PRICES Appetizers: $12–$19. Dinner Entrées: $30–$57. Kids: $9–$17.

OVERVIEW Jiko isn't afraid to use a liberal amount of exotic spices on many of its constantly changing menu items. Flatbreads, which are typically topped with things like duck confit or shrimp, virtually always impress. Filet mignon, fresh fish, and short ribs are menu mainstays. Kids have a wide range of options from macaroni-and-cheese or cheese pizza to fresh grilled fish and grilled steak. The main dining room, themed to the opening scenes from *The Lion King*, is elegant and reserved. This is one of the best date-night restaurants on property. Request a window table deep inside the restaurant to get away from the lobby noise.

Sanaa

In the Kidani Village wing (at Kidani, take the elevator to the first floor)
CUISINE African/Indian. **HOURS** *Lunch* 11:30am-3pm; *Dinner* 5–9:30pm.
DDP Yes.
PRICES Lunch/Dinner Appetizers: $9–$18. Lunch Entrées: $14–$28. Dinner
Entrées: $19–$34. Kids: $10–$13.
OVERVIEW Sanaa features expansive savanna views in a fun, low-key
dining room themed to an African spice market. The Indian Bread Service
with nine accompaniments is not to be missed. Excellent Tandoori options
reliably come in under $20, in addition to slightly more expensive chicken
and steak. Kids' options are a little out there and include items like Butter
Chicken and Shrimp with Quinoa. The lounge is open until midnight.
Request a window table during daylight for the best views.
Note: In late 2016, Sanaa began serving quick service breakfast from 7-10am.
While there's a little bit of African flair to a couple of the items offered,
the meal is served as a convenience to Kidani Village guests that would
otherwise have to travel to The Mara at Jambo House for hot breakfast. It's
a nice option for guests staying at Kidani, but don't travel out of your way
to dine here in the morning, particularly considering most of the animals
aren't released onto the savanna until later in the day.

DINING AT DISNEY'S BEACH CLUB RESORT

Beaches and Cream Soda Shop

Behind Stormalong Bay
CUISINE American burgers, sandwiches, and ice cream. **HOURS** 11am–11pm.
DDP Yes.
PRICES Lunch/Dinner Entrées: $13–$18 Kids: $9–$11.
OVERVIEW Themed to a boardwalk-style ice cream shop, Beaches and
Cream offers inexpensive burger and sandwich fare in a fun, bright setting. Most people eating here visit for the giant ice cream sundaes, which
arrive with a ton of fun toppings. The restaurant began accepting reservations in late 2013, cutting down waits from as much as two hours to
just a few minutes. The restaurant also closed for a refurbishment in the
middle of 2019, reopening on December 26, 2019 in a much larger, and
arguably blander, space. While we miss the quaintness of the original,
guests may appreciate being able to more easily secure reservations, and
the kitchen is now able to execute an expanded menu more consistently.
The $32 Kitchen Sink Dessert, featuring eight scoops of ice cream, and an
entire bottle of whipped cream, is a favorite tradition of many returning
visitors. An ice-cream to-go window is also available..

Cape May Café

Character meal (breakfast only); inside the lobby to the left of check-in
CUISINE American character breakfast with Minnie, Goofy, Donald, and
Daisy in beach outfits. Dinner buffet is heavy on seafood. **DDP** Yes.

HOURS AND PRICES *Breakfast* (7:30–11:00am): $44 adults, $26 kids. *Dinner* (5–9pm): $58 adults, $31 kids.

OVERVIEW Like the rest of the resort, Cape May Café is themed to a comfortable beachside setting with inviting pastel colors. Breakfast is a character affair with the usual suspects like waffles and pancakes, in addition to elevated offerings like smoked salmon, creamy cheddar grits, and sliced capicola. Dinner is more expensive and characterless, with an emphasis on seafood paella, peel-and-eat shrimp, snow crab legs, salmon, clams, and mussels, in addition to salads and roasted meats. Kid options include chicken nuggets and macaroni. Both meals are above average, though the lack of Mickey at breakfast is disappointing.

DINING AT DISNEY'S BOARDWALK

Big River Grille and Brewing Works

On the end, near Jellyrolls

CUISINE American. **HOURS** 11am–11pm. **DDP** Yes.

PRICES Lunch/Dinner Appetizers: $5–$15. Entrées: $12–$27. Kids: $9.

OVERVIEW Big River is the only working brewpub on property, offering five beers brewed on-site, in addition to a robust menu featuring less expensive sandwich fare along with more expensive steaks and ribs. The less expensive burgers and sandwiches are more reliable than the more expensive items. Beer is unique and decent, but not up to snuff compared to some of the better bottled craft brews available at other restaurants. Diners can sit inside the family-friendly restaurant or outside on the boardwalk overlooking Crescent Lake. Most sports and beer fans will want to take a look at ESPN Club a few hundred feet away. The restaurant otherwise has very little kid appeal, though its menu includes similar burgers and sandwiches.

ESPN Club

Closest to Epcot

CUISINE American. **HOURS** 11am or 12pm–11pm. **DDP** Yes.

PRICES Lunch/Dinner Appetizers: $9–$23. Entrées: $15–$28. Kids: $9–$12.

OVERVIEW With around 100 video monitors showing every televised sporting event imaginable, ESPN is heaven for anyone looking to catch a game while on vacation. Food and drink are better and more varied than you might expect, though the entrées are primarily burgers and sandwiches. ESPN Club is popular during major sporting events and all day Saturday and Sunday during football season.

Flying Fish

To the right of Trattoria al Forno.

CUISINE Steak and Seafood. **HOURS** 5–9:30pm. **DDP** 2 Credits.

PRICES Appetizers: $13–$19. Entrées: $33–$59. Kids: $13–$23.

OVERVIEW Flying Fish reopened in August 2016 in the same location on the BoardWalk. The focus is still on fresh seasonal flavors, locally sourced ingredients, and sustainable seafood, but the interior replaces the whimsy of its predecessor with a more luxurious, sophisticated look. Because Flying Fish can't rely on fireworks views or some other gimmick, the focus is entirely on the food, which elevates it above most Disney signature restaurants on quality and presentation. The luxurious touches inside and expansion of the cocktail list also make this a great date night restaurant, but kids may not connect with the subtle details.

Trattoria al Forno

Character meal (breakfast only); in between Flying Fish and ESPN Club

CUISINE Italian-inspired character breakfast with Ariel, Eric, Rapunzel, and Flynn Rider. Dinner is Italian-inspired. HOURS *Breakfast 7:30–12:05pm; Dinner 5–10pm.* DDP Yes.

PRICES Character Breakfast: $38 adults, $24 kids. Dinner Appetizers: $9–$17. Personal Pizzas: $19–$22. Dinner Entrées: $22–$42. Kids: $12–$15.

OVERVIEW Trattoria al Forno replaced Kouzzina by Cat Cora in December 2014, bringing the number of Italian restaurants in the area to four. The dinner menu focuses on Italian classics like fried calamari, shaved Italian carved meats, baked lasagna, and chicken breast alla parmigiana, in addition to wood-grilled steak and innovative pizzas. On April 2, 2017, Rapunzel, Flynn, Ariel, and Eric began hosting a character breakfast with some Italian touches. The meal begins with a fresh fruit salad or mixed berry parfait to accompany a "frying pan of pastries including braided bread." That's followed by choice of entrée including a Calzone with scrambled Eggs, Soppressata, Bacon, Sausage, Blend of Cheeses and Sunday Gravy or Oak-Grilled Steak with Cheesy Egg Torte, Asparagus, Crispy Onions and Roasted Potatoes. This is the only location where Flynn and Eric typically greet guests and it's proving to be one of the most difficult reservations to secure. While we like breakfast a lot, dinner food and service are typically better at the other Italian restaurants, though Trattoria remains the most casual.

DINING AT DISNEY'S CARIBBEAN BEACH RESORT

Sebastian's Bistro

Behind Old Port Royale, the resort's main building

CUISINE Caribbean and Latin-inspired. HOURS 5–10pm. DDP Yes.

PRICES Appetizers: $9–$14. Entrées: $19–$34. Kids: $11–$13.

OVERVIEW Bright, airy, and heavy on sea breeze tones, Sebastian's Bistro took over for Shutters in October 2018. The atmosphere is casual with a menu heavy on Latin influences and featuring the usual assortment of chicken, steak, and pork accompanied by a variety of black beans, yucca, rice, and plantains. While the restaurant opened with lunch service, it has since been eliminated. With a keen attention to detail and a lot of interesting flavors, Sebastian's is a convenient choice for guests staying at Caribbean Beach or Riviera, but we wouldn't necessarily recommend going out of your way to visit.

DINING AT DISNEY'S CONTEMPORARY RESORT

California Grill

Check in on 2nd floor, ride designated elevator to the restaurant on the 15th floor

CUISINE American, Sushi. **HOURS** 5–10pm. **DDP** 2 credits.

PRICES Appetizers: $16–$24. Sushi: $20–$28. Dinner Entrées: $36–$65. Kids: $12–$19.

OVERVIEW California Grill underwent renovations throughout much of 2013, but the restaurant retains its emphasis on $50 steaks, in addition to many of the same excellent, albeit pricey, sushi dishes. Best known for its panoramic view of Magic Kingdom, and the nighttime fireworks from the 15th floor, consider scheduling a meal about an hour before the show begins to enjoy appetizers and a drink before it gets underway. Guests may watch the show from their table or head outside to the balcony. It's first come, first served at the large bar and lounge area in the middle of the restaurant, making it perfect for drinks and appetizers closer to when the restaurant opens. Check on the second floor for availability. California Grill is great for a date night, but kids are more common than at other signature restaurants due to the excellent fireworks view. Kids may choose between cheese pizza, pasta, chicken, or grilled beef tenderloin.

Disney introduced a weekly Sunday brunch in early 2016 at a cost of $101 for adults and $60 for those between the ages of 3 and 11. Diners have an opportunity to interact with chefs during the meal as they prepare dishes in the open kitchen. Arrive hungry as there is an all-you-care-to-enjoy component with small bites and sushi, in addition to a plated entrée that includes the likes of Grilled Hanger Steak or Eggs Benedict with Butter-poached Maine Lobster. A complimentary sparkling wine cocktail will be served as the host walks you to your table and they are bottomless throughout the meal. It's going to be a splurge for most, but the experience can't be replicated anywhere else.

Chef Mickey's

Character meal, 4th floor Concourse

CUISINE American. Character meal with Mickey, Minnie, Goofy, Donald, and Pluto in chef gear. **DDP** Yes.

HOURS AND PRICES *Breakfast* (7–11:15am): $52 adults, $31 kids. *Brunch* (11:30am–2:30pm): $52 adults, $31 kids. *Dinner* (5–9:30pm): $63 adults, $37 kids.

OVERVIEW Consistently the most popular and one of the most expensive single-credit character meals on property, this is the only place you'll find Mickey, Minnie, Donald, Goofy, and Pluto together greeting diners tableside. Meals are a crowded, raucous affair with the monorail whizzing by just one floor up, but kids don't seem to mind and parents are happy to take pictures of the Fab Five without having to wait an hour in the sun. Breakfast is the strongest and least expensive meal with all of the usual suspects, including a make-your-own Mickey Waffle bar. Brunch swaps things like oatmeal for peel-and-eat shrimp and salads in place of cereals, in addition to carved ham instead of bacon and ribs and salmon instead of biscuits and pancakes. Dinner food quality is below average, but there's a wide variety of roasted meats, soups, and salads, in addition to an all-you-can-eat ice cream bar. Brunch may be a good option for those looking to take some time away from the parks during the busy afternoons and also makes securing a reservation easier. Visit only if the characters are important.

The Wave of American Flavors

First floor on the left, past the check-in area

CUISINE American. **HOURS** Breakfast 7:30–11am; Lunch 11:30am–2pm; Dinner 5–9:30pm. **DDP** Yes.

PRICES Breakfast Entrées: $12–$17. Breakfast Buffet: $27 adult, $15 kid. Lunch/Dinner Appetizers: $9–$17. Lunch Entrées: $14–$20. Dinner Entrées: $18–$34. Kids: $9–$13.

OVERVIEW With more emphasis on healthy food and fresh, locally sourced ingredients than almost any other restaurant on property, The Wave offers an innovative menu for all three meals. The breakfast buffet is excellent, with a wide array of fresh fruit, made-to-order omelets, a smoked salmon bar, and all the traditional accompaniments like pancakes, sausage, and waffles. Less hungry patrons can order a la carte for not much more than the counter-service Contempo Café upstairs. Lunch focuses mostly on sandwiches, burgers, and salads under $20. Only a few tables are usually occupied unless convention goers take over the space. Dinner brings near signature quality fare at one-credit prices. Same-day reservations are usually easy to secure.

DINING AT DISNEY'S CORONADO SPRINGS RESORT

Maya Grill

Inside the main building, down the hall to the right of El Mercado de Coronado, formerly Pepper Market

CUISINE Mexican. **HOURS** 5–10pm. **DDP** Yes.

PRICES Appetizers: $6–$13. Dinner Entrées: $18–$28. Two-Person Platters: $48–$59. Kids: $7–$10.

OVERVIEW Operated by the same company as the so-so restaurants in Epcot's Mexico Pavilion, Maya Grill recently updated its menu to be more in line with La Hacienda de San Angel. In fact, it offers two of the same platters – one featuring steak, chicken al pastor, and chorizo and the other with shrimp, fish, scallops, and vegetables. Other Tex-Mex-style entrees include beef short ribs, shrimp tacos, and fajitas. Kids are unlikely to connect with the restaurant's loosely themed Mayan motifs of fire, sun, and water, but their menu includes some interesting options like a quesadilla, tacos, and grilled fish, in addition to chicken tenders and mac 'n cheese.

Toledo - Tapas, Steak, and Seafood

The 16th floor of the Gran Destino Tower

CUISINE Steak, Seafood, Small Plates. **HOURS** 5–10pm. **DDP** Yes.

PRICES Appetizers: $3–$18. Entrées: $28–$89. Kids: $10–$14.

OVERVIEW Seating is all indoors at this rooftop restaurant on top of the Gran Destino Tower with panoramic views of Coronado Springs down below and the theme parks in the distance. Toledo tries to do a lot, offering a variety of Pintxos, or "small snacks," for just three dollars each, in addition to a wide assortment of Spanish charcuterie and cheeses. Appetizers follow with selections that include head-on garlic shrimp and charred octopus, both of which we recommend. From the entree list, we like the scallops with fava hummus and yogurt powder, along with the hanger steak accompanied by crushed new potatoes. The red wine-braised chicken, which is a huge portion, is also served on top of a bed of delicious roasted tomato 'bomba' rice. We'd skip the pork chop and Manhattan filet. Frankly, we were a bit disappointed by the views - only a few tables enjoy much of one and the theme parks are a good ways off in the distance, making fireworks views much less impressive than California Grill. The atmosphere inside the restaurant is neatest after dark, when the olive trees growing in the center lead the eyes up to the beautiful mosaic-covered vaulted glass ceiling overhead. Toledo just opened in July 2019, so it may take some time for it to get its footing. Until then, there are better destination restaurants, but anyone looking for an upscale meal without needing to leave the resort should give it a good look. We like the Dahlia Lounge next door, too.

DINING AT DISNEY'S
FORT WILDERNESS RESORT AND CAMPGROUND

Hoop-Dee-Doo Musical Revue

Dinner show at Pioneer Hall, near the boat dock

CUISINE Fried chicken, ribs, and all the fixins. Includes unlimited beer and wine for those 21 and older. **HOURS** Usually three shows daily: 4pm, 6:15pm, and 8:30pm. **DDP** 2 credits.

PRICES Hoop Dee Doo has tables in three price categories. Category 1, which we recommend, is $72 for adults, and $43 for kids. Category 2 ($67/$39) and especially Category 3 tables ($64/38) are more distant from the main stage.

OVERVIEW Run more than 35,000 times over the last 40-or-so years, Hoop-Dee-Doo is as much of a Walt Disney World institution as chicken nuggets and Peter Pan's Flight. While expensive at first blush, your admission includes all-you-care-to-eat fried chicken, ribs, corn, salad, baked beans, corn bread, and strawberry shortcake, in addition to unlimited soft drinks, sangria, house wine, and beer. And, of course, the two-hour, kid-friendly Western musical remains the star of the show. Expect a lot of banjos, sing-a-longs, and audience participation in what ends up being a hokey, joke-filled experience where nobody takes themselves seriously. Take the boat from Magic Kingdom if possible for an easy walk to Pioneer

Hall. Those arriving via Disney bus will need to transfer to the internal shuttle for transportation to the show, which can take an extra 20 minutes.

Trail's End

Pioneer Hall, near the boat dock

CUISINE American/BBQ. **HOURS** Breakfast 7:30am–12pm; Dinner 4:30–9:30pm. **DDP** Yes.

PRICES Breakfast Buffet: $29 adult, $16 kids. Weekend Brunch: $32 adult, $17 kids. Dinner Buffet: $39 adult, $21 kids.

OVERVIEW Consistently the cheapest Disney World buffet at breakfast and dinner, Trail's End serves up country cooking in Disney's most casual sit-down restaurant. Breakfast is satisfying with a spread of the usual Mickey waffles, pancakes, pastries, bacon, sausage, etc., in addition to unique items like Pulled Pork Eggs Benedict and brisket mash. On Saturdays and Sundays, a weekend brunch is served with many of the same dishes as breakfast, in addition to made-to-order omelets, fried chicken, and macaroni & cheese, for a few more dollars than breakfast. The dinner buffet consists of much of the same food as the much more expensive family-style dinner at Whispering Canyon Café at Wilderness Lodge. Enjoy all-you-care-to-eat peel and eat shrimp, pulled pork, baked beans, chili, brisket, and more. While not necessarily a destination restaurant, Trail's End is a fantastic, economical choice for those staying at the campground.

DINING AT DISNEY'S GRAND FLORIDIAN RESORT & SPA

1900 Park Fare

Character meal, just inside the first-floor entrance on the left

CUISINE American. Character meal with Mary Poppins, Mad Hatter, Alice, Winnie the Pooh, and Tigger for breakfast. Dinner has Cinderella, Prince Charming, Lady Tremaine, Anastasia, and Drizella. All characters may not appear. **DDP** Yes.

HOURS AND PRICES *Breakfast Buffet* (8–11:50am): $47 adults, $28 kids. *Dinner Buffet* (4–9pm): $63 adults, $37 kids.

OVERVIEW 1900 Park Fare's Victorian theme is carried out subtly throughout the restaurant with carousel animals placed around the massive dining room. A calliope, or steam organ, is the focal point, hanging high above the buffet area. The restaurant is otherwise nondescript for the most part—loud, and without windows. Food is quite good for a buffet. Breakfast includes specialties like corned beef hash, smoked salmon lox, and hickory-smoked ham, in addition to the usual. Dinner brings a large selection of salads and roasted meats, as well as spice-crusted salmon, shrimp scampi, and roasted root vegetable gratin. Don't forget the strawberry soup. The five very different characters present at each meal otherwise steal the show, as they visit every table taking pictures and mingling with guests.

Citricos

Second floor of the main building, near Mizner's

CUISINE American/Mediterranean. **HOURS** 5–9:30pm. **DDP** 2 credits.

PRICES Appetizers: $12–$18. Dinner Entrées: $32-$51. Kids: $9–$16.

OVERVIEW Citricos is Grand Floridian's best signature restaurant, serving inspired steak and seafood with a Mediterranean twist. Old World furnishings and mosaic-tiled floors invite guests into a restaurant that is just fancy enough that everyone feels welcome, yet an air of glamour and prestige permeates throughout. Seasonal changes bring out the freshest flavors on a menu focused on some of the best fish, seafood, and beef available on property. Kids can choose from basics like cheese pizza and macaroni and cheese, or go big with steak or shrimp. Views out the expansive windows are pleasant, but don't provide much of a theme park or fireworks view.

Grand Floridian Café

First floor, all the way back on the left

CUISINE American. **HOURS** Breakfast 7:30–11am; Lunch 11:05am–2pm; Dinner 5–9pm. **DDP** Yes.

PRICES Breakfast Entrées: $9–$21. Lunch/Dinner Appetizers: $10–$16. Lunch Entrées: $15–$27. Dinner Entrées: $16–$34. Kids: $10–$15.

OVERVIEW It's usually easy to secure reservations at Grand Floridian's least expensive, most casual restaurant, subtly themed to the Victorian era with charming views of the rose gardens outside. Unlike the signature restaurants, nobody will bat an eye if you arrive wearing fanny packs and Mickey ears. The restaurant is unique in that it serves its entire breakfast and lunch menus from 7:30am through 2pm, so guests have the option of ordering breakfast and lunch options throughout the morning and afternoon. We like the flexibility of being able to order Lobster Eggs Benedict at 1pm or a Shrimp Cocktail at 8am when the mood strikes. You never know when you'll be up late editing a guidebook. Dinner is a relatively inexpensive proposition with most entrees under $25, including Shrimp & Grits and a Lobster Thermidor Burger. We appreciate the relaxed atmosphere and the ease of the overall experience, but it's not necessarily a destination restaurant unless you want to take advantage of some of the resort's other amenities. Kids won't be impressed by the ambiance, but they can get in on the action with salmon, cheese pizza, chicken, and meaty mac 'n cheese.

Narcoossee's

Located outside, near the boat dock

CUISINE Steak and Seafood. **HOURS** 5–9:30pm. **DDP** 2 credits.

PRICES Appetizers: $14–$22. Dinner Entrées: $29–$72. Kids: $12–$18.

OVERVIEW Narcoossee's doesn't really do anything better than other signature restaurants, which puts it far down our list of Disney's best expensive eateries. While it does position itself on the water, the patio outside is obscured during fireworks time by guests standing there, so it's virtually impossible to enjoy the view from inside the restaurant. The view from the California Grill's 15th floor observation deck is far more spectacular. The menu isn't particularly innovative either, with Citricos offering more flavorful options and superior ingredients. Those serious about their seafood want to take a closer look at Flying Fish. The atmosphere is on the bland side of things at what Disney describes as an "elegant waterfront retreat" with basic wood furniture and standard wood floors. It might work as an upscale take on casual fish and chips, but it isn't the sort of spot where spending a lot of money feels natural. On the plus side, what is offered is typically executed well by the kitchen and prices have become a bit more manageable in recent memory, though steak and lobster will still easily set you back $50+.

Victoria and Albert's

Second floor of the main building, near Citricos

CUISINE Fine Dining; **HOURS** One seating between 5:30–7:35pm. **DDP** No.

PRICES $235/person eight-course Prix Fixe menu.

OVERVIEW Victoria & Albert's, boasting the AAA Five Diamond Award every year since 2000, is unlike any other restaurant on property. With a seven-course menu that starts at $235 per person, it's also the most expensive. The restaurant does not serve children under the age of ten in the main dining room and there is a strict dress code: men must wear dinner jackets with dress pants or slacks and shoes. Ties are optional. Women may wear a cocktail dress, nice dress, dressy pant suit, or a skirt with a blouse. The 18-table restaurant is otherwise equal parts intimate and opulent, with reliably impeccable service from the inviting staff. Menus change daily, but Chef Hunnel reliably offers Australian Kobe-style beef tenderloin, Holland white asparagus, braised oxtail, Imperial osetra caviar, and other fine ingredients. Desserts, overseen by the venerable Erich Herbitschek, are excellent. While expensive, Victoria & Albert's may be the best value on property. Strongly consider the wine pairings with seven healthy pours of fine wines perfectly paired to each selection. V&A's is not for everyone, but it doesn't get any better than this for those celebrating something special.

DINING AT DISNEY'S OLD KEY WEST RESORT

Olivia's

Next to the gift shop, across the way from check-in

CUISINE American. **HOURS** Breakfast 7:30–10:30am; Lunch 11:30–4:55pm; Dinner 5–10pm. **DDP** Yes.

PRICES Breakfast Entrées: $14–$18. Lunch/Dinner Appetizers: $8–$16. Lunch Entrées: $15–$25. Dinner Entrées: $20–$37. Kids: $10–$11.

OVERVIEW Nautically themed with wooden fish and pictures of past guests adorning the walls, Olivia's is one of the friendliest restaurants on property. Breakfast is excellent with specialties like Crab Cake Eggs Benedict with Key Lime Hollandaise. Standard fare includes pancake, waffle, and egg platters. Guests staying at the resort may want to take advantage of a relaxing, relatively inexpensive lunch with a number of burgers and sandwiches coming in under $20, in addition to some heavier entrees like steak or fried chicken around the $25 mark. Dinner remains casual, but bring higher-priced items that include prime rib and a seafood stew. Order at least one conch fritter appetizer. Kids enjoy this colorful, boisterous restaurant with their menu of pasta, fish, or chicken. While not a destination restaurant for most visitors, anyone staying here should plan at least one meal back at the resort. Outdoor patio seating is available.

DINING AT DISNEY'S POLYNESIAN VILLAGE RESORT

'Ohana

Character meal (breakfast only), on second floor of main building

CUISINE Character breakfast with Mickey, Pluto, Lilo, and Stitch. Dinner (served family style) is heavy on meat. **DDP** Yes.

HOURS AND PRICES *Breakfast* (7:30am–noon): $44 adults, $26 kids. *Dinner* (3:30–10pm): $58 adults, $31 kids.

OVERVIEW Characters stop by for the Polynesian-themed breakfast served family-style. Scrambled eggs, Mickey waffles, fried potatoes, pork sausage, bacon, and biscuits will all be delivered in copious quantities throughout the meal. It's a limited selection compared to buffets, but it does the trick and the characters are friendly. Dinner starts with pineapple-coconut bread and salad and continues with honey-coriander chicken wings and potstickers. Skewers with sweet-n-sour chicken, marinated sirloin steak, and spicy grilled peel-n-eat shrimp follow with stir-fried vegetables and lo mein as accompaniments. The restaurant is incredibly loud, particularly at dinner when staff members lead kids in games and parades throughout the meal. Very few tables have window views of Magic Kingdom. (Protip: It's 'Ohana. Not O'hana. Or O'hana's. Just, 'Ohana. It means "family".)

Kona Café

Second floor of main building

CUISINE American, Pan-Asian. **HOURS** Breakfast: 7:30–11am; Lunch: 12:10–2:55pm; Dinner; 5–9:45pm. **DDP** Yes.

PRICES Breakfast Entrées: $12–$16. Lunch/Dinner Appetizers: $10–$18. Lunch Entrées: $16–$32. Dinner Entrées: $16–$40. Sushi: $16-$28. Kids: $9–$12.

OVERVIEW Regular visitors have long considered Kona a hidden gem – an easy, reasonably-priced, accessible meal in a sea of hoity-toity options at the likes of the Grand Floridian and Contemporary. Breakfast is very much still that, offering a menu that includes the iconic Tonga Toast (banana-stuffed sourdough French toast rolled in cinnamon sugar and served with a strawberry compote), in addition to Macadamia-Nut Pancakes and a traditional Loco Moco, consisting of a tower of rice, grilled hamburger patty, house-made chorizo gravy, two eggs-any style, and topped with Tomato Salsa, in addition to omelets and other traditional favorites. Lunch is a departure from what has been typically offered, replacing favorites like the Island Steak and Crispy Chicken with more expensive Dashi Noodle Bowls and Duck Fried Rice with Leg Confit. Dinner is even more unrecognizable with specialty sushi rolls that start at $26 and steaks, served without sides, running $35+ without any Polynesian flourishes to speak of. Less expensive items remain, but it's difficult to recommend this restaurant, located just off the main lobby, with a menu that tries to do much more than the kitchen can reliably execute. We still recommend breakfast whole-heartedly. Lunch and dinner may impress as well on the low-end of the price spectrum, but this isn't where we'd go for a $40 steak.

Spirit of Aloha

Dinner show, in dedicated space on the Grand Floridian side

CUISINE American/Polynesian. **HOURS** Usually two shows Tuesday-Saturday at 5:15pm and 8:15pm. **DDP** 2 credits.

PRICES The Spirit of Aloha show offers tables in three price categories. Category 1, which we recommend, is $78 for adults, and $46 for kids. Category 2 ($74/$44) and Category 3 ($66/$39) are distant from the main stage.

OVERVIEW Food is okay at this Polynesian luau and dinner show, which follows the story of a young woman returning home after spending time as a city girl on the mainland. All-you-care-to-enjoy Island pulled pork, BBQ ribs, roasted chicken, and Polynesian rice are served family-style alongside fresh salad with honey-lime vinaigrette, seasonal vegetables, and pineapple-coconut bread. Complimentary beer and wine are served, though it may be difficult to flag down a server for a refill. Kids receive chicken nuggets with tater tots, cheese pizza, and either grilled chicken or mahi mahi with rice and green beans. The show has its moments, with an outstanding fire-dancing and sword-eating finale, but at over two hours, it drags in places. With the amount of better entertainment already seen at the parks, the Luau is going to be superfluous for many, and, at $70/adult, is an expensive proposition.

Trader Sam's Grog Grotto

Past Captain Cook's in the main building and outside on the patio

CUISINE Polynesian, Sushi. **HOURS** 3pm–12am; 21+ only after 8pm. **DDP** No.

PRICES Appetizers/Small Plates: $10–$15.

OVERVIEW Trader Sam's Grog Grotto features two distinct areas married under a single banner. The outdoor, open air Tiki Terrace offers a surprisingly relaxing atmosphere among swaying palm trees, fountains, and live ukulele music. Inside, the bar that officially seats just about 50 people is whimsically themed and full of interactive artifacts from around the mysterious South Seas. Due to the bar's low capacity, Sam's usually uses a pager system to alert prospective imbibers that space is available inside. Wait times can be quoted as high as two or more hours on the weekends, but are usually short or nonexistent on weeknights, particularly after 9pm. Staff will remind those under 21 that they should prepare to leave by the 8pm cutoff. Food tends to be better and more varied upstairs at Tambu Lounge and Kona Café, though you might want to order one of the small bites with drinks inside or out on the patio. Our favorite drink is the souvenir HippopotoMai-Tai, which includes a take-home Tiki glass for around $25. Be careful with the souvenir Uh-Oa, which will run you north of $40, and the Nautilus, which arrives over $50. Other drinks like the Tropical Dark and Stormy are closer to $10, but don't include a souvenir glass.

DINING AT DISNEY'S PORT ORLEANS RIVERSIDE RESORT

Boatwright's

Inside the main building, near the quick service
CUISINE Cajun/American. **HOURS** 5–9pm. **DDP** Yes.
PRICES Appetizers: $8–$13. Dinner Entrées: $19–$36. Kids: $9–$12.
OVERVIEW Loosely themed to a shipyard warehouse with the skeletal hull of a fishing boat suspended overhead, Boatwright's is a casual restaurant just off the main lobby. The menu revolves around typical southern favorites like crawfish, grits, jambalaya, and Nashville hot chicken. An all-you-care-to-enjoy platter is also available with ribs, hot chicken, smoked sausage, and barbecued beef brisket, with mashed potatoes, macaroni and cheese, sweet corn, and green beans. It's a nice variety of food and a good choice for those who arrive hungriest. Most of the Cajun entrees are under-seasoned and bland. Boatwright's is excellent for guests who unexpectedly find themselves back at the resort, but do make sure you have reservations because waits can be surprisingly long, particularly on weekends in lousy weather.

DINING AT DISNEY'S RIVIERA RESORT

Disney's Riviera Resort will open on December 16, and bring with it several new dining venues. "Topolino's Terrace – Flavors of the Riviera" is the name of the table service restaurant, which will play host to a character meal featuring Mickey Mouse, Minnie Mouse, Donald Duck, and Daisy Duck during breakfast. Pastries are shared and each person chooses an entrée from a selection that includes grilled steak, smoked salmon, and a sausage hash. Dinner at this indoor rooftop terrace is a signature affair with a focus on French and Italian cuisine. Diners will enjoy "a modern interpretation of the textures, colors, carved details and stonework found in ancient villages along the Riviera" as they feast on appetizers like escargot and ricotta, followed by a list of entrees that includes hand-crafted pastas, veal, fish, lamb, filet mignon, and more. We expect the view of the nighttime spectaculars to be as good as the food.

Primo Piatto is the name of the quick service, which should be perfect for a quick snack or casual meal with a menu heavy on sandwiches and salads. Le Petit Café, which shares its name with the restaurant in *The Aristocats*, will be a small coffee shop that serves a variety of baked goods, in addition to beer, wine, cocktails, and savory bites beginning in the afternoon. Bar Riva is the open-air pool bar, specializing in frozen cocktails and spritzers, along with hearty hamburgers and a variety of small plates.

We expect Topolino's to be incredibly popular, particularly for breakfast. The Riviera is just one Skyliner stop away from Epcot and also on the system that services Pop Century, Art of Animation, Caribbean Beach, and Hollywood Studios, making for some relatively convenient transportation options from a variety of locations on property.

DINING AT DISNEY'S SARATOGA SPRINGS RESORT & SPA

The Turf Club Bar & Grill

Inside the main building, beyond the quick service

CUISINE American. **HOURS** 5–9:30pm. **DDP** Yes.

PRICES Appetizers: $9–$13. Dinner Entrées: $20–$36. Kids: $9–$12.

OVERVIEW Turf Club is themed to a turn-of-the-century, upstate New York racetrack clubhouse. Wood-paneled walls and dark wood furniture provide a gentlemanly ambiance with views of Lake Buena Vista Golf Club below and Disney Springs in the distance. It's not the most inviting restaurant, particularly with kids, but it's a great choice for couples looking for a more intimate experience, and riders will find the displayed horse tack delightful. Kids may enjoy the covered patio seating outside more. The menu leans toward steak, lamb, and pork. Start with the Turf Club Signature Grilled Romaine Salad and Buffalo Chicken Dip. Kids choose between entrees like prime rib and grilled fish, or something more basic, like a hot dog or cheeseburger. The Saratoga Cocktail with Maker's Mark Bourbon and Mint Julep with Woodford Reserve are a nice departure from most cocktail menus heavy on flavored vodkas and light rum.

DINING AT DISNEY'S WILDERNESS LODGE

Story Book Dining at Artist Point

Character meal, back of main building

CUISINE American. Character meal with Snow White, Evil Queen, Dopey, and Grumpy. **HOURS** 4–9pm. **DDP** Yes.

PRICES Adults: $63. Kids: $37.

OVERVIEW Those who visited Artist Point before the December 2018 switchover to Storybook Dining won't recognize much of what used to be a quiet, understated respite that was one of the easiest reservations to snag at the last minute. Storybook Dining is far more vibrant, much more popular, and set loosely inside of an enchanted, forest-themed dining room. Snow White, Grumpy, and Dopey happily greet diners tableside, taking pictures with guests, signing autographs, and occasionally breaking into dance. Evil Queen waits for the end of your meal, when you'll be invited to meet and take pictures with her in the middle of the restaurant. Food at what is now a three course, prix fixe meal is still quite good, beginning with a trio of shared appetizers that may include a bisque, shrimp cocktail, and hot savory pie. Entrée choices remain elegant with the likes of prime rib, pork shank, roasted chicken, butter-poached fish, and gnocchi. Dessert follows with four individual desserts shared among the group, perfectly-themed to the meal. Kids enjoy the same appetizers and desserts as the rest of the group, while their entrée choices are usually a bit simpler, offering items like grilled chicken, pasta with marinara, prime rib, and a vegetarian selection like a steamed bao bun. This is one of our favorite new character meals, blending in some fun characters that aren't otherwise meetable in a fun setting with some great food.

Whispering Canyon Café

Just inside the main entrance, on the left

CUISINE American. **HOURS** Breakfast: 7:30–11:15am; Lunch: 11:45am–2:30pm; Dinner: 5–10pm. **DDP** Yes.

PRICES Breakfast Entrées: $11–$22. Lunch/Dinner Appetizers: $9–$12. Lunch Entrées: $14–$24. Dinner Entrées: $19–$35. Kids: $8–$16.

OVERVIEW Whispering Canyon Café is like a Western-themed 50's Prime Time Café. While the antics have been toned down in recent years, guests requesting a bottle of ketchup will find that 25 bottles from around the restaurant appear. Don't be surprised if your drink refill comes in a gallon jug or a two-ounce miniature jar, depending on how generous your server is feeling. All-you-care-to-enjoy platters are the most popular here with a selection that has improved in recent memory. Breakfast brings the choice of one of three skillets, with your selection ultimately depending on how much meat you'd like with your accompaniments that include home fries, bacon, sausage, biscuits, and Mickey waffles. Traditional entrees like omelets, waffles, and frittatas are also on the menu. Lunch and dinner both feature the usual barbecue skillet with pulled pork, ribs, chicken, mashed potatoes, corn, and green beans. At dinner, salmon, sausage, brisket, piggy wings, and more sides are also available. For lunch and dinner, a vegan skillet is offered with barbecue jackfruit, beefless tips, Beyond Sausage products, and more. Less expensive a la carte appetizers and entrees are also available and all skillets are served alongside bottomless cornbread. We like Whispering Canyon for its fun, casual atmosphere, but be prepared for a little hijinks.

DINING AT DISNEY'S YACHT CLUB RESORT

Ale & Compass Restaurant

Off the main lobby

CUISINE New England-inspired American. **HOURS** Breakfast 7:30–11am; Lunch 11:30am–2pm; Dinner 5–9pm. **DDP** Yes.

PRICES Breakfast Entrées: $12–$19. Breakfast Buffet: $24. Lunch/Dinner Appetizers: $9–$15. Lunch Entrées: $13–$20. Dinner Entrées: $17–$34. Kids: $9–$13.

OVERVIEW Ale & Compass opened in place of Captain's Grille in late 2017 with a renewed emphasis on New England comfort food in a slightly upscale setting heavy on royal navy blues and details reminiscent of a lighthouse. All three meals are casual with breakfast bringing delicious entrees like salted caramel-apple French toast and dark chocolate waffles, in addition to mainstays like a ham & cheese omelet or American breakfast. Lunch is our favorite meal, delicious and relaxing with a terrific fish & chips and hearty Maine lobster roll. Since opening, dinner prices have come down as quality has improved and we now recommend evening meals as well with an excellent Seafood Pot Pie stuffed full of scallops, shrimp, and lump crab meat for around $25, in addition to the Coastal Clambake and Cabernet-braised Short Ribs for under $30 each. There are more interesting restaurants in the Crescent Lake area, but Ale & Compass is a no-fuss option if you're looking for an easy, pleasant experience.

Yachtsman Steakhouse

Back of lobby

CUISINE American. **HOURS** 5–9:30pm. **DDP** 2 credits.

PRICES Appetizers: $12–$19. Dinner Entrées: $34–$57. Kids: $9–$13.

OVERVIEW Yachtsman takes its meat more seriously than any other Disney resort restaurant on property, though recent additions like the BOATHOUSE, STK Orlando, and Morimoto Asia to Disney Springs make it much more difficult to definitively award it "best steak". Steaks are aged, trimmed, and hand cut on site before being prepared on an oak-fired grill in the open kitchen. The traditional steakhouse setting is heavy on wood with elegant white linens topping every table. While all steaks come in over $45, the high quality of the meat and the elevated service bring guests back again and again. The restaurant is not the best with young kids in tow, as there's little about the restaurant that will keep them occupied, but they may choose from pasta, chicken, steak, or fish. Consider the restaurant for an intimate meal or special occasion, particularly with someone who knows their meat.

CHAPTER EIGHT

Which Tickets to Buy and How Much to Budget

"What should we budget?" is the hardest simple question for this book to answer. This is because smaller families, families whose kids are younger, families staying at a less expensive hotel, families going during a less expensive set of dates, and families on shorter trips will pay less. Larger families, families where everyone is over nine, families staying at a more expensive hotel, families going during a more expensive period, and families on longer trips will pay more.

- A parent and one younger child, with three days of tickets and three nights in a value resort during one of the less expensive periods, could spend as little as $1,500 in Orlando.
- Add another parent and another younger child and this trip jumps to $2,600.
- Stretch the visit out to the 8 nights and 9 days we recommend for "only visits" and the in-Orlando price exceeds $5,500.
- Stay this long in one of the more expensive deluxe resorts instead, and the price is more than $9,000.
- Shift to the times of the year to visit and add $3,000 more.

(All the figures are before transportation costs and souvenirs.)

The good news is that budgeting for a specific trip is relatively straightforward, with most costs set and paid far in advance of arrival.

This chapter discusses the ins and outs of budgeting. We'll walk you through how to establish what you can expect to pay for each component of your trip, whether it includes just one adult and one child on a tight budget over a few days, or a week-long extended family blow-out.

We open with a discussion of the one major budget issue we haven't discussed yet: theme park tickets with their various add-ons and related costs. The section that follows covers estimating your budget based on your dates, resort hotel, group, etc. Then we cover budgets for "only" trips, several ways to reduce costs, and even a few reasons to spend even more!

Disney World Tickets and Prices

On October 16, 2018, Disney World moved to a new date-based ticket pricing approach. (The former "Magic Your Way" tickets purchased before then are still usable based on the terms with which they were sold.) 2020 ticket prices came out in June 2019—we expect at least one more price increase for these. New Disney World theme park ticket prices vary based on how many park days they are purchased for, as they always have; prices now also vary depending on the first day of use they are eligible for. Moreover, both prices and eligible use dates can vary depending on which ticket type you buy, and even how you buy them.

So you now have to make four decisions before buying your tickets:

- Buying as part of a package or separately, and if separately, on-line or at the gate
- Whether to go with a base ticket, a Park Hopper ticket, or a Park Hopper Plus ticket
- The number of ticket days
- Your targeted first day of eligible use of these tickets, and the first day they will actually be used to visit a park—which are not always the same dates

There are two bits of good news here. First, you can always add features to a not-yet-expired version of one of these tickets, so if you start with a six day base theme park ticket, and then decide halfway through your vacation that you really needed an eight-day Park Hopper ticket, Disney World will allow you to pay the price difference to upgrade your base theme park ticket. So the risk of buying too little ticket is low. Second, you have us to guide you through the process!

To actually purchase a ticket, you have to know answers to all four of the questions above. But, because everything can be seen as a variant of the base "1 Park Per Day" theme park tickets, we will start with that, and then build on it.

WHAT IS A "1 PARK PER DAY" THEME PARK TICKET?

What Disney calls "1 Park Per Day" tickets—which to save a tree we call "base tickets"—are tickets good for one park per day for between one and ten ticket days. On any ticket day, you gain unlimited entrances and exits to one single theme park during its regular operating hours. So on one day you can go to Magic Kingdom, leave and return, and on a different day you can go to Epcot, leave, and return again. What you can't do with base tickets is go to two different parks in the same day—for that you need the Park Hopper add-on, discussed below. For any given ticket length and eligibility period, base tickets are the least expensive tickets available to the general public.

WHAT OTHER TICKET TYPES ARE AVAILABLE?

In addition to base tickets, you can also buy two types of add-ons to base tickets, and a third modifier to base tickets that takes out some of their restrictions.

- The "Park Hopper" add-on gives you the ability to visit more than one park in a day. Returning visitors commonly enjoy the extra flexibility that Hoppers give them, but we counsel first-timers to only add them after they are sure they need them. Each Disney park takes more than a day to see, and travel between parks can take longer than first-timers might imagine. Adding a Park Hopper costs an additional flat fee for the entire length of the ticket. For a one day ticket, it costs (including tax—all of our numbers include tax) $63.90. Adding a Hopper to a two or three day ticket costs a flat fee of $74.55, and adding it to a three to ten day ticket costs a flat fee of $85.20.

- The "Park Hopper Plus" option is an add-on to a Hopper ticket—you cannot add it to a base ticket. It allows, in addition to the number of theme park days you've selected, and hopping among them, a specific number of visits to Disney World's "minor" venues, such as its water parks, mini-golf offerings, and nine-hole golf at Oak Trails. This add-on costs a flat fee of $26.63 per ticket, and allows you a number of visits to the minor venues equal to the number of days in your base ticket, except for one day tickets, where you get two. Returning visitors planning multiple visits to the minor venues—especially the water parks—can gain real value out of this add on, especially if they had already planned to buy a hopper. First timers generally will gain more value by focusing any extra time they have either on rest or on the theme parks, rather than on the minor parks.

- The "Flexible Date" ticket is a variant of all the options above. Selecting it frees you from the narrow usage windows and expiration dates that the other options have—which we will discuss more below. These tickets expire December 31 of the calendar year after they are purchased, and can have their first use for any date in that window. Because they can have their first use during any date in that window, including the highest-priced dates, they are priced a little higher than what would otherwise be the highest not-flexible price of the year.

- The main other option available to everyone is Annual Passes, of which there are various types, which provide unlimited entry to the parks over most or all of the upcoming 12 months. Narrower populations—most significantly Florida residents, visitors from the UK, and members of the US Armed Forces—can often find different or special offers. Check the Disney World website for eligibility, prices and terms of these.

HOW SHOULD THESE TICKETS BE BOUGHT?

Base tickets and their add-ons can be purchased separately, or as part of a Disney World package that also includes a Disney World hotel room.

If purchased separately, they can be purchased on-line or at the gate. Tickets of three days or longer purchased separately will be $21.30 more expensive if purchased at the gate rather than online. Base, Hopper, and

Hopper Plus tickets purchased as part of a package will be the same price as tickets purchased separately online, but have either the same or a better usage window than tickets purchased separately. So if you are also planning to book a Disney-owned hotel room, in many cases it will be best to purchase your tickets as part of a package; if you are purchasing three day or longer tickets separately, buy them online.

WHAT ARE THE ELIGIBLE USAGE PERIODS?

Base, Hopper, and Hopper Plus tickets must have their first day of eligible use identified before you can purchase them. Except for one day tickets, which must be used that exact day, these tickets come with varying usage windows—that is, for example, you don't have to use a four-day ticket on four precisely consecutive days. This lets you fit in days off, visits to other Orlando attractions, water park visits, etc., and lets you roll a bit with family or weather issues.

- Base and Hopper tickets not purchased as part of a package have the following usage allotments: two and three day tickets get two extra days for use; four through seven day tickets get three extra days; eight through ten day tickets get four extra days. So if you buy a three day ticket whose first day of eligible use is May 3, 2020, you can use this ticket any three days of the five-day period that begins May 3 and ends May 7.

- Park Hopper Plus tickets get one additional day of use—making it easier to fit the water parks or mini golf into your visit. So the three day ticket in the above example would be usable through May 8.

- Base, Hopper, and Hopper Plus tickets purchased as part of a package get a usage period of whatever is longer—the usage periods noted above, or the length of the hotel reservation they are booked with, figured as the number of booked nights plus one. So if you bought the same three day May 3 ticket noted above as part of a seven night Disney hotel package, your usage period would be eight days (seven nights plus one), extending through May 10.

- Flexible Date tickets have a usage period of 14 days—so you can begin the use of this ticket anytime during its eligible period (for tickets bought in 2020, that means through December 31, 2021) and use whatever additional days you bought anytime the thirteen days after.

WHAT ARE THE PRICES AND HOW DO THEY VARY?

If you buy Base, Hopper, and Hopper Plus tickets, the price of the tickets will vary based on the length of the ticket, whether it is for someone ten or older or three to nine years old at the time of their visit (kids younger than three are free), and, new as of October 2018, when the first day of eligible use is.

- Prices per day always go down with longer tickets compared to shorter tickets with the same first eligible day. While the new date-based pricing means how much they go down will vary over the year, typically the least expensive days to add are days five through ten, each of which costs typically over 2020 just $9-17 per day to add. The first ticket day, and days two through four, cost an arm and a leg.

- Tickets for kids three to nine cost ~$5 to ~$20 less per ticket than tickets for those ten and older, with the larger saving applying to longer tickets.

- More profoundly, the ticket price also varies depending on the first start date. In the longer ticket lengths—five days and longer—in 2020 prices for tickets of the same length vary over the course of the year on average about $150—that's a $600 difference for a family of four. See the table below for the price range by length for base tickets.

Basically, tickets are more expensive during the times when it is most convenient for families with school-age kids to go, so they will be typically higher during holiday periods, common vacation periods, and over weekends. The most expensive tickets in 2020 are in the second half of December. For longer tickets, the least expensive tickets are during the common semester-beginning periods of much of January, some of February, and later August through most of September; there's also a period in the first half of May that sees lower prices.

Shorter visits have a less predictable set of higher and lower prices. As with longer tickets, they will be higher near and during common vacation periods; also, shorter visits whose eligible usage period

Disney World 2020 Ticket Prices One Park Per Day		
Number of Ticket Days	Lowest Price	Highest Price
1	116	169
2	228	330
3	335	476
4	430	601
5	442	607
6	454	613
7	462	619
8	477	630
9	489	642
10	501	650

Includes tax; prices for those 3-9 years old may be lower

We expect prices to increase over these levels in 2020

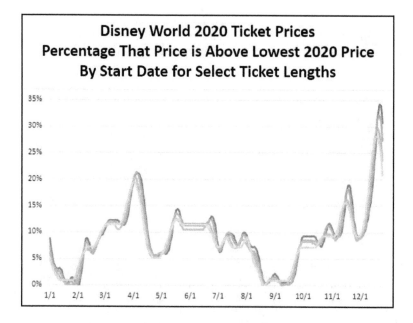

Disney World 2020 Ticket Prices
Percentage That Price is Above Lowest 2020 Price
By Start Date for Select Ticket Lengths

includes weekends will see higher prices most times of the year than visits near the same time whose usage period includes only weekday dates.

To see exact prices for your potential dates go to Disney's website at https://disneyworld.disney.go.com/admission/tickets (or navigate their from your My Disney Experience account—at the upper left, click "Parks & Tickets," and from the drop-down menu, go down to "Admissions" and under it select "Theme Park Tickets"), and select your ticket type. From there a monthly calendar will open. After you first select the number of ticket days desired, the calendar will show you the average daily ticket prices by first day of eligible use for every day for which ticket prices have been released. These prices are rounded, and pre-tax, but will illuminate for you the various prices for various possible start dates.

If you have many potential dates you could visit, then the chart below might be helpful for honing in on the lowest ticket prices during the periods available to you. It shows the price for each day of 2020 of four different ticket lengths—four, six, eight, and ten days. (We selected this subset because if we included all ten possible ticket lengths, it would be a mess, and we do care about you).

WHAT FIRST ELIGIBLE DAY SHOULD BE TARGETED?

Because usage periods for all ticket lengths greater than one day are longer than the number of ticket days, and because average daily prices can be different from day to day, some may find ticket savings by picking as their first eligible day a date somewhat earlier than the first day they plan to be in a theme park.

Some of the most extreme examples of this are near Christmas. If you are committed to the parks the five days beginning 12/20/20, a 5 day ticket that begins 12/20 will cost you $531.79. But a five day ticket whose first day of eligible use is 12/17 can also be used for the five days beginning 12/20, and will cost $494.59. That's a savings of almost $40 per ticket--or $150 for a family of four. An eight person family would save around $300 from this choice (and the parents should get a different hobby...) Note that this won't work if you are buying a package—if you have a package, your first day of eligible use will be set as the day you check in to your hotel.

WHAT'S THE PRICE TO ADD A DAY?

Back in the olden days—that is, before October 16, 2018—it was straight-forward to figure out the extra cost of a ticket a day longer. For example, adding a sixth through a tenth day cost a flat $10.65 per ticket per day.

Now that prices vary so much over the course of the year, you can only know for sure the costs of adding days by comparing tickets of varying lengths with the same start days. On average, the cost to add days five through ten is around $9 to $17, but for any specific date, it can vary from a dollar to more than $30 per day.

Estimating Budgets

Now that we've determined the cost of theme park tickets, let's add them to the resort and dining costs discussed in Chapters 5 and 7, and consider the following variables:

- **DATES OF THE VISIT** Walt Disney World prices for hotel rooms vary tremendously over the year, and ticket prices vary moderately.

- **GROUP SIZE / AGE STRUCTURE AT CHECK-IN DATE** Kids less than three years old don't require theme park admission and aren't charged at buffets. Kids from three to nine are charged a little less than older folk for theme park tickets, and a lot less for kids' meals and kids' buffets. Kids ten and older as of the check-in date are charged the same as adults for theme park tickets and the Dining Plan. With the exception of the Disney Vacation Club rooms and the Fort Wilderness campground, Disney includes two guests age 18 or older in the room at the base price. Additional guests over the age of 18 will be charged $10–$35 per night extra, depending on the resort level.

- **TARGETED HOTEL** Walt Disney World hotel rooms are available for prices just over $110 per night to well over $600 per night.

- **TRANSPORTATION COSTS** These vary greatly depending on mode and length of travel.

- **TIPS, SNACKS, SOUVENIRS, AND OTHER EXTRAS** Add about $25 per person, per night.

Now that we have an idea about when and for how long we want to visit, let's input our information and get an idea of how much it's all going to cost. Visit your My Disney Experience account, click at the top Places to Stay and input your check-in date, check-out date, and party size. Pick your desired hotel and room/view type.

The next page lists tickets and the add-ons discussed previously in the chapter. Select the tickets and then click Dining Plan. Note the cost with and without the Plan. While we don't recommend the Dining Plan in most situations, it does give a general idea about what it will cost to eat one quick service and one table service meal per day, in addition to a snack or two. Don't worry if this number seems too high—we'll cover discounts and ways to save money shortly.

Saving Money on a Disney World Visit

Money-saving opportunities depend on when you go and where you stay:

- When you go matters because Disney changes resort and ticket pricing multiple times over the course of the year. Staying in the same exact standard-view room at the Polynesian for eight nights during the most expensive time of the year can cost $2,900 more than it would cost during the cheapest period.
- Where you stay matters because Walt Disney World has resorts priced at many different levels. Staying eight nights at the Polynesian instead of Art of Animation during the lower cost season will cost almost $3,300 more.
- Combining these effects—staying eight nights at the Poly during the highest cost time of the year instead of at Art of Animation during the lowest cost time of the year—costs a whopping $6,200 more for the same family with the same theme park tickets!

So the takeaways for the first-time family visitor:

- On a tight budget, consider sticking with one of Disney's less expensive on-property resorts like All-Star Movies, Art of Animation or Pop Century.
- Think carefully about what is really getting in the way of going during one of the less expensive periods. Is it possible to pull the kids out of school to visit when crowds and prices are much lower?

Because Disney controls the entire supply of theme park tickets, discounts from reputable sources are slim. Check officialticketcenter.com for some of the best discounts on multi-day tickets. Fortunately, major savings may be available on other aspects of your vacation:

- Keep an eye out for deals available to the general public—typically room rate discounts, but sometimes a version of the Dining Plan for free—especially in September. Find them at yourfirstvisit.net/deals or at Disney World's Special Offer web page as they are announced. These discounts are often available to Disney Visa card holders a few days before they become available to everyone else. Visit disneyrewards.com for more information.
- Use special discounts that you quality for, the most valuable of which is the Armed Forces Salute, which has been extended for 2020. See militarydisneytips.com for more. There may also be discounts for Florida residents, Annual Passholders, international guests, and others.
- Access Disney Vacation Club rooms for a lot less by renting points from owners who won't be using them—this is a particular boon for

large families, who have the most difficulty finding Disney-owned accommodations at reasonable prices. Visit dvcrequest.com for pricing and options.

- Consider staying offsite, especially with large groups. As noted in Chapter 5, there are some takeaways on the convenience side of things, but it may be the most viable option for some groups, and the savings can be substantial. It's hard to find reasonably priced Disney-owned options on-site for groups larger than four people, and even more difficult for groups larger than five. You'll find lots of ideas at yourfirstvisit.net/large-families, but the least expensive way to stay will be offsite.

For a family of four, all ten or older, and staying in a standard room in 2020 in one of Disney's All-Star value resorts:

- For about $3,500, you can expect to stay for two nights and spend three days in the parks all of 2020, and stay three nights and spend four days in the parks about a third of the year;
- For about $4,500, a four-night stay with five days in the parks works all but the last two weeks of December, and a five-night / six-day stay works almost half the year; or
- For about $5,500, a five-night stay with six days in the parks is doable all of 2020, and most of the year so is a six-night stay with seven days in the parks.

To budget your own trip, add to these figures transportation, souvenirs, treats, extras and a contingency fund in case prices—especially ticket prices—go up again before you book.

Chapter Four covers resort and ticket pricing in-depth. Visit during less expensive seasons to pay the lowest prices or budget a little more if you're visiting during peak or holiday seasons. Also take some time to price out a couple of potential trips on DIsneyWorld.com. You might be surprised how much prices differ from week to week.

Spending Even More at Disney World

There's almost no limit to what could be spent on a first visit to Walt Disney World, with a fat enough wallet and sufficient desire to thin it. For example, how about a couple of newly-published authors as really expensive tour guides?

For a fuller list, see "The Comfortable Guide to Walt Disney World" on yourfirstvisit.net/comfortable. But a shorter list of extra spending that may significantly increase comfort levels on a first visit includes:

- **RENTING A CAR** Disney's Magical Express (discussed in Chapter 9) will transport your group back and forth from the airport, but it requires that guests return to their resort for pickup no later than three hours before the flight is scheduled to leave. With a car, you can potentially leave for the airport directly from the theme park. On property, Disney's transportation system will get you from your Disney hotel to the parks, but a rental car reduces waits, increases flexibility, and offers a more comfortable, private ride. Transport to all the parks but the Magic Kingdom is faster by car than by Disney bus: it's the only simple way to get from most resort hotels—especially values and moderates—to another for dining, etc.; it's the only easy way to get to the non-Disney parks; and it makes shopping, off-site dining, and other activities much easier. All that said, in the spring of 2018 for the first time the Disney resorts started charging for overnight parking, so there's that additional expense. Moreover, Uber, Lyft, and Disney's high-priced Lyft based alternative, the Minnie Vans, make life without a rental car easier, and the resorts served by the Disney Skyliner gondola system have an alternative to buses for getting to Hollywood Studios and Epcot.

- **STAYING A FEW DAYS LONGER** Adding two or three days to a trip (and planning on relaxing those days) can make your vacation much more comfortable. A Disney World trip is like a backpacking expedition—lots of walking, lots of energy used, lots of early mornings. A few more days off can make a world of difference.

- **GETTING A MULTI-SPACE ROOM** Even the happiest families can tire of staying together in a single room. Several Disney lodging options—mostly at the expensive deluxe resorts—give you more space. Consider (in order of increasing prices) deluxe rooms at the Wilderness Lodge, one and two bedroom villas at the Disney Vacation Club resorts, and suites at all the deluxe resorts. Much lower priced— but still expensive—multi-room options are Family Suites at All-Star Music and at Art of Animation, and the Cabins at Fort Wilderness. Many—but not all—of these options include full kitchens as well.

None of these are inexpensive...but they might make a real difference to comfort!

Pricing out a Walt Disney World vacation is daunting. The good news is that once you've arrived, most everything is already taken care of and you can let loose and enjoy your trip. In fact, if you've added the Dining Plan, the only additional costs most guests encounter in Orlando is souvenirs (and there will be souvenirs), tips, and a few treats. With the ability to save a substantial amount of money on resort costs and a few dollars on tickets, it's easy to design around just about any budget.

CHAPTER NINE

How to Set Everything Up and Get Everything Done

There are three key dates to consider:

- For those staying at a Disney-owned resort, restaurant reservations open for booking 180 days before their arrival date, and can be booked for that date and the next 9 days.

- For everyone else, restaurant reservations open for booking 180 days before a potential dining date

- For those staying at a Disney-owned resort, the Swan or Dolphin, Shades of Green, Four Seasons, the Hilton Orlando Bonnet Creek, the Waldorf Astoria Orlando, or a Disney Springs Resort Area hotel, FastPass+ reservations can be booked beginning 60 days before their arrival date.

- For everyone else, FastPass+ reservations can be booked beginning 30 days before planned use.

Building a to-do list is keyed to these dates because booking as early as possibly will result in the widest selection of experiences being available.

The first section of this chapter outlines how to sign up for and use Disney's new My Disney Experience mobile app and website. From there, we'll walk through customizing MagicBands and setting up FastPass+.

Tailored to-do lists are available for each of the sample itineraries available at yourfirstvisit.net/itineraries. For guests building custom itineraries, the second section of this chapter discusses putting together a to-do list to make sure everything is booked as easily and conveniently as possible.

My Disney Experience, FastPass+, and MagicBands

MY DISNEY EXPERIENCE

If you don't already have a My Disney Experience (MDE) account, sign up for one by visiting disneyworld.com and clicking the "sign in or create account" link on the top center of the screen. An account is required to make dining and FastPass+ reservations, in addition to customizing

MagicBands and keeping track of each component of your vacation online.

If you already have an account and booked a trip through the website while logged in, you should already see these reservations upon signing in. If not, link them manually by clicking "My Reservations and Tickets" under the My Disney Experience dropdown menu (located in the top right under the search box) and input the confirmation numbers and ticket IDs.

If people on the reservation are missing, click from the same MDE dropdown menu, "My Family and Friends". Once the new screen opens, click the little "Add a Guest" button on the right side of the page. Type the names of the missing people, and, if applicable, their ticket IDs. If you have trouble, try tech support—at (407) 939-5277—and have the ticket and reservation numbers of the missing elements at hand.

BOOKING FASTPASS+ AHEAD OF YOUR ARRIVAL

FastPass+ can be booked in advance by everyone with a valid "Magic Your Way" ticket or annual pass. Guests staying in Disney-owned resorts or other eligible hotels can begin booking FastPass+ 60 days before their arrival date. Guests staying elsewhere can book up to 30 days before planned use. FastPass+ strategy is covered in depth back in Chapter 6.

Booking FastPass+ as soon as eligible is advantageous because the most attractions and times will be available. Each FastPass+ experience has a limited number of slots. Fewer and fewer experiences will be available as a specific visit date approaches because more and more people have gone online and secured their choices.

Read Chapter 6, if you haven't already, and decide which FastPass+ experiences and times you'd like to book. Beginning at 7am, exactly 60 days out, you can sign into your MDE account on disneyworld.com and complete the following steps:

- At the top right hover over the words "My Disney Experience." From the drop down that emerges, click FastPass+

- Then you add, one at a time, FastPass+ up to a total of three per ticket per day. You no longer need to book exactly three per day.

- Because not all members of the group are required to select the same FastPass+ experiences, first you select the people for whom you are scheduling for your FastPass+.

- Then you pick the date, and then at the bottom of same page, the park. Rides and possible times for your FastPass+ that day will then show on your screen.

- Note that there are tabs above where you can target morning, afternoon, and evening. Attractions only available in the evening will still show, even if you picked morning. By clicking the rightmost tab, you can even target a specific time.

- By default, the system will show only up to three time choices for each ride. But note that under each ride's name is a link "View Details and More Times." Click it, and if available you'll see a lot more times to pick from. Tap the time you want, and hit the green "Confirm" button at the lower left of the next screen.

- Your FastPass+ may conflict with another time you've picked, or even a set of FastPass+ at a different park. If so, you'll get an error screen. If you lose track of the FastPass+ you've already booked for that day, most pages have a link "My Plans" in the top left. Click that and a pop up of your plans will show up. Scroll down to the appropriate day to see what's conflicting, then X out the pop-up and fix it.

- Once you have a successful "confirm," you will be given the choice of continuing that day or working on a different day. Either way, you will start at the beginning with the people involved for whom you are scheduling a FastPass. Continue until you are done booking all your FastPass+ for everyone!

Times and experiences may be changed as often as wished (limited, though, to what is available at the time you change them), up through the last hour the theme park is open on the day you're visiting. If you run into problems, try tech support at (407) 939-5277.

MAGICBANDS

For those staying at a Disney-owned resort, MagicBands play many roles on a trip. Most importantly, they are room keys, park tickets, the link to using your Dining Plan credits, the link to FastPass+, and, if charging privileges are enabled, a means to charge back to the room.

They contain no personal data—rather, all they have encoded within them is a unique numeric identifier which Disney uses to link up databases in its own systems behind the scenes.

MagicBands are waterproof and hypoallergenic, and don't even need to be worn on a wrist—you can stick them in a pocket or purse and just wave them about when needed. Many need to take them off and wave them about anyway since not all the readers work perfectly when they are on a wrist, especially hotel room locks.

The color and names printed on the MagicBands can be customized online at disneyworld.com after booking. To do so, log in to your MDE account at disneyworld.com and select MagicBands and Cards from the My Disney Experience dropdown menu. Confirm the shipping address, then select MagicBands one by one for the people in your party. For each MagicBand, pick a color and customize the name, which is limited to nine characters including spaces. So "easyWDW" fits, but not "yourfirstvisit.net". Colors can be the same among your group, so long as the names are different. Well, names can be the same, too...but why would you do that?

MagicBands will be shipped directly to the U.S. address of your choice if they're customized at least 10 days (at press time) before the arrival date. MagicBands customized closer to the check-in date will be available at check-in at the resort. Disney does not ship MagicBands internationally, which means all visitors without a U.S. address will pick up their MagicBands at check-in. If you fail to customize the MagicBands at all, grey MagicBands will be waiting at the resort at check-in.

Those not staying at a Disney-owned resort can purchase MagicBands on site, with current pricing at $14.99 and up. The MagicBands of such visitors are linked at the time of purchase to a theme park ticket, and the MagicBand can then be used for FastPass+. Note that a MagicBand is not required to use FastPass+ (a ticket, of course, is required) and off-site guests can simply scan their ticket instead of a Band. There are no charging privileges for off-site guests, so you'll need to keep cash or a credit card handy.

Disney World To-Do List

Tailored To-Do lists are available for each of the itineraries located at yourfirstvisit.net/itineraries. For more general guidelines, see below:

MORE THAN 181 DAYS BEFORE YOUR PLANNED ARRIVAL DATE

- Double-check budget (Chapter 8), dates (Chapter 4), intended hotel (Chapter 5), intended dates in each park (Chapter 6), intended dining venues (Chapter 7), and transportation choices and their availability for the planned dates.
- Make transportation arrangements as necessary, including any flight or rental car reservations.
- Create your My Disney Experience account and add your group members to it.
- If staying at a Disney-owned hotel, book your hotel and purchase your tickets. Call 407-939-7675 to book by phone (optimal, because this allows you to tell the reservationist which area at a resort you want to be in, if you have a preference) or go to your MyDisneyExperience account to use Disney's online system. At the same time, you'll have the opportunity to sign up for Disney's Magical Express service that transports Disney-owned hotel guests from Orlando International (but not Sanford) Airport directly to their hotel. Don't worry if you don't have your flight details set. You can come back to this page later or call 866-599-0951 to set it up. Disney hotel reservations can be made over the phone up to 499 days before an arrival date. Online, the system may only show reservations available through the end of the calendar year, particularly if you try to book for the next year more than six months in advance. Call Disney reservations at 407-939-7675 if your dates aren't available online but you are within 499 days of your arrival date.
- If not staying at a Disney resort, buy your tickets from within your My Disney Experience account—this increases the chance that they will be properly linked. Alternatively, purchase tickets from an authorized reseller and link them manually.

EXACTLY 6AM EST, EXACTLY 180 DAYS BEFORE ARRIVAL DATE

Log on to DisneyWorld.com/dining by at least 5:50am EST, and have your highest priority reservation all set up on the page. Keep refreshing, as you will be let in as soon as Disney's system decides it is 6am. Make as many of the following hardest-to-get reservations that are on your itinerary, in the order listed:

- Be Our Guest Restaurant [Magic Kingdom]
- California Grill brunch
- Artist Point dinner [Wilderness Lodge]
- Trattoria al Forno breakfast [Boardwalk]
- Cinderella's Royal Table [Magic Kingdom]
- Chef Mickey's [Contemporary Resort]
- 'Ohana [Polynesian Resort]
- Akershus Royal Banquet Hall [Epcot]
- 1900 Park Fare Dinner [Grand Floridian Resort]
- California Grill dinner [Contemporary Resort]

For other restaurants, booking at 6am 180+ days in advance isn't necessary, but doing so will guarantee a desired day and time.

If you have trouble online, call (407) WDW-DINE (939-3463) to book reservations offline, beginning at 7am EST on the same date.

60 DAYS BEFORE ARRIVAL DATE (IF STAYING AT DISNEY-OWNED RESORT OR OTHER ELIGIBLE HOTEL)

- Beginning (if you choose) at 7am, go to your My Disney Experience account and set up your FastPass+ selections.
- If staying at a Disney-owned resort, do online resort check in, requesting any special location or amenity preferences.
- If staying at a Disney-owned resort, customize MagicBands.

30 DAYS BEFORE FIRST PARK VISIT (IF STAYING ANYWHERE ELSE)

Beginning (if you choose) at 7am, go to your My Disney Experience account and set up your FastPass+.

NOTES ON PACKING, ETC., BEFORE YOU LEAVE

- If you have them, bring your MagicBands in your carry-ons or wear them on your wrists.
- If you use Disney's Magical Express, you do not need to collect your bags at the Orlando airport unless you choose to, arrive late in the evening/at night (between 10 pm and 5 am), or are an international traveler. Disney will obtain them for you (without the bags ever going to baggage claim) and deliver them directly to your room. Your bags will likely arrive at your hotel hours after you do. Plan to pack an appropriate change of clothes for Orlando weather, medications, etc., in a carry-on. Follow the instructions in the Magical Express packet you will receive in the mail regarding both tagging your bags pre-departure and where to go at the Orlando airport to find the bus to your resort. Magical Express check-in is located on the B side of Level 1. If you arrive on the A side or pick up your luggage yourself on the A side, you will need to walk over to the B side. Note that this is only possible on Level 3. There is no way to walk from the A side to the B side on any other level.

- Bring copies/printouts of your room reservation, confirmation numbers, and any tickets for special events you may have received in the mail.

- When you arrive at the hotel, if you used Online Check-in, look for the special Online Check-in line, and get into it.

We're almost there! Setting up dining and FastPass+ reservations can be stressful and frustrating, but you're armed with the best possible strategy. Once the reservations are booked, there's little to worry about.

CHAPTER TEN

Where to Go Next

Congratulations! You either skipped to the end of the book to find out if the princess really does end up with the prince, or have now read so much great Disney World information that there's really no need to actually go on the vacation. And this book isn't even billed as a money saver. Oh, you still want to go, and you want to be kept up to date on any changes? We weren't expecting that, but we might still be able to help.

First of all, take advantage of our new free update program! We will update this 2020 edition several times between its initial 2019 publication date and the late summer of 2020, when our 2021 edition will come out. For the 2020 edition of this guide, we are offering free updates!

To get on the list for updates to the 2020 edition forward your confirming Amazon email (that is, the email titled "Amazon.com order of The easy Guide to Your Walt Disney World Visit") to easyguidewdw@gmail.com, and then, whenever a new update of the 2020 edition comes out, we will email you instructions on how to get yours (as a PDF).

Then, for changes between updates, bookmark yourfirstvisit.net/easy-guide-2020-changes.

From there, easyWDW.com is your best chance to see what's going on inside the theme parks as it happens. With weekly visits, thousands of pictures, up-to-date info on operating schedule changes, and ideal touring strategies, there's no other website in the world like it. If you'd like to join other WDW fans and have an opportunity to ask Josh questions about your trip directly, sign up for the forums at easywdw.com/forums.

Pay close attention to yourfirstvisit.net for new material aimed squarely at first-timers who both may never return and also don't necessarily want to spend a lot of time planning. Advice there for such visitors is very specific, but always comes with next best options ranked in order for those who can't, or won't, follow Dave's specific advice. The site is particularly helpful for choosing among hotels. Read it, and easywdw.com, too, and your life will be fulfilled.

We sincerely hope this book helped you plan a special trip full of the best that Walt Disney World offers. Get out there and put everything you learned into action. And after you've left Disney World and come back home—leave us comments at yourfirstvisit.net and easywdw.com to let us know how it went!

Acknowledgments

Dave would like to thank those who helped with this book and the years of work that led up to it:

- This book would not have been possible without the encouragement and skills of Bob McLain and Theme Park Press.
- And it wouldn't have been too good without my co-author Josh Humphrey. The best Disney World thinker of his generation, Josh has made this book more than twice as good as it would have been without him, thanks to his capability and stubbornness.
- Gratitude to my family—Amy, Ted, and Alex—who once again let a Walt Disney World project divert my time and attention.
- Many thanks to a list of people whose support over the years made the work that led to this book possible: Steve Bell, Joe Black, Tom Bricker, Lee Cockerell, Mary Conor DeFazio, Beth Pickel Doda, Faith Dority, Mike Ellis, Kristen Hoetzel-Go, Jackie Hutnik, Allison Jones, Linda Stevens Jones, Kathleen Kelly, Karen Landry, Kuleen Lashly, Sarah Harvey Mitchell, Julie Neal, Steve Seifert, Len Testa, Carl Trent, and Jodi Whisenhunt.
- Last, but not least, thanks to the readers ofyourfirstvisit.net—more than ten million of them—you all inspire me every day.

Josh would like to thank:

- My mom and dad for smiling as their (favorite) son crossed the country to try and chase down yet another dream.
- Dave Shute for bringing me this posh book deal, in addition to providing the foundation and structure for everything in it.
- Everyone that's ever recommended easyWDW to a friend, colleague, family member, or fellow DISboards member. Your continued support is what drives everything I do. Thank you.

About the Authors

Dave by day co-leads Hopewell, a farm-based residential treatment program for adults with severe mental illness. At night and on weekends he writes yourfirstvisit.net, and, lately, Disney World guidebooks. All the time he's a husband, dad, son, and brother. He has a BA from the University of Chicago, and both an MA in English Literature and MBA from the University of Virginia, where he also completed the majority of work for a PhD in English Literature. He spent almost a decade as a strategy consultant at McKinsey & Co., Inc., and since then has largely operated as an independent strategy consultant. He founded yourfirstvisit.net in 2009—the first Disney World site aimed squarely at first-time visitors who may never return. He visits Disney World six to ten times a year, and in 2019 he stayed in his 160th different Disney World-owned hotel room.

Josh grew up in Seattle, Washington, the only known city to adequately prepare a person for Orlando's wet summers. He was fascinated by Disney theme parks long before his first visit to Disneyland at age eight. He started easywdw.com in the spring of 2010 as an outlet to help visitors maximize their theme park experience with practical, hands-on advice. He lives just 15 minutes from Magic Kingdom's gates and records more than a hundred theme park visits every year, each with the express intent of uncovering ways to better enjoy everything the parks offer. In his spare time, he enjoys dressing his Duffy the Disney Bear in fabulous outfits, taking his dog to the park, and the occasional single malt scotch.

About Theme Park Press

Theme Park Press publishes books primarily about the Disney company, its history, culture, films, animation, and theme parks, as well as theme parks in general.

Our authors include noted historians, animators, Imagineers, and experts in the theme park industry.

We also publish many books by first-time authors, with topics ranging from fiction to theme park guides.

And we're always looking for new talent. If you'd like to write for us, or if you're interested in the many other titles in our catalog, please visit:

www.ThemeParkPress.com

• •

Theme Park Press Newsletter

Subscribe to our free email newsletter and enjoy:

- ◆ Free book downloads and giveaways
- ◆ Access to excerpts from our many books
- ◆ Announcements of forthcoming releases
- ◆ Exclusive additional content and chapters
- ◆ And more good stuff available nowhere else

To subscribe, visit www.ThemeParkPress.com, or send email to newsletter@themeparkpress.com.

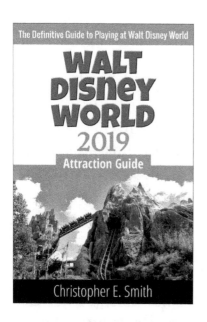

Read more about these books
and our many other titles at:

www.ThemeParkPress.com

CPSIA information can be obtained
at www.ICGtesting.com
Printed in the USA
LVHW022002240120
644726LV00012B/1420